Accessible Housing for South Asia

Amitabh Kundu · Tomaz Ponce Dentinho ·
Habibullah Magsi · Kanika Basu ·
Sumana Bandyopadhyay
Editors

Accessible Housing for South Asia

Needs, Implementation and Impacts

Springer

Editors
Amitabh Kundu
Research and Information System for Developing Countries, World Resources Institute India
New Delhi, India

Habibullah Magsi
Sindh Agriculture University
Tandojam, Pakistan

Sumana Bandyopadhyay
University of Calcutta
Kolkata, India

Tomaz Ponce Dentinho
University of the Azores
Angra do Heroísmo, Portugal

Kanika Basu
Housing and Urban Development Corporation
New Delhi, India

ISBN 978-3-030-88880-0 ISBN 978-3-030-88881-7 (eBook)
https://doi.org/10.1007/978-3-030-88881-7

This Springer imprint is published by the registered company Springer Nature Switzerland AG
The registered company address is: Gewerbestrasse 11, 6330 Cham, Switzerland

Contents

Contributors

Ateeq Ahmed Department of Economics and Development Studies, University of Swat, Swat, Khyber Pakhtunkhwa, Pakistan

Naureen Akhtar University Gillani Law College, B.Z.U, Multan, Pakistan

Asraful Alam Department of Geography, Serampore Girls' College, University of Calcutta, Hooghly, West Bengal, India

Atif Bilal Aslam Department of City and Regional Planning, University of Engineering and Technology, Lahore, Pakistan

Sumana Bandyopadhyay Department of Geography, University of Calcutta, Kolkata, India

Kanika Basu Housing and Urban Development Corporation, Goverment of India, New Delhi, India

Alfredo Cartone Department of Economic Studies, University G. D'Annunzio of Chieti Pescara, Pescara, Italy

Tomaz Ponce Dentinho Centre for Applied Economics of the Atlantic, University of Azores, Angra do Heroísmo, Portugal

Fawzia Farzana Urban and Rural Planning Discipline, Khulna University, Khulna, Bangladesh

Pritam Ghosh Department of Geography, University of Calcutta, Kolkata, West Bengal, India;
Department of Geography, Ramsaday College, Amta, Howrah, West Bengal, India

Rao Imran Habib University Gillani Law College, B.Z.U, Multan, Pakistan

Vineeta Hariharan Senior Urbanisation and Public Policy Expert, New Delhi, India

Samrat Hore Department of Statistics, Tripura University, Agartala, Tripura, India

Anwar Hussain Department of Economics and Development Studies, University of Swat, Swat, Khyber Pakhtunkhwa, Pakistan

Wajahat Hussain School of Economics, Quaid-i-Azam University, Islamabad, Pakistan

Nasir Javed Urban Development Specialist, Lahore, Punjab, Pakistan

Binod Khadka Government of Nepal, National Reconstruction Authority, MOUD, DLPIU, Okhaldhunga, Nepal, India

Amitabh Kundu Distinguished Fellow, Research and Information System for Developing Countries, New Delhi, India;
Senior Fellow, World Resources Institute, New Delhi, India

Attia Madni Faculty of Shariah and Law, International Islamic University, Islamabad, Pakistan

Habibullah Magsi Department of Agricultural Economics, University of Hyderabad, Hyderabad, Pakistan

Darshini Mahadevia School of Arts and Sciences, Ahmedabad University, Ahmedabad, India

Sana Malik Housing Research Center, University of Management & Technology, Lahore, Pakistan

Ishita Mandal Department of Geography, University of Calcutta, Kolkata, India

Sangeeta Maunav Human Settlements Management Institute, HUDCO, Government of India, New Delhi, India

Saptarshi Mitra Department of Geography and Disaster Management, Tripura University, Agartala, Tripura, India

Dinabandhu Mondal Centre for the Study of Regional Development, School of Social Sciences, Jawaharlal Nehru University, New Delhi, India

Sree Lakshmi Nambiar Policy Student (Institute of Public Policy), Chennai, India

Lila Nyaichyai Central Department of Library and Information Science, Tribhuvan University, Kathmandu, Nepal

Ruhizal Roosli School of Housing, Building and Planning, Universiti Sains Malaysia, Penang, Malaysia

Debodatta Saha Department of Geography, Bijoy Krishna Girls' College, Howrah, India

Joydeep Saha Department of Geography, Bijoy Krishna Girls' College, Howrah, West Bengal, India

Syeda Sani-e-Zahra Naqvi Urban Development Specialist, Lahore, Punjab, Pakistan

Lakshminarayan Satpati Department of Geography & Director, UGC-HRDC, University of Calcutta, Kolkata, India

Hans Schenk University of Amsterdam, Amsterdam, The Netherlands

Krittika Uniyal The Environmental Governance and Territorial Development Institute, University of Geneva, Geneva, Switzerland

Abbreviations

ABD	Area-Based Development
AHP	Affordable Housing in Partnership
AMRUT	Atal Mission for Rejuvenation and Urban Transformation
AUWSP	Accelerated Urban Water Supply Programme
BBMP	Bruhat Bengaluru Mahanagara Palike
BLC	Beneficiary-Led Construction
BPL	Below Poverty Line
BRP	Bhashantek Rehabilitation Project
BSUP	Basic Service for the Urban Poor
CAB	Consumers Association of Bangladesh
CDP	City Development Plan
CGI	Corrugated Galvanised Iron
CLSS	Credit-Linked Subsidy Scheme
CRS	Corporate Social Responsibility
DCHB	District Census Hand Books
DDA	Delhi Development Authority
DGHC	Darjiling Gorkha Hill Council
DHS	Demographic and Health Surveys
DMIC	Delhi-Mumbai Industrial Corridor
DPC	Damp-Proof Course
DUDBC	Department of Urban Development and Building Construction
EIUS	Environmental Improvement of Urban Slums
FBL	Freed Bonded Labourers
FSI	Floor Space Index
GGI	Gender Gap Index
GOI	Government of India
GoN	Government of Nepal
GoP	Government of Pakistan
HBFC	Housing Building Finance Corporation
HDI	Human Development Index
HFC	Housing Finance Companies

I/NGO	International Non-Governmental Organizations
IAY	Indira Awaas Yojana
ICT	Information and Communication Technology
IDSMT	Integrated Development Scheme for Small and Medium Towns
IHSDP	Integrated Housing and Slum Development Programme
ISAL	Informal Subdivision of Agricultural Land
ISSR	In-situ Slum Rehabilitation
JRY	Jawahar Rozgar Yojana
KSDB	Karnataka Slum Development Board
KTT	Khu Tap The
LISA	Local Indicator of Spatial Association
LTV	Loan to value ratio
MDG	Millennium Development Goals
MFI	Micro-Finance Institutions
MHADA	Maharashtra Housing & Area Development Authority
MHUPA	Ministry of Housing and Urban Poverty Alleviation
MIG	Middle Income Group
MoFALD	Ministry of Federal Affairs and Local Development
MoHUA	Ministry of Housing and Urban Affairs
MRT	Mandatory Rule of Thumb
NAS	National Accounts Statistics
NBFC	Non-Banking Finance Companies
NBO	National Building Organisation
NDRF	National Disaster Response Framework
NHA	National Housing Authority
NHB	National Housing Bank
NHP	National Housing Policy
NPHP	Naya Pakistan Housing Program
NRA	National Reconstruction Authority
NSC	Non-Scheduled Caste
NSDP	National Slum Development Programme
NSS	National Sample Surveys
NSSO	National Sample Survey Organisation
NULM	National Urban Livelihood Mission
ODP	Open Developed Plots
PDNA	Post Disaster Needs Assessment
PMRC	Pakistan Mortgage Refinance Company
POA	Plan of Action
PPP	Public-Private Partnership
RC	Reinforced Concrete
REHAB	Real Estate and Housing Association of Bangladesh
RFCTLARR	Right to Fair Compensation and Transparency in Land Acquisition, Rehabilitation and Resettlement
RLEGP	Rural Landless Employment Guarantee Programme
RMBSO	Recovery of Mortgage-Backed Security Ordinance

RWA	Residents Welfare Association
SBP	State bank of Pakistan
SC	Scheduled Caste
SCM	Smart Cities Mission
SEM	Shared Equity Model
SEZ	Special Economic Zones
SFB	Small Finance Banks
SHG	Women Self Help Groups
SJSRY	Swarna Jayanti Shahri Rojgar Yojana
SLNA	State Level Nodal Agency
SMP	Siliguri Mahakuma Parishad
SPV	Special-purpose Vehicle
SRA	Slum Redevelopment Authority
ST	Scheduled Tribe
TDR	Transfer of Development Rights
TOD	Transit-Oriented-Development
UBSP	Urban Basic Services for the Poor
UDI	Urban Development Index
UIDSSMT	Urban Infrastructure Development Scheme for Small and Medium Towns
UIG	Urban Infrastructure and Governance
ULB	Urban Local Bodies
UNDG	UN-Inter-Agency Development Group
URMM	Unreinforced Mud-Bonded Masonry
USHA	Urban Statistics for Human Resource and Assessment
VAMBAY	Valmiki Ambedkar Awaas Yojana
VAT	Value-Added Tax

List of Figures

List of Tables

Chapter 1
Introduction to Accessible Housing

Amitabh Kundu, Kanika Basu, Habibullah Magsi, Sumana Bandyopadhyay, and Tomaz Ponce Dentinho

Abstract This introductory chapter of the book aims to present the recurring issue of market and policy failures in accessible housing and aims to highlight the unanswered questions and issues addressed by the contributors of the book. The mismatch between non-spatialized policy aims and the strongly spatialized demand for houses at the local level frames the analysis of the various chapters that try to address the problem of the impacts of urbanization with concentration leading to a demand-supply mismatch the presentation of the various parts and chapters of the book justify on the one hand the recommendation to look at the connections of housing policies with the spatialized demand and supply of housing and on the other hand the need to understand and monitor the uncontrolled urbanization and concentration phenomena.

Keywords Sustainable Development Goals · Sustainable cities and communities · Housing market and policy failures

---

The perspectives and views expressed in these chapter are only those of the authors and not necessarily reflect the views of any institution.

A. Kundu
Distinguished Fellow, Research and Information System for Developing Countries and Senior Fellow, WRI India, New Delhi, India

K. Basu
Joint General Manager, Housing and Urban Development Corporation, Goverment of India, New Delhi, India

H. Magsi
Professor, Department of Agricultural Economics, University of Hyderabad, Hyderabad, Pakistan

S. Bandyopadhyay
Professor, Department of Geography, University of Calcutta, Kolkata, India

T. P. Dentinho (✉)
Professor, Centre for Applied Economics of the Atlantic, University of Azores, Angra do Heroísmo, Portugal
e-mail: tomas.lc.dentinho@uac.pt

A. Kundu et al. (eds.), *Accessible Housing for South Asia*,
https://doi.org/10.1007/978-3-030-88881-7_1

1.1 Shelter: A Basic Need and a Key Element in Human Security

The world is as unequal as it gets, and out of nowhere came the great leveller of all times. As the pandemic gripped the world, we began to realize that there are elements in nature that make the richest as vulnerable as the poorest. Development, modernization, highest GDP's and per capita incomes ceased to matter as the most advanced countries struggled as much as did the poorest economies, to save their population from the deadly virus. More than a year has passed and we are yet to know when the world will be secure again. The matter of human security is as brittle as glass. Long-term changes like climate change and biodiversity losses superimposed by natural hazards, poverty and inequality loom larger before us than ever before.

Shelter is one of the key aspects of human security and that too a basic human need that still remains a challenge in many poor countries of the world. UN-Habitat (2015) estimates that as of 2015, "330 million households are financially stretched by housing costs; this number could grow to 440 million by 2025." The number would be higher if 'houseless people' living on the street would be added to this category. The 'lion's share' of the absolute housing shortage is in developing nations, mainly in South Asian and African countries.

Housing is a basic human need, which many argue, is one of the most important inputs to improve livelihoods. Today, particularly in developing nations, housing is one of the most dynamic infrastructures, attributed mainly to rapid urbanization driven by large-scale rural to urban migration. The scale varies but the pervasive presence of inadequate and congested housing, slums and houseless population in urban centres all across the world, bears testimony to the fact that adequate housing is still a distant dream for millions of people.

Adequate housing being a cornerstone for social equity and environmental sustainability, its failure is a threat to sustainable urbanization, and a complex challenge. Addressing housing needs requires legislative, financial and technical support and involves multiple stakeholders, noting that the task of housing for all does not only entail the additional households created due to in-migration in urban places but also involves rehabilitation of Internally displaced persons and replenishment of housing stock lost to frequently recurrent natural disasters like flood, cyclones and earthquake.

The housing challenge has received UN recognition through its mention in both Millennium Development Goals (MDGs) as well as the recently adopted Sustainable Development Goals, SDG 11: which aim to, by 2030, "ensure access for all for adequate, safe and affordable housing and basic services and upgrade slums." The UN documents that 1.6 billion people live in inadequate housing, and thus focuses upon affordable housing as one of the key Sustainable Development Goals [SDG11]. Notwithstanding the varied policy and program response from governments in different countries and endeavours by international agencies, achievements are limited with little or no evidence of large-scale positive impact on the urban housing sector, especially for the working class and the low-income groups. Joan Clos, Executive Director of the UN Habitat Programme, ruefully admitted in his

World Habitat Day (2021) speech that "Handing over housing to the market has proved a failure in providing affordable and adequate housing for all," and went on to remind us that "We all remember well that housing was at the epicentre of the eruption of the global economic crisis of 2008, instead of being at the heart of the urban policy."

1.2 What Lies Ahead?

The 2020 report on SDG's (UN, 2020) give a grim reminder of the times ahead as an impact of the pandemic:

(a) "An estimated 71 million people are expected to be pushed back into extreme poverty in 2020, the first rise in global poverty since 1998. Lost incomes, limited social protection and rising prices mean even those who were previously secure could find themselves at risk of poverty and hunger."
(b) "the more than one billion slum dwellers worldwide are acutely at risk from the effects of COVID-19, suffering from a lack of adequate housing, no running water at home, shared toilets, little or no waste management systems, overcrowded public transport and limited access to formal health care facilities."

The above warnings are more than relevant to the Global South in general and to South Asia in particular. Though newspapers and journals are carrying articles on rental stress on a large section of the population in the developed countries like Australia, where the job-keepers changing to job seekers bring down rental affordability by 56% (Casey & Ralston, 2021). Approximately, 10.5% of Americans paid their rents 3 months later and 4% were evicted due to non-payment (Grinstein et al., 2020); and this was the early part of the pandemic. When WHO Guidelines convey, "Stay at home"—what does it mean for the 1.77 million homeless Indians (Census 2011)? On the other hand, when "social distancing" is prescribed what are the options for 8–10-member families in slums? We are still grappling with information on how the pandemic threw thousands of migrant workers, daily wage earners and small enterprise owners in the throes of poverty, hunger and homelessness. Notwithstanding this, we have attempted to compile this book on Accessible Housing in South Asia with a collection of essays on the South Asian scenario in the pre-condition to the pandemic.

1.3 What is Said and What is Missing?

Access to housing associates usually with the public provision of houses to those in need. Nevertheless, it is known that access to houses should include not only the attributes of the houses (Des Rosiers et. al., 1999) but also many other features. Neighborhood attributes (median income, school dropouts, density, suspended particles, sulphur dioxins), public service benefits and costs (property tax, parking, pedestrian paths), accessibility to services and amenities (CBD, ocean, river, recreation, school, hospital, commercial area) (Li & Brown, 1980), earthquake and flooding risks (Keskin, 2008), speculative premiums (Calmasur, 2016) and access to transport networks (Wu et. al., 2018).

Looking at the diffusion literature on housing policies, we tried to see if the concepts "access to." clearly related to the demand for housing, do show up. Looking at Table 1.1 it is clear that access to natural resources like land and water, adapted spaces of buildings and infrastructures, production and consumption facilities, capital and Finance and citizenship. Nevertheless, they are non-spatialized expressions and, contrary to what is seen in the estimates of the value of houses, seldom there is any reference about the distance to these amenities that complement each house. Actually, they are just a list of requirements impossible to fulfill all if not by the constraints of space.

1.4 The Major Issues Discussed in This Book

This book tries to address these mismatches by looking at three major issues related to Housing in South Asia: (a) demands and needs in space and time; (b) financial capabilities and policy implementation; and (c) socio-economic and environmental impacts of housing. Through various case studies across South Asia, the book analyses the process of delivering of houses, the issues related to access to employment, markets and services, the cumulative effects on gentrification, exclusion and spatial justice and the long-term outcomes concerning economic, social and environmental sustainability of the urban tissue.

The book covers the myriad aspects of the issues of access and provisioning of housing in South Asia. It has been the endeavour of the editorial team to bring together planning professionals, experts and veteran academicians as well as doctoral researchers in an attempt to take both macro and micro views in discussing the many facets of housing as a basic need and an amenity. The enigma that prevails in the South Asian context is the annual ritualistic launching of policies and programmes by the Government over the years, while millions remain homeless. Is it not time to seek doable solutions? Identify the gaps in policy-making and execution and bring in the political will to break the barriers to execution—by removing gaps in assessment and review of whether the investments and policies goals are achievable and accessible to the poor.

This chapter introduces the theme and justification of the book. Chapter 2, written by Amitabh Kundu, provides a critical overview in the characterization of slums in India and suggests the creation of an index of tenability defined with inclusivity. Chapter 3 authored by Hans Schenk adopts a historical perspective on housing policies in India moving from an unreachable proposal of improved urban shelter to a

Table 1.1 Housing and accessibility

	Access to				
	Natural resources	Adapted spaces	Production and consumption	Capital and Finance	Citizenship
Irazábal (2009)	Water, land, sea	Housing, transports,	Trade, jobs, services	Capital	Culture
Nenova (2010)	Land	Housing, transports	Housing market	Finance	
UN (2011)	Water, Resources	Shelter, technology, energy	Services, Jobs, Information	Credit	
Mitlin et al. (2011)				Credit	
Jha et al. (2012)	Waterresources	Technology	Information	Credit	
World Bank Group (2015)	Water	Sanitation, energy Housing	Basic services		
Thorn et al. (2015)	Water	Sanitation	Goods and services		
Michael (2015)	Water, Resources	Sanitation	Services		
Jain et al (2015)	Resources, land	Technology, Telecommunications, electricity, sanitation, Infrastructures	Services		Social networks
Hoelzel (2016)	Land	Housing, Electricity	Mobility, education, jobs	Mortgages	
Ellis and Roberts (2016)	Water, land	Housing, Ports	Education, Jobs, information	Finance	Benefits of agglomeration. participation
Counihan (2017)	Water, property		Basic services		
Kundu and Kumar (2018)	Land, amenities	Electricity			

segregation process between new urbanizations and slum areas. In Chap. 4, Pritam Ghosh, Debodatta Saha and Alfredo Cartone relate temporary houses in Indian districts to income distribution, gender and rurality. Fawzia Farzana, in Chap. 5, show evidence of housing segregation associated with urbanization in Dhaka, Bangladesh. As highlighted in Chap. 6 urbanization with segregation is also present in Pakistan where, according to Anwar Hussain, Ateeq Ahmed and Wajahat Hussain, the rise of urban land and housing prices regarding average income are creating problems of housing affordability.

Asraful Alam, Lakshminarayan Satpati and Ishita Mandal, in Chap. 7, address the quality of rural houses and argue for a proper identification of beneficiaries, a judicious combination of modern technology with traditional knowledge, effective community participation and cost-effective project implementation and maintenance. Chapter 8 written by Dinabandhu Mondal and Joydeep Saha defend that housing policies should not be a target to slums but to the specificities of each city. Chapter 9, authored by Binod Khadka from Nepal, focuses on the importance of construction materials not only for the quality of the houses but also for their resilience to earthquakes in "A road to recovery: Housing reconstruction in Bhaktapur Nepal post the 2015 Gorkha Earthquake". Chapter 10, also on Nepal and the impact of the Gorkha Earthquake, points out that the security of vulnerable communities should be the focus of attention in housing policies. Darshini Mahadevia, in Chap. 11, deconstructs the idea of Smart City while focusing on the redevelopment of slums in Ahmedabad. Chapter 12, written by Nasir Javed, Syeda Sani and Zahra Naqvi reveal market and policy failures in housing progresses in Pakistan. Atif Bilal Aslam in Chap. 13 analyzes the effects of remittances investments in the housing market. Chapter 14 written by Naureen Akhtar, Rao Imran Habib and Attia Madni reveals the importance of housing finances by looking at the Mortgage-Backed Security Model of Naya Pakistan Housing Program. The rural housing programme in West Bengal in India is crictially assessed by Saptarshi Mitra and Samrat Hore in Chap. 15 that shows clear performance variations across time and space. In Chap. 16, Sangeeta Maunav looks into 61 towns of Bangalore to conclude that access to land and finance are crucial to address the issues of urban poor. Chapter 17, authored by Sana Malik and Ruhizal Roosli, looks at the important issue of housing finance in Pakistan. Finally, Vineeta Hariharan in Chap. 18 suggests key issues and recommendations for housing policies in different countries of South Asia.

1.5 Conclusion

Poverty alleviation is pointed by many poor people to be the others' duty and the others provide multiple policies to remove poverty. There are poor people in slums and out of slums but poverty is a direct reflection upon housing for both the slum and non-slum poor. How to address housing poverty? Is it to provide access to water, land and amenities? Is it enough to build houses, transport and energy networks? Can it be done by providing access to the labour market and to private and public goods and services? Instead, what is required is access to cheap financing schemes? What about participation and citizenship?

What we can strangely perceive from the various chapters is that there are empty houses in speculation and highly densified slums; and to address that suitable property tax systems, based on the cost of infrastructured space might promote the use of empty private houses. The problem is when those houses are provided by public entities in the wrong place; where there are land, water, houses, transport and energy but no markets for labour, goods and services and no adequate institutions for social and political proximity.

References

Calmasur, G. (2016) Determining factors affecting housing prices in Turkey with Hedonic Pricing Model. In *International Conference on Business and Economics Studies, February 25–28, 2016, Washington D.C., USA*. ISSN 2469-7540.

Casey, S., & Ralston, L. (2021). Retrieved June 21, 2021, from https://theconversation.com/at-least-2-6-million-people-face-poverty-when-covid-payments-end-and-rental-stress-soars-157244. (4.15.IST).

Census. (2011). https://censusindia.gov.in/2011-common/censusdata2011.html

Counihan, C. H. (2017). An incremental intervention in Jakarta: An empowering infrastructural approach for upgrading informal settlements. Landscape Architecture Masters Theses Collection. 1. Retrieved from https://scholarworks.umass.edu/la_theses/1.

Des Rosiers, F., Thériault, M., & Villeneuve, P. Y. (1999). Sorting out access and neighbourhood factors in hedonic price modelling: An application to the Quebec City metropolitan area. Paper presented at the Sixth European Real Estate Society Conference Athens, 23–25 June 1999

Ellis, P., & Roberts, M. (2016). Leveraging urbanization in South Asia. Managing spatial transformation for prosperity and livability. International Bank for Reconstruction and Development, The World Bank.

Grinstein, M., et al. (2020). https://www.brookings.edu/blog/up-front/2020/06/01/housing-hardships-reach-unprecedented-heights-during-the-covid-19-pandemic/

Hoelzel, F. (2016). Which way, Lagos? In: Heinrich Böll Foundation/Fabulous Urban (Eds.), Urban planning processes in Lagos. Policies, Laws, Planning Instruments, Strategies and Actors of Urban Projects, Urban Development, and Urban Services in Africa's Largest City. Lagos. Retrieved July 18, 2016, from https://ng.boell.org/sites/default/files/160206_urban_planning_processes_digital_new.pdf.

Irazábal, C. (2009). Revisiting urban planning in Latin America and the Caribbean. Regional study prepared for Revisiting Urban Planning: Global Report on Human Settlements 2009. http://www.unhabitat.org/grhs/2009.

Jain, G., Jigyasu, R., Gajjar, S. P., & Malladi, T. (2015). Cities provide transformational opportunity to Reduce Risk Accumulation. RF-IIHS Paper on Indian Urban Risk and Resilience. Indian Institute for Human Settlements, Bangalore.

Jha, A. K., Lamond, J. E., Proverbs, D. (2012). Cities and Flooding: A guide to integrated urban flood risk management for the 21st Century. The World Bank.

Keskin, B. (2008). (2008), Hedonic analysis of price in the Istanbul housing market. *International Journal of Strategic Property Management, 12*, 125–138.

Kundu, A., & Kumar, A. (2018). Social Housing. Analysis of housing vertical interventions for urban poor in large cities of Andhra Pradesh. 2018 Copenhagen Consensus Center2018 Copenhagen Consensus Center.

Li, M. M., Brown, J. (1980). Micro-neighborhood externalities and hedonic housing prices. *Land Economics, 56*(2).

Michael, J. O. (2015). *An evaluation of slum upgrading schemes in Nairobi County*. School of Environmental Studies of Kenyatta University.

Mitlin, D., Satterthwaite, D., & Bartlett, S. (2011). Capital, capacities and collaboration: the multiple roles of community savings in addressing urban poverty. Human Settlements Working Paper Series. Poverty Reduction in Urban Areas–34. Human Settlements Group. International Institute for Environment and Development (IIED).

Nenova, T. (2010). *Expanding housing finance to the underserved in South Asia*. The International Bank for Reconstruction and Development. The World Bank

Schwarm, W., & Cutker, H. (2003). Building small city and town SAMS and CGE models. *Review if Urban and Regional Development Studies*, *15*(2), 133–147.

Thorn, J., Thornton, T. F., & Helfgott, A. (2015). Autonomous adaptation to global environmental change in peri-urban settlements: Evidence of a growing culture of innovation and revitalisation in Mathare Valley Slums, Nairobi. *Global Environmental Change, 31*(2015), 121–131.

UN. (2011). Report of the Fifth Asia-Pacific Urban Forum. Bangkok, Thailand.

UN-Habitat. (2015). Habitat III Policy Paper Framework 10–Housing Policies, 31 December 2015 (not edited version). file:///C:/Users/tomazdentinho/Downloads/PU10%20-%20HABITAT%20III%20POLICY%20PAPER%20FRAMEWORK.pdf.

UN. (2020). The sustainable development goals report 2020. https://unstats.un.org/sdgs/report/2020/The-Sustainable-Development-Goals-Report-2020.pdf.

World Bank Group. (2015). Global Practice on Social, Urban, Rural and Resilience. (July 2015). www.worldbank.org/urban.

World Habitat Day. (2021). Accelerating urban action for a carbon-free world. Concept Note. https://urbanoctober.unhabitat.org/sites/default/files/2021-06/World_Habitat_Day_2021.pdf.

Wu, H., Jiao, H., Yu, Y., Li, Z., Peng, Z., Liu, L., & Zend, Z. (2018). Influence factors and regression model of urban housing prices based on internet open access data. *Sustainability*, *2018*(10), 1676. https://doi.org/10.3390/su10051676.

Chapter 2
Housing for All: From Rhetoric to A Reality Check on Slum Statistics for Operationalization of Flagship Missions in India

Amitabh Kundu

Abstract A negative perspective on slums in the domains of urban planning and data collection has been responsible for the process of exclusionary urbanization in India, whereby residents are evicted and relocated to the peripheries. Owing to not having a sharp focus on the tenurial security and tenability of slums, only a small percentage of the targeted populations has been brought under the development missions of government, resulting in the eviction of slum population, segmentation of cities and degenerated peripheralization. There is an urgent need for expanding the scope and coverage of information, collected by Population Census and NSSO as well as restructuring their framework of data generation. Also, a system to collect and collate slum-related information, generated through regular administrative work during the implementation of development schemes, in a temporally and cross-sectionally comparable manner must be set up. This would help in monitoring the key indicators of SDG 11 that envisage access to adequate, safe and affordable housing and basic services to all, thereby promoting inclusive and sustainable urbanization. The number of slums in India that have been identified using government notification and legal sanctions as being *tenable* for in situ development is much less than that recognized or projected at the policy level. A positive perspective on slums, built through an index of tenability, defined inclusively, would greatly enhance the scope of state intervention and address the needs of a much larger segment of India's deprived population.

Keywords Slum statistics in India · Inclusive urbanization · SDG 11 · Slum vulnerability · Notification of slums · Tenability index and in situ upgradation

2.1 Introduction

Data gathering on slums in India has generally been purpose specific and ad hoc in nature as it is often taken up, by a researcher or a research team, using personal, national or international patronage, mostly at the city level. Unfortunately, these organizations have gone in for sponsoring independent surveys at micro and meso levels

A. Kundu (✉)
Senior Fellow, World Resources Institute, New Delhi, India

A. Kundu et al. (eds.), *Accessible Housing for South Asia*,
https://doi.org/10.1007/978-3-030-88881-7_2

rather than strengthening the existing information system, generated by regional and national agencies, having greater comparability over time and space. The data obtained through these surveys, understandably, have serious limitations of providing one-time snapshots and restrictive coverage and, therefore, limited usability in policymaking. Much of the data remain in archives and the larger bodies of planners and researchers do not generally have access to and even knowledge about these.

Collecting comparable and robust statistics on the living conditions of slum dwellers, including their access to basic amenities in different states and the size class of urban centres, gain importance in the context of the housing and sanitation missions, launched by the government. It is, however, important to note that the state has withdrawn in a significant way from the arena of urban planning and housing as greater reliance is placed on private agencies and their partnership with the public sector. This has opened the doors even wider, for vested interests and pressure groups to interfere in designing and implementing the missions/ programmes, using data sets that are neither verified nor verifiable with any degree of statistical rigour. The data challenge for operationalizing the national-level missions, thus, cannot be exaggerated.

Given this scenario, the present paper takes stock of the existing data on housing and slum conditions, identifies the data gaps and proposes measures to clean these up for greater usability. The key objectives are to review the concept of slums, as used in official literature and policy documents, highlight the deficiencies in the available database, and propose institutional arrangements for their effective use in policy formulation and implementation.

The second and third sections of the paper, which follow the present introductory section, overview the definitions of slums proposed at a global level and by Indian national agencies. The next section discusses the deficiencies in the slum statistics in India, available from national sources and puts forward a perspective for strengthening them, addressing the problems of temporal and cross-sectional non-comparability. The following section presents the need for, and importance of slum vulnerability indices in formulating urban development strategy for promoting inclusive development. In addition, it overviews the methodology proposed by a committee set up by the Ministry of Housing and Urban Poverty Alleviation (MHUPA 2014) to construct such an index and discusses its six dimensions and their constituent indicators.

The sixth section focuses on tenability as an important additional dimension and makes a case for bringing it in, either as a part of the slum vulnerability index or by constructing a parallel index as a measure of vulnerability analysis, as proposed by the MHUPA Committee. The basic idea is to design a methodology that can be used at the micro level to identify slums for in situ up-gradation, as envisaged in many of the "flagship missions" that have such high political and social visibility in the country. The impropriety of considering only those slums that are notified by the government for up-gradation as being potentially tenable, and the inadequacy of the information available from the National Sample Survey for operationalizing this concept, are discussed empirically.

Operationalization of the concept of tenability of slums in the context of in situ up-gradation of slum settlements has been done in the next section. It proposes a methodology for building a slum tenability index, using the available secondary data, that can be used at a micro level to identify the tenable slums, as envisaged in PMAY, for easing the problem of land availability for in situ up-gradation. It discusses its potential use in designing and monitoring slum upgrading schemes, and additional data requirements for doing this regularly for selected large cities. It is argued that the inclusion of a positive indicator of tenability, replacing the negative indicators of illegality, and defining it with inclusivity, would increase the coverage of deprived slum dwellers under state-sponsored missions. The final section puts forward a perspective for the way forward in terms of both policy formation and its implementation, to incorporate the goal of incorporating positivity and inclusivity in the slum development strategy.

2.2 Defining Slums at Global Level

The United Nations System entrusted UN HABITAT (2003) with the responsibility to assist Members States monitor and gradually attain the Target 11: "Cities without Slum". This is one of the three targets of the MDG Goal 7 of *Ensuring Environmental Sustainability*. It prescribes that "by 2020, significant improvement is to be achieved in the lives of 100 million slum dwellers".

To facilitate monitoring of this target, UN-HABITAT (2012) has attempted to define relevant indicators, in consultation with activists, practitioners and policy-makers, having experience in the field of slum improvement and urban poverty. This became necessary since there was no internationally recognized operational definition of slums.

Target 11 initially had just two indicators 'security of tenure' and 'improvement in sanitation facilities', indicators 31 and 32, respectively, that articulate the basic vulnerability in the slums. The UN-Inter-Agency Development Group (UNDG) on MDGs subsequently expressed concern that tenure and sanitation do not adequately constitute a complete response to the target of 'improving the lives of 100 million slum dwellers'. UN-HABITAT, thereafter, proposed to develop a comprehensive definition to respond directly to the challenge of Target 11. It finally came out with five factors, each reflecting an aspect of vulnerability suffered by the slum dwellers, as noted below:

1. Insecure residential status,
2. Inadequate access to safe water,
3. Inadequate access to sanitation and other infrastructure,
4. The poor structural quality of housing,
5. Overcrowding.

As per this definition, a neighbourhood is classified as a slum if more than half of the households in the area suffer from one or more shelter deprivations, as defined by the five indicators. It is important to note that while the UN system has tried to define slums focusing on deprivations across physical, social and economic dimensions, it has posited insecurity of tenure as the key parameter. The characterization of slums in terms of sub-standard living conditions, overcrowding, inadequate public infrastructure, deficiency in economic assets, etc. becomes less important in the face of the fact that the slum dwellers mostly have no legal right on the piece of land, they are occupying and consequently have no incentive to invest for improving the local environment. The lack of security of tenure should, therefore, the most important vulnerability in defining the slums.

2.3 Slum Definitions in India

Information on slums was collected since 1981 and published in the Census Reports but this was done without the Registrar General of India providing a specific criterion for their identification. Before the Census of 2001, slum data were collected not by canvassing questionnaires at household or slum level but by putting questions to town-level authorities enquiring if there were slums within their jurisdiction. Most states and many cities in India defined slums as per their Acts, to provide services and launching improvement programmes. The information provided by these authorities were compiled by the Directorate of Census Operations and put in the Town Directory in the District Census Hand Books (DCHB). Since the information was based on the available records with the Town Authorities and not generated through field-level operations of the Census, these were not comparable over time and across states, as admitted also by the Census authorities.

The 2001 Census was the first in which the Registrar General of India (RGI) was directly involved in the collection and reporting of slum data at the national, state and settlement level. It collected data from urban settlements having a population of 50,000 and above. Apart from the slums *notified* under the State and city Acts, some areas are *recognized* by the state government agencies as slums but not notified as so. For the first time, it tried to formulate a proper definition and brought the slums belonging to both categories within the purview of its definition. Besides that, it stipulated the third category. Any cluster of at least 300 populations or about 60–70 households, living in a compact area in poorly built structures/congested tenements and lacking in access to basic amenities was identified as a slum. It noted that these people are living in unhygienic environments, usually with inadequate infrastructure and lacking in proper sanitary and drinking water facilities. The definition, thus, was based on negativity in physical terms and did not mention their vulnerability due to not having title to land or security of tenure as addressing this was not a part of the government's development agenda (see Denis et al., 2012). It may be noted that slum data for 1151 towns with a population between 20,000 and 50,000 were collected subsequently (along with 170 additional towns having a population above 50,000) by the Census in response to a specific request from the Ministry of Housing and Urban Poverty Alleviation. The coverage in the 2001 Census was thus all slums, irrespective of whether they were notified or recognized but restricted to urban settlements with a population of 20,000 and above.

The Census of 2011 adopted a definition of slums similar to that of 2001 although it differed from it in terms of coverage. The data was collected/compiled from all the statutory towns irrespective of their population size. However, 19 non-statutory towns from Delhi and one from Uttar Pradesh were also included. Importantly, it counted slums in 2613 out of 4041 statutory towns, covering 'notified slums', 'recognized slums' and 'identified slums' as was done in 2001. For the third category, slums were identified using the same definition as in 2001. The data collected in 2011 are, however, more elaborate. While the Census of 2001 gives slum information on only the demographic dimensions, the Census 2011 provides data also on access to basic amenities and locational characteristics.

National Sample Survey Organisation (NSSO) collected slum data in its surveys conducted in 1976–77, 1993, 2002 and 2012. While the 1976–77 survey had two major categories—Declared and Undeclared slums—1993 (49th round), 2002 (58th round) and 2012 (69th round) surveys defined slums as notified and non-notified.[1] The coverage under the new categories was similar to those of declared and undeclared slums. Notified slums covered the areas declared as slums by the respective municipalities, corporations, local bodies or development authorities". Undeclared slums were defined in the 1976–77 survey as clusters of 25 kutcha (non-permanent) structures with inadequate access to sanitation and water. In the later surveys, non-notified slums were defined as a cluster of 20 households with pre-defining criteria as overcrowding, inadequate access to sanitation and drinking water and unhygienic living conditions.

Unfortunately, there were no specific quantitative criteria or cut-off points adopted by different states and cities for notification of slums. As a result, assessment of livability conditions in the NSS surveys for notification of slums remains subjective, rendering the data non-comparable over space and time. Slum population grew in size through areal expansion and densification of slum settlements. The other reason for this increase was more and more states and cities coming forward to recognize and report the existence and emergence of slums. In the absence of a systematic procedure to update slum profile and detect new informal growth/settlements, official figures of slum population have been underestimated, since a large number of undeclared slums remained outside the notification/recognition process and hence were excluded in the enumeration.

The other major drawback of the NSS data is the inadequate number of slums surveyed, which in turn makes the task of generating robust estimates of the characteristics of slums difficult at the city level as also for small states. This is because NSSO conducts the slum surveys as part of its larger survey on housing conditions and does not have an adequate sample size of slum households.

[1] NSSO's 58th round provides slum household data conducted during July-December, 2002 with an all India coverage, published in it Report on "*Housing Condition in India: Household Amenities and Other Characteristics*". The 69th round of NSSO slum complied slum data at household level, covering the same period during 2012, available in their Report "*Drinking Water, Sanitation, Hygiene and Housing Condition in India*".

Urban development is a state subject, the challenge of building a cross-sectionally comparable database is enormous since the identification of municipal corporations, towns and slums vary as per the state legislation and ordinances. The definition of slum varies across urban local bodies even within the states, resulting in different criteria being adopted for notification of slums in different cities, creating discrepancies in the official data for inter-state and inter-city comparability. This makes cross-validation of information across cities and states, making comparative assessments and macro-level generalizations almost impossible.

The problem gets compounded as there is a lack of an effective mechanism for notification and de-notification of slums on a regular and scientific basis. Notifications are often done as per the demand emerging from various housing and slum improvement programmes, carrying a high subsidy component, to be implemented by State Governments. Notification facilitates the agencies to implement the programmes since that gives certain statutory rights to the state and local agencies over the slum land. Implementation of programmes, launched by the Union Governments, becomes difficult due to these varying formalities.

It is important to note that NSSO provides the data on slums and slum households generally in 5-year intervals through its regular sample survey using its definition. The state is the lowest unit for which the data is published. City-level estimates are not published by NSSO due to the small sample size, except in the case of a few metropolitan cities. However, the unit-level data are available based on which, it is possible to generate estimates for megacities or NSS regions. Unfortunately, the standard errors of the estimates generally work out to be too high to be useful in the making of any important policy decision.

This overview makes it evident that an acceptable, unique and complete identification of all urban slums in the country has not been possible due to conceptual and administrative problems. Pronab Sen Committee (MHUPA, 2010), set up to address the definitional anomalies and giving robust estimates of present and projected slum population, unfortunately, too, failed in achieving the objectives. It defined slum as "a compact settlement of at least 20 households with a collection of poorly built tenements, mostly of temporary nature, crowded together usually with inadequate sanitary and drinking water facilities in unhygienic conditions". This definition has commonality with all the diverse definitions used by different data-gathering agencies in the country, except that it adopted the threshold number of 20 households which is below the level defined by Census and NSSO. It neither specified the criteria for quantitatively capturing the different characteristics of slums noted above nor tried to provide the rationale for them. Most importantly, it did not draw attention to the economic contribution of the slum population and efficiency in their use of land, etc. and ignored the aspect of the security of tenure that could have provided a positive perspective for launching slum development programmes in the country.

2.4 Limitations of Data Availability from National Sources and the Need for Strengthening the System

The main sources of data regarding slums in India are the decennial population and housing census and the National Sample Surveys (NSS), as noted above. Information from both sources is available regularly that can help in studying the living conditions in the urban slums over time, at the macro-level, although their coverage and methodology differ significantly. These two are the independent external sources that can help evaluate and validate the claims of outcome and success of government agencies, implementing various schemes launched at the national and state level.

While the Census can provide detailed data on slums in the statutory towns of 2011 and hopefully for 2023, when the next Census is likely to be conducted, a detailed socio-economic survey covering the inter-census period could have been considered by NSS providing similar details and a few other socio-economic characteristics of the population living therein. This would have provided a few temporally comparable indicators needed for capturing a macro picture of the slum situation in the country and the improvements brought about through programmatic interventions, as also helped international comparisons in the context of the SDG.

It has been argued that the lack of holistic and equity-based urban planning, based on comprehensive slum data has led to the large-scale exclusion of the vulnerable population, resulting in segmentation of cities, the concentration of poor in certain areas and degenerated peripheralization. Miserable living and working conditions in slums or squatter settlements are the most visible manifestations of such exclusionary development, which is reflected also in a declining trend in the share of rural poor in the Rural-Urban migration stream.

For building a holistic picture of the slum situation emerging over the years, both Census and NSS must bring the notified and recognized slums, as defined by the State Acts, within their definitional purview. In addition, the non-notified and undeclared slums, exhibiting unhygienic living conditions, the inadequacy of basic amenities, etc. must also be included employing definitive criteria based on a certain threshold percentage of households, suffering from deprivation.

It is important to note that massive data on slums flow out of urban administration and development schemes and urban local bodies, besides those provided by the two official agencies, noted above. This information must be compiled using the latest ICT, including mobile-based applications, through a network, linked with the state-level urban information system. It would also be necessary to have a complete geo-referenced registry or directory of all urban slums so that analyses across space and time become possible. Space technology can also be used for mapping slums within urban areas. The necessary capacity for this should be developed in National Building Organisation (NBO). Importantly, NBO has collected a large amount of data under its USHA scheme, which should be made easily available to researchers and administrators. A critical analysis of the strength and weaknesses of this rich data source is yet to be undertaken. This needs to be taken up as a priority task by the NBO.

Availability of comparable data across the cities, states and over time is an issue, as discussed above. As per the Ministry of Housing and Urban Poverty Alleviation's committee, headed by Dr Pronab Sen, the slum population was projected to go up from 63 million in 2001 to 93 million in 2011. Population Census of India, however, records about 65 million slum dwellers for the later year. This implies a significant decline in the percentage of the slum population during the decade. The gap between the projected and recorded figures of slum population in 2011 could be attributed to poor coverage in the 2011 Census and an exclusionary urbanization process. Micro-level evidence from across the country suggests that the deficit of 18 million slum population in 2011 can indeed be attributed to both the factors; apathy of the Census organization to identify slum population and exclusionary urban growth, inhibiting expansion and emergence of slums, particularly in large cities.

Due to these data inconsistencies concerning slums, the Government of India, (Ministry of Statistics and Programme Implementation) was not able to accurately benchmark the country's progress towards the UN MDG Target 11 of achieving "significant improvement in the lives of at least 100 million slum dwellers", in its monitoring Report in the year 2014. While the Report records data deficits in several areas of development, in the context of slum statistics, it simply notes that "reliable data do not exist". This certainly is a sad commentary on the state of slum statistics in India. It also reflects the negativity of the framework of slum research and an absence of a positive perspective in favour of in situ slum improvement.

2.5 Need for Slum Development Indices for the Identifying States and Cities for Priority in Intervention

The governments, both at central and state levels, have, from time to time, recognized the necessity of operationalizing the concept of slum deprivation and slum vulnerability leading to building indices capturing the levels of deprivation in physical, social and economic dimensions, to prioritize the programmatic interventions. The indices are considered important also for assessing the changes in deprivation/vulnerability over time which, in turn, helps monitor the progress of slum-related programmes and taking the corrective steps in implementation. For monitoring the outcomes of the various slum development policies and programmes, such indices need to be constructed at regular intervals. There is, indeed, a felt need for working out these slum-related indices in the ministries and departments concerned with urban development for fund allocation and determining priority areas for intervention.

Importantly, an attempt has been made by a committee appointed by the Ministry of Housing and Urban Poverty Alleviation (MHUPA), headed by Amitabh Kundu in 2014, to construct a slum index using the data available from various official sources. The idea was to present the status of select states and cities in terms of slum vulnerability at two points in time. Accordingly, indices articulating slum situations were prepared for 2001 and 2011 for all States and UTs. City-level indices were also worked out for 46 cities that had a population above a million in 2011 and 22 such cities in 2001. The differences between the composite indices for 2001 and 2011 reflect the improvement or deterioration in the slum situation over the decade. It is suggested that such indices can be developed at the state level and for all urban centres at regular intervals by obtaining the required data from the concerned agencies. The index can be used by administrators and policymakers, besides the academics, for better designing the programmes and schemes, monitoring their implementation and taking corrective actions, as and when required, in a transparent manner. Most importantly, the Committee also found that 95.9% of the households covered in the study live in slums that can be considered tenable and, therefore, could be upgraded in situ. It further recommended that tenability must be an important component of the index, constructed for identifying slums to be taken up for up-gradation since the use of tenability criterion in an ad hoc manner results in the exclusion of a large number of slums, urgently requiring state attention. The recommendations of the Committee, unfortunately, did not receive active consideration of the policymakers understandably because of an absence of political will to provide the title to the land occupied by the slum dwellers.

2.6 Tenability: An Unexplored Dimension in Slum Studies

The negative framework in the slum studies in India has often led to the conclusion that keeping the slums at their present location poses a threat to the health of not only the slum population but also to the entire city. This has led to programmes of eviction and relocation of slums, generally outside the city limits. Such measures are often justified by referring to the different types of livelihood and community networks, often created by the slum population, that are not possible in the heart of the city. It is argued that they comprise largely the displaced rural population "who would find the city peripheries to be more congenial for their economic pursuits and styles of living".

A myth has, thus, been built that the slum population prefer locations outside the city limits for their livelihood and habitation. This, however, has been busted not only by rigorous field-based studies but also by the strong and often violent resistance by slum dwellers to initiatives of relocation. This is basically because they do not want to be delinked from the economic and social network of the earlier locations and thereby face the absence of employment opportunities in the periphery. Consequently, in situ up-gradation versus relocation of slums has become the central issue of debate in slum related interventions (De, 2017). Taking note of the disenchantment with the programmes of relocation, many of the Union Government Programmes including Rajiv Awas Yojana, Jawaharlal Nehru National Urban Renewal Mission, Prime Minister's Away Yojana have thankfully been forced to accept that up-gradation must take place at the site of the slum itself and not through eviction or displacement.

Given this macro context, it is important to propose an alternate definition of slum vulnerability, incorporating the concept of tenability and an appropriate system of data generation. It is extremely important to bring in tenurial vulnerability formally into the slum development analysis at the inception stage rather than leaving it to the stage of implementation. This would help to determine the magnitude of the slum population that can be covered under a programme and check whether that matches with what is envisaged or promised by the policy at a macro level and if any amendment in the legal system is required for the purpose. Furthermore, this would allow or necessitate determining the criterion of security of tenure in the context of the mission and vision of the government, instead of leaving it to the legal setup and implementing agencies at the grass-root level. The exercise would also rescue the definition of slums from a negativist framework by adding a positive indicator of tenurial security.

The criterion of legal right to the land, which constitutes the basis of the UN-Habitat definition, has unfortunately not been brought within the definitional framework of vulnerability indices in India, as noted above. There has been no empirical investigation or political questioning of the land tenure issue while designing the relevant schemes. This is kept under the carpet and brought out only at the final stage, just to exclude the slums where tenurial security for the slum population does not exist. This has resulted in the exclusion of a large number of slums with high vulnerability, permitting only a small number of slums to take advantage of the programmes.

The agencies owning the slum land - not only the private bodies but also even government agencies, at central, state and municipal levels - strongly resent and resist their land being taken up for slum development, making a plea that the land has been designated for other priority use. Sometimes the argument is that the land under the slums are not suited for human habitation and, therefore, must be left vacant.

A convenient argument has, thus, flowed out of the negative framework of slum studies that a large proportion of the slum population lives in non-tenable areas that cannot be developed or regularized for habitation. The local authorities have pleaded their inability to resolve this conflict and launch in situ slum development programmes as envisioned under the schemes at the national or state level. Such claims, nonetheless, require empirical verification.

Tenability refers to the possibility of "maintaining, holding or sustaining" a settlement at a particular site. At a programmatic level, unfortunately, it is confused with notification, stipulating that notified sites are "tenable" and vice-versa. It is important that NSS and Census do not identify slums as tenable and non-tenable but only as being notified and non-notified. However, it does note its location, as to whether it is near a drain, or railway line, quality of land for habitation etc. The information is not based on households' responses but is gathered from key informants in each slum, included in the survey. However, based on this information, government agencies have mostly not notified these as slums and therefore treated them as "non-tenable" at programmatic level.

An examination of the data sources indicates that the official data on notified and non-notified slums do not help calculate a tenability Index. From Table 2.1, it can be seen that there is no appreciable difference in the quality of the micro environment

Table 2.1 Location of notified and non-notified slums (%)

Indicator	Notified		Non-notified	
	69th	65th	69th	65th
Owned by railway	3	3	9	6
Owned privately	48	38	42	44
Surrounded by an industrial area	7	6	11	10
Near drain, railway or river	40	42	38	47
Approach motorable road/path	83	75	75	69
Waterlogging of the approach road	35	36	29	45
No drainage	11	10	45	23
Number of Slums in sample	441	365	440	365

Source Committee Analysis, based on NSS (69th round) Survey on "Key Indicators of Urban Slum 2012" and NSS (65th round) Survey on "Some Characteristics of Urban Slum 2008–09"

between the non-notified and notified slums. This raises questions about considering non-notified slums as non-tenable. One observes that most of the non-notified slums are approachable by motorable roads as much as the notified slums. In the context of other amenities, the Table shows that many among the non-notified slums have access to services while several notified slums do not have that. The differences in terms of their location on the river bed, on sides of rail track and approachability by motorable roads are not significant. It is nonetheless true that a resident of a notified slum has a higher likelihood of receiving government support for basic amenities, such as street lighting, drinking water and garbage collection. The notification also appears to incentivize households to invest in their dwellings, as manifest in the higher proportion of *pucca* houses and in-house latrines.

An analysis of the access to basic amenities reinforces the above conclusions about the difference between the notified and non-notified slums bring statistically non-significant (Table 2.2). The same is true in terms of social characteristics, as presented in Table 2.3. Minorities and SC/ST households are over-represented in slums but that is the case in both notified and non-notified slums. The proportions of households with freehold and written contracts in the two categories of slums are comparable, though the figure has decreased appreciably in non-notified slums over time. A large majority report being in the area for a decade or more and claim to have documentary evidence for that in both types of slums. The data on latrines further reinforce the earlier conclusions regarding the absence of significant differences between the two types of slums. Finally, one of the definite indicators of "non-tenability"', viz. flooding, is seen to be similar across notified and non-notified slums.

The above overview of the physical and social conditions in the two categories of slums, based on NSSO data leads to immediate rejection of the idea of equating notification with tenability. The official use of the concept of "tenability"' based on this idea has indeed been restrictive, not allowing adequate slum population to be brought under the purview of the ongoing housing and slum development programmes.

Table 2.2 Access to basic services—notified and non-notified slums (%)

Share of slums	Notified		Non-notified	
	69th	65th	69th	65th
Pucca houses	85	64	42	50
Semi-pucca houses	11	30	34	29
Drinking water from the tap	82	79	64	77
Most residents have no latrine	16	10	42	20
Waterlogging	37	33	43	44
Electricity in both streets and houses	86	76	55	53
Garbage collection by the municipality	80	75	49	55
Garbage collected at least once a week	90	77	89	59
Presence of association	26	28	13	20
Number of slums in sample	441	365	440	365

Source Committee Analysis, based on NSS (69th round) Survey on "Key Indicators of Urban Slum 2012" and NSS (65th round) Survey on "Some Characteristics of Urban Slum 2008–09"

Table 2.3 Household characteristics of notified and non-notified slums (%)

Indicator (share of households)	Notified Slum		Non-Notified Slum		Non-slum Urban	
	69th	65th	69th	65th	69th	65th
Religious minority	25	26	26	22	19	19
ST/SC	30	34	33	33	16	16
Freehold and written contract	62	63	54	62	67	65
Access to motorable, lighted road	53	47	37	35	66	58
Household exclusive latrine	43	30	27	23	67	62
No latrine access	13	16	26	24	8	10
In the area 10 years and more	71		67		59	
Insufficient water supply	12		11		10	
Experience flood in the past 5 years	10		12		5	
Stomach problem in last month	14		12		13	
Official document noting the area of living	88		85			
Number of households in sample	3,176	3,957	2,142	3,553	36,633	48,085

Source Committee Analysis, based on NSS (69th round) Survey on Key Indicators of Drinking Water, Sanitation, Hygiene and Housing Condition in India 2012 and NSS (65th round) Survey on Housing Condition and Amenities in India, 2008–09

2.7 A Framework for Constructing Slum Development Indices Focusing on Tenability

Given the urgency of policy intervention for slum improvement, recognized both at the global and national level, and the current usage of notification criteria to exclude a large number of slum settlements in an ad-hoc manner, a framework for constructing a formal vulnerability index has been proposed in this section, having a built-in component of slum tenability, using the available data from secondary sources, at the state and city level. Adoption of this framework is likely to increase the scope and coverage of intervention by the central and state governments in slum improvement.

After reviewing the definitions viz. UN-HABITAT as also those of the Census, NSSO and the Pronab Sen Committee, and understanding their limitations and scope for improvement, an attempt has been made here to assess slum vulnerability based on six dimensions. The details of the dimensions and their constituent indicators are given in Table 2.4. It is important to mention that the list of indicators proposed here is illustrative. It is given here only to suggest that such indices can be developed at the State level and possibly for all urban centres of the country, based on a much larger database, than attempted here.

1. The magnitude of slum population
2. Availability of basic household amenities
3. Housing conditions articulated through temporary, semi-permanent and permanent structures
4. Possession of household assets
5. Access to banking services
6. Social dimensions: Coverage of SC/ST population, literacy rate and availability of health facilities.

The indicators under each of the six identified dimensions of vulnerability have been chosen based on a review of the available research studies, keeping the current development policies in the context. The indicators can be constructed using the data sources, the robustness of which is well established. The rationale for the adoption of each of the dimensions of vulnerability and their indicators are given below.

It is important to note that similar indices were constructed for 2001 and 2011 at the state and city level by the MHUPA Committee (2014), mentioned above.

Because NSS provides no robust data regarding tenurial security at the household level, MHUPA through the National Buildings Organisation (NBO), carried out surveys between 2008–09 and 2011–12 in 988 cities/towns, having population more than 40,000 (as per 2001 census) throughout the country, under the Urban Statistics for Human Resource and Assessment (USHA) scheme. Using this data set, the MHUPA Committee (2014) had proposed to identify tenable slums as those having a certain percentage of households "who have recognized tenure rights, e.g., *patta*, possession certificate, occupancy right, etc.". Accepting this framework, a slum can be defined as tenable if:

Table 2.4 Dimensions of vulnerability, constituent indicators and their rationale

Dimensions and sub-parameters		Rationale
1. Magnitude of the slum Population		This is an important dimension capturing the slum magnitude in terms of population and households. The dimension through its various indicators articulates the volume of the slums in the state concerning the total number of slums in the State. The implicit assumption in choosing the dimension is that the larger the slum proportion, the greater is the vulnerability
(i)	Percentage Slum Household of State/Total urban household of state. (from Census)	This captures the scale of the slum population concerning the urban population in the State
(ii)	Percentage of Slum HHs to Total Urban HHs. (From NSSO Housing Condition Survey)	The scope and coverage of the NSS survey are different from that of the Census. To bring this additional information that might be captured by NSS, an indicator similar to the first indicator based on Census data, has been included under this dimension
(iii)	Percentage of non-notified slum Enumeration Blocks (EB) in the state/Total no of slums EB in the state. (from Census 2011)	The inclusion of this index is based on the assumption that non notified slums are those that have come up recently and are in a worse condition compared to notified slums. As census 2011 slum data is regarding EB, it is important to measure the magnitude based on the EB data
2. Availability of basic household Amenities		The non-availability of basic amenities is an important aspect of deprivation in the slums. This is a part of the UN-HABITAT definition as well
3. Housing condition		
(i)	Percentage of HHs living in kutcha and semi-pucca houses + Percentage of HHs reporting housing condition to be bad (NSS) + Percentage of HHs living in dilapidated houses (Census)	Robustness of the physical structure of the house is an important indicator stipulated by UN-HABITAT and this is incorporated in the index by taking the average of the percentage of households with kutcha and semi-pucca structures, the percentage living 'bad' houses and that of HHs in dilapidated houses

(continued)

Table 2.4 (continued)

Dimensions and sub-parameters		Rationale
(ii)	Percentage of HH by no. of married couples without exclusive dwelling room	Overcrowding or congestion is another important factor considered by the UN-HABITAT to measure the deprivation in slums. The indicator like the percentage of HHs having one or more married couple sharing their room with an adult can be taken as an indicator of overcrowding
(iii)	The average number of persons living in a room in slum HHs (Room Density)	UN-HABITAT defines overcrowding as the proportion of HHs with more than two people per room. The indicator of the number of persons per room in slum HH can be taken as a good indicator of room density in a slum HH
4. Assets in slum households		Although the UN-HABITAT stipulated assessment of slum status concerning the physical parameters related to housing and availability of basic amenities, the Committee considered the inclusion of assets owned by the slum HHs as an important dimension in the slum index, for taking a holistic view. Consequently, the indicators relating to possession of assets like TV and bicycle have been considered relevant for determining economic vulnerability
(i)	Percentage of HHs with no television	
(ii)	Percentage of HHs with no bicycle	
(iii)	Percentage of HH with No Scooter/Motorcycle/Moped	
(iv)	Percentage of HH with No Mobile	
(v)	Percentage of HH with No asset	
5. Social dimensions		Though the UN-HABITAT definition does not explicitly mention aspects of social vulnerability, the Committee considered that as important for inclusion in the slum index for making the framework holistic. The social composition of the slum population often determines the perception and attitude of civic authorities and common people, adding to their vulnerability
(i)	Percentage of SC & ST slum population in the State to total Slum Population in the state	The percentage of the SC/ST population in the slums is an important indicator of the level of vulnerability due to social prejudices against them

(continued)

Table 2.4 (continued)

Dimensions and sub-parameters		Rationale
(ii)	Percentage illiterate persons in the slums	The percentage of illiterate within slums, especially female illiteracy is an important indicator of slum vulnerability as these are strongly correlated with several indicators of socio-economic development
(iii)	Percentage of illiterate females in the slums	
6. Availing banking services by slum HHs		The literature on slum vulnerability mostly tends to ignore the economic conditions of the slum HHs. The Committee considered these to be important as these often manifest in the physical conditions of the housing and the neighbourhood. Since the only economic indicator that could be constructed using the available data from national sources is access to banking facilities, this has been included to assess economic vulnerability
(i)	Percentage of HH not availing banking services	

Source Census/NSSO/Slum Committee Analysis

(a) It is notified, regardless of location;
(b) It is located in an area classified as "Others (non-Hazardous/Non-Objectionable)", even if it is not notified;
(c) If at least 10% of households in the slum report having *patta (land title)*, possession certificate of occupancy rights, even if it is not notified and not located in an area classified as "Others (non-Hazardous/Non-Objectionable)".

The rationale for considering the third indicator is that in many non-notified slums, several households report having *patta*, possession certificate or occupancy rights. A positive approach to slum development would then be to consider all households in these slums as having a prima facie claim for *patta* or occupancy right. One would argue that if a slum has been declared fit for habitation by the concerned authorities for a certain percentage of the people, it cannot be declared unsafe and hazardous for others. Also, if a site is amenable to human habitation, the default mode of development there should be in situ up-gradation.

Based on this premise, the slums, wherein the number of slum households, who have recognized tenure rights, e.g. *patta*, possession certificate and occupancy right is over 10% of the total non-rental slum households, could be considered tenable. This index indicates the extent to which the state or city can extend tenure rights to those who are *prima facie* eligible to make such a claim and have the potential to be recognized or given such tenure rights. The 10% threshold was used to take care of sampling and reporting errors.

Table 2.5 Percentage of households having/not having tenurial rights in tenable and non-tenable slums

Classification of location		Patta/possession certificate/ Occupancy right	Encroacher on private/public land and others	Renter	Total
Tenable	Notified	10.2	3.2	5.6	18.9
	Non-notified	29.4	11.6	12.0	52.9
Usually 'Untenable'	Notified	8.1	3.8	4.3	16.2
	Non-notified	4.7	5.2	2.1	12.0
	Of which, not satisfying condition "(c)"	0.1	3.5	0.5	4.1
Total		52.3	23.8	23.9	100.0

Source Slum Index Committee Analysis, based on USHA Survey

Information on possession of patta or land title is not collected in the NSSO rounds. To address the aspect of tenability at the household level, it is possible to use the data collected under the USHA scheme. Under USHA, information about slums regarding their notification and location—establishing whether the safety of the neighbourhoods is compromised by major transport routes, drains, railway lines, rivers or other water bodies, stormwater drains, or other potentially hazardous or objectionable factors—are collected. Applying the threefold criteria discussed above, 95.9% of the slum households have been found to be living in slums that are tenable and hence are appropriate for in situ up-gradation.

As seen in Table 2.5, only 10.2% of slum-dwellers in the sample have Patta/ Possession Certificate/ Occupancy Right in the notified slums that are usually considered "tenable". This works out to be about 54% of the total households of 18.9% in tenable notified slums. The corresponding figure in the case of non-notified tenable slums is slightly higher—56%. In the case of the slums considered untenable, one observes that 50% of the slum dwellers in the notified slums have *patta*, possession certificates, etc. The corresponding figure in the non-notified non-tenable slums is 39%. The analysis shows that most of these households can be considered eligible for in situ up-gradation through the application of the threefold criteria.

Under the current government programmes, only 18.9% of the slum households that are in notified slums at tenable sites would be considered eligible for in situ up-gradation. However, the definition of tenability proposed here would lead to the inclusion of an additional 77% of households. Only 4.1% of slum households are in locations that are empirically "untenable".

The final composite index of Slum Vulnerability must, then, be constructed by combining the aspect of slum tenability along with the six dimensions of vulnerability, as discussed above. Alternately, a separate index on tenability can be developed and analysed along with other six dimensions of slum vulnerability in an institutionalized manner to select slums for in situ up-gradation.

2.8 Conclusions and the Way Forward

The slum population in India was projected to increase from 63 million in 2001 to 93 million in 2011. The 2011 Census, however, reported the figure to be only 65 million. Negative perspectives on slums, in the domains of data collection and urban planning, have been responsible for a process of exclusionary urbanization, whereby residents are evicted from slums and relocated to the peripheries and outside the city limits. Because urban planners and politicians have not had a sharp focus on the tenurial security and tenability of slums, and have defined these in an extremely restrictive manner, only a small percentage of the targeted populations has been brought under the development missions of government. The absence of an equity consideration in planning, based on an inclusive definition of tenability, is responsible for the large-scale exclusion of potential slum populations, segmentation of cities and degenerated peripheralization (see Kundu et al. (2002) and Kundu (2012)).

The Census and NSSO regularly provide information on housing conditions, access to amenities and other aspects of slum life that help in analysing inter-state and inter-city variations in the conditions in urban slums, and changes over time. The problem with the census data, however, is its coverage of only a limited set of items and its temporal non-comparability. NSSO, on the other hand, has the problem of a small sample size, inadequate for generating robust estimates at the city level. These problems need to be addressed by restructuring the system of data generation by NSSO, adding a few new items in the questionnaires and increasing the sample size in selected cities. In addition, the creation of a system to collect and collate information generated through regular administrative work during the implementation of development schemes (such as the USHA) in a temporally and cross-sectionally comparable manner, is required urgently. The strengths and weaknesses of such datasets, generated by the concerned ministries of the Government, need to be identified and their problems addressed. Cleaning up these data, making them cross-sectionally and temporally comparable, and bringing them into the public domain will help in better designing and implementing a comprehensive slum development strategy. Also, this would help in monitoring the key indicators of SDG 11 that envisage access to adequate, safe and affordable housing and basic services to all, thereby promoting inclusive and sustainable urbanization (see Mitlin & Patel, 2005).

The number of slums in India that have been identified using government notification and legal sanctions as being *tenable* under various government missions is much less than that recognized or projected at the policy level. The indices of slum vulnerability and tenability constructed by MHUPA's Committee in 2014, which applied an inclusive reading of slum development data, shows that potential slum beneficiaries are several times the population that is currently being targeted for in situ redevelopment. A positive perspective on slums, built on an index of tenability defined inclusively, would greatly enhance the scope of state intervention and address the needs of a much larger segment of India's deprived population.

References

Census of India. (2011). General population tables, government of India, New Delhi.

De, I. (2017). Slum improvement in India: Determinants and approaches. *Housing Studies, 32*(7), 990–1013.

Denis, E., Mukhopadhyay, P., & Zerah, M. H. (2012). Subaltern urbanisation in India. *Economic and Political Weekly, 47*(30), 52–62.

Kundu, A. (2012). Dynamics of growth and process of degenerated peripheralisation in Delhi: an analysis of socioeconomic, segmentation and differentiation in micro environment. In P. J. Marcotullio & G. McGranahan (Eds.), *Scaling urban environmental challenges: From local to global and back* (pp. 156–179). London: Earthscan Publications.

Kundu, A.K., Pradhan, B. K., & Subramanian, A. (2002). Dichotomy or continuum: analysis of impact of urban centres on their periphery. *Economic and Political Weekly, 37*(50), 5039–5046 (2002).

MHUPA. (2010). *Report of the Committee on Slum Statistics/Census* (Pronab Sen Committee Report). New Delhi: Government of India, 2010.

MHUPA. (2014). *Report of the Committee on Slum Index* (Amitabh Kundu Committee Report). New Delhi, Government of India, 2015.

Mitlin, D., & Patel, S. (2005). Working for rights from the grassroots. *Alliance, 10*(3), 27–28.

UN-HABITAT. (2003). *Guide to monitoring target 11: improving the lives of 100 million slum dwellers. Progress towards the millennium development goals.* Nairobi: UN-HABITAT.

UN-HABITAT. (2012). *State of thewWorld's cities 2012–2013: Prosperity of cities.* Nairobi: UN-HABITAT.

Chapter 3
India's Poor and Better-Off Urban Citizens: Cycles of Proximity and Segregation

Hans Schenk

Abstract After India's independence in 1947 sought its leaders to provide the country's urban slum dwellers with acceptable, accessible and affordable housing. A major question was where this acceptable, i.e. decent housing should be built. Slum dwellers had to live in accessible locations, close to their inner-city worksites, while land in inner cities appeared too expensive to provide for affordable housing. It took some 15 years before the failures of this policy were accepted. Increasing negative opinions regarding the urban poor helped from the 1960s onwards to make slum dwellers themselves responsible for their housing needs: the state withdrew largely from its welfare-oriented housing policies. Self-help housing projects in urban peripheries were developed, while in some existing slums marginal in situ improvements took place. The resulting increased spatial segregation of the urban poor from their work locations resulted however in large-scale subaltern return movements by erstwhile slum dwellers from the urban fringes to the places where they used to live, belonged and had found a livelihood. A new impetus to remove the urban poor from inner-city locations emerged after the introduction of India's liberalized economic policies in the 1990s that fostered (foreign) investments in prestigious real estate. New luxury residential and commercial complexes replaced slums and slum dwellers were once again pushed out of the city. The question remains whether they will again be able to return to the places where they came from, or whether they have to find new types of survival in the peripheries of India's cities.

Keywords Housing policy · Slums · Urban segregation · India

H. Schenk (✉)
University of Amsterdam, Amsterdam, The Netherlands

A. Kundu et al. (eds.), *Accessible Housing for South Asia*,
https://doi.org/10.1007/978-3-030-88881-7_3

3.1 Introduction: Towards Acceptable, Accessible and Affordable Urban Housing for All

In 1946, on the eve of India's independence in 1947, the colonial Ministry of Health published a rather depressing report on the state of urban housing:

> Housing conditions in India present a deplorable picture. The impression that we have gained during our tours indicate extremely unsatisfactory conditions of housing in some rural and urban areas and, in particular, appalling conditions of overcrowding in industrial centres. The single-room tenement is a common feature of even of the many more recently constructed housing accommodation in industrial areas. Such tenements often house more than one family and, in many cases, have to serve as living-room, kitchen and bed-room. The sanitation of these dwellings is usually inadequate and of a very rudimentary nature. Thousands are without any home or shelter and have to live and sleep on pavements, verandahs, open spaces, under trees, in cowsheds or in any temporary shelter.[1]

It was hence no surprise that the new Indian rulers, from Jawaharlal Nehru, its undisputed leader till his death in 1964, to a range of bearers of authority, and members of advisory committees, advocated for the removal of the overcrowded and dilapidated tenements and the makeshift huts in India's towns and cities, and the construction of acceptable, accessible and affordable housing. Nehru said how painful it was to him to see the huts on either side of the road in Madras. He was quoted to be appalled at the slums in Kanpur and thought that these should be burned down. He criticized the tenements for the industrial workers when he visited Bombay (see for details: Schenk, 2020, 2021).

3.1.1 *Acceptable Housing Standards*

How were these desires operationalized? A convenient key is formulated in 1955 in the editorial of the prestigious Journal of the Indian Institute of Town Planners. It was stated that standards for housing should be at least a: "… two-roomed house with adequate sanitary facilities", and that: "Sub-standard housing is but a step towards slums" (Quoted in Jha, 1986, p. 19). A Study Group on Greater Bombay,[2] appointed by the Bombay State in 1958, chose almost the same words in recommending minimum accommodation for a family but added the provisioning of a separate kitchen (Study Group for Greater Bombay, 1959, p. 57).[3]

---

[1] Government of India, Ministry of Health, Report of the Health Survey and Development Committee, 1946. Quoted in Singh (1978, p. 2).

[2] Bombay State was in 1960 bifurcated into two states: Maharashtra (with the city of Bombay) and Gujarat.

[3] The Study Group added, however, surprisingly that it might be necessary to lower down this standard of accommodation temporarily, and it went on by stating that it might be necessary as a transitional measure to rest content with single-room tenements (p. 58).

The initial mood among the architects of India's development was hence to improve the housing conditions of large segments of its urban population, by formulating minimum standards as per the appeal made by Nehru and others. Where this accommodation should be built? "Near to factories, shops and workshops where the inhabitants of tenements and huts live", was the obvious answer. A short distance to work (and some access to drinking water and basic sanitation) was of overriding importance for labourers, after long working hours and often without means of transport. But, as shall also be seen in this paper, such an initial answer is too easy and naive. It underestimates the historic, but enduring "uneasiness" of close urban co-habitation of poor and better-off citizens. Structural inequality between several urban communities manifests itself not merely in the geographical distance but also in terms of mistrust and fear of others, notably the poor or lower castes in urban India. Time and again it has been observed that in the past the poor, or lower castes, had to be satisfied with the spatial leftovers after the fulfilment of the residential needs and desires of the better off. Thus, civil lines were built for the colonial elites (where also the Indian better-off found a place), away from the areas of the urban poor, who were looked upon as: "… inherently insanitary in their habits … rustic misfits" (Gooptu, 2001, p. 69). When the new colonial capital of New Delhi was lavishly developed, Old Delhi was "forgotten", while remarking: "keep the rats of the old city out of the new".[4]

Keeping these precautionary remarks in mind, I come to the crux of this chapter: where should acceptable dwellings for all citizens living in dilapidated tenements and makeshift huts be built? Should improvements and new constructions take place on the spot, or somewhere else? Space and distance are critical areas of concern in this paper. But spatial proximity and spatial segregation are linked to more fundamental, but parallel societal concepts of inclusivity and exclusivity in determining urban structures. Sapana Doshi reminds us that: "Eviction and resettlement practices reflecting both inclusive and exclusionary notions of belonging have contoured the boundaries of urban citizenship among slum-residents" (Doshi, 2015, p. 230). Though the focus will remain on the spatial aspects of acceptable housing in this chapter, the idea of belonging, of being included in, or being excluded from, the larger urban structures and processes are present in the background, and will now and then come to the fore.

3.1.2 *Affordable, Acceptable and Accessible Shelter for All Urban Citizens*

There is no single answer to the question of where acceptable, affordable and accessible housing for all in India's towns and cities should be provided, given the variety of the living conditions of slum dwellers, and the diversity in the physical structures of

[4] These words are said to be spoken by New Delhi's chief architect and planner, Lutyens, and recorded by Goodfriend (1982, p. 473).

their dwelling units. Appearances of slums could range from single-room dwellings with shared facilities in multi-storeyed overcrowded and dilapidated buildings to huts built by squatters, erected with any available material, on any available place.[5]

There seems, however, to exist a common ground in the search for an answer to the question of where improved housing for poor urban citizens should be located. Tenement buildings and huts have in common that they were largely built near the places of work of their respective inhabitants. This characteristic can clearly be seen in Madras until a few decades after independence when land to build huts was still available. Relatively large squatter settlements in the North of the city where industries were concentrated, housed predominantly industrial workers, while in the South such settlements were small and evenly dispersed over this part of the city. They accommodated the household servants, washermen and -women, gardeners, street sellers, etc. working for the middle-class neighbourhoods in the South (see de Bruijne and Schenk, 1992, passim). This historically grown pattern of the common citizens to live close to their worksites, has hence resulted in the emergence of slums in high- and middle-income neighbourhoods and subsequently in redevelopment programmes on-the-spot in Madras and other cities with available land.

However, the available literature indicates that such in situ improvements would generally imply high-rise housing solutions to accommodate the large slum population in a limited space. Land is scarce and expensive in the central parts of many urban places in India. The costs of high-rise housing solutions would be prohibitive for most of the targeted categories of the urban population, even with sizeable public financial support, or when generous subsidies were included in the balance sheets of private builders (see Schenk, 2020, for details). Some employers, however, invested in a subsidized shelter for their workers, reasoning that both workers and employers would benefit from improved shelters near the work sites. Paul Wiebe writes about Madras that: "Industries have done much for their employees in the way of housing and the provision of facilities", and gives a few examples (Wiebe, 1975, p. 32).[6] Kunj Patel gives examples of Bombay mill owners subsidizing the rents of their tenements for their workers, and she observes that: "The Killick management regards housing as a part of its welfare activities" … as … "every effort is being made to provide good accommodation for the workers", but these examples are exceptional as she states in general that from the side of employers: "no appreciable efforts have been forthcoming" regarding the housing problem of their workers (Patel, 1963, p. 76).

[5] I have chosen to use here as much as possible the generic word 'slum'. I have, where possible, ignored often made specifications of housing, such as those into types of building material of a shelter, or of its legal status in the complicated urban rules and regulations and landownership. I have similarly deliberately chosen not to categorize the inhabitants in areas of sub-standard dwellings in terms of legitimacy, etc. for improvement or clearance, etc. Such specification form not seldom a distraction manoeuvre from the core issue: the existence of extremely bad shelter, usually used by extremely poor citizens.

[6] This statement has, however, been contradicted in an anonymous article in the Economic Weekly of 25 June 1949, p. 11 in which it is stated that few employers are willing to co-operate with the Government and to participate in schemes of industrial housing which will impose additional burdens to them.

R. K. Trivedi, who analysed 1961-census data on slums in Ahmedabad, is outright in pointing out the grave and chronic shelter conditions in the slums in this city and calls for drastic action. "The State, the local authorities and the employers whose duty it is to provide a comfortable living to their employees must rise to the occasion and discharge their responsibilities without further delay" (Trivedi, 1970, p. 213).

In summary, the idea that in situ shelter improvement projects for urban workers is a viable option has not been operationalized on any sizable scale, particularly in the private sector, despite some early exceptions. What remains are the cynical words of Kamal Nayan Kabra to defy the: "incapability of the large mass of urban populations to be able to own or hire a structure which may be called a house" (Kabra, 1975, p. 21). The focus of public authorities, hence has rather been on re-settlement and re-housing projects elsewhere, as the costs of erecting shelters away from the urban centres are lower: the land is less costly. Most of the available jobs, however, could be found in urban centres. Hence, sailing between the Scylla and the Charybdis of costs and distances characterizes much of the struggle among poor citizens to survive in urban India, and is of central concern throughout this paper.

3.1.3 Phases of Affordable, Accessible and Acceptable Realities for Poor Urban Citizens

In this chapter overviews of the dominant and subaltern approaches to the question of the location of affordable, accessible and acceptable shelter for poor citizens are discussed. Several phases in these approaches can be distinguished. In the first phase, discussed in the next paragraph, only costs and distances to work-places are considered. This phase coincides more or less with the first 3 Five-Year Plans in India (1951–1966) when optimism about India's future was plainly articulated. India was to become a secular society, free of caste and community-linked prejudices—particularly towards the "ritually unclean" Harijans, who often performed the most unattractive but essential urban activities.

The public sector played an important role in shaping this future, envisioning shelter for all its urban citizens, an approach which in retrospect has been considered as Nehruvian socialism. The next phase—coming to the fore in the subsequent paragraph—is more complex. Disappointments with the functioning of state institutions in charge of housing paved the way for a development scenario with greater roles and responsibilities given to individuals to realize their shelter, in collaboration with these institutions. This period started in the early 1960s and lasted till the launched New Economic policy in 1991. This new policy has been analysed in a final paragraph, focusing on the current, ongoing role of the urban middle classes and elites in shaping and improving their housing and environment facilitated by the private sector, at the expense of the urban poor. The importance of available urban land for housing has led to a series of interludes spread between the more time-bound paragraphs, in which I elaborate on land, both in the Indian context and under conditions of existing full public ownership of urban land in Hanoi.

There is another way to characterize the mentioned phases. Each phase has provided a fresh impulse for spatial segregation between the inhabitants of substandard shelter and other categories of India's urban population. But spatial segregation has, however, in each phase been contested: poor citizens tried to return to their jobs, their neighbourhoods, even their dilapidated shelters. In the first phase is this segregation accompanied by optimism regarding the provision of new, better and eventually more accessible shelter for poor urban citizens in the mainstream of high expectations of India's welfare politics. The second phase sought primarily individual contributions to better shelter conditions, which were often far from where the urban poor would like to live. This period is as well characterized by an increase of manifest feelings of mistrust for "nearby" urban poor. In the third phase could urban middle-classes in major cities, with the help of public and private capital inputs, express to be "fed up" with the nearby urban poor, and push them away from their living surroundings. In between the high tide waves leading to spatial segregation are periods of a lower tide, when many of the dislodged citizens came back, accompanied by more and more expelled rural migrants.

3.2 Public Housing: Where and for Whom?

What happened during the first few decades of interventions in the urban housing stocks in terms of proximity and segregation? I shall start this discussion with a few examples. In 1949 started the central government its Industrial Housing Scheme. In this scheme were industrialist financially encouraged to finance housing projects for their workers against low rents (to a maximum of 10% of their wages). The government decided three years later even to subsidize industrial employers up to 20% of the construction costs of houses they had built for a concessional rent to their—what was named "genuine" workers. In major cities such as Bombay, with a heavy concentration of cotton mills and their workers, who were usually housed in nearby tenement buildings (*chawls*) in the centre of the city, was urban land extremely scarce and expensive. This scheme hence implied that houses had to be built far from central Bombay. And far away from the cotton mills as well, as industrialists were not willing to move their factories to the urban outskirts, and they were not pressed to do so.[7] Nigel Harris, commenting on such remote housing projects during the 1950s,

[7] The Study Group on Greater Bombay argued that removal of existing industries would impair their production capacity, and stated that from the point of view of the general economy of the country any such impairment of the productive capacity or the competitive position of industrial units would be highly undesirable. (1959, p. 28). Harris is, however, of the opinion that, though the industry is in quantitative terms important (48% of the industrial labour force), it is old and declining, situated in obsolete mills in downtown Bombay. He writes that apart from the sheer existence of the mills in Bombay—which is in his opinion a rather powerful argument—there do not seem compelling

however, remarks: "Peripheral housing is practical only at income levels which make commuting feasible" (Harris, 1978, p. 31). And, apart from distances, there are the high costs of such new accommodation for the tenants. The calculations made by Andrea Menefee Singh and Alfred de Souza and many other researchers on the costs of any tenement housing in Calcutta and Delhi lead to their conclusion that: "… such housing must be highly subsidized, and …. finding the resources for such large-scale subsidies does not seem even remotely possible" (Singh and De Souza, 1980, p. 47). Did slum dwellers, hence move to a house in the urban peripheries? Sisodia concludes in an evaluation of the housing and urban development components of the Second Five Year Plan (1956–1961), that: "Although a fraction of [the] slum dwellers moved out of their habitation for a couple of years as a result of the subsidised industrial housing scheme, yet, on the whole, the slum problem continued as it was" (Sisodia, 2006, p. 392). Resettlement proved to be far, too far and also expensive, too expensive. Ordinary mill workers were often unable to pay the rents, and this doubled the problem—"illegal" occupancies, and sub-letting, leading eventually to the gradual transformation of such a project into a (lower) middle-class housing area. The originally targeted labourers mostly went back to a form of sub-standard shelter nearby their mills or tried to do so—for better or for worse.

This sad scenario became unfortunately too often a reality. But in a project in Bombay which was focused on the resettlement of slum dwellers, things went even worse. "Most eviction campaigns" … writes Weinstein, "… were undertaken without the accompanying rehousing and residents were typically rendered homeless by the actions" (Weinstein, 2014, p. 60), and far away from their sources of livelihood. In a large project in Delhi in the late 1950s under the so-called *jhuggi-jhompri*–huts—scheme, over 50,000 families[8] were forcefully moved from their central locations and provided plots of about 20 square meters in the urban periphery on which they were supposed to construct temporary shelters, awaiting permanent housing.[9] "[T]he inability of the households to remain in the periphery led to approximately 25% of them selling their plots illegally and returning to their place of employment", writes Geoffrey Payne. He adds that the plots were subsequently developed by the new, generally middle-income residents (Payne, 1977, p. 67). Ashish Bose remarks that "We think that the only way to solve the squatter problem is to demolish unauthorized structures and settle the people in the periphery of the city, a process which never works" (Bose, 1973, p. 234). The attempted segregation between evicted families and their places of work made Nigel Harris comment in terms of its impracticality, but Ashish Bose went further. He wrote emotionally that "… social justice demands that people who have cars should *not* live within walking distance of their offices

economic reasons why the mills should be there, and strong reasons why they should not (Harris, 1978, p. 82).

[8] The numbers given in several studies vary, however, widely.

[9] See Tarlo (2000) for a detailed analysis of this "J-J" scheme. *Jhuggi-jhompri* refers to huts, but the programme refers actually to huts or filthy shacks of poor material. She adds that these dwellings are mostly located in forsaken and insanitary places, such as bordering railway lines, open drains, open spaces earmarked for dumping refuse, etc. (Tarlo, p. 53). An apologetic defence by one of the main actors involved in the J-J programme, is given by Jagmohan (1978).

and people who are not rich enough even to afford cycles should *not* be put 20 miles away from the city. Poor people must live near their places of work ... regardless of land values" (Bose, 1973, p. 237).[10]

The trade-off between the lower cost of resettlement in the urban periphery and the advantage for workers finding shelter near work sites is not only an issue in large metropolises such as Bombay. For example, a study on a sub-standard living area in a smaller city, Vijayawada in the then state of Andhra Pradesh, with just over 300,000 inhabitants in 1971, presents the same picture of failed re-settlement. The authors, K. Ranga Rao and M.S.A Rao, describe how a sizeable number of re-settled households sold or rented out their new plots, as there were no jobs nearby the re-settlement area: "... the long distances from the places of work or from the main commercial areas, where only the uneducated slum dwellers could seek employment" made them return to the slums where they came from. "Many such plots are now occupied by middle-class families", add the authors (Rao & Rao, 1984, p. 103). The unavoidable conclusion is that attempts to re-house or re-settle poor urban citizens have failed. And furthermore, not many such planned housing complexes for industrial workers could after all be built, due to paucity of funds.

A rare example of housing projects whereby accessibility and affordability were given due attention can be found in Madras. In 1946, the Madras City Improvement Trust, established with the task to develop activities regarding housing and planning, initially sold plots to middle- and higher-income groups. However, since the late 1940s, it launched so-called Open Developed Plots (ODP) schemes for hut dwellers who were displaced for urban development projects. These schemes were not developed in the outskirts of Madras but on available pockets of land within the city. Between the late 1940s and the early 1960s, 8,430 plots were made available for rent in 28 projects, covering about 50,000 inhabitants. Early schemes had common sanitary facilities, but subsequently, private toilet-cum-bathroom units were constructed. Most schemes were developed mixing ODP-plots with houses for middle- and higher-income groups. Cross-subsidization made it possible to reduce the costs of the plots and the provided infrastructure for the former hut dwellers. Research in 1988 in five ODP-schemes revealed that even after 30–40 years, most of the original inhabitants still lived in their hutments or houses on the assigned plots (see Schenk, Ten Holder & Mulders, 1989, for details).

[10] Italics in original. Twenty miles (say 30 kms) sounds extreme, but the sociologist S. S. Jha mentions a resettlement project in Bombay, whereby dwellers of to-be demolished huts were simply thrown into the streets or carried by the busloads not less than 25 miles away, just to be dropped like refuse into a piece of reclaimed land that was infested by mosquitoes, snakes and wild dogs (Jha, 1986, p. 101),

3.3 Interlude: Land

Spatial proximity between work and living, and costs and time of travel, were the key concerns of the social scientists who analysed urban housing issues in post-colonial India. A common denominator in such analyses was how to make urban land–including land near the places of work –sufficiently accessible to all citizens and how to control its price? Cross-subsidization of land, as practised in Madras, is one such option. Other suggestions include relocation of work sites close to the residential areas of the workers, "so that they are not uprooted from their fields of employment" (Sisodia, 2006, p. 397).[11] Controlling rents, imposing ceilings on urban landownership, acquisition of vacant lands, etc. figure among the policy recommendations made by economists, sociologists, administrators, etc. Time and again, suggestions have also been made to check speculation of land prices. The Urban Land Ceiling Act of 1976, which aimed at curbing private landownership and which was expected for a long time as a satisfactory answer to excessive prices of land, appeared highly inadequate since it had several loopholes and consequently, became a rich source of corruption, and profitable speculation in the imperfect land market. "This act has failed to achieve its main aim all over the country ..." concludes Jha, and he adds "*... the Act is being implemented more through its provisions about exemptions and less through its main provisions*"(Jha, 1986, p. 30; italics by Jha). Gadkari concludes that "the majority of our urban areas are exempt from this Act" and points that "local pressure which makes it difficult for municipalities to acquire land of local people" (Gadkari, 1981, p. 401). Some have openly opposed the imposition of a ceiling on landholding. "It might lower land values to some extent", writes Ashish Bose, but not enough for the urban poor to get access to land. However, he adds, "A new set of rich people will replace another". A ceiling will then prove to be an exercise in futility (Bose, 1973, p. 238).

More radical proposals focus on getting full public control over all urban land—Ashish Bose seems to support such proposals—and even including privately constructed houses for renting purposes. G. B. Krishna Rao argues that a take-over of all vacant land outside the built-up urban areas against a financial compensation might be a better tool to achieve an orderly urban development than the Urban Land Ceiling Act could offer (Rao, 1981, p. 257), while S. S. Jha concludes that a "first essential step towards a rational housing policy in a city like Bombay would be total government control, without any ambiguity, on the vacant land in the city" (Jha, 1986, p. 43). Even a "government of India note on urban land policy", envisages nationalization of urban land, as is noted and highlighted by Kabra (1975):

> It is only through substantial stock of readily available land and its timely disposal that a public authority can influence and control the land prices and regulate balanced use. **Public ownership of land in a big way is thus indispensable.** It is desirable too because such a measure conforms to one of the most significant ingredients of the socialist pattern of

[11] As soft is the in the preparatory studies for the Delhi Master Plan, (in effect in 1962) worded plea (quoted by Sayed S. Shafi) for an optimum location of work centres in relation to housing in Delhi without even trying to substantiate this optimum (Shafi, 1981, p. 62).

society, namely progressive expansion of the public sector. In fact t**he logical next step in this process is the nationalisation of all urban land. That would, of course, provide the ideal setting for urban planning** (Kabra, 1975, pp. 58–59).[12]

This proposal has, however, not taken a dominant position in debates on land policy in the context of India's urban future.[13] Here and there, it has, however, been mentioned. The leader of the politically dominant Congress Party, Indira Gandhi, had brought the issue of nationalization of urban land into a broad political arena as she made an electoral pledge to nationalize urban land in 1972. Nigel Harris believes that such pronouncements "could presumably make possible a serious approach to housing in the city [of Bombay]". He added—as subdued as usual in his book on Bombay's socio-economic history—between brackets: "so far, not implemented" (Harris, 1978, p. 34). Jha concludes, regarding Bombay, that "in the absence of political will the Government cannot solve the accommodation problem" … that the poor … "in the city face" (Jha, 1986, p. 439).

Surprisingly, the discussion on a land policy does not take into account that in some cities land became under full public ownership. In the context of Delhi's Master Plan 1961–1981, all land that was stipulated to be developed for urban development, was indeed acquired by the central government and passed on to the local government. A large part of it has subsequently been assigned to the Delhi Development Authority (DDA), in charge of residential (re-)development. It had to auction plots of residential land to higher and lower-income groups, taking care that auctioned land should also become available to poor citizens. The DDA has, however, according to Nilima Verma, used its monopoly powers to earn as much as possible by creating a paucity in the availability of land and selling it preferably to higher income categories, to the detriment of the poor (see Verma, 1981, for details). Moreover, and directly relevant for the basic question posed in this paper "where" the poor could find affordable, accessible and acceptable housing, is the conclusion that also a spatial bias was noted, since the "more influential among the riches cornered plots in attractive localities", as shown by Somnath Basu in his detailed study of the role of the DDA in the provision of residential land in Delhi (Basu, 1994, p. 219). Public control of land in this situation unfortunately was no guarantee for a fair spatial housing policy. Public ownership of urban land remains, however, a feasible proposition to enhance the proximity between working and improved living for all urban citizens, despite the experiences in Delhi. In another sidestep, let me briefly describe some relevant approaches in Hanoi, Vietnam.

[12] Bold by Kabra. This author does not give particulars of this note (year, author, source, etc.).

[13] It has also been criticized by some. Rudolf C. Heredia remarks that socialisation of land may actually create greater insecurity by subjecting people to the vagaries of party bosses and Government bureaucrats, but he does, regrettably, not substantiate this statement (1986, p. 34).

3.4 Interlude: Hanoi, "The Ideal Setting for Urban Planning"

After a fierce war won Vietnam independence in 1954 establishing in the North of the former French colony a socialist regime. All land was nationalized, except plots of a few hundred square meters which were kept at the disposal of peasants. With Soviet, Chinese and East European financial and technical support, this regime sought to transform the colonial capital Hanoi from a "consumers" city to a "producers" city, in line with the communist approach to development. For Hanoi this meant, building of several factories. It was decided very soon that these factories must be built near to be developed housing estates that should accommodate their workers and other civil servants. Consequently, from about 1960 onwards massive housing estates were built at walking distances from clusters of industrial enterprises (and government offices), a few kilometres away from the historic core of Hanoi. The basic idea was to create self-supporting neighbourhoods of—in the order of magnitude—7,000 to 15,000 inhabitants each. These neighbourhoods consist of several three- to five-storeyed apartment blocks with initially mostly single room tenements of about 20 m^2 each, but later having larger units with two rooms. The tenements in the early built apartment blocks had shared sanitary arrangements: toilets and washing places. Cooking facilities were minimal and collective as well, as dining could take place in factory canteens. Moreover, in many of the housing estates, collective dining facilities were provided. The Vietnamese terms *Khu Tap The*—collective area—indicates the character of these planned neighbourhoods. The KTT comprised some basic shops, kindergarten, schools and a medical post. The tenements were managed by the nearby enterprises and rented out to their workers against nominal rents of one or two per cent of their monthly wages that could meet only the costs of maintenance.

The design of the neighbourhoods was a mixture of modernist town planning concepts and Soviet ideas. The modernist ideas were visible in the ample open spaces between the tenement blocks, thus providing for sufficient fresh air and sunlight.[14] The desire to design self-contained neighbourhoods, "with inhabitant living independent from the city", as an architect in Hanoi once explained to me, originated both in the "*mikroraion*" built in the Soviet Union as well as in the by the American architect Perry designed neighbourhood units in the 1930s. Over 400 housing blocks in KTT units were erected between 1960 and 1980 without the curse of inflating costs of land for construction. They housed not only industrial workers but also a staff of ministries, to a total of about 30% of the urban population. Inter-industry or inter-department labour mobility was rare, while husband and wife mostly worked for the same employer. The proximity of working and living sites was, therefore, very high.

---

[14] These ideas originated from the experiences with nineteenth-century West European urban slums: crowded, dark dwellings without any access to fresh air and daylight. The acquired insights during the nineteenth century about the relations between the incidence of diseases such as cholera and plague and "foul air" and "foul water"' contributed to wishes among town planners and others to develop more healthy dwellings for urban workers.

The satisfaction among the dwellers in the KTT-neighbourhoods was high during the first decades of the development in North Vietnam; also since their new dwellings were mostly better than their earlier ones. Most workers came from slum-like dwellings in Hanoi or from dilapidated huts in nearby villages. Satisfaction levels, however, decreased when after the reunification of North and South Vietnam in 1975, and the end of the protracted "war economy", the citizens of Hanoi became tired of the sacrifices which the war had forced them to make and wanted more luxury and space than the KTT tenements could offer. From 1986 onwards, when Vietnam's economy was re-styled towards a market economy, the tenements fell a bit in disgrace, their wealthier occupants moving out to private housing.[15]

3.5 Back to India: Housing Needed and Unwanted Poor

The elimination of the land factor as a component part of the comparative cost calculations in housing developments in Hanoi shows that spatial proximity between working and living is feasible. This supports the proposition that nationalisztion of urban land opens up a new dimension in urban planning and housing the poor. However, the ways in which the Delhi Development Authority dealt with its monopoly of landownership show that there are several factors between land and the poor. These factors go far beyond the scope of this chapter but it is evident that the nationalization of urban land has not reached a mainstream discussion in India, despite Mrs. Indira Gandhi's pledge.

Spatial proximity and spatial segregation are conditioned by market-dominated pricing of urban land where a host of socio-political factors play a role. I intend here to enter the field of attitudes, opinions, etc. that explains, or co-explains the forces leading to segregation of residential areas between the poor and other–dominant–categories of the urban society. It has been noted above that most of the urban poor try to find shelter as close as possible to their sources of income. I, therefore, turn now to the better-off in urban areas, including the providers of their income or their shelter. Is the optimism, expressed by young India's leaders for providing acceptable housing for all citizens shared by many citizens? Or has the historical inequality in living arrangements between the poor and better-off urban citizens been internalized in human minds and behaviour? In short, what are the factors at stake and what pervades the thinking of the better-off in the cities and towns of India?

[15] See for details on socialist housing; Schenk, Hans (2021), *Rise and Fall of Socialist Housing in Hanoi*. In Hans Schenk & Trinh Duy Luan, Socialist Housing in Hanoi, Exploring its collective living quarters and experiences of a resident family. (pp. 15–151) Hanoi: Social Sciences Publishing House.

3.5.1 Needed and Unwanted Poor

The sociologist Paul Wiebe signals that landowners in Madras do not oppose the growth of slums on their lands and many profit from it, as they: "… collect a little on the side from the occupants" (Wiebe, 1975, p. 32). The existence of slums is also profitable for those politicians who act as advocates of a continuation of existing slum communities by the exchange of votes against a promised bore well or latrine, to be installed in a slum, when elected in some council. I quoted an NGO worker in Bangalore, where I did research on "living in slums", saying, "A politician will never arrange … too many improvements, otherwise he has no more grip over the population" (Schenk, 2001, p. 274). The existence of these vote-banks is, however, almost casually mentioned by many researchers, as if it is to be accepted as given.[16] "Providers" of income, middle-class—or at least less poor households, have a direct relation with slum dwellers. They hire their labour, their services and buy the merchandise nearby slum dwellers sell and all these activities promote proximity. But one has to be more precise. The dominant position of these "providers" can be summed up as "OK, we want labourers, goods, and services for daily requirements nearby, but not too many, not too much, and on our terms". An example will clarify this proposition.

One of the above-mentioned ODP-schemes in Madras, the CIT-Colony, was developed in 1948. It was small and counted only 20 plots, all located in a fashionable middle- and upper-class area in the South of the city and spread more or less in between private plots. From the 1970s onwards, large slum improvement projects have been taken up in Madras, usually involving re-location. However, this colony seemed to have been "forgotten". All original inhabitants or their descendants still lived there after 40 years. The following illustrates this:

> The inhabitants have strong footings in the surrounding area. They almost all work there: the men as gardeners, rickshaw pullers, coolies and watchmen, and the women as domestic servants. Thus they are bound to keep strong ties with their surroundings and they can probably rely on sufficient societal protection to stay … [T]he interests of the local elites in Madras require sufficient labour nearby to run their households in a cheap way. The CIT Colony offers a good example of the advantage of having servants around the corner and consequently of a de facto security for these servants (Schenk, Ten Holder & Mulders, 1989, p. 117).

The middle-class residents in Madras who had a small slum nearby, thus, expressed their wish to have servants around the corner. But they also put forward their accompanying "terms" - the desire "… not to be confronted too much with the presence of these 'servants'". In other words, they sought "invisible nearness", or "slum pockets hidden in interior parts of residential blocks or tucked behind urban estates" (de Bruijne & Schenk, 1992, p. 11).

Employers may react similarly. I spoke in the 1970s to an entrepreneur in Alleppey (Kerala) who told me that his workers had to come to his enterprise when they heard

[16] I found an exception in research by Neelima Risbud of slum improvement activities undertaken by the Bhopal Municipality during the 1980s. She compared two time-lines: one of local elections, and another one of provided slum improvements. She concluded that between elections the improvement works in slums in Bhopal distinctly slowed down (1990, p. 52).

the sound of a coming truck. Employers want labourers around when required but not too many. There exists in the minds of employers the understanding that there should be a spatial balance between demand and supply of labourers. Subsequently, a distinction can be made, and has been made, between needed–and wanted–labour and unwanted surpluses.[17] Within the margins of this balance are the ideas of proximity, and even close proximity, for the needed labour developed, along with ideas of separation of the unwanted surplus, often voiced in the form of disgust for inferior lower caste fellow citizens. The balance is understandably unstable but has primarily been kept alive by those who were directly concerned with needed versus unwanted poor in their daily proceedings. Processes of "modernity" in a very tangible way and noticeable on a daily scale can easily disturb this uneasy balance.

> One could see on the luggage belts in the arrival halls of international airports such as the ones I saw in Madras, in the 1980s, the luggage of flights from countries with low taxes on luxury items: heavy packages containing even washing machines or fridges or vacuum cleaners. Washing machines and the like need the personal attention of a lady of the house, at the detriment of a *dhobi*–washerman or–women–or a household servant. On could see in the streets of Madras the first supermarkets, fashionable places where, again, the lady of the house bought the often prepacked and imported food, at the detriment of the roadside shop or a mobile food vendor. Servants, *dhobis*, vendors, serving a neighbourhood, were to become superfluous and their services were not put any more on the balance against the possible nuisance of their nearby existence.

The experiences of those who were daily involved influence the ideas—perhaps emerging ideas—about issues of proximity and segregation among others as well. In the harsh words of sociologist Shashi Shekhar Jha "A city tolerates its slum dwellers up to the period they can be utilized as cheap labour and the maintenance of their habitat does not involve any significant expenditure of public funds…But now it seems this reserve army of cheap labour has really grown and expanded itself well beyond the utilising capacity of the city's employers" (Jha, 1986, p. 144 and p. 5, respectively). This emerging calculation has gone hand-in-glove with a gradual manifestation of fear and dislike for less needed urban poor among the better-off in Indian cities. This growing mistrust found its way in the discussion about poor urban citizens, emerging since the early 1960s. Two names that have become almost iconic ones in these discussions, should be mentioned: those of Oscar Lewis and John F. C. Turner.

> I shall not enter in detail here in the ideas of Lewis and Turner and of those of their many followers.[18] A few words are, however, necessary. Based on research in Mexico in the 1950s, Oscar Lewis developed his concept of the 'culture of poverty' among the urban poor, aptly condensed by Paul Wiebe as: "… the disengagement of the poor with respect to the major institutions of the society"(Wiebe, 1975, p. 10). Turner contributed to these discussions, as is widely recognised, by his thesis that the poor are perfectly capable to build their own shelter

[17] It goes beyond the scope of this paper to elaborate this concept. It has been explored in a recent thorough study on the formation of slums during Bombay's colonial era, notably focusing on the plague at the end of the nineteenth century, by Chhabria (2019).

[18] A convenient recent overview of their ideas in the context of worldwide slums can be found in Mayne (2017).

and just need some public support in the form of a place to stay and the provision of basic infrastructure. Summarized, he nursed and popularized the idea of do-it-yourself housing, sometimes also named aided self-help housing as a panacea for urban slumdwellers.

Lewis and Turner can best be considered as symbols of the emerging Indian ideas on the location of better housing of the urban poor living in slums. These symbols mark in the first place a change in the attitude among policy-makers in support of minimal urban housing during the early years after independence.[19] They also mark the second phase in India's involvement with urban housing. The second phase saw a shift from the objective of a double-roomed house for all to an attitude of getting concerned and even annoyed by all those urban citizens who could not avail of such a house. The concern is worded by the sociologist M. S. Dhadave in his study in a medium-sized urban place, Gulbarga, in Karnataka. He hypothesizes that slum dwellers have marginal relations with the rest of society. He concludes that slum dwellers are indeed alienated from others in society and expresses his concern about this trend for the whole society. He concludes that "...integration is the need of the hour" (Dhadave, 1989, p. 10 and pp. 195–199). The annoyance of the well off in the cities is expressed by others like Gopal Bhargava who articulates "As the squatters continue to increase in number, their influence and resistance to ouster grows, and as officials demonstrate their inability to grapple with the issue, still more immigrants move in to take advantage of official helplessness or acquiescence" (Bhargava, 1981, p. 210). An extract taken by the sociologists A. R. Desai and S. Devadas Pillai from a study undertaken by the Department of Economics at the University of Bombay in 1959 states that an investigation in an area of huts in Bombay showed that the dwellers: "had lost sense of moral values and social codes" (Desai and Devadas Pillai, 1970, pp. 174–175).

The fear for the growing numbers of urban poor and more or less homeless co-citizens led to policies based upon ascribed negative personal characteristics of these groups. Jha reports the measures adopted by the Municipal Corporation of Bombay in 1954 to clear "areas unfit for human habitation" as they are considered as places where "'undesirable' people live and often live a life as a 'lawless citizen'" (Jha, 1986, p. 23). One could say that such ideas of a "culture of poverty"' provided the ideological underpinning for the removal of unwanted urban poor from the more central urban areas. There are however other, more optimistic, and perhaps more pragmatic voices opposing the notions of moral-less and lawless squatters. "The squatter community is not an aggregation of rootless people living in shacks and huts. It is a community of fellow-migrants", states the sociologist Tapan K. Majumdar in his study on low-income citizens of Delhi. The anthropologist Christiane Brosius, also analysing Delhi's slum situation, comments that "these colonies were often tolerated, if not perceived, as a part of civil society that had to be carried along and uplifted"

[19] It is striking that even Prime Minister Jawaharlal Nehru, the ideological leader of India's desire to build "decent" houses for all its urban citizens, should have said – according to Gopal Bhargava, that if you cannot provide buildings for those dwelling in slums, you should give them an open space to live in, and give at least some social services, like good sanitation and water supply. The rest will follow. (Bhargava, 1981, p. 215). Particulars about this assumed statement are not given by Bhargava.

(Respectively Majumdar, 1983, p. v; and Brosius, 2010, p. 134). Wiebe remarks that Lewis himself did not find a "culture of poverty"" in his later research in India, and indeed, Wiebe concludes in his research in Madras that the people in his research area: "need to be recognized as able to function effectively, resourcefully, and in organized ways. They need to be recognized as able to understand their own needs and expectations" (Wiebe, 1975, p. 166). Similarly, the sociologist K. Raman Unni remembers the words of the architect Charles Correa who "has pointed out that the poor, given freedom and space, have traditions and the capacity for a judicious choice of houses within their means" (Unni, 1978, p. 221). In the preamble of the chapter on housing and slum clearance of a Report on the Development Plan for Greater Bombay 1964, it is noted that "The natural crave of these people [hutment dwellers, HS] is to look forward to the promises the future holds for them, to more hygienic and decent living conditions" (Greater Bombay, Municipal Corporation, 1964, p. 85). And, again in Bombay, it was stated in the Regional Plan for Bombay Metropolitan Region 1970–91 that the needed slum improvement "should inculcate in the population a spirit of civic consciousness and of cleanliness" (Bombay Regional Planning Board, 1974, p. 137). This optimism leads smoothly to the ideas of Turner regarding self-help housing, as well as to the idea that living in improved slums would contribute to greater civic consciousness.

Slums have been improved in many cities. Rather peripheral locations and extremely modest improvement packages have proven to be a 'guarantee' against processes of gentrification in such slums: "informal" sales of a hut to slightly less poor citizens. More attractively located slums and/or more ambitious improvement programmes, have proven to become likely "gentrified" (see Robben (1984) for details on improved slums in Madras). Site-and-services schemes have often been developed in the urban outskirts, and they have often been designed for slightly less-poor citizens.

3.5.2 Stench, Eyesores and Public Health

Another source of inspiration to "deal" with sub-standard housing areas is evoked by the organs of sense: the stench of a slum, or the eyesore that it might offer. Soon after independence Jha reports a discussion between the then Chief Minister of Bombay State and the Mayor of Bombay Municipality noting that they aspired: "to create another 'Paris' out of this city of Bombay. For the realisation of this dream", Jha continues "…the slum dwellers of Bombay, 'the eyesore of the city, the shanty-ugly looking spots on the face of the beautiful city' needed to be transferred to the outskirts of the main city". Jha adds that the municipality "took a decision to work towards the materialization of this dream": two areas made available for about 70,000 evicted slum dwellers in the city 35 km away from the municipal limits (Jha, 1986, pp. 4–5).[20]

[20] Jha gives no reference for the quotation of the shared dream of the Chief Minister and the Mayor.

> A similar clearance of a centrally located slum in Delhi - between the banks of the Yamuna river and the walls of the old city of Shahjahanabad – took place in 1967, where the: "... sacred character of the Nigam Bodh Ghat,[21] the natural beauty of the Riverfront and its green land use" had become: "a vast stinking slum with about 6,000 squatters, scores of cattle dairies and about 700 non-conforming industries and godowns." The then President of India, Rajendra Prasad, accompanied by a few diplomats ("... who could hardly stand the stench, filth and flies all around." as Jagmohan – the author of this story - adds to augment to the painting of the setting) sent a letter to the local authority and asked for immediate steps to be taken to remove the slum. Jagmohan, had to add with some nausea that it took years before the authorities braved this "stranglehold of the politics of slums" and cleared the area. Jagmohan does not tell where the squatters went to (Jagmohan, 1978, pp. 31–32).[22]

This cleaning along the Yamuna river proved to be a try-out for the large-scale demolitions that took place during the Emergency. Prime Minister Indira Gandhi is quoted to have said during this period: "We have to clean up the country. If your house is dirty, you don't leave it like that. You clean it up with a duster and a broom".[23]

Were these clearances after all just undertaken to remove stench and eyesores? There is more than just irritated eyes and noses. One may say that the sensual dimensions of removed sub-standard areas are an exponent of a broader concern: that of public health. Aspects of health and the absence of sanitation (water supply, waste treatment, toilets, roads, etc.) in slums of all kinds and shapes are often casually mentioned by researchers and others, and rarely taken as a central focus of research as pointed out by Amitabh Kundu in his study on the access to basic amenities by poor urban inhabitants (Kundu, 1993). Aspects of health and public health are, however, used as arguments for in situ improvements. This concern has a long history. The fear for transmittable diseases such as cholera and the bubonic plague has, as has been widely documented, for many years influenced the rules of urban land use, both in colonial and post-colonial India, notably during epidemic outbreaks of such diseases (see e.g., Kidambi 2007 and Chhabria 2019). The fear is still present. Aditya Nigam argues in retrospect for the 1970s that the elimination of the breeding grounds of fear instilling diseases was used as an argument to control urban space.

> There is no doubt that the early efforts at town planning in Delhi were all characterized by this fear of disease. The document by the Town and Country Planning Organization ... in the 1970s, implemented with an unprecedented brutality during the Emergency, and witness in the large-scale demolitions of urban slums, was framed by this fear. It was the designation of these areas as 'plague spots' and 'dens of vice' that underlay the entire discourse of town planning (Nigam, 2001, pp. 42–43).

---

[21] Nigam Bodh is a crematorium site, to be reached via a *ghat*, a series of steps towards the Yamuna river.

[22] The dwellers went eventually to a Trans-Jamuna resettlement colony, named Welcome. See Tarlo (2000) for details in her excellent analysis of the re-settlement colony.

[23] Quoted in Weinstein (2014), p. 67. She refers to a publication by Hansen in 2001. Weinstein adds, however: "The dusters and brooms used in Bombay, as in Delhi and other cities ... were bulldozers and *lathi* sticks used to demolish slums and evict poor residents".

3.5.3 *The Cycle of Eviction*

Summarizing this phase leads unavoidably to the conclusion that–barring a few exceptions, such as the mentioned experiences with the in situ improvement of sub-standard housing areas in Madras–authorities tried to segregate the citizens who were living under sub-standard conditions spatially from others in the centres of urban places during the 1960s, 1970s and 1980s. Segregation took alternating place, I must add, interchanged by periods of relative quietness with regard to the eviction of poorly housed slum dwellers and their re-settlement elsewhere, alternated with hectic clearance activities. During the 19 months of the Emergency in India, Bombay saw widespread evictions, under the banner of cleaning up the city, as done in Delhi. Again, in the middle of the 1980s, attempts were made to clear the city's sidewalks from those living on these pavements. Liza Weinstein characterizes this periodical history of public actions towards sub-standard housing in Bombay as "… cyclical, comprising violent insurgencies carried out alongside and interspersed with more benevolent programmatic interventions" (Weinstein, 2014, p. 66).[24]

Sometimes evictions were enduring in the sense that the evicted and thus spatially segregated citizens, stayed where they were shifted, but more often than not evictions proved to be futile. Many, most perhaps, re-settled or re-housed citizens came back as soon as possible and as close as possible to where (their original) jobs were, and tried to resume their prior social and economic relations, based upon unequal proximity. Meanwhile, new migrants kept coming and joined them, altogether leading to the mushrooming of the usual slums in Delhi, Bombay and dozens of other large cities, even more than before. However, more fundamental changes made their entry into urban India in the subsequent years, as discussed in the following paragraph.

3.6 Capital and the Urban Middle Class: Pushing the Urban Poor to the Periphery Again

Observers have noticed changes in the expressions, perceptions and attitudes among the citizens in Indian cities from the 1980s onwards. First, there were more intense feelings and attitudes among regularly housed citizens, (the word "colony" is often used to describe their housing blocks or neighbourhoods) towards their less fortunate fellow citizens. These feelings are even more evident in the changing attitudes among these citizens towards public institutions and politicians dealing with housing, land use and related urban issues. A growing annoyance—anger even—with the state was seen among these citizens—who identified themselves as belonging to the "middle class" and even glorified this "label" as the "Great Indian Middle Class". The annoyance among this middle-class was fuelled by its perception of a non-balanced pro-poor state, governed by corrupt politicians, who depended on their vote-banks. Such

[24] Weinstein gives a useful comprehensive overview of the history of Bombay's policies regarding sub-standard housing, and their reactions.

politicians were seen as representing more the widespread and populous housing areas of poor citizens than the sparser populated colonies of the better-off. These politicians prevented, in their views, clearance of slums or arranged to save illegal settlements from eviction within sight of the middle-class colonies.[25] A new perspective was gradually unfolding on the better-off: the "market", as brought to India by domestic and foreign capital,

A big-bang change, according to some, was the strengthening of the free global market, following the decision of the central government to "liberalize" the economy in 1991, or in the proper jargon, to "adjust it structurally".[26] The much-needed IMF-loans were tied to a reduction of the costly developmental role of the state since 1947. The free entry of foreign capital to invest where profits were seen in the emerging markets, notably those of real estate, was welcomed with open hands. It was also hoped that capital injections into the city through this process would lead to the transformation of urban spaces that were hitherto used for sub-standard housing, for more profitable (and more beautiful) usages. And, as far as Delhi is concerned, finally, there was hope that an emerging "slum-free" national capital would acquire the "world-class" status that it is entitled to by some.[27]

3.6.1 Bhagidari: A Soft Middle-Class Coup Disguised as a Partnership

The sociologist Sanjay Srivastava states that the middle-class interests needed: "a renegotiation of the relationship with the state which ... has been popularly understood to be 'pro-poor'. It must be noted that the engagements with the state are since the early 1990s taking place against the background of increasingly intense engagements with the market" (Srivastava, 2015, p. 89). These renegotiations are shaped in Delhi and other cities through the Residents Welfare Associations (RWAs). What are these associations?

> The urban geographer D. Asher Ghertner introduces the RWAs to the reader of his book on Delhi's transformation towards a 'world-class' city with the following dialogue: "Before 2000, the acronym RWA would have left almost any Delhi resident guessing." Ghertner mentions a respondent who during an interview says "'R-W-what? I don't know what that is'. When I said it was a neighbourhood association – the resident's welfare association – that exists in residential colonies like his, his response was 'Yeah. My dad's in one of those. It's for senior citizens, right?'" (Ghertner, 2015, p. 45).

[25] I. Milbert raises the question whether "slums as 'cities within cities' should not be acknowledged as separate entities and ... should not be constituted as separate electoral constituencies". The point has remained theoretical, Milbert adds, as it did not reflect political realities. (2008, p. 204).

[26] Other observers point at the culmination of an already loosening grip of "Nehruvian socialism" on the economy and the growing market-sector during the 1980s.

[27] Similar developments took place in other major Indian cities. Since my data base is for this topic mainly confined to Delhi, I have not included developments in Mumbai (Bombay), Kolkata (Calcutta), etc.

Delhi's RWAs were indeed rather relaxed associations of residents in one or more housing blocks, preferably around an interior open space. The members used to install a watchman and refuse collectors, and looked after the collective interior garden, etc. But there have been changes in the role and functioning of the RWAs over the years. One could see, as Srivastava writes, that during the 1980s, gates were installed and maintained by the RWAs, marking physical demarcation of a residential locality. "The gates were the earliest visible signs of the RWA's increasing public presence as a formal entity in urban affairs". In hindsight, this was a small first step, just a visible sign of the presence and the power of RWA's. However, as Srivastava subsequently points out, this also marked "de facto privatization of public thoroughfares in residential localities by the installation of large iron gates ..." (Srivastava, 2015, p. 113).

The annoyance among many Delhi citizens with the perceived "pro-poor" attitude of the public authorities, was officially supported and even stirred up by Sheila Dikshit, the Chief Minister of Delhi State.[28] On the 8th of March 2000, she, in a television broadcast, blamed "poor migrants for crime in Delhi, drawing an association between migrants, slums, and most problems of the city" (Verma, 2002, p. 109). In the same year, she proposed a solution to "most problems" by stipulating the participation of Delhi's citizens in the development of the city through the RWAs. This system was baptized as *Bhagidari*: partnership, and was institutionalized as a special branch of the state administration, right in the office of the Chief Minister. Three types of central stakeholders were envisaged in the development-through-partnership under the *bhagidari* system: "market/industrial associations, bureaucrats placed in various departments; and the RWAs established in officially planned residential colonies, membership being open only to those owning property in the colony" (Ghertner, 2015, p. 58). RWA's, concludes Christiane Brosius, should then be seen as "moral communities that shape new forms of neighbourhood locality, inclusion of members of their class and exclusion of 'non-citizens'". In this manner, RWA's became the dominant pressure group, and, as Brosius remarks, "Members of the middle classes seemed to have the 'given' right to actively participate in the making of public opinion" (Brosius, 2010, p. 107 and p. 134, respectively).

Bhagidari meant a far-reaching two-stage missile. Its design out-manoeuvred politicians, notably those whose powers depended on their vote-banks. They could prevent or correct the measures that were conflicting with the interest of the organized middle class, to the detriment of their poor electorate.[29] It gave heavy-weight advisory powers to the middle class as new formal development partners. *Bhagidari* can in this way be considered as a "soft coup" of local governance, bringing power to the propertied urban middle classes (representing, according to Ghertner, less than 25% of the urban population only) (Ghertner, 2015, p. 77). It was an effective coup in the

[28] Delhi State is a city-state consisting of the Delhi municipality and a surrounding rural belt.

[29] The daily newspaper "Indian Express" of the 3rd of February 1999, opened its electronic version with an account by Kota Neelima of the reactions of Members of the Legislative Assembly, (MLA) of Delhi State, on a demolition in New Delhi under the heading: "MLAs panic as their vote banks are demolished".

Indian urban context "where the bourgeoisie is so clearly in the ascendant, and the bureaucracy such a willing accomplice", writes Janaki Nair referring to developments in Bangalore (Nair, 2013, p. 46), but equally valid for Delhi. The RWAs in effect became: "the key vehicle for articulating an exclusionary urban politics of space" (Srivastava, 2015, p. 113) and actually "reinforcing the city's divide between formal and informal human settlements" (Milbert, 2008, p. 204). How did this soft coup look like?

3.6.2 Two Faces of the Partnership: Words and Deeds

The coup had two faces. The first face fostered, showed and promoted the idea that if Delhi had to become a world-class city, it needed investments: in its infrastructure, in its environment and in impressive real estate. Only in that way, an environment for substantial inflow of multinationals, from Sony to Nokia, together with international banks and related financial companies and consultancy firms, till fast food chains can be created. They indeed came, and built fancy offices on auctioned public land, and so did the myriad companies of supporting activities such as hotels and shopping malls: "displaying familiar signs of giant global chains that mark any first-world city" (Nigam, 2001, p. 41). The entry of the investors from world-class cities is manifest on the streets. Srivastava, after having given an exposition of the shopping malls that house supermarkets and fast-food restaurants, focuses in flowery words at street level: "If the street is to be transformed—cleansed—through a transnational commodity-broom, the street corner is also becoming linked to a network of national and global spaces": discount supermarkets, fair price shops (Srivastava, 2015, p. 218). The city prepared itself also for proper reception of the expected foreign guests for the Commonwealth Games of 2010, resulting in the removal of slums near monuments and other (potential) tourist spots. Jagmohan, during the period of Emergency in the late seventies a spider in the web of massive slum clearances in Delhi acted in the early years of the twenty-first century as minister of Tourism in the Central Government. He advocated in this capacity the demolition of slums near a historic monument with a crushing logic: "Why should a foreign tourist visit Humayun's Tomb if it is surrounded by slum clusters?".[30]

Delhi's major waterbody, the Yamuna river, got also special attention. Karen Coelho makes an important observation for Chennai which is equally valid the Yamuna in Delhi and water bodies in many other cities: "Waterbodies and waterways are now, above all, emblems of the city's aspiration to world-class status. Waterfront development, beautification, and eco-restorations are idioms through which cities position themselves in the global arena as direct strategies for capital accumulation through real estate value" (Coelho, 2013, pp. 146–147). And last but not the least, the world-class cities need multi-star high-rise condominiums as residential spaces for foreign experts, consultants and the well-to-do non-resident Indians (NRI's) from

[30] The Hindu, of 7 September 2001, quoted in Schenk, 2004, p. 105.

the Gulf or the West, as and when they return, and the wealthy local citizens. Small private cities have been built for this purpose in Gurgaon and Greater Noida. At the same time, however, massive residential buildings and five-star estates are found in prime locations in Delhi that used to house poor citizens.[31]

This is the shining face. The other face looks ugly since it emerges by responding to the questions of exactly how and where the spaces for modern development are to be found for the cities to acquire world-class status. The answer was simple: spaces are to be created by clearing the ugly and insanitary slums occupying prime places where the urban poor had settled for years. It is at this junction that *bhagidari* became an indispensable instrument. I return to the grandiose upgrading of the banks of the Yamuna river, initiated by the tourism ministry of Delhi-State and labelled by the Delhi High Court as "a 'clean-up' drive, necessary to prevent the conversion of the Yamuna 'into a huge sewage drain".[32] Srivastava makes the following notes from his visit to a settlement along its bank, called Brahmpuri.

> Taking a road near the building of the Slum Wing of the Delhi Municipal Corporation towards the nearby river: "a right turn down a sloping laneway leads to an area known as 'Pehla Pushta' (the First Embankment). Here, the land is at the same level – and sometimes lower than – the riverbed. Brahmpuri is a mish-mash of lanes, garbage dumps, decrepit government schools, myriad shops operating from houses, irregular house numbers, grass-less parks, open air plastic and paper recycling shops, casually parked water tankers, and, on hot days, curtains of flies that swarm around moving and still bodies (Srivastava, 2015, p. 155).

There were dozens of such localities along the Yamuna and cleared during the early years of the new millennium. Some say that 300,000–400,000 people living there were evicted between 2001 and 2006.[33] Most men and women here worked as head-loaders, rickshaw-pullers, domestic servants, ragpickers, etc. somewhere nearby, or were involved in waste recycling, tanning, electroplating and quite some other workshops in and around the settlements.[34] In 2006, the Delhi Development Authority could declare proudly that 7,300 hectares of land had been 'reclaimed' out

[31] Convenient overviews of the promotion of multi-star residential complexes are given by Dupont (2005), Brosius (2010) and Searle (2016), and will not be discussed here.

[32] Ghertner (2015), p. 120. Delhi's Water Board officially announced in 2007, however, that the main causes of pollution are the twenty-two open drains that carry untreated sewage from mostly middle-class residential colonies across the city directly into the river. (Ghertner, 2013, p. 269).

[33] Figures by Brosius (2010, p. 137 and p. 133, respectively. But beware of figures; others mention 200,000 in 2004; or even 200,000 in 2004 (Ghertner, 2015, p. 96), or even over 150,000 (Menon-Sen, 2006) on top of the 20,000 evicted families (say: 100,000 persons) in 2000 (Dasgupta, 2014, p. 238). Others are more cautious and come to significantly lower figures: 200,000 for the whole of Delhi between 2000 and 2006 (Bhan and Shivanand, 2013, p. 56).

[34] Sharan mentions that there were by 2000 some 93,000 industries in slums, urban villages, resettlement colonies and other areas were hey should not have been, including those along the Yamuna. He mentions that "sealing" occurred frequently, such as between 2,856 and 4,000 between November 2000 and January 2001 (2014, pp. 204–205). I have not come across any form of coordination between the evictions of residents with those of work sites. It seems that no systematic attempts have been undertaken to locate evicted workshops, etc. as much as possible near locations of re-settled workers.

of which three per cent was to be used for residential and commercial purposes and not less than 85 per cent for the "creation of green spaces, water sports, a racecourse, tourist cottages, camping sites and pleasure parks" (Brosius, 2010 p. 138).

Bhagidari did more. It inspired also less spectacular actions than the one along the river, but which occurred more often. The Residents Welfare Associations which were to take part in *bhagidari* became well-motivated to complain formally and openly with relevant authorities about slums in their vicinity and demand their demolitions. This was noteworthy as the actions of RWAs made a significant departure from the past. Since the 1970s, the judicial institutions had been intervening by facilitating access for less privileged persons by passing judgments in the form of a 'Public Interest Litigation' (PIL)'.[35] This was a great saviour of poor citizens as the PILs were used by the judiciary to halt or postpone slum demolitions, arguing as Ghertner writes that the judicial actions were" to protect the 'right to life' of the community or by noting that slums were actively settled by state agents and were the product of a planning system that failed to provide the low-income housing mandated by the Master Plan" (Ghertner, 2015, p. 12). Gautam Bhan gives an elaborate account of the workings of the PILs, and mentions a court ruling in 1985 (in Tamil Nadu) which stated that "alternative accommodation must be provided before evictions can take place". Even India's highest judicial institution, the Supreme Court in 1989 observes that: "'reasonable residence is an indispensable necessity' for human development and the fulfilment of the Right to Life" (Bhan, 2016, p. 113).

However, the tide turned, around the turn of the century. The Supreme Court ruled in 2002 that the state should hurry in cleaning the city: "In Delhi, which is the capital of the country and which should be its showpiece, no effective initiative of any kind has been taken by the numerous governmental agencies operating there in cleaning up the city". The ruling elaborated on the bad sanitary conditions in parts of Delhi, but then "displaced the source of the problem from a lack of proper sanitation and services to the innate character of slum dwellers"(Quoted in Ghertner, 2015, p. 104). This ruling paved the way for many subsequent rulings by lower courts. Nigam mentions an (ill-)famous court ruling which stated that "the health of some is more important than the livelihood of others" (Nigam, 2001, p. 43).

The disgust of, and fear for the urban poor were no new phenomenon in Delhi. It, however, seems that the checks against too openly expressed sentiments had faded away due to court rulings since the early twenty-first century. Hence, conflicts could easily escalate and transcend the stage of gossip and be brought successfully to court by the members of the RWAs. These rulings motivated RWAs not even to ask, but simply to demand the removal of such nearby ugly and foul-smelling housing areas for the poor, in order to live in a world-class place. I give an example.

> A conflict broke out between the residents of the Ashok Vihar colony and the dwellers of the neighbouring unauthorized settlement over the use of a park. "The residents of the ... slums", writes Aditya Nigam, "... in the absence of any proper sanitation facilities, often used the

[35] The Litigations serve to reach legal and constitutional rights to a "person or ... class of persons who by reason of poverty, helplessness or disability or socially or economically disadvantages position is unable to reach the court for relief. (Gidwani, 2013, p. 182).

park for the purposes of defecation" The conflict escalated and ended at Delhi's High Court which ruled that: (a) the slum dwellers cannot be guaranteed basic amenities, as they were above all "'lawbreakers, unauthorized occupants of public land'". (b) the provision of both infrastructure or relocation would be seen as an invitation to others to come to Delhi, and (c) the Delhi Development Plan--was wasting money of taxpayers in favour of lawbreakers (Nigam, 2005, pp. 246–247).

Consequently, hundreds of thousands of men, women and children were thrown out of the city, or at least out of its inner parts. A few could stay in the still available servant's quarters of the mansions in central Delhi or in the Southern parts of the city. Some others could hope to stay in projects of land-sharing in which developers were given a free hand in developing financially attractive real estate by reserving a part of the acquired land for re-housing the original settlers or at least some among them. This was, for example, the case in the centrally located Kathputli Colony (see Chalana and Rishi 2016, Rishi and Syal 2020). But the dominant measures taken regarding the dwellers of slums and their shelters were eviction. Bhan concludes that the fundamental nature of citizenship as it has evolved in the early years of the twenty-first century, is characterized by "a site and a moment not of equity and insurgence, but of inequality, impoverishment and differentiation. Claims to the city are, in fact, being made not by basti [slum dwelling, HS] residents but by an elite insurgent urban citizen" (Bhan, 2016, p. 182). Another conclusion is derived from the analyses of Gautam Bhan and Swathi Shivanand. These researchers found, based on their field investigations in 2009 that 24% of the land of evicted slums between 1990 and 2007 was still vacant. They write - unavoidably angered "The presence of so many vacant land parcels that were used productively by the poor for housing and shelter before their 'reclamation' is not just an indicator of the futility of so much of the displacement that has taken place in Delhi, but also makes a case for re-hauling the state's policy towards the land it owns and redefining the basis of the priorities on use of public land" (Bhan & Shivanand, 2013, p. 57).

Like earlier waves of evictions of slum dwellers, the present period exhibits a calming down of the intensity of evictions. "As millennium Delhi wound to a close, the world-class city had lost its luster", observes Ghertner (2015, p. 187). More important, perhaps, was an unexpected ruling by Delhi's High Court in 2010 that "'jhuggi dwellers are not to be treated as secondary citizens. … They are the citizens who help the rest of the city to live a decent life, they deserve protection and the respect of the rights to life and dignity which the Constitution guarantees them'" (Dupont, 2005, p. 86). Subsequent rules ordered that evictions could only take place when a place with the needed amenities was available. These rulings brought Delhi back to the pre-2002 era and heralded so to say changes in the way Delhi became governed the next few years. These years saw changes in the political power structure of the city and time-and-again solemn promises were made to make India "slum free", within a few years, accompanied by grand designs to solve the problem of slums. Such promises have, however, made no great impacts on the slum dwellers—either those in the city, re-housed or awaiting action—or re-settled in the urban periphery.

3.6.3 Re-Settlement: Far Away, But a New Start?

> We have come from the village to the city for work. Now see what they have done. They have thrown us out into the village again (Rao, 2013, p.1).

Delhi witnessed during the 1990s and the first decade of the twenty-first century another massive exodus of citizens who were spatially segregated from their means of livelihood. The exodus diminished during the second decade, but questions remain: where did they go? What happened to them, could they find new sources of livelihood? Were there any sort of site-and-services like provisions? Bhan and Shivanand estimate that over 97,000 families, i.e. about half a million persons, have been evicted between 1990 and 2007. But only about a quarter of a million persons have actually been resettled (Bhan & Shivanand, 2013, p. 57). These figures raise the subsequent question: where did the others go? At a local level, Ursula Rao gives an answer to the question of numbers as well as to its irrelevancy. She tells the story of Amit, who lived in a slum near Yamuna river as a regular casual worker and now in a re-settlement colony some 40 kms away from the centre of Delhi.

> He discontinued this activity after resettlement. Six hours travel back and forth into the city … with no guarantee of work on any given day was untenable. …. During the resettlement process many people failed to secure a plot in spite of possessing the necessary documentation. Amit was among them. He mobilized 1200 affected families … became their representative and took the case to court. ... He was overjoyed when they won the case in 2007. Yet the judgement was never implemented. To consolidate his position as leader and improve his economic situation, Amit opened a roadside stall selling building materials, an ideal business in an emerging colony. It lasted for two years before it was destroyed during a police raid that cleared all 'illegal' constructions.

The story goes on via an illegally bought plot, another shop, failed access to the ration shop for subsidized food though he continues to live below the poverty line. All this makes Rao conclude that "Amit's life is saturated with illegalities produced at the conjuncture between needy citizens and fractured state interventions" (Rao, 2013, pp. 10–11). Illegalities are of course not confined to re-settlers, but these have a deeper impact on lives in exigencies of existential upheavals like forced re-settling. Spatial segregation thus marks a break from an earlier inclusive existence, though based on the severe inequalities for ensuring a livelihood. Similar stories have been told by many others depicting the further losses of the already meagre erstwhile means of livelihood, as well as the additional losses of an earlier social embedding.

The urban periphery of Delhi is not only populated by re-settled urban poor. Villages around the built-up area, and within the territory of Delhi-State exist for a long.[36] Many have become encircled by the expanding city and have become "urban villages". Others are still surrounded by agricultural land and are hence called "rural villages". Re-settlement colonies have often started near rural villages on land that public authorities in Delhi bought from farmers. The relations between villagers and re-settlers may be tense, as I heard in the far North of the periphery.

---

[36] I follow the description and analysis of Bentinck (2000) on the urbanisation in Alipur Block in the Northern part of Delhi's fringe.

> I wrote, after a visit in the far North of the periphery: "A small pond next to the village is traditionally used for irrigation purposes. The DDA [Delhi Development Authority, in charge of the re-settling] used it as the end-station of a sewerage system in the re-settlement colony; the pond is now severely polluted. The few men and women in the village who are engaged in the scarce non-agricultural jobs in the area meet the competition of newcomers from the colony" (Schenk, 2004, p. 107).

Private developers and industrial entrepreneurs have bought land near the villages and started workshops and factories, even built sheds for their workers: often single men who migrated from far-away places. Developers have also tried their luck and developed illegally "unauthorised colonies" which may attract eventually even lower-middle-class newcomers and get regularized: formally accepted by the state authorities. Slums started and developed similarly on publicly owned land. These often hectic developments in Delhi's fringes[37] might—at first sight—suggest that there exist opportunities to start a new future for evicted slum dwellers from Delhi. Is not the neo-liberal doctrine, in the words of Ursula Rao, aiming to direct poor people: "… away from welfare payments, towards programs that educate poor people, discipline them and entice them, to self-activate and become entrepreneurs who take advantage of opportunities provided by the official market"(Rao, 2013, p. 6). Well, looking at the map of Greater Delhi, there is indeed a convergence between the new re-settlements and unauthorized colonies and slums on the one hand, and the locations of new and proposed workshops, etc. on the other. A market is likely to be found there. But as I wrote earlier: "… map wisdom can be far remote from field realities. A small-scale employer does not recruit workers as such: he recruits known workers, from his native area, speaking the same language, being perhaps related, being a patron in dependency relations, etc." (Schenk, 2004, p. 109). The re-settled slum dwellers from Delhi's inner city have hence no easy access to work.

Thus, an often-found reality in re-settlement colonies is that women have lost their former jobs, often as household servants. Work has gone too far away. Kalyani Menon-Sen records the account of a woman in a re-settlers colony, in 2004: "One of her employers even offered her accommodation, but she could not accept because she has to look after her old husband and young grand-daughter" (Menon-Sen, 2006, p. 1970). Often, though, husbands try to keep their old job, even when commuting is costly and time-consuming. I was told in 2002 in a re-settlement colony that many men lost their jobs as well, as their employers found it more convenient to recruit fresh boys and men from their networks in their places of origin. Exclusion may hence follow spatial segregation. Others stayed on the work premises during the week and came home once a week (Schenk, 2004, p. 109). The advent of multi-nationals in Delhi's periphery, in Gurgaon in the neighbouring state of Haryana, and Noida and Greater Noida in Uttar Pradesh, satellite towns of the capital city, tells a similar story of exclusion. However, here social relations (or the lack of these) do not play a major role, which is reserved for 'modernity'. Vasudevan tells how—barring a very few exemptions—new companies in Greater Noida recruit their staff.

---

37 Amitabh Kundu speaks even of a "degenerated periphery", in a documentary video-movie (Nelissen and Schenk, 2002).

"But almost every other company in Greater Noida makes no attempt to train and employ local youth, preferring to continue to transport buses full of employees up to the farthest corners of NCR [National Capital Region, HS]. The Yamaha spokesperson told me, 'At about 5 p.m., the road outside Yamaha is totally jammed. Forty-five buses take off in 10 min to drop employees back to their homes in Noida, Delhi, Ghaziabad, etc." Vasudevan continues: "When a big multinational company sets up shop in a rural farmland and disengages with its surroundings, it is a lethal social cocktail. The villagers see a glass-and-chrome office building …., well-to-do sahibs driving in and out of the factory in smart cars, foreigners arriving for meetings … They realise that they have been left out of the action. They approach the company for jobs, but are rejected because they are not skilled enough." However, traces of the traditional ideas of recruitment are still there: "Every service is given to a contractor who hires people from Chhattisgarh, Bihar and Jharkhand to be security guards and window cleaners (Vasudevan, 2013, p. 157).

Though Vasudevan's account pertains to "original" villagers, her observations are equally valid for the slum dwellers who entered the fringe areas of Delhi, or of other cities for that matter. Eviction from inner cities has not meant integration in a new social environment in the urban periphery. What stands, for the time being at least, is just enduring spatial segregation.

I have another glance at the map of Delhi—or rather a glance at a sequence of imaginary maps drawn over time, say with an interval of five years—and see the removal of many urban poor from the central locations, and the emergence of quite some impressive residential estates which are apparently meant for well-to-do citizens. At the same time, one can see the gradual population increase in the periphery, which includes many poor newcomers. A closer look reveals that the urban middle classes and elites can often be found in a piece of an imaginary cake, originating in New Delhi's elitist government quarter, and mainly extending to the Southwest and the South of the centre, the ill-famous farmhouses and eventually Gurgaon. Resettlement locations are predominantly in the Northwest and the East..[38] I found this geographical dichotomy very rigid: "squatters in the South (and in the central areas) are easily chased away, and relatively [easily] tolerated elsewhere", (Schenk, 2004, p. 108) pointing at a frightening trend of solid socio-spatial segregation.

Delhi's wave of evictions of the early twenty-first century has certainly been influenced by India's liberalized economy, world-class dreams and a major international sports event. Another comparative interlude to Hanoi, after a similar economic liberalization, is relevant.

3.7 A Final Interlude: Hanoi's Urban and Rural Villages

Vietnam had to follow the prescriptions from the IMF to adjust its development-oriented policies, six years ahead of India. The country had to stop most of its welfare programmes, including the heavily subsidized provision of housing to its urban workers. It also liberalized its economy and paved the way for what has been

[38] For Jagmohan form these locations the core of his stubborn dream of a revolutionary Ninth Delhi (1978).

coined as 'popular housing', housing by the people. But unlike the Indian case of popular housing as a form of building of huts and the like by its poor themselves, in Vietnam, it became an activity undertaken by–say–everybody who had the opportunity, the means, and the motives to have their houses built or improved. The hectic building activities that took place across the city since the late 1980s covered existing houses and new ones and took place without much state control or even coordination. Popular housing promoted spatial inequality. The better-off among the residents in the socialist housing blocks (KTT, see above) tended to move outwards towards the urban fringe in search of more and better living accommodation, while the poorer residents remained in their KTT-apartments. The emptied apartments in the tenement buildings were often filled up by illegal subletting to rural immigrants, students, etc. The buildings currently show the signs of neglect: maintenance and repair get little attention.

The state tried simultaneously to attract foreign capital to invest in real estate. It was, therefore, necessary to expropriate agricultural land. Farmers were compensated for this loss and promised to be absorbed in new urban jobs. This, unfortunately, did not happen much, as their skills did often not match those required for urban jobs. A first gated community, for instance, was built in the first decade of this century on agricultural land, while the usual 'star' hotels, appeared at attractive locations.

The expropriation of agricultural land did not take place in, and immediately around the many villages around Hanoi. Such land—often in plots of up to a few hundred square meters—was considered as "belonging" to the villagers, to put up a small house, grow and sell vegetables, maintain a fishpond, etc. Following changes towards a more liberal policy regarding the transfers of land-use rights, villagers could "sell" smaller or larger parts of their plots. Buyers were often urbanites in search of land and given the imbalance between demand and supply of usable land, high prices could be asked for a small plot of sometimes less than 50 square meters. Consequently, built houses were small and tall, along narrow and winding village lanes with inadequate sanitary facilities. These 'New Urban Villages' as they became coined are strewn around the city and now appear as strange "pre-historical" dots on a map: small irregularly formed village roads and buildings in between the formal lay-outs of formal and glossy urban extensions: the "New Urban Areas".

Land has become an issue in planning, both at the side of the relevant authorities and at the side of those who could sell or buy "users-rights" to land which still remains state-owned. This process that evolved since the 1990s leads to well-known outcomes such as land hoarding, speculation, brokers in land transactions, etc. unknown in North Vietnam, since the socialist revolution. The villagers are certainly no outsiders in these emerging transactions, even though shrewd urban brokers profited most. Many villagers could start a business undertaking or invest in a posh house. The process of change in the New Urban Villages brought about initial forms of spatial segregation. The financially better-off Hanoians tend to move to Hanoi's periphery, while those who could neither catch up with the opportunities provided by the markets, nor could find a job in the shrinking public sector, remained in the central parts of the city.[39] Significant spatial re-arrangements, thus, took place under influence of the market, though in a different manner than in Delhi. The periphery of Hanoi is not at all a site of rejected migrants.

3.8 Final Remarks

Looking back at the three-quarters of a century of concern with citizens living in slums in India's towns and cities, one can see that this concern has oscillated over times. There have been waves of intense attempts to change their situation, alternated by seemingly smoother periods. But though the waves have a rather similar appearance, their generating powers varied greatly. The first wave started immediately after India's independence in 1947 and got momentum during the 1950s. It was generated by India's inclusive, secular and welfare politics. Slums were considered as an unbearable stain on these politics, resulting in the design of decent houses for all in the development plans of that time. However, the realisation of the failures of the construction of accessible, affordable and acceptable housing, paved the way for a new approach, from the 1960s onwards. The authorities laid the responsibilities of the failures of the 1950s on the shoulders of the slum dwellers themselves. They should be more involved in improving their living conditions, and hence the second wave centred around self-help solutions. It lasted definitely until the late 1970s but it continued with lesser intensity till the 1990s. It resulted in large-scale spatial segregation of the urban poor from their means of survival in inner cities and their re-settling in some way or the other in peripheral urban areas and was largely motivated by disgust among the well-off citizens for those living in slums. This wave resulted in some kind of subaltern movements back by slum dwellers from the fringes to the central areas where they used to live, used to belong, and had found a livelihood.

A third wave started with India's new market-oriented economic policies, since the 1990s. In addition to the simmering and perhaps even more intensified disgust of the elites for slum dwellers, the former cherished the desire to catch up with the consumerism of the capitalist world. The logic of the global market ordained that land occupied by slums could, for better and higher profitability, be used for a shopping mall, a star-residential estate, or a multinational consultancy office. Hence, the slums were segregated (again) from where their dwellers worked. In Delhi, even massive money and energy were spent in removing the slums for giving an upgraded look of the city for the Commonwealth Games of 2010. What took place in Delhi happened also in Mumbai, Chennai, Bangalore, Kolkata, etc. The key question remains: will the inhabitants in re-settlement colonies once more succeed in returning to the inner cities where they have had their living and access to basic amenities? Or will the power of capital be stronger than the earlier ones of disgust and fear and utopian

[39] A useful guide through the history of villagers around Hanoi dealing with their land is given by Danielle Labbé, 2014, *Land Politics and Livelihoods on the Margins of Hanoi, 1920–2010*, Vancouver, University of Columbia Press.

welfare, and will the urban slum dwellers, who lived close to their employment sources in the centre of the city, have now to settle for new types of proximity to livelihoods in peripheral urban colonies?

References

Basu, S. (1994) *Land use and land prices in semi-controlled land market: A case study of Delhi*. Ph. D. Thesis, Centre for the Study of Regional Development, School of Social Sciences, Jawaharlal Nehru University, New Delhi.

Bentinck, J. (2000) *Unruly Urbanisation on Delhi's Fringe, changing patterns of land use and livelihood*. Ph. D. Thesis, Groningen, University of Groningen/Utrecht, Netherlands Geographical Studies, No. 270.

Bhan, G. (2016) *In the Public's Interest, evictions, citizenship, and inequality in contemporary Delhi*. Athens (Georgia): University of Georgia Press.

Bhan, G., & Shivanand, S. (2013) (Un)Settling the City, analysing displacement in Delhi from 1990 to 2007. *Economic and Political Weekly, XLVIII*(13) 54–61.

Bhargava, G. (1981). Slums of Urban India: Planning and policy framework. In G. Bhargava (Ed.), *Urban Problems and Policy Perspectives* (pp. 197–216). Abhinav Publications.

Bombay Metropolitan Regional Planning Board. (1974). *Regional Plan for Bombay Metropolitan Region 1970–91*, Poona, Government of Maharashtra.

Bose, A. (1973). *(1974), Studies in India's urbanization, 1901–1971*. New Delhi: Tata McGraw-Hill.

Brosius, C. (2010). *India's Middle Class, New forms of urban leisure, consumption and prosperity*. London: Routledge.

de Bruijne, G. A., & Schenk, H. (1992). Where do the poor live? An analysis of residential patterns of poor inhabitants in Indina cities. *The Indian Geographical Journal, 67*(2), 1–16.

Chalana, M., & Rishi, S. (2016). Making sense of the order in Delhi's Kathputti colony. In M. Chalana & J. Hou (Eds.), *Messy urbanism, understanding the "other" cities of Asia* (pp. 154–174). Hong Kong: Hong Kong University Press.

Chhabria, S. (2019). *Making the modern slum, the power of capital in colonial Bombay*. Seattle: University of Washington Press.

Coelho, K. (2013). From the frying pan to the floodplain: Negotiating land, water, and fire in Chennai's development. In A. Rademacher, & K. Sivaramakrishnan (Eds.), *Ecologies of Urbanism in India, metropolitan civility and sustainability* (pp. 145–168). Hong Kong: Hong Kong University Press.

Dasgupta, R. (2014). *Capital, the eruption of Delhi*. New York: Penguin Books.

Desai, A. R., & Devadas Pillai, S. (1970) Housing conditions in slums in greater Bombay, from a study by the Dept. of Economics. In A. R. Desai, & S. Devadas Pillai (Eds.), *Slums and Urbanization* (pp. 171–175). Bombay: Popular Prakashan.

Dhadave, M. S. (1989). *Sociology of slum*. New Delhi: Archives Books.

Doshi, S, (2015) Resettlement ecologies: environmental subjectivity and graduated citizenship in Mumbai. In A. Rademacher, K. Sivaramakrishnan (Eds.), *Ecologies of Urbanism in India, metropolitan civility and sustainability* (pp. 225–248). Hong Kong: Hong Kong University Press.

Dupont, V. (2005). The idea of a new chic Delhi through publicity hype. In R. Koshla (Ed.), *The idea of Delhi* (pp. 70–94). Mumbai: Marg Publications.

Gadkari, S. S. (1981). Financing urban development. In G. Bhargava (Ed.), *Urban problems and policy perspectives* (pp. 386–407). New Delhi: Abhinav Publications.

Ghertner, D. A. (2013) Nuisance Talk: Middle-class discourses of a slum-free Delhi. In A. Rademacher, & K. Sivaramakrishnan (Eds.), *Ecologies of Urbanism in India, Metropolitan civility and sustainability* (pp.249–275). Hong Kong: Hong Kong University Press.

Ghertner, D. A. (2015) *Rule by Aesthetics, World-class city making in Delhi*, New York: Oxford University Press.

Gidwani, V. (2013). Value struggles: waste work and urban ecology in Delhi. In A. Rademacher, & K. Sivaramakrishnan (Eds.), *Ecologies of Urbanism in India, metropolitan civility and sustainability* (pp. 169–200). Hong Kong: Hong Kong University Press.

Goodfriend, D. E. (1982). Shahjahanabad–Old Delhi: tradition and planned changer. *Ekistics*, no. 297,1, November/December.

Gooptu, N. (2001). *The politics of the urban poor in early twentieth-century India*. Cambridge: Cambridge University Press.

Gerater Bombay, Municipal Corporation. (1964). *Report on the development plan for greater Bombay 1964*. Bombay: Government Central Press.

Harris, N. (1978) *Economic Development, Cities and Planning: the case of Bombay*. Bombay, etc.: Oxford University Press.

Heredia, R. C. (1986) *Settlements and Shelter, Alternative housing for the urban poor in Bombay*, New Delhi: Indian Social Institute.

Jagmohan. (1978). *Island of truth*. New Delhi: Vikas Publishing House.

Jha, S. S. (1986). *The structure of urban poverty*. Bombay, Popular Prakashan.

Kabra, K. N. (1975). *Urban land and housing policies, ceiling and socialisation*, New Delhi: People's Publishing House.

Kidambi, P. (2007). *The making of an Indian metropolis, colonial governance and public culture in Bombay, 1890–1920*. Aldershot: Ashgate.

Kundu, A. (1993). *In the Name of the Urban Poor, access to basic amenities*. Sage.

Majumdar, T. K. (1983). *Urbanizing poor, a sociological study of low-income migrant communities in the metropolitan city of Delhi*. New Delhi: Lancers Publishers.

Mayne, A. (2017). *History of a global Slums, the injustice*. London: Reaktion Books.

Menon-Sen, K. (2006). Better to have died than to live like this, 2006. In *Economic and Political Weekly*, May 20, (pp. 1969–1974).

Milbert, I. (2008). Law, urban politics and the role of intermediaries in Delhi. In, I. S. A. Baud, & J. de Wit, (Eds.), *New Forms of Urban Governance in India* (pp. 177–212). New Delhi: Sage Publications India.

Nelissen, B., & Schenk, H. (2002). *Delhi, towards a new urban order*. Amsterdam: Debert Media. (Video).

Nair, J. (2013). Is there an 'Indian' urbanism. In A Rademacher, K. Sivaramakrishnan (Eds.), *Ecologies of urbanism in India, metropolitan civility and sustainability* (pp. 44–70). Hong Kong: Hong Kong University Press.

Nigam, A. (2001) *Dislocating Delhi, a city in the 1990s*, Sarai reader. http://www.sarai.net/journal.

Nigam, A. (2005). Civil society and its 'Underground': Explorations in the notion of 'political society.' In R. Bhargava & H. Reifeld (Eds.), *Civil society, public sphere and citizenship, dialogues and perspectives* (pp. 236–259). New Delhi: Sage Publication.

Patel, K. (1963). *Rural Labour in Industrial Bombay*, Bombay: Popular Prakashan.

Payne, G. K. (1977). *Urban housing in the third world*. London: Leonard Hill.

Rao, G. B. K. (1981). Urban land (Ceiling and Regulation) Act (1976): Will it fulfil goals of urban development. In G. Bhargava (Ed.), *Urban problems and policy perspectives* (pp. 238–258). New Delhi: Abhinav Publications.

Rao, K. R., & Rao, M. S. A. (1984). *Cities and slums, a study of a squatters' settlement in the city of Vijayawada*. Delhi: Concept Publishing Company.

Rao, U. (2013). Tolerated Encroachment, resettlement policies and the negotiations of the licit/illicit divide in an Indian metropolis. *Cultural Anthropology, 28*(4), 760–779.

Risbud, N. (1990). Government support for popular settlements in Bhopal. In *Open House International*, (Vol. 15, No. 4, pp. 49–53) 'Housing and Urban Development in India'.

Rishi, S., & Syal, S. (2020) Megacities and slums, learning from Delhi's experience. In D. Rukmana (Ed.), *The Routledge handbook of planning megacities in the global south* (pp. 191–201). Abingdon: Routledge.

Robben, P. (1984) *Improvement and the better-off, displacement as a consequence of squatter settlement upgrading, a case study of Madras*. Geografische en Planologische Studies, no. 24, Amsterdam, Vrije Universiteit.

Schenk, H. (2001). Slums and government authorities: The Karnataka slum clearance board. In H. Schenk (Ed.), *Living in India's slums, a case study of Bangalore* (pp. 263–280). New Delhi, Manohar/IDPAD.

Schenk, H. (2004). Towards Apartheid? Policies of segregation and deprivation in Delhi. In K. R. Gupta (Ed.), *Urban development debates in the new millennium, studies in revisited theories and redefined praxes* (Vol. 1, pp. 96–114). New Delhi: Atlantic Publishers and Distributors.

Schenk, H. (2020, 2021). *Housing India's urban poor 1800–1965*. New Delhi, Manohar, (2020)/London, Routledge (2021).

Schenk, H., Ten Holder C., & Mulders, R. (1989). Open developed plots and sites & services, experiences and lessons from Madras, India. *Indian Geographical Journal, 664*(2), 107–126. (December).

Searle, L. G. (2016). *Landscapes of Accumulation, Real estate and the Neoliberal imagination in contemporary India*. Chicago: University of Chicago Press.

Shafi, S. S. (1981). Planning the Indian metropolis: Some reconsiderations. In G. Bhargava (Ed.), *Urban problems and policy perspectives* (pp. 47–76). New Delhi: Abhinav Publications.

Sharan, A. (2014). *In the City, Out of Place, nuisance, pollution and dwelling in Delhi, c. 1850–2000*, New Delhi: Oxford University Press.

Singh, A. M., & de Souza, A. (1980). *The urban poor, slum and pavement dwellers in the major cities of India*. New Delhi: Manohar.

Singh, K. N. (1978). *Urban development in India*. New Delhi: Abhinav Publications.

Sisodia, O. P. (2006). Urban poverty in Five Year Plans. In S. Ali (Ed.), *Managing urban poverty* (pp. 378–431). New Delhi: Uppal Publishing House.

Srivastava, S. (2015). *Entangled urbanism, slum, gated community and shopping mall in Delhi and Gurgaon*. New Delhi: Oxford University Press.

Study Group on Greater Bombay. (1959). *Report of the Study Group on Greater Bombay*. Report to the Government of Bombay, Bombay Government Central Press.

Tarlo, E. (2000) Welcome to history: A resettlement colony in the making. In V. Dupont, E. Tarlo, & D. Vidal (Eds.), *Delhi: Urban Space and Human* Destinies (pp. 51–72). New Delhi: Manohar/Centre des Sciences Humaines.

Trivedi, R. K. (1970). Slum areas of Ahmedabad city. In A. R. Desai, S. Devadas Pillai (Eds.), *Slums and* urbanization (pp. 211–214) Bombay: Popular Prakashan.

Unni, K. R. (1978). Slum relocation and urban planning: some social concerns. In A. de Souza (Ed.), *The Indian city, poverty, ecology and urban development* (pp. 215–231) New Delhi: Manohar.

Vasudevan, V. (2013). *Urban villager, life in an Indian satellite town*. New Delhi: Sage.

Verma, G. D. (2002). *Slumming India, a chronicle of slums and their saviours*. New Delhi: Penguin Books.

Verma, N. (1981). Urban land acquisition: Certain emerging issues. In G. Bhargava (Ed.), *Urban problems and policy perspectives* (pp. 259–272). New Delhi: Abhinav Publications.

Weinstein, L. (2014). *The Durable Slum, Dharavi and the right to stay put in globalizing Mumbai*. Minneapolis: University of Minneapolis Press.

Wiebe, P. (1975). *Social life in an Indian slum*. Delhi: Vikas Publishing House.

Chapter 4
Housing Inequality by Social Groups, Gender, and Place of Residence: A District-Level Geospatial Analysis in India

Pritam Ghosh, Debodatta Saha, and Alfredo Cartone

Abstract The association of economic growth in India with the increase of inequality level during the past few decades is an open controversy. After 74 years of independence, about 12% of houses are still temporary (Census of India, in Census of India instruction manual for houselisting and housing census. Ministry of Home Affair, Government of India, https://censusindia.gov.in/2011-Documents/HouselistingEnglish.pdf) whereas, a protected, liveable, resilient, and sustainable house is considered as one of the basic human needs. The primary aim of the study is to identify the pattern of distribution of temporary houses along with inequalities between socially marginalized and non-marginalized groups, female- and male-headed households, and rural and urban residences. The research also tries to show the distribution of spatial clusters of the neighbouring districts with a relatively larger *proportion* and *disparity* of temporary housing in these three dimensions. The inequality has been calculated as the percentage difference of temporary housing between the two categories being each dimension entirely based on the house-listing database, Census of India, (Census of India in Census of India instruction manual for houselisting and housing census. Ministry of Home Affair, Government of India. https://censusindia.gov.in/2011-Documents/HouselistingEnglish.pdf). Choropleth mapping, quadrant analysis, and spatial statistics techniques (Global Moran's I and Univariate and Bivariate LISA) have been used for the identification of spatial clusters of districts with a higher proportion of temporary housing along with higher degree of inequality. This study reveals that the proportion of temporary housing is higher among the districts along the eastern coastal, north-eastern, central north, and the western part of the country. Consecutive clusters of 101, 94, and 90 districts are identified ($P < 0.05$)

P. Ghosh (✉)
Department of Geography, University of Calcutta, 35, Ballygunge Circular Road, Kolkata, West Bengal 700019, India

Department of Geography, Ramsaday College, Amta, Howrah, West Bengal 711401, India

D. Saha
Department of Geography, Bijoy Krishna Girls' College, 5/3, Mahatma Gandhi Road, Howrah 711101, India

A. Cartone
Department of Economic Studies, University G. D'Annunzio of Chieti Pescara, Pescara, Italy

A. Kundu et al. (eds.), *Accessible Housing for South Asia*,
https://doi.org/10.1007/978-3-030-88881-7_4

with a relatively higher percentage of total temporary housing in an association with higher level of inequality in the previously mentioned three dimensions, respectively. The clusters of 17 districts are identified in different parts of Odisha, Tamil Nadu, and Jharkhand, where the share of temporary houses to total houses and the proportion of temporary housing among socially marginalized groups, female-headed households, and rural areas are higher.

Keywords Temporary housing · Marginalized and Non-marginalized · Gender Difference · Rural-urban inequality · Spatial statistics · India

4.1 Introduction

The association of economic development in India with the increase of inequality during the past few decades is an open controversy. Previous researchers have shown the growing economic inequality of India (Ahluwalia, 2002; Sen et al., 2005; Pal et al., 2007), where a weaker section of the society cannot access basic human amenities, even adequate housing (Srinivasan et al., 2004; Mohanan et al., 2008; Dreze et al., 2013; Kumar, 2014, 2017; Ghosh et al., 2021). Presently, providing affordable housing to the weaker section of society has become a socio-political issue.

The Government of India (GOI) through different programmes like Indira Awaas Yojana (1985), Jawaharlal Nehru National Urban Renewal Mission (2005), Rajiv Awaas Yojana (2011) has taken the initiative to provide affordable housing in urban and rural areas. However, after 74 years of independence, around 10 million houses are dilapidated and 29 million are still noticed temporary, (Census of India, 2011) whereas protected, liveable, resilient, and sustainable house is one of the basic human needs. The owners of these temporary houses mostly belong to economically poor families from socially backward communities. In this context, according to the Indian census, a temporary house structure indicates a house made of temporary material. Hence, temporary housing is a significant indicator of housing deprivation (Ghosh et al., 2021).

India reflects a huge local and regional disparity and diversity in terms of human development, socio-economic growth, development (Fusco et al., 2019; Jose, 2019; Bakshi et al., 2015; Kundu et al., 2013; Roy, 2012; Dholakia, 2003; Kurian, 2000; Ghosh, 2018; Ghosh & Rohatgi, 2018), quality of living as well as household basic amenities (Kumar, 2017; Mondal, 2020; Ghosh et al., 2021; Ghosh, Hossain and Alam, 2021). With the increasing facilities and opportunities, existing socio-economic inequality is highly increasing between rural and urban areas (Deaton and Draze, 2002; Sen et al., 2004). Several researchers (Das et al., 2012; Shafiquallah, 2011; Narayanamoorthy et al., 2010) have already recognized the rural-urban divide from different socio-economic aspects over India. Chaudhuri & Roy, (2017) showed the spatial pattern of rural-urban disparity in terms of drinking water and sanitation facilities of households in India.

Moreover, more inequality from the aspects of well-being exists among different social groups in Indian society (Thorat et al., 2007, 2009; Desai & Dubey, 2011).

Kumar (2014, 2015a, b, c) has shown the existing disparity in basic housing amenities among different social groups in India. Among those different dimensions, the existence of gender inequality in Indian society is also clearly reflected when India ranked 112th out of 153 countries with a score of 0.668 on the World Economic Forum's Global Gender Gap Index (GGI) (WEF, 2020). Desai (1994) has shown the different aspects of women's deprivations in India. According to Sustainable Development Goal (SDG) 01 to reduce poverty and exposure and vulnerability to climate-related extreme events and other socio-economic, environmental shocks and disasters, sustainable, resilient, and permanent housing need to build up for the owner of these temporary houses in India. In order to make human settlements inclusive, safe, resilient, and sustainable (see SDG 11), it is necessary to assure adequate, affordable 'Housing and Basic Service' for all the citizens. However, the existence of a gender divide in India is also nested with the lack of affordable and adequate housing.

Further, the attention to the spatial dimension of territorial inequality is a significant aspect to take into account (Panzera & Postiglione, 2020) and spatial patterns of temporary housing are significant to policymakers, as they can highlight spatial clusters and critical situations. Therefore, to fulfil the goal of gender equality (SDG 05) and reduced inequality (SDG 10) among social groups, gender, community in terms of housing condition and, district-wide analyses of housing inequality are also significant. In this direction, more evidence is needed for central and local governments to initiate proper policies to fulfil SDGs by 2030 and put forward the nation in the global platform.

Particularly, in the case of housing, the presence of spatial effects (Anselin, 1988) plays a pivotal role. The spatial effect distribution of the proportion and disparity of temporary housing is immensely important because the planners can identify spatially disadvantaged districts. Recently several researchers have already concluded that spatial dependency influence different socio-economic and demographic issues (Crowder & South, 2008; Millward, 2008; Baumont, 2009; Taiwo & Ahmed, 2015; Chaudhuri & Roy, 2017; Wang & Chi, 2017; Cartone & Postiglione, 2020; Ghosh & Cartone, 2020). Hence, the extent of spatial effects in the distribution of housing quality has also been examined in different regional level studies in India (Haque et al., 2020; Mondal, 2020).

Given those issues, the main aim of this study is to identify the distribution of temporary houses along with inequalities among social groups, gender, and place of residence. In this context, to identify the distribution of spatial clusters of the neighbouring districts of the relatively higher burden of temporary housing along with a higher level of disparity between socially marginalized-non-marginalized groups, female-male headed-households, and rural-urban residence through spatial statistics. To the best of our knowledge, this is the first comprehensive effort to measure the district level inequality of temporary housing in India based on three dimensions; socially marginalized and privileged groups, male and female-headed households, and rural and urban areas. Hence, different dimensions at the basis of inequality are analysed and explored in their spatial attributes using Global Moran's I, Univariate and Bivariate LISA. The objective is to provide a further picture of how different dimensions of inequality interact on territories, create interdependencies and structural differences, whose analysis can provide a better understanding of ad hoc strategies.

4.2 Material and Methods

4.2.1 Database

The latest House listing and Housing census data, 2011 are employed to develop this study. The database of total temporary houses among SC/ST households has been selected from 'HH 13: Households by type of structure of the census household occupied (Total SC/ST) House listing and housing census data tables (Total, SC/ST)'. The male–female-headed household data has been collected from female-headed households by the type of structure of the census household occupied (excluding institutional household) 'Houses, household amenities and assets among female-headed household'.

4.2.2 Measures and Dimensions of Housing Inequality

For analysing the inequality of housing, the selection of 'structure of census houses', as a parameter is very logical as by definition it is very clear that in this category the total housing scenario such as the condition of houses (good, liveable, dilapidated), the material of the roof, wall, the floor are included. Households by types of structure of the census houses occupied are categorized into: 1. Permanent 2. Semi-permanent 3. Temporary. According to the census commission, India, Temporary Houses specifies 'Houses with wall and roof made of temporary material. Wall can be made of Grass, Thatch, Bamboo, etc., Plastic, Polythene, Mud, Unburnt brick, or Wood. The roof can be made of Grass, Thatch, Bamboo, Wood, Mud, Plastic or Polythene'.

Further, we have not only identified the unequal distribution of households but also—and most importantly—highlighted the most deprived clusters of districts to uplift their condition for the fulfilment of SDGs (SDG 01, 11). By not using the broad category 'Structure of household' or permanent household, specifically temporary household is chosen as the main variable. This variable has been previously considered as an indicator of housing quality (Mondal, 2020; Das and Mistri, 2013).

Temporary housing inequality in this study has been measured in three dimensions, like inequality of temporary housing between (a) socially marginalized and socially non-marginalized groups, (b) male-headed and female-headed households and (c) rural and urban residential areas. In this context, we have considered scheduled tribes and scheduled caste populations as socially marginalized groups. The 'Scheduled Caste' and 'Schedule Tribe' are the socially disadvantaged social groups recognized by the President of India according to article numbers 341 and 342 of the Constitution of India (MOPPP, 2019).

4.2.3 Analytical Strategies

Firstly, we determined the district-wide temporary housing inequality with the help of an absolute percentage difference between two selected groups of each dimension. It can be explained as follows:

$$\text{Diffence between the groups} = \left[\left(\frac{X_{td}}{X_{hd}}\right) - \left(\frac{Y_{td}}{Y_{hd}}\right)\right] * 100$$

Here, X_{td} indicate the number of temporary housing among socially marginalized groups, female-headed household and total number of temporary houses in rural areas in the district 'd'. X_h refers to the total number of households among respective categories (e.g. socially marginalized groups, female-headed households, and rural households in(d) districts). Y_t is the number of temporary house among socially non-marginalized groups, male-headed households and urban areas of the districts 'd', Y_h is the total number of households among socially privileged groups and female-headed or urban households in that district.

In this context, as we have taken a socially marginalized group, female-headed house, and rural houses as base categories to determine inequality by percentage difference, the positive inequality value denotes a higher prevalence of temporary housing among base categories. Alternatively, negative inequality values are indicating more ownership of temporary housing among socially privileged groups, male-headed households, and urban areas than the selected base categories.

Secondly, the district level temporary housing proportion and disparity in terms of each dimension have been represented by the histogram (for all India level) and box plots (for State level). After that, we mapped the district-wise percentage of temporary housing and the housing disparity between social groups, gender, and place of residence.

Along with that, we have also employed spatial statistics techniques to understand spatial dependency (Moran, 1948) and spatial heterogeneity in the concentration and disparity of temporary housing in every dimension. We applied Global Moran's I index of spatial autocorrelation (Anselin, 1988) and Moran's scatter plots (Anselin, 1995, 1996) to investigate the spatial dependency of temporary housing distribution and disparity. It can be expressed as follows:

$$I_x = \frac{n}{\sum_i \sum_j w_{ij}} \frac{\sum_i \sum_j w_{ij}(x_j - \overline{x})(x_i - \overline{x})}{\sum_i (x_2 - \overline{x})^2}$$

where n is the number of districts under analysis, x_i is the value of the variable of interest in the considered districts i,$\overline{x}$ is the calculated mean of the variable x_i understudy, and w_{ij} are the entries of a $\boldsymbol{W}$ contiguity matrix indicating spatial neighbourhood between i and j. Moran's I value varies from -1 to $+\ 1$, where a positive value indicates positive spatial autocorrelation, while a negative depicts negative spatial autocorrelation. In this context, different weighting methods can be selected, such as contiguity-based (queen and rook) and distance-based weights (distance band and k-nearest neighbour weights) used to generate the spatial weightage of different locations. After comparing, for robustness, different weighting matrices calculated by the queen, rook, and k-nearest neighbour (k value ranged from 3 to 8), we used k-nearest neighbour ($k = 5$) weight matrices as it produced the highest Moran's I value in this study.

To represent the specific spatial pattern of the selected variable (distribution and disparity of temporary housing) in the study area univariate Local Indicator of Spatial Association (LISA) has also been adopted. LISA statistics focus on spatial heterogeneity and they show the extent of local spatial autocorrelations (High–High and Low–Low) and the presence of spatial outliers (High–Low and Low–High). These local indicators of spatial association denote the local clusters of similar or dissimilar variable values in a set of observations. The Local Moran's statistics can be expressed as a decomposition of the global Moran's I as the following:

$$I(i)_x = \frac{n(x_i - \overline{x})\sum_j w_{ij}(x_j - \overline{x})}{\sum_i (x_i - \overline{x})^2}, j \neq i$$

where n is the number of the district under analysis, x_i is the variable under study, $\overline{x}$= the calculated mean of the selected variable x_i, and w_{ij} are the entries of $\boldsymbol{W}$.

To get a more extensive picture of the phenomenon, we have adopted a 'quadrant analysis' technique to categorize the districts in terms of the proportion of temporary housing along with the inequality in each dimension. The method has been applied previously in different research on health and social geography to categorize different spatial units (Ghosh et al., 2021; Liou et al., 2020; Mazumdar, 2010). Because it was too difficult to draw lines over the closely placed scatter dots of temporary housing and housing disparity value of three selected dimensions of the districts. Here we used the median value of the percentage of temporary housing as a threshold value for the demarcation of quadrants. The districts consisting of the share of temporary housing over the threshold value have been identified as 'High' and below the threshold value coded as 'Low'. On the other hand, in the case of inequality, we have fixed '0' as the threshold value for the demarcation of the quadrants. The districts comprising the housing inequality of more and less than the threshold value indicate the positive and negative disparity respectively. Therefore, the first quadrant (I) is characterized by a higher share of temporary housing along with a higher proportion of temporary housing among socially marginalized groups, female-headed households, and in rural areas (Positive inequality) than privileged groups, male-headed households, and urban areas, respectively. The second quadrant (II) is characterized by a higher concentration of temporary housing along with more prevalence of temporary housing among socially privileged groups, male-headed households, and urban areas (Negative inequality) than the selected base categories. The third quadrant (IV) is characterized by a lower percentage of temporary houses along with negative disparity. The fourth quadrant (III) is representing a lower percentage of temporary houses with a higher level of positive disparity in temporary housing.

Along with that we also adopted bi-variate LISA and scatter plots to represent the relationship between the spatial lag of the inequality of temporary housing with the proportion of temporary housing of different districts in India. We have applied this spatial technique to identify specifically those districts that are significant in terms of the relationship between the proportion of temporary housing and the spatial lag of the inequality of temporary housing. Bivariate Moran's I can be written as the following:

$$I_{x,y} = \frac{n}{\sum_i \sum_j w_{ij}} \frac{\sum_i \sum_j w_{ij}(y_j - \overline{y})(x_i - \overline{x})}{\sum_i (x_2 - \overline{x})^2}$$

where y_j is a generic spatially distributed temporary housing inequality, $\overline{y}$ its mean, X is the proportion of temporary housing, and the rest same as above. Bivariate Moran's I show the presence of spatial effects linked to inequality of temporary housing. Analytical Strategies has been shown through a schematic diagram (Fig. 4.1).

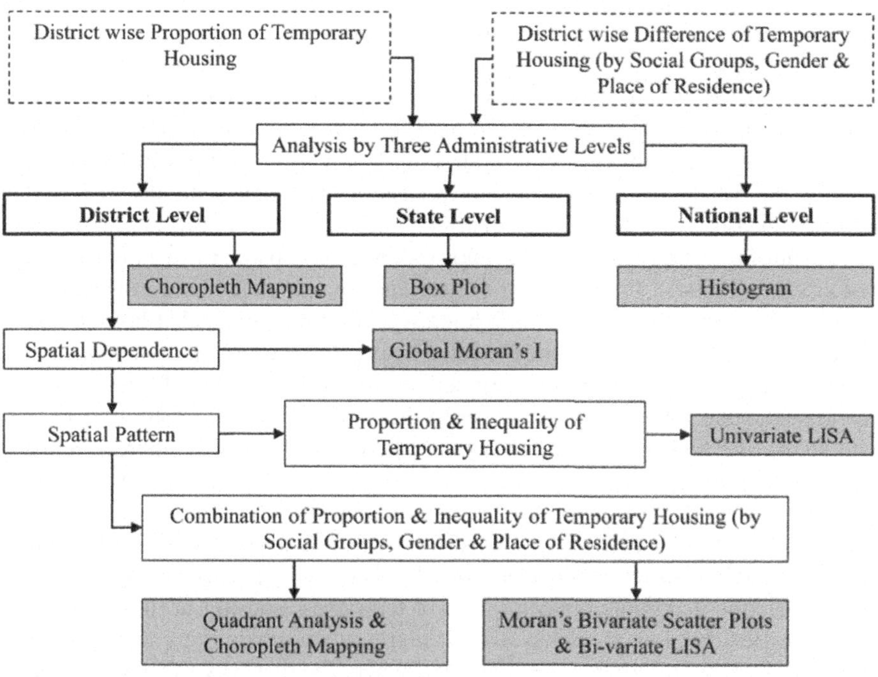

Fig. 4.1 Methodological framework of the present study

Calculations, cartographic representation, and mapping have been conducted with the help of Microsoft Excel,2013, IBM SPSS 23, QGIS 2.8.1, GeoDa and Plot.ly, etc Software. Location and administrative setup of Indian states, union territories and 640 districts has been represented in Appendix 1.

4.3 Results

4.3.1 District-Wise Inequalities in Temporary Housing: A National and State Level View

District-wise proportion and disparity of temporary housing from the dimensions of social groups, gender, and place of residence in India have been represented by Fig. 4.2. The central tendency of every dimension of inequality is found to be positive, which indicates the proportion of temporary housing is comparatively higher among socially marginalized groups, female-headed households, and rural areas as compared to the respective selected alternate categories in major portions of districts of India. The proportion of temporary housing varies from 0.064% (Rudraprayag in Uttarakhand State) to 76.70% (Tirap in Arunachal Pradesh State, Northeast India) in the various districts of India. The range of temporary housing disparity is maximum between rural and urban areas (from −26.18 to 62.54%) followed by the disparity between social groups (from −34.81 to 47.20%) and gender (from −22.07 to 10.72%).

The inequality in temporary housing among social groups is positively highest in the Tirap district, where the proportion of temporary housing is higher (83.65%) among socially marginalized groups than socially privileged groups (36.46%). Alternatively, the Senapati district from north-eastern Nagaland state shows a higher negative disparity (−32.81%). This district shows a higher proportion of temporary housing among socially privileged groups (53.50%) compared to socially marginalized groups (18.69%). In the case of female-headed and male-headed ownership of temporary housing, the proportion is highest among female-headed households in Rayagada district Odisha state, and lowest in Lawngtlai district Mizoram as compared to male-headed households in that respective district. In the case of female-headed and male-headed ownership of temporary housing, Rayagada district in Odisha state shows the highest positive disparity, where the share of temporary housing among female-headed and male-headed households are 39.72% and 29%, respectively. Lawngtlai district, Mizoram, is identified as maximum negative inequality, where the proportion of temporary houses among male-headed households is much higher (56.54%) than female-headed households (34.46%). This Lawngtlai district also reaches the maximum concentration of temporary housing in rural areas than the urban. Besides, Leh (Ladakh) district represents a maximum concentration of temporary housing in urban areas than rural where the disparity of rural temporary housing than urban areas is −26.18.

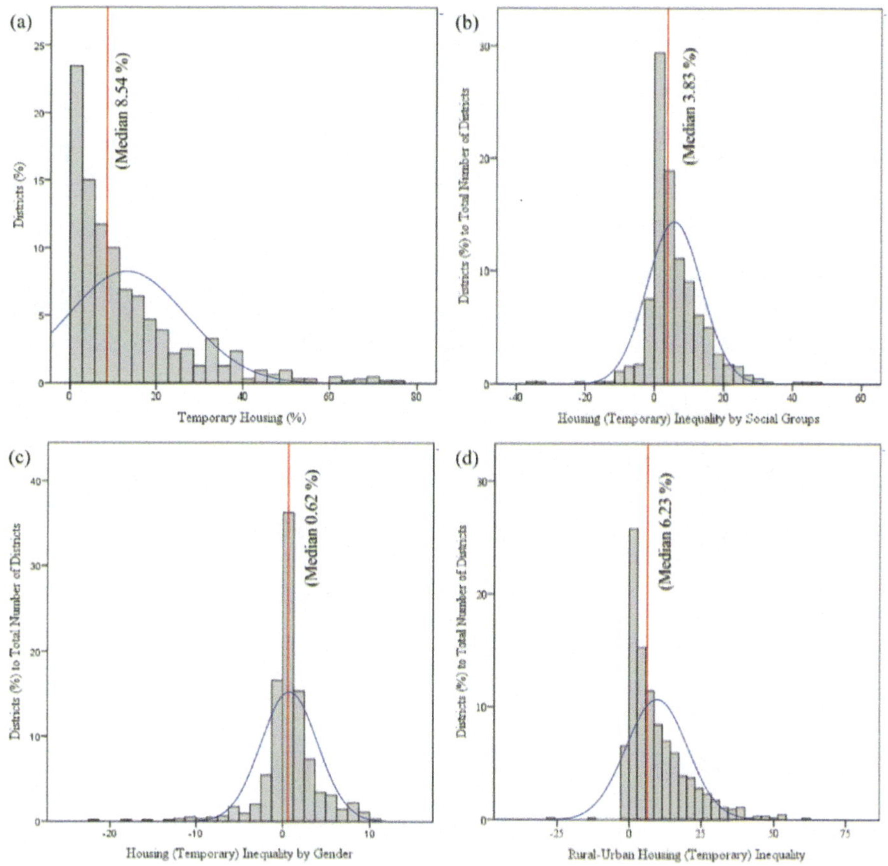

Fig. 4.2 **a** Distribution of district-wise proportion of temporary housing in India, 2011. Inequality of temporary housing by **b** social groups, **c** gender, and **d** place of residence

To summarize the information and highlight the extent of disparities, the state-level view of district-wide temporary housing disparity has been represented by a boxplot (Fig. 4.3). From the aspect of temporary housing inequality between social groups, the inter-state disparity is found to be positively higher in Tripura, Odisha, Bihar, Puducherry, Meghalaya, and Arunachal Pradesh. At the same time, the intra-state range of disparity is higher in Arunachal Pradesh, Manipur, Meghalaya, Nagaland, etc. For the case of temporary housing disparity between female and male-headed households, inter-state positively high disparity is in Andhra Pradesh, Tamil Nadu, Puducherry, and Odisha, etc. and negatively high in Mizoram, Meghalaya, Nagaland, Arunachal Pradesh, Assam, Tripura, etc. Northeast Indian states. The variation of temporary housing disparity by place of residence is existing in all the states to a different extent. This range of variation is higher in Jammu & Kashmir, Mizoram, and Nagaland and lower in Haryana, Gujarat, Goa, Daman &

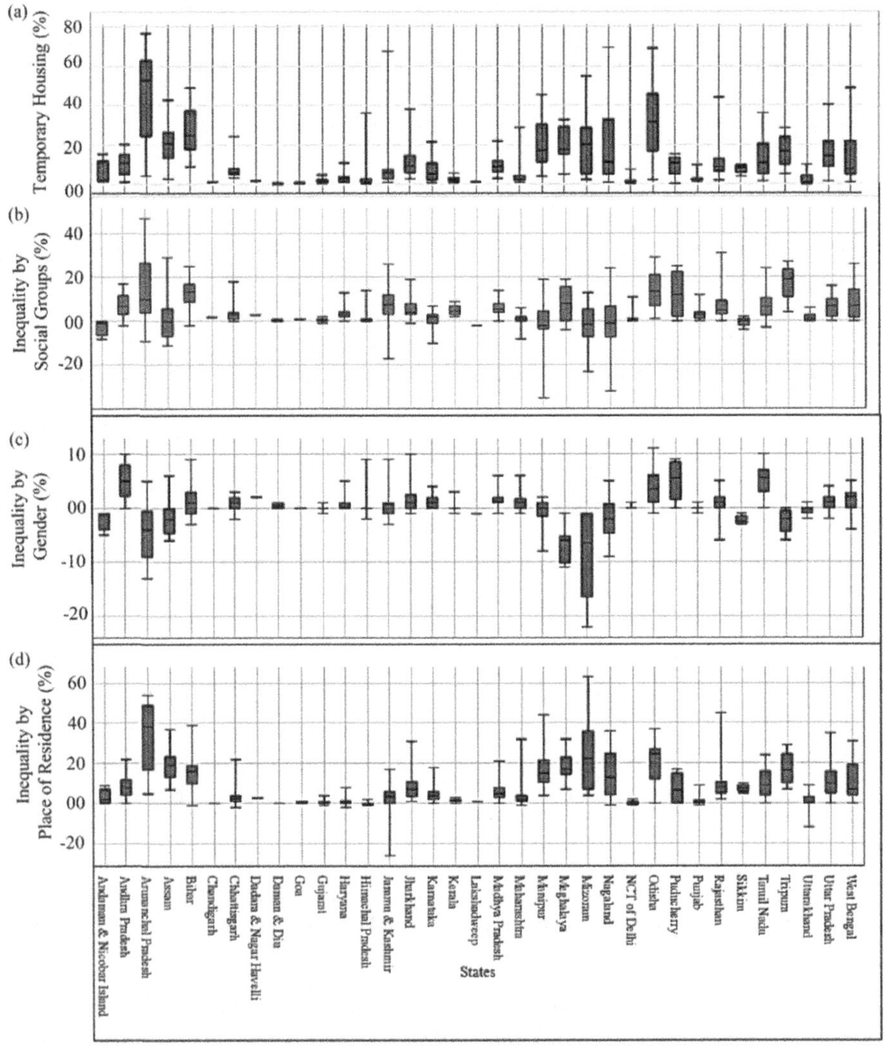

Fig. 4.3 **a** District-wise proportion and inequality of temporary housing by **b** social groups, **c** gender, **d** place of residence in India, state-level view (2011)

Diu, Himachal Pradesh, etc. Inter-state housing disparity, in this case, is also positively higher in Arunachal Pradesh, Mizoram, Odisha, and Assam compared to the other states, which indicates the concentration of more temporary housing in rural areas than urban.

4.3.2 Geospatial Pattern of District-Wise Proportion and Inequality in Temporary Housing

Before performing spatial analysis, it is important to visualize spatial patterns, which could be returned by plotting the variables under analysis. Here the distribution and the disparity of temporary housing in three-selected dimensions have been represented through choropleth maps at the district level (Fig. 4.4). After that, to understand spatial dependence, spatial clustering, and the disparity of temporary housing we performed a global Moran's I index with Local Indicator of Spatial Association (LISA) map. Two types of spatial clusters (High–High and Low–Low) and two types of spatial outliers (High–Low and Low–High) are noticeable in the distribution and disparity of temporary housing in LISA maps.

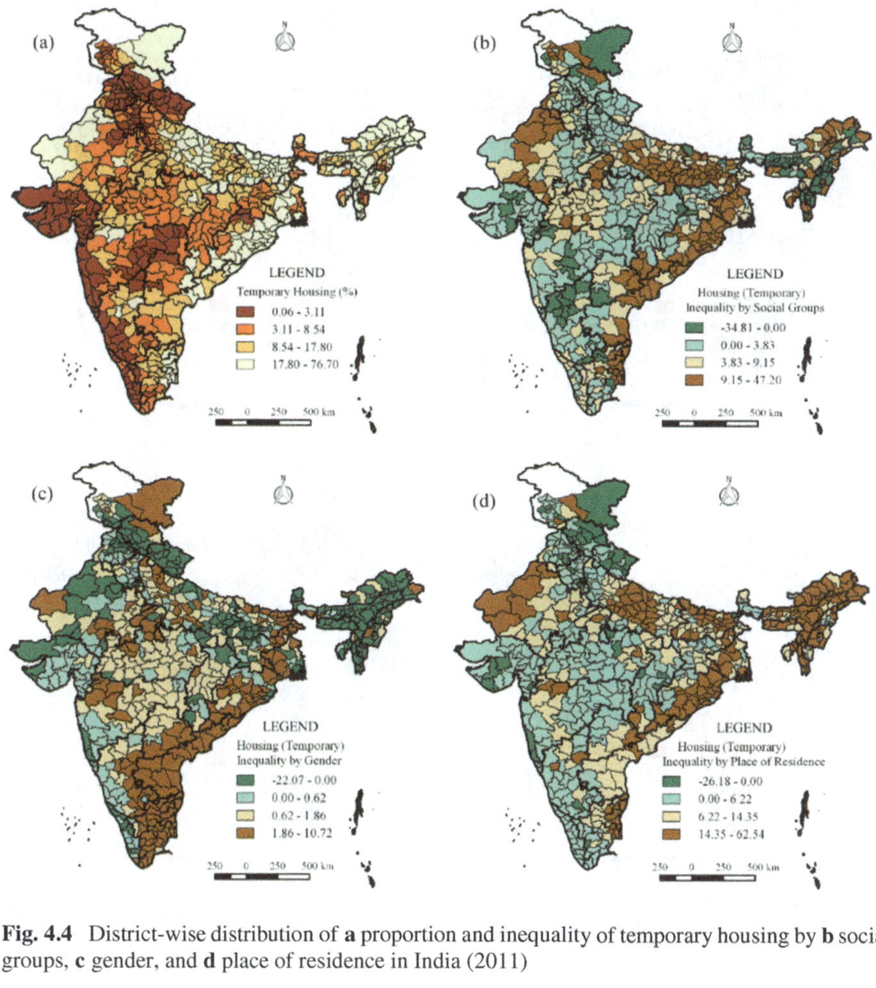

Fig. 4.4 District-wise distribution of **a** proportion and inequality of temporary housing by **b** social groups, **c** gender, and **d** place of residence in India (2011)

The Global Moran's I value (0.642) for the distribution of temporary housing indicates that there is a presence of high significant ($P < 0.05$) spatial effects. Further, the LISA map shows (Fig. 4.5) that there is a cluster (High–High) of 79 districts concentrated over the eastern coastal region (Odisha coast) and north-eastern and northern central parts (Bihar, Uttar Pradesh) of India, with a relatively high percentage of temporary housing surrounded by similar conditions of districts. Alternatively, significant clusters of 178 districts with a lower percentage of temporary housing are found to be concentrated over the southwestern coastal part and northern parts surrounding the capital city, Delhi of India.

The disparity of temporary housing in the selected three dimensions also shows significant spatial dependence. In the case of temporary housing inequality between

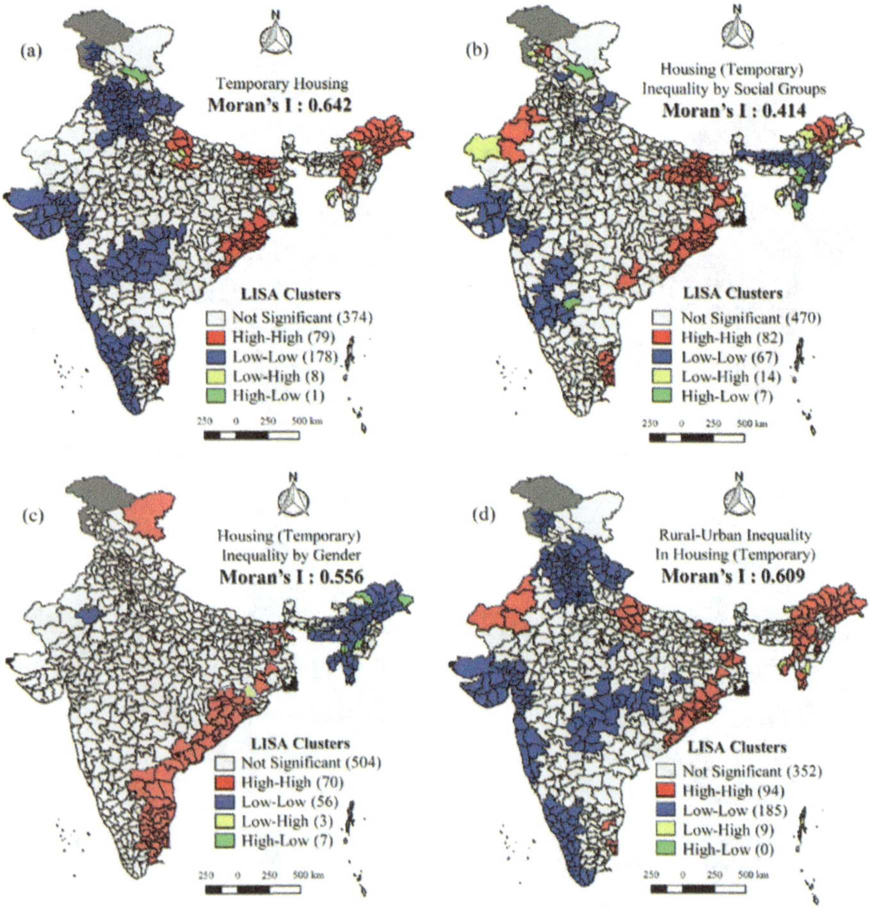

Fig. 4.5 Geospatial heterogeneity of district wise **a** total temporary housing and inequality of temporary housing by **b** social groups, **b** genders, and **c** place of residence in India (2011)

the social groups, spatial dependency calculated by Moran's I is 0.414 ($P < 0.05$). In fact, the higher proportion of temporary housing ownership among socially marginalized groups compared to the privileged groups (High–High clusters) is higher over the districts situated along the eastern coast of India. This positive disparity is also found to be higher in some districts situated in the extreme north-eastern part, and northern central part of the country.

The spatial dependence of the distribution of gender disparity in temporary housing is relevant (Moran's I = 0.556; $P < 0.05$). While turning to LISA groups, the greater coverage of temporary housing among female-headed households compared to the male-headed household (High–High Cluster) is found among the districts situated along the east coastal region from the extreme south location of India. Conversely, the districts in the north-eastern states (56 districts) show the higher deprivation of male-headed households in terms of ownership of temporary housing compared to the female-headed households. This feature shows how spatial techniques at a refined scale can capture influence between regions not merely embedded into economic or commuting flows, but that also involve social aspects due to cultural characteristics.

Lastly, the Global Moran's I value of rural-urban disparity is the highest (Moran's I = 0.609) among these three-selected dimensions of temporary housing. The concentration of temporary houses in the rural area is much higher than urban areas among those districts situated along the eastern coastal zone, northeast and central north (Uttar Pradesh) part, and some districts of western Rajasthan in India. Alternatively, the concentration of temporary housing in urban areas compared to rural areas is found to be higher among the districts situated along the western coast and northern region. This feature may be particularly linked to the concentration of slum houses in the urban areas. However, the level of urban deprivation from the aspect of temporary housing is relatively lower than the deprivation in rural areas.

4.3.3 Categorization of Districts by Inequalities and Overall Burden of Temporary Housing

The distribution of temporary housing along with the level of disparity has been represented at the district level through scatterplots (Fig. 4.6). There is a moderate positive correlation (Pearson $r2 = 0.475$; $P < 0.01$ (2-tailed)) between the share of total temporary housing and disparity between social groups. The scatter dots of the districts have been categorized into four quadrants. The scatter plot of district-wise proportion of temporary housing along with the disparity between socially marginalized and non-marginalized groups has been reported in Fig. 4.6a.

The spatial distribution of these 640 districts along with their quadrant memberships has been mapped (Fig. 4.6b). There are 273 districts fallen in quadrant zone I, characterized by a higher proportion of temporary housing among socially marginalized groups along with a higher proportion of total temporary housing. On the other

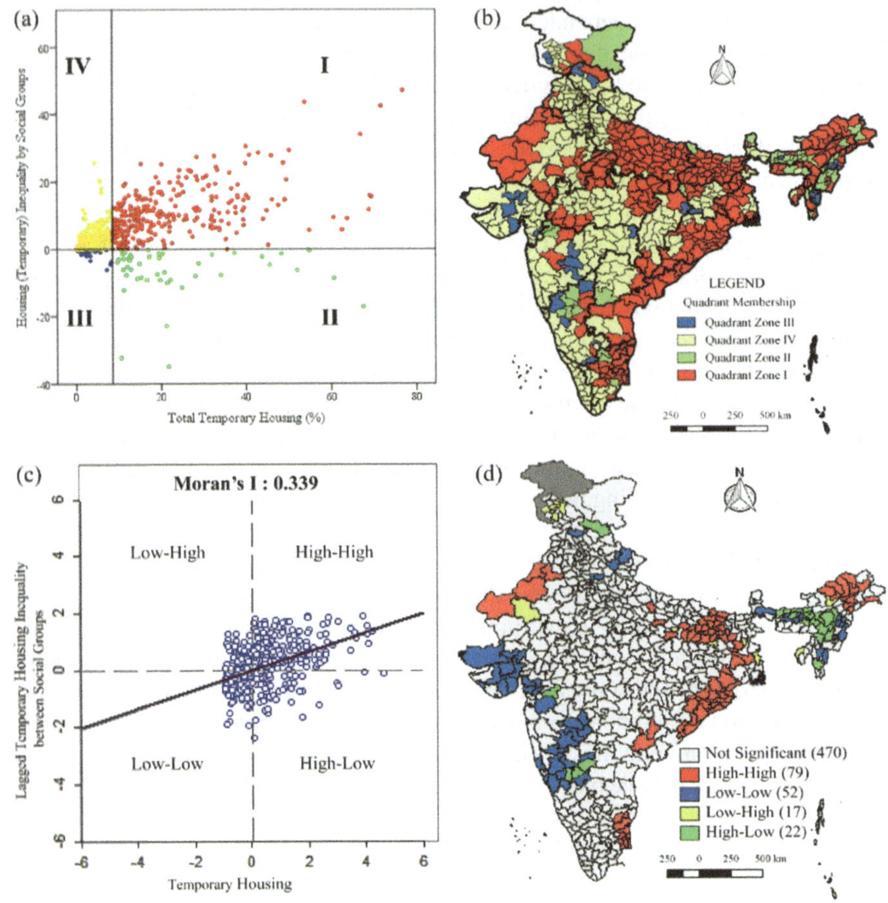

Fig. 4.6 Categorization of the Indian districts based on the geospatial correlation between proportion and the inequality of temporary housing between socially marginalized and non-marginalized groups

hand, there are also 43 districts (Quadrant Zone II) with a higher proportion of temporary housing and a relatively higher proportion of temporary housing among socially non-marginalized groups. Quadrant zone IV consists of 286 districts that represent a comparatively lower proportion of total temporary housing and higher ownership of temporary housing among socially marginalized groups compared to socially non-marginalized groups. Only 34 districts are fallen in Quadrant zone III, characterized by a relatively lower proportion of temporary housing and a higher proportion of temporary housing among socially non-marginalized groups.

Interestingly, the spatial link between the proportion of temporary housing and the spatial lag of the temporary disparity between social groups has also been represented through Moran's scatter plot and bi-variate LISA cluster mapping (Fig. 4.6c and d).

What emerges is the significant presence of local instabilities in this link. Hence, a cluster including 101 districts with a higher proportion and higher disparity of temporary housing between social groups is present. Among these, 79 districts are characterized by more coverage of temporary housing among socially marginalized groups than privileged groups.

By looking at the Moran's scatterplot (Fig. 4.7c), no significant global spatial correlation appears between total proportion and the disparity of temporary housing by gender. This relationship has also been represented through a scatter plot with quadrant zones (Fig. 4.7a). The spatial distribution of these districts from these four quadrant zones has been represented in Fig. 4.7b. There are 214 scatter dots in quadrant zone-I indicating the district with a higher percentage of temporary

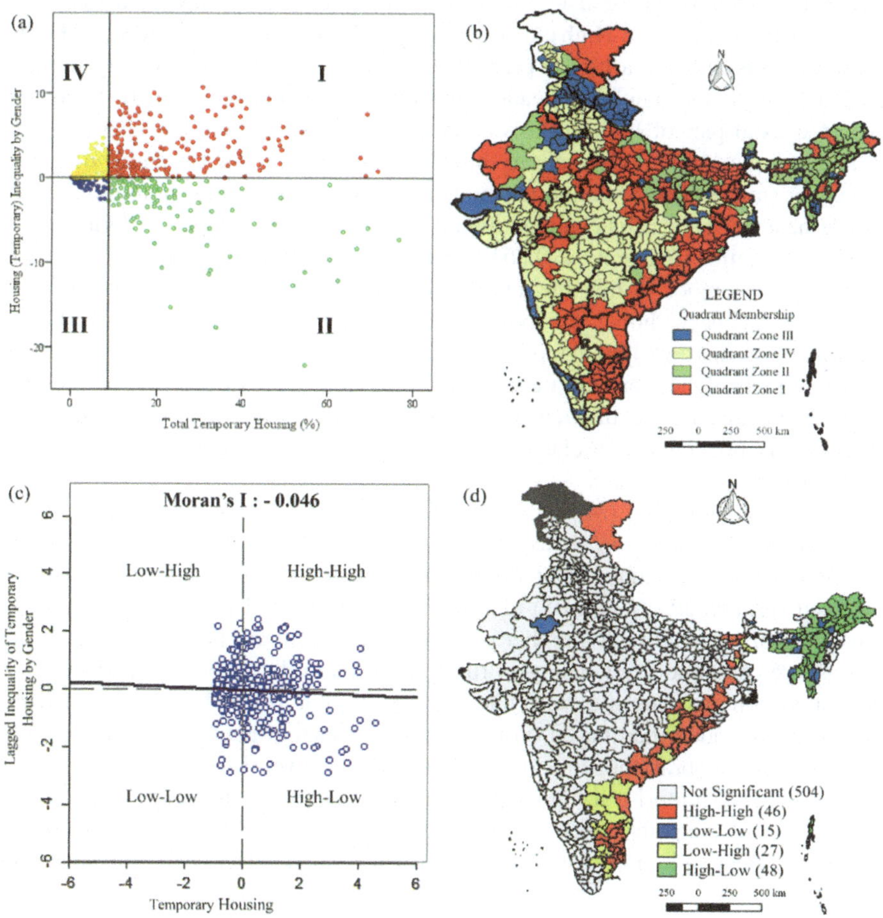

Fig. 4.7 Categorization of the Indian districts based on the geospatial correlation between proportion and the inequality of temporary housing between male-headed and female-headed households

housing and more coverage of temporary housing among female-headed households than male-headed. Similarly, 106 districts from zone II represent a higher percentage of temporary housing and a relatively higher proportion of temporary housing among male-headed households compared to female-headed. Total 83 districts from zone III shows a lower prevalence of temporary housing and a lower proportion of temporary housing among male-headed households than female. A brunch of 237 districts from quadrant zone IV indicates a relatively lower percentage of temporary housing along with a higher proportion among female-headed households than male-headed. The Global Moran's I (−0.046) value indicates the random distribution of the districts with the proportion of temporary housing in association with district-wise lagged temporary housing disparity by gender.

Bivariate LISA map identified 46 districts ($P < 0.05$) characterized by a higher percentage of temporary housing along with a higher positive lagged disparity of temporary housing (High–High cluster) among male and female-headed households. These districts indicate a higher proportion of temporary housing among female-headed households than male-headed and are located discontinuously along the eastern coastal part of India. In this context, 48 districts ($P < 0.05$) characterized by a higher percentage of temporary housing along with lagged negative disparity by gender (more share of temporary housing among male-headed households than female-headed) have also been identified over the north-eastern part of India.

The association (Pearson $r = 0.851$; $P < 0.01$ (2-tailed)) between the district-wide proportion of temporary housing and the rural-urban disparity is very strong. This correlation has been shown by a scatter plot with quadrant zones in Fig. 4.8a. The majority of the district (316) in India shows a higher percentage of temporary housing and a relatively higher concentration of temporary housing in rural areas compared to urban. There are only four districts from (quadrant zone II) representing a higher share of temporary housing and a relatively higher proportion in urban areas compared to the rural areas.

The global Moran's I (Moran's I = 0.591; $P < 0.05$) value indicates relatively high spatial dependency in terms of the proportion of total temporary housing in association with a spatial lag of urban-rural inequality. A cluster of 89 districts has been significantly ($P < 0.05$) identified from bivariate LISA map (High–High cluster), characterized with a higher prevalence of temporary housing along with a more share of temporary housing in rural areas than urban, concentrated over the eastern coastal area, north-eastern and northern middle part. The districts of India have also been identified based on the spatial correlation between proportion and inequality of temporary housing at a 99% confidence level (Fig. 4.9).

The districts comprise a higher proportion of temporary housing along with a higher level of inequality between socially marginalized-privileged groups, male- and female-headed households, and rural-urban residence has been represented in Table 4.1.

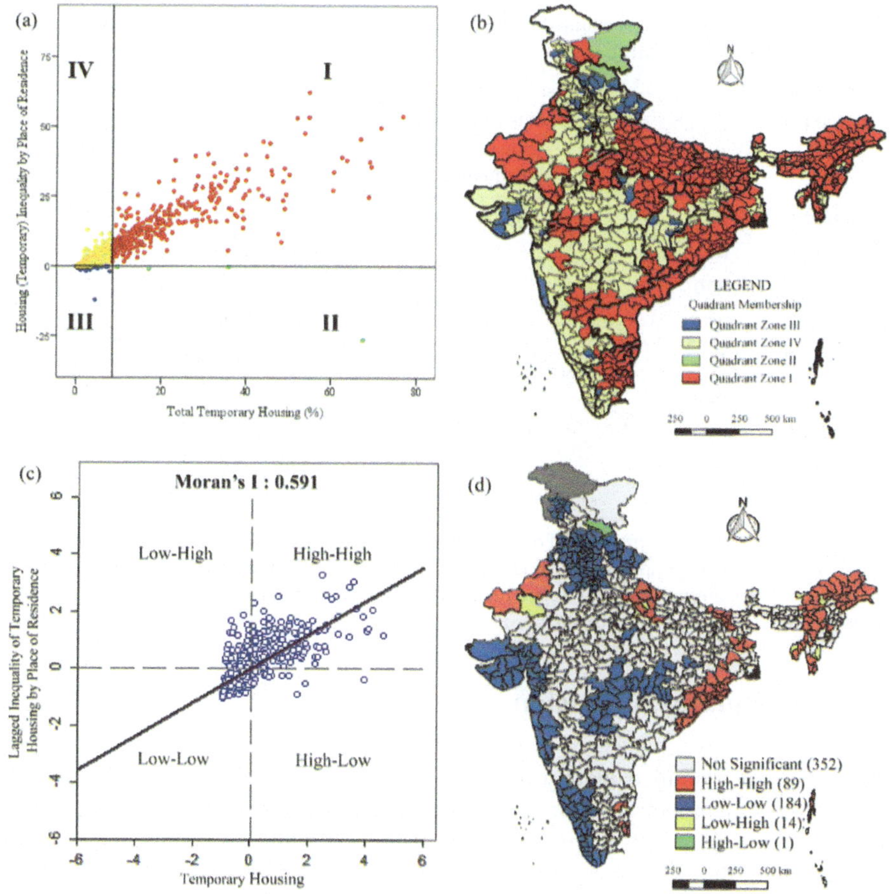

Fig. 4.8 Categorization of the Indian districts based on the geospatial correlation between proportion and the inequality of temporary housing between rural and urban areas

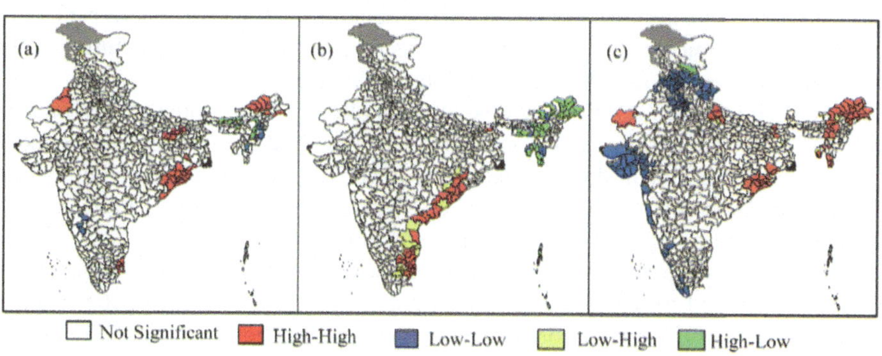

Fig. 4.9 Spatial clusters of Indian districts based on proportion and inequality of temporary housing by **a** social groups, **b** genders, and **c** place of residence with 99% confidence level

Table 4.1 Number of districts counted in the clusters of a higher proportion of temporary housing with a higher level of inequality

Quadrant analysis		Spatial cluster analysis			
Quadrant zone	Number of district	Dimension of housing (temporary) inequality	Hot spot	Number of districts	
				95% CI	99% CI
Quadrant I	273	Social Groups	High–High	79	42
Quadrant II	47		High–Low	22	11
Total	320		Total	101	53
Quadrant I	214	Gender	High–High	46	29
Quadrant II	106		High–Low	48	31
Total	320		Total	94	60
Quadrant I	316	Place of residence	High–High	89	50
Quadrant II	4		High–Low	1	1
Total	320		Total	90	51

Notes Quadrant I: A higher proportion of Temporary Housing and Positive Inequality; Quadrant II: A higher proportion of Temporary Housing and Positive Inequality; High–High = Higher proportion of Temporary Housing and Higher Lagged Inequality; High-Low = Higher proportion of Temporary Housing and Lower Lagged Inequality

4.4 Concluding Discussion

The study has identified mainly four things about the distribution and inequality distribution of temporary housing over 640 Indian districts. First, the proportion of temporary housing varies among different districts of India. Generally, the districts situated along the western coast and northern portion consist of significantly lower proportion, whereas the eastern coast, north-eastern, northern middle part shows a higher proportion of temporary housing. To survive in the Himalayan hilly topography and humid monsoonal climate the people of north-eastern India have adapted the temporary housing material based on the abundant local flora. There is also an influence of tradition and culture on the housing material and architecture among different tribal societies of this region (Kolkman and Balcknburn, 2014; Das et al., 2012; Ghosh et al., 2021). Besides this, clusters of districts are found to be concentrated over Odisha, Bihar, and some parts of Uttar Pradesh. These states ranked lower in terms of human development. The lower level of human development of these states (Suryanarayana, 2011; Das & Mistri, 2013; Jose, 2019) indicates the poor standard of living as well as housing structure.

On the other hand, the cluster of the districts with less temporary housing is found to be concentrated over Delhi and surrounding states. It is because of the 'spread effect' (Myrdal, 1957) of economic development among the neighbouring districts, based on the proximity from the main capital city Delhi. A higher level of development in these districts has made housing conditions better. Some researchers (Kundu et al., 2002; Krishna and Bajpai, 2011; Sharma, 2016; Mondal, 2020; Ghosh et al.,

2021; Ghosh, Hossain and Alam, 2021) previously explained a similar matter in the case of India. Along with that, clusters of districts consisting of a lower proportion of temporary housing are found to be concentrated over the extreme north-western part, surrounding the capital city of Jammu Kashmir, Srinagar. The proximity and functional connection to the capital city Srinagar has risen the level of development of these neighbouring districts, which led to the better housing structure in those districts. Similarly, the concentration of a cluster of districts consisting lower proportion of temporary housing, along the western coastline part from Gujrat to the extreme southern point of India may be found due to the higher level of development, the standard of living of these states, and location of different cities (Suryanarayana, 2011; Das & Mistri, 2013).

Another relevant issue that led us to focus on, the districts consisting of the deprivation among the socially marginalized groups in terms of ownership of temporary housing as compared to the privileged groups. The ownership of temporary housing is not only found to be more among socially marginalized groups and female-headed households in the majority of the districts. There are also many districts in India where the proportion of temporary housing is higher among socially privileged groups and male-headed households compared to socially marginalized groups and female-headed households, respectively.

Further, a third feature that emerges from our analysis is related to rural-urban temporary housing disparity, the proportion of temporary housing is higher in rural areas than urban in the (more than 90%) majority of the districts. However, the magnitude of this inequality varies in different districts in India. This struck rural-urban differences is one of the most significant obstacles for the progress of a developing nation like India (Chaudhuri & Roy, 2017).

Finally, the result also indicates the poor housing structure in rural areas than urban along with a huge gap between urban and rural residential areas in providing housing facilities. Consequently, it suggests urgent reforms in government policies and subsidies to provide adequate, sustainable housing to the rural people.

In 2015, Pradhan Mantri Awas Yojana (Urban & Rural) (1915) has been launched by the Government of India, considering the theme 'Housing for all by 2022' to provide affordable housing for the economically weaker section, lower and middle-income groups of the society. Many people in the country have already been benefited from this programme. More initiative and investment need to be taken in this context to bring every family of the country under their affordable shelters. Our study emphasis more on space-specific strategies and initiatives considering the fulfilment of SDGs 01, 05, 10, and 11 by 2030.

Finally, deepening spatial aspects highlights how relationships between various aspects of disparities are very unstable over space, which leads policymakers to be extremely careful and cooperate with local levels. For instance, the percentage of temporary housing is much higher in the eastern coastal districts than western. The frequency of prevalence of different natural hazards like cyclones, floods is more in eastern coastal districts. The study suggests more initiatives to improvise the resilience and adaptive capacity by improving the housing condition of these most vulnerable districts (SDGs 01, 11). In this direction, our study separately identified the districts comprised of a higher proportion of temporary housing along with higher deprivation among socially marginalized groups, female-headed and rural households as compared to socially privileged groups, a male-headed and urban household in terms of ownership of temporary housing and vice versa. Therefore, considering SDGs (5, 10) our study suggests proper initiative and investment for these districts to reduce inequality among social groups, gender, and place of residence firstly by providing affordable housing to the more deprived social, demographic groups or areas.

Appendix

See Fig. 4.10.

Fig. 4.10 Administrative setup of the States, Union territories and the districts in India (Source: World Map and India Map: GADM database of Global Administrative Area)

References

Ahluwalia, M. S. (2002). State-level performance under economic reforms in India. In A. Krueger (Ed.), *Economic policy reforms and the Indian Economy* (pp. 91–128). University of Chicago Press.

Anselin, L. (1988). Lagrange multiplier test diagnostics for spatial dependence and spatial heterogeneity. *Geographical Analysis, 20*(1), 1–17.

Anselin, L. (1995). Local Indicators of Spatial Association—LISA. *Geographical Analysis, 27*, 93–115.

Anselin, L. (1996). The Moran scatterplot as an ESDA tool to assess local instability in Spatial Association. In M. Fischer, H. Scholten, & D. Unwin (Eds.), *Spatial analytical perspectives on GIS in environmental and socio-economic sciences* (pp. 111–125). Taylor and Francis.

Anselin, L. (2010). Thirty years of spatial econometrics. *Papers in Regional Science, 89*(1), 3–25.

Anselin, L., Sridharan, S., & Gholston, S. (2007). Using exploratory spatial data analysis to leverage social indicator databases: The discovery of interesting patterns. *Social Indicators Research, 82*, 287–309.

Anselin, L., Syabri, I., & Kho, Y. (2010). GeoDa: An introduction to spatial data analysis. In *Handbook of applied spatial analysis* (pp. 73–89). Berlin, Heidelberg: Springer.

Bakshi, S., Chawla, A., & Shah, M. (2015). Regional disparities in India: A moving frontier. *Economic and Political Weekly, 50*(1), 44–52.

Baumont, C. (2009). Spatial effects of urban public policies on housing values. *Papers in Regional Science, 88*(2), 301–326.

Cartone, A., & Postiglione, P. (2020). Principal component analysis for geographical data: the role of spatial effects in the definition of composite indicators. *Spatial Economic Analysis*, 1–22. https://doi.org/10.1080/17421772.2020.1775876.

Census of India. (2011). *Census of India instruction manual for houselisting and housing census*. Ministry of Home Affair, Government of India. https://censusindia.gov.in/2011-Documents/HouselistingEnglish.pdf.

Chaudhuri, S., & Roy, M. (2017). Rural-urban spatial inequality in water and sanitation facilities in India: A cross-sectional study from household to national level. *Applied Geography, 85*, 27–38. https://doi.org/10.1016/j.apgeog.2017.05.003

Crowder, K., & South, S. J. (2008). Spatial dynamics of white flight: The effects of local and extra-local racial conditions on neighbourhood out-migration. *American Sociological Review, 73*(5), 792–812.

Das, D., & Pathak, M. (2012). The growing rural-urban disparity in India: A growing issue. *International Journal of Advancements in Research and Technology, 1*(5),1e7.

Das, B., & Mistri, A. (2013). Household quality of living in the Indian States: Analysis of 2011 Census. *Environment and Urbanization Asia, 4*(1), 151–171. https://doi.org/10.1177/0975425313477759

Das, P., Korde, C., Sudhakar, P., & Satya, S. (2012). Traditional bamboo houses of North-Eastern Region: A field study of Assam & Mizoram. *Key Engineering Materials, 517, 197–202*. https://doi.org/10.4028/www.scientific.net/KEM.517.197.

Deaton, A., Dreze, J. (2002). Poverty and Inequality in India: A Re-Examination. *Economic and Political Weekly, 37*(36), 3729–3748. http://www.jstor.org/stable/4412578.

Desai, S., & Dubey, A. (2011). Caste in 21st century India: Competing narratives. *Economic and Political Weekly*, 40–49.

Desai, S. (1994). Gender inequalities and Demographic Behaviour, India. *The Population Council*, New York.

Dholakia, R. H. (2003). Regional disparity in economic and human development in India. *Economic and Political Weekly, 38*(39), 4166–4172. https://www.jstor.org/stable/4414081.

Dreze, J., & Sen, A. (2013). *An uncertain glory: India and its contradictions*. Penguin Books.

Fusco, G., & Perez, J. (2019). Bayesian network clustering and self-organizing maps under the test of Indian districts. A comparison. *Cybergeo: European Journal of Geography, 887*.

Ghosh, P. (2018). Spatial analysis and assessment of child health risk and vulnerability in West Bengal: A geo-medical study. *Eastern Geographer, 24*(1), 136–148.

Ghosh, P., & Rohatgi, P. (2018). Status of maternal healthcare service utilization in West Bengal. *International Journal of Innovative Knowledge Concepts, 6*(8), 22–30. https://doi.org/10.11.25835/IJIK-147.

Ghosh, P., & Cartone, A. (2020). A Spatio-temporal analysis of COVID-19 outbreak in Italy. *Regional Science Policy & Practice, 12*, 1047–1062. https://doi.org/10.1111/rsp3.12376.

Ghosh, P., Alam, A., Ghosal, N., & Saha, D. (2021). A geospatial analysis of temporary housing inequality among socially marginalized and privileged groups in India. *Regional Science Policy & Practice, 13*(2), 1–22. https://doi.org/10.1111/rsp3.12425

Ghosh, P., Hossain, M., & Alam, A. (2021). Water, Sanitation, and Hygiene (WASH) Poverty in India: A district-level geospatial assessment. *Regional Science Policy & Practice, 1–21*. https://doi.org/10.1111/rsp3.12468.

Haque, I., Rana, J., & Patel, P. P. (2020). Location matters: Unravelling the spatial dimensions of neighbourhood level housing quality in Kolkata, India. *Habitat International, 99*(102157). https://doi.org/10.1016/j.habitatint.2020.102157.

Jose, A. (2019). India's regional disparity and its policy responses. *Journal of Public Affairs*, e1933. https://doi.org/10.1002/pa.1933.

Kolkman, R., & Blackburn, S. (2014). *Tribal architecture in Northeast India*. (Leiden, Boston: BRILL). ISBN 978-90-04-26392-5.

Krishna, A., & Bajpai, D. (2011). Lineal spread and radial dissipation: experiencing growth in rural India, 1993–2005. *Economic and Political Weekly, xlvI*(38), 44–51.

Kumar, A. (2014). Access to basic amenities: Aspects of caste, ethnicity and poverty in rural and urban India—1993 to 2008–2009. *Journal of Land and Rural Studies, 2*(1), 127–148. https://doi.org/10.1177/2321024913515113

Kumar, A. (2015a). Disparities in access to basic amenities across caste, ethnicity and classes in rural and urban India. *Social Change and Development, 12*(1), 20–45.

Kumar, A. (2015b). Indian urban households' access to basic amenities: Deprivations, disparities and determinants. *Margin—The Journal of Applied Economic Research, 9*(3), 278–305. https://doi.org/10.1177/0973801015579754.

Kumar, A. (2015c). Rural households' access to basic amenities in India: Deprivation and socio-economic exclusions. *Social Change, 45*(4), 561–586. https://doi.org/10.1177/0049085715602789.

Kumar, A. (2017). Households' toilet facility in rural India: Socio-spatial analysis. *Indian Journal of Human Development, 11*(2), 1–20. https://doi.org/10.1177/0973703017716602

Kurian, N. J. (2000). Widening regional disparities in India: Some indicators. *Economic and Political Weekly, 35*(7), 538–550.

Kundu, A., Mohanan, P. C., & Varghese, K. (2013). *Spatial and Social Inequalities in human development: India in the global context* (pp. 1–44). UNDP.

Kundu, A., Pradhan, B. K., & Subramanian, A. (2002). Dichotomy or continuum: Analysis of the impact of urban centres on their periphery. *Economic and Political Weekly, 37*(50), 5039–5046. https://www.jstor.org/stable/4412965.

Liou, L., Kim, R., & Subramanian, S. V. (2020). Identifying geospatial patterns in wealth disparity in child malnutrition across 640 districts in India. *SSM—Population Health, 10* (2020). https://doi.org/10.1016/j.ssmph.2019.100524.

Mazumdar, S. (2010). Determinants of inequality in child malnutrition in India. *Asian Population Studies, 6*, 307–333. https://doi.org/10.1080/17441730.2010.512763

Millward, H. (2008). Evolution of population densities: Five Canadian cities. *Urban Geography, 29*(7), 616–638, 1971–2001.

Mondal, S. (2020). Modelling the spatial pattern of household quality of living in West Bengal: An approach of hotspot and cluster analysis. *Modeling Earth Systems and Environment, 6*, 833–851. https://doi.org/10.1007/s40808-020-00711-2

Moran, P. (1948). The interpolation of statistical maps. *Journal of the Royal Statistical Society B, 10*, 243–251.
Mohanan, P. C., & Chakraborty, S. (2008). Inter-state comparisons of housing conditions—A study based on NSS 58th round. *Sarvekshana, 94*(28), 13–23.
Myrdal, G. (1957). *Economic theory and under-development regions.* Gerald Duckworth.
Narayanamoorthy, A., & Hanjra, M. A. (2010). What contributes to the disparity in rural-urban poverty in Tamil Nadu?: A district-level analysis. *Indian Journal of Agricultural Economics, 65*(2), 228e244.
Pal, P., & Ghosh, J. (2007). *Inequality in India: A survey of recent trends.* Economic and Social Affairs, DESA Working Paper No. 45, ST/ESA/2007/DWP/45, pp. 1–27.
Panzera, D., & Postiglione, P. (2020). Measuring the Spatial Dimension of Regional Inequality: An Approach Based on the Gini Correlation Measure. *Social Indicators Research, 148*, 379–394. https://doi.org/10.1007/s11205-019-02208-7.
Roy, S. (2012). *Regional disparities in growth and human development in India.* ISID Working Paper, No 2012/05.
Roy, D., & Mondal, A. (2015). Rural urban disparity of literacy in Murshidabad District, WB, India. *International Research Journal of Social Sciences, 4*(7), 19e23.
Sen, A., & Himanshu. (2004). Poverty and Inequality in India: II: Widening Disparities during the 1990s. *Economic and Political Weekly, 39*(39), 4361–4375. http://www.jstor.org/stable/4415594.
Sen, A., & Himanshu. (2005). *Poverty and inequality in India: Getting closer to the truth* (pp. 1–77).
Shafiquallah, S. (2011). Regional analysis of urban-rural differentials in literacy in Uttar Pradesh, India. *Journal of Geography and Regional Planning, 4*(5), 287e296.
Sharma, A. (2016). Urban proximity and spatial pattern of land use and development in rural India. *The Journal of Development Studies, 52*(11), 1593–1611.https://doi.org/10.1080/00220388.2016.1166207.
Srinivasan, K., & Mohanty, S. K. (2004). Deprivation of basic amenities by caste and religion: Empirical study using NFHS data. *Economic and Political Weekly, 39*(07), 728–735.
Suryanarayana, M. H., Agarwal, A., & Seeta Prabhu, K. (2011). *Inequality-adjusted human development index for India's states.* New Delhi: United Nations Development Program.
Taiwo, O. J., & Ahmed, F. (2015). Geographical analysis of voter apathy in presidential elections between 1999 and 2011 in Nigeria. *African Geographical Review, 34*(3), 250–268.
Thorat, S., & Newman, K. S. (2007). Caste and economic discrimination: Causes, consequences and remedies. *Economics and Political Weekly, 41*, 41–45.
Thorat, S., & Newman, K. (Eds.). (2009). *Blocked by caste: Economic discrimination in modern India.* Oxford University Press.
Wang, D., & Chi, G. (2017). Different places, different stories: A study of the spatial heterogeneity of county level fertility in China. *Demographic Research, 37*, 493–526.
World Economic Forum. (WEF, 2020). Global Gender Gap Report 2020, World Economic Forum, Geneva.

Chapter 5
Neoliberalism and Housing Affordability Crisis in Dhaka Where Market-Enabling Efforts Failed

Fawzia Farzana

Abstract The rise of neoliberalism was instigated by the failures of welfare states in the western world in the 1970s. Policies were formulated to 'extend market discipline, competition, and commodification throughout all sectors of society' because of the diminishing profitability by the mass production concept of Fordism and increasing public budget deficits. As a result, the social good housing was commodified too and considered as an investment asset globally. Such transformation has intensely influenced the right to adequate housing endorsed by the constitutions across the world. The neoliberal policies have shaped the housing provision system worldwide, where the private market has been considered as the absolute provider of housing for all income groups according to demand but not need. From the literature, the most prominent characteristics of the neoliberal housing market have been identified as: 1. Homeownership focused housing provision to uphold asset base welfare system; 2. 'Unlocking land values and new geographies of the cities'and 3. Affordability crisis. Thatcherism and Reaganism aggressively implemented neoliberal reforms in the 1980s which gradually influenced most of the countries in the world. Neoliberalism was introduced in developing and underdeveloped countries through Structural Adjustment Programs (SAPs) and measures to reduce budget deficits. Bangladesh accepted the SAP reform packages as the aid conditionality of IMF in the early 1980s and initiated denationalization of industries. The study has analysed the impacts of neoliberal policies on housing provision in Dhaka according to identified three prominent neoliberal housing market characteristics and the malfunction market enabling roles of the state that ultimately resulted in acute housing affordability crisis for limited-income households. The findings are based on secondary and grey materials, which have been analysed and validated by key personnel interviews. The findings will have some policy implications to tackle the housing affordability crisis of Dhaka.

Keywords Bangladesh · Privatization · Asset-based welfare · Gentrification

F. Farzana (✉)
Urban and Rural Planning Discipline, Khulna University, Khulna, Bangladesh

A. Kundu et al. (eds.), *Accessible Housing for South Asia*,
https://doi.org/10.1007/978-3-030-88881-7_5

5.1 Introduction

The intellectual inception of neoliberalism happened through the post-war writings of Friedrich Hayek and Milton Friedman, where they criticized the central economic planning of National Socialism and Totalitarianism. However, neoliberalism got focused during the late 1970s and early 1980s as a political strategy to deal with the global recession that resulted from the failures of welfare states in the western world during the preceding decade. Harvey (2005) refers to neoliberalism as 'in the first instance a theory of political economic practices that proposes that human wellbeing can best be advanced by liberating individual entrepreneurial freedoms and skills within an institutional framework characterized by private property rights, free markets and free trade. Thatcherism and Reaganism aggressively implemented neoliberal reforms in the 1980s which gradually influenced most of the countries in the world. Neoliberalism was introduced in the Third World countries through Structural Adjustment Programs (SAPs) with the help of international neoliberal agents (Brenner & Theodore, 2002). Bangladesh accepted the SAP reform packages as the aid conditionality of IMF in the early 1980s and initiated denationalization of industries.

Neoliberalism advocated the opening of the market which emphasized channelling the private sector wealth for housing provision. Components of this neo-liberal housing policy including privatization, reduction of subsidies, elimination of rent controls, liberalization of private housing and mortgage provision and relaxation of planning controls have intensely influenced the right to adequate housing endorsed by the constitutions across the world (Wang et al., 2012).

This paper is targeted at identifying the relation between neoliberalism and the housing affordability crisis in Dhaka by analysing the political-economic transformation of Bangladesh towards neoliberalism. To develop the conceptual framework, the next section discusses the characteristics of the neoliberal housing market from the literature on both central and peripheral countries of the world. An intensive literature review has been done to come up with the most prominent housing provision characteristics which then used for a systematic review to delineate the neoliberal impacts in the housing sector of the capital Dhaka. Sections 5.3 and 5.4 will discuss the adaptation of neoliberal political-economic policies in Bangladesh and the impact of such policies on housing provision and malfunctioning market enabling initiatives of the state of the capital Dhaka. The impacts are identified, and state initiatives are analysed through a systematic review of journal papers, books and grey materials and the findings have been validated by key informant interviews.[1]

[1] Key informants include housing experts, developers and professionals from state housing agencies. The name and designation have not been provided here due to page limitation.

5.2 Neoliberalism and Housing: International Perspective

Neoliberalism has reshaped the housing provisions, in slightly different ways, in both developed and developing countries and the East Asian developmental states where government regulations strictly controlled the neoliberal transformation (Brenner & Theodore, 2002; Doling & Ronald, 2010; Gough, 2002; Harvey, 2005; Peck & Tickell, 2002). This section discusses the neoliberal reforms of housing provisions and their impacts concerning different categories of world cities.

Neoliberalism induced the restructuring of western welfare states adopted a new welfare idea known as an 'asset-based or property-based welfare system' (Rolnik, 2013; Ronald, 2008; Watson, 2009). In this system, individuals are responsible for their own welfare needs where they are encouraged to invest in financial and property assets that ensure short-term or long-term financial gains. According to this theory, such investments can be utilized for generating supplementary incomes to support welfare needs when income is reduced, most commonly, after being retired from work.

As a strategy of an asset-based approach to welfare, developed countries like the UK and eastern Europe started to sell public rental housing to the occupiers at a subsidized rate to increase homeownership. Other initiatives to encourage homeownership, through speeding up the neoliberal housing market, include liberalization of rent control and financing of homeownership (Rolnik, 2013). However, the strategies to increase homeownership taken under asset-based welfare system set apart the interests of two groups of the population, one who had already ensured ownership of property with an interest in the constant increase in house prices and the other, who are seeking access to housing, have demand for a house price reduction or the improvement of home purchase affordability (Doling & Ford, 2007; Ronald, 2008; Watson, 2009).

Globalization has affected Asian developmental states since the 1980s and since Economic Crisis in the late 1990s, the neoliberal ideology intruded into through IMF and World Bank economic rescue packages (Hundt, 2015). The homeownership percentage among urban citizens of China in 2010 indicates concurrent pervasive housing commodification and privatization (Wu, 2015). The initiatives by the Chinese government for affordable housing such as the waiver of land charges and formation of mortgage market ultimately favoured the high-income households only (Wang et al., 2012). However, the state control did compel the work-units (employers) to buy housing from the market for allocating among employees as in-kind benefits which helped, to some extent, increase homeownership among lower-income households too (Logan et al., 2009). The study by Doling (2002) on eight East Asian developmental states summarizes the varying government interventions to increase homeownership as the asset-based welfare component of neoliberalism. The governments in Singapore and Hong Kong exercise the roles of housing providers and developers. However, in Singapore, public housing is for sale while in Hong Kong it is mostly for rental. Japan, Korea, and Taiwan intervene in the housing market selectively and depends on subsidy to ensure housing accessibility of citizens under the market framework. In the case of Japan, to encourage homeownership, the state launched a series of new loan systems like a stem loan system with lower repayments during the first five years, a two-generational loan system, and a supplementary loan system (Lee et al., 2003). While the other developmental states like Indonesia, Malaysia, and Thailand are successful in increasing homeownership where the government intervention is to promote self-help strategies (Doling, 2002).

Neoliberalism was initiated in developing countries arguably in the 1980s where the key roles were played by the international agencies like the World Bank and IMF with the Structural Adjustment Programs (SAPs). In the case of developing nations, the neoliberal policy recommended ownership as the best housing tenure option, however, they transferred the responsibility of housing provision from the public sector to the private market. As a result, both the state and private developers became reluctant to be involved in the unprofitable low-income housing market. In Ghana, as suggested by the SAPs and Economic Recovery Projects in the early 1980s, the public rental houses and the vacant land acquired for such housing projects were sold out to individuals (not the initially targeted low-income households) and developers accordingly (Songsore et al., 2004; Tipple, 1994).

India was liberalized lately in 1991 through SAPs where housing was seen as an asset in an asset-based welfare system. To encourage homeownership, a series of fiscal incentives was announced in successive 'housing-friendly budgets' in the late 1990s and housing finance institutions were restructured to make home loans affordable. All these incentives to increase homeownership have created a bubble in the housing market in India. However, the housing market largely caters to India's high and upper-middle-income households; the housing needs of the lower-middle-income households and the poor have never been served by the market (Chakrabarti, 2001; Deshpande, 2004).

The literature on different categories of neoliberal cities reveals that the foremost strategy of neoliberal housing provision is to increase **homeownership under the asset-based approach** to welfare.

Neoliberal urbanism is a form of urbanism where the logic of building cities is formed according to the dynamics of global capitalism. The growth of large global cities under neoliberal urbanism gives an artificially and immensely increased value to the land in specific areas. When the buildings, founded on such lands give reduced returns than the potentials, gentrification is initiated to unlock the land values. Due to increased rents the working group or the poor of those areas face displacement (Smith, 2002). Gentrification across the Western countries happened due to the penetration by global finance (Smith, 2002). Gentrification happens in British and European cities in the name of 'urban regeneration', which is presented as a positive and necessary environmental strategy. Urban regeneration generally involves displacement, too. Nevertheless, the strategies for urban regeneration do not address the fate of the displaced people and recognize their right to the proposed revitalized city (Smith, 2002). The urban regeneration or gentrification matches with David Harvey's concept of 'accumulation by dispossession', where neoliberal capitalist policies help the accumulation of wealth by a few by dispossessing less powerful entities of their properties. The gentrification cases of the United States can be considered as examples of dispossession too where condominiums and shopping malls were developed by displacing long-term residents through the abuse of rights of eminent domain (Harvey, 2004).

The degree of state intervention in the gentrification process is much higher in East Asia (Lee et al., 2003). In the case of developmental states, gentrification resulted from state-led redevelopment projects. However, in recent years, the traditional 'market-based' form of gentrification in Western countries has emerged in developmental states too (Shin, 2009; Wong, 2006). According to Harvey (2005), the trajectory of change has been different in cities where liberal urban policies did not govern the development during much of the twentieth century, yet a similar direction was led by a competitive urban strategy to attract global finance through the gentrification of old centres. The big cities of third world countries like India, Ghana, Kenya, Nigeria or Zimbabwe all forcefully evicted residents as a result of neoliberal urbanism that provokes regeneration through gentrification to make them the destinations of choice for global investments (Smith, 2002; COHRE, 2006; Afenah, 2009). So, **unlocking land values through gentrification** is considered here as another influential neoliberal strategy that caters to the price appreciation of land and property and constrains the accessibility of the households who are financially not capable of enjoying the luxury of neoliberal urbanism.

The asset-based welfare system, gentrification resulted from the increased significance of prime cities for global capital accumulation and the centrality of the housing market in the new urban economy have resulted in the **housing affordability crisis** in global cities. Though it was argued that general national incomes would grow due to the new neoliberal macroeconomic policies and more people will be able to afford to house supplied by the market, things never happened in that way. Urban housing markets have become elitist arenas where low-income inhabitants have been threatened in their 'right to the city' (Kadi & Ronald, 2014; Rolnik, 2013).

Neoliberal schemes in the UK like the Right-to-buy scheme for selling out of council housing, buy-to-let mortgage scheme or get-rich-quick scheme through tax rebate for landlords are the most significant causes of today's unaffordable housing. Urban 'regeneration' policies adopted in the UK continue to provide luxurious housing options by demolishing affordable ones (Dorling, 2014; Hodkinson, 2012). In the developmental states, when the planned economy phase (1950–1977) ended, the real estate sector witnessed the similar asset price appreciation like in cities of the developed world only with a few exceptions where state interventions helped the low-income households by the provision of affordable housing (Shin, 2009; Wong, 2006). The affordability crisis affects the cities in the developing world most aggressively because of increased income inequalities resulting from neoliberal policies as well as due to super expensive land and housing properties and unaffordable mortgage finances resulting from the propensity of relying entirely on market forces of demand and supply and withdrawal of public initiatives from housing provisions (Deshpande, 2004; Harvey, 2005).

5.3 Neoliberal Dhaka: The Megacity Resulted from Uneven Geographical Development

Bangladesh accepted the SAP reform packages as the aid conditionality of IMF in the early 1980s to overcome serious macroeconomic imbalances resulted due to the unavailability of credit provided by DFIs, worsening of external aid environment and sluggishness in national resource mobilization. Structural adjustment was introduced in Bangladesh in December 1980 as the conditionality clause of IMF for the provision of Extended Fund Facilities followed by Structural Adjustment Facilities and Enhanced Structural Adjustment Facility throughout the consecutive two decades. As suggested in SAP, massive privatization started where the government supported the development of the private sector through deregulation of the economy, formation of disinvestments board and formulation of new industrial policy to support the private sector. The state also decided to make financial support provided by DFIs available for private entrepreneurs (Quadir, 2000). Nevertheless, most of the state-owned enterprises were sold to businessmen at 'give-away' prices in a very non-transparent manner. Moreover, subsidized credits were provided to the buyers from the public fund. This non-transparent manner developed a 'symbiotic relationship' between the government and the business. As a result, though the SAP policy packages strongly believed that rapid privatization would eventually boost the overall production the production performance of these privatized units were never encouraging (Sobhan, 1991). Instead, the implementation of reform measures resulted in the increasing trend of wealth accumulation by the business elites, who have associations with the administration, through the exploitation of public resources (Quadir, 2000; Nuruzzaman, 2004; Abdullah, 1991).

One of the themes of neoliberalism that Harvey explores is the phenomenon of uneven spatial development which results in extreme inequality between regions (Harvey, 2005). In the case of Bangladesh, the only epicentre of economic power and activity in the capital Dhaka. As a result of globalization and neoliberalism, by 2005, the number of active garments factory were around 3500, whereas in 1980 there was nearly a zero base. Because of its long-term regional primacy, Dhaka offered already developed infrastructural and logistical conditions that favoured the establishment of industries and as a result, it was the main site of the progress of the garments industry. In 2005 the total employment created by the garments sector was about 2 million people only in Dhaka (World Bank, 2005).

Since the 1980s, residential and governmental buildings, cultural and financial institutions, shopping centres, and movie theatres have been concentrated in Dhaka at an immense rate. Due to pro-privatization policies, private schools, universities, clinics, hospitals, diagnostic centres mushroomed in the capital Dhaka. By 2009, there were 51 private universities with several disciplines where a total of 200,939 students were studying. Along with students, these private universities also have created huge numbers of job opportunities in Dhaka (Kabir, 2012). In the context of the health sector, the contrast of Dhaka with other major cities of the country can be realized by the fact that the population per bed is 4174 in secondary and other tertiary care hospitals in Dhaka division while in Chattogram and Khulna Divisions the figure is 8054 and 7300, respectively. Both private health and education sectors have created huge job opportunities as well as attractions to live in Dhaka with the belief of getting necessary services. The Figure 5.2 shows the volumes of life-time in-migration into the districts of Bangladesh. Of all migration reported, 59% was towards the Dhaka Metropolitan Area (DMA).

Due to the failure of essential decentralization programs, the divergence between Dhaka and other cities and villages, with perilous socio-economic situations, was exacerbated furthermore (Bertuzzo, 2014). According to the holy constitution, the government is obliged to reduce the gap between cities and villages as well as to reduce the regional imbalances. However, it is not reflected in the dissemination of public funds. The fiscal allocation made in the budgets from the financial year 2006–07 to 2008–09 (regional allocation was indicated only in these fiscal years, otherwise the annual budget only provides sectoral allocations) reveal that the Dhaka division has attracted the highest share (36.73%) of public funds (Fig. 5.3). Due to the disparity between Dhaka and the other parts of the country, the capital has been receiving the bulk share of internal migrants over the years (Fig. 5.2). Due to in-migration, its population grew from 1 to 10 million within three decades and now after almost five decades, it has become around 20 million, of which 84% are migrants (BBS, 2011). This section has described how the free market economy and lack of decentralization of development have accelerated the transformation of Dhaka into a megacity. While the neoliberal housing policy impacts on the housing provision of this megacity are described in the following part of this paper.

5.4 Neoliberalism and Housing Provision in the Capital Dhaka

Since the early 80s, when Bangladesh accepted the SAP reform packages, there was a shift in the state's housing initiatives. The state emphasized the provision of serviced land rather than the construction of high-quality housing. Moreover, lower standards were adopted in housing provision and measures to improve cost recovery were introduced too (Choguill, 1993). The direct implications of neoliberalism can be traced back to 1993 when National Housing Policy was formulated that annexed the recommendations of the World Bank. The policy recommended the role of the state as the enabler to promote and facilitate the provision of shelter through the market. The following sections describe the impacts of neoliberalism on the housing provision of Dhaka and the malfunction enabling roles of the state under the three most significant aspects of neoliberal housing provision derived from the literature review (Fig. 5.1).

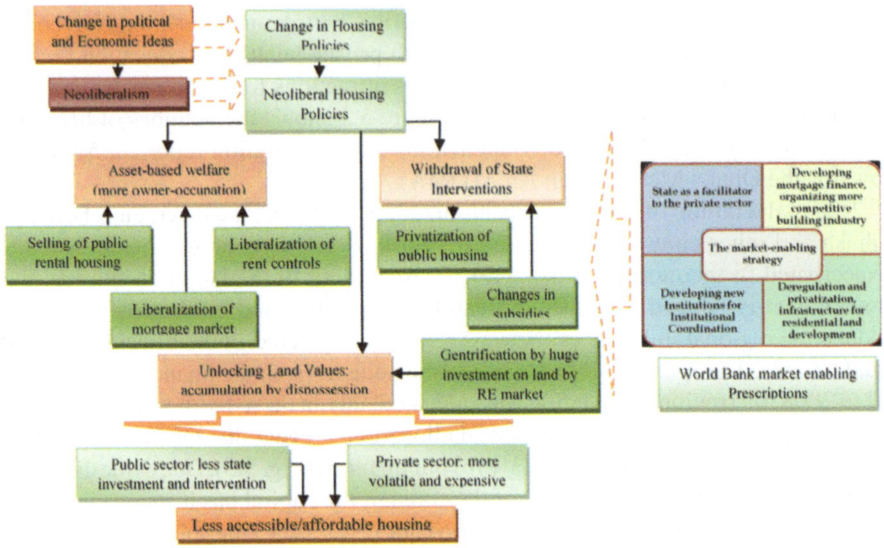

Fig. 5.1 Impacts of neoliberalism on housing provision. *Source* Adapted from Hervey (2005), Wu (2015); Hodkinson (2012), Brenner and Theodore (2002), Rolnik (2013)

5.4.1 Homeownership

After the adoption of neoliberal housing strategies as the by-product of SAPs, the concept of cooperative housing in the first five-year plan (1973–1978) was abandoned, public rental housing for government employees was less emphasized.[2] Afterwards, the other neoliberal component in the Third Five-Year Plan (1985–1990) was the transfer of at least a proportion of the government-owned housing stock to private ownership. The plan suggested selling around 12,000 houses that were rented out by the state at subsidized rates (Choguill, 1993). Such suggestions made by the development plans match with the concurrent trends of encouraging homeownership in asset-based welfare systems under neoliberalism.

The beginning of the 90s can be marked as the kick-off point for the private housing market in the capital Dhaka. Since 1991, housing was started to be considered as an industry and the Real Estate and Housing Association of Bangladesh (REHAB) was formed to safeguard the interests of the stakeholders and strengthen the role of the industry. In 1993, REHAB members supplied 436 flats which grew to 5090 flats in 2004 and in 2015 the figure was 15,000 (Ahmed et al., 2017). Dismantling of

[2] Most of the rental apartments for govt. employees as, for example, in Motijheel, Azimpur or Baily road Officer's Colonies were developed in provincial capital Dhaka during Pakistan period. Though public rental housing contributed only 8% of total housing need of this group, such initiatives were further deprioritized when the Second Five-Year Plan (1980–1985) mentions that 'unjustified construction of staff housing should be stopped given the resource constraints and other pressing needs'. And the Fifth Five-Year Plan envisions not on rental housing rather on construction of flats for sale on hire-purchase basis for govt. employees.

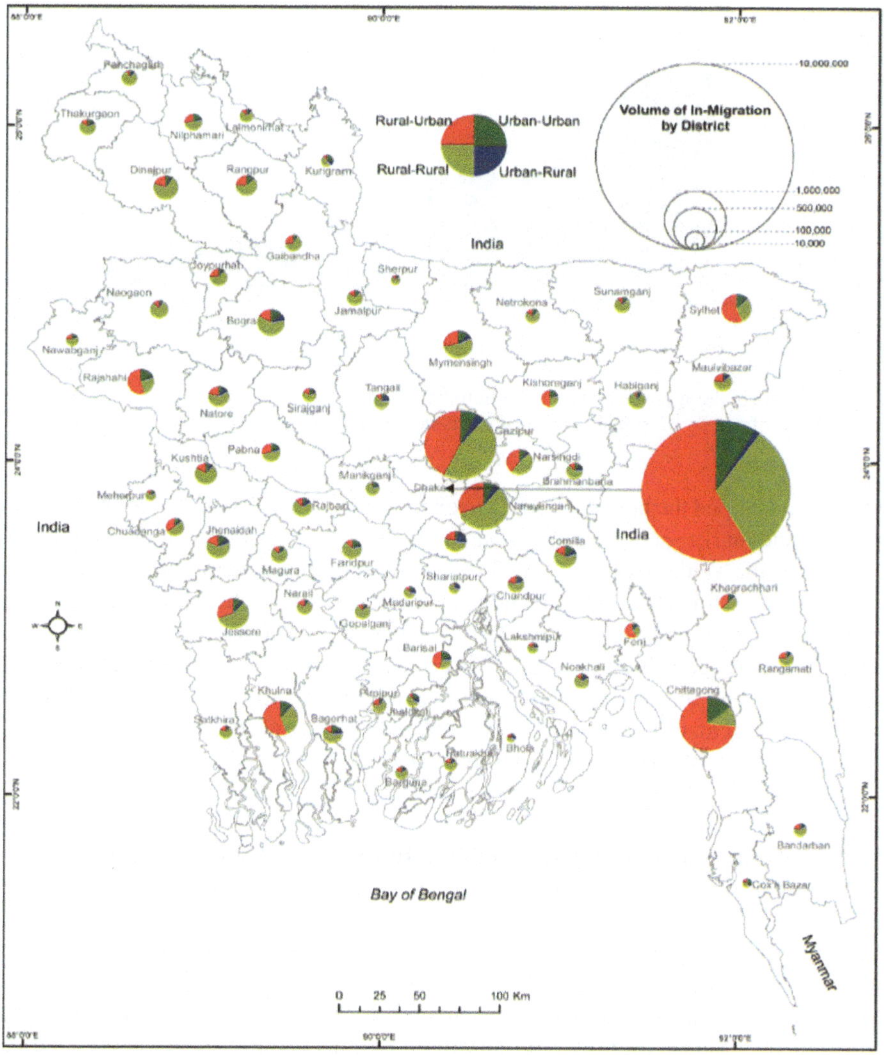

Fig. 5.2 Life-time migration at the district level, 2011 census. *Source* BBS (2011)

rent ceiling was recommended in asset-based welfare for unrestricted price appreciation of property to encourage homeownership as well as boost up the property market (Rolnik, 2013, Ronald et al., 2016). Though Premises Rent Control Act was developed in 1991, just before the adoption of the 'market enabling' housing policy in 1993, to safeguard the interests of renters, its application is almost non-existent (BIGD, 2017). The other simultaneous strategy to promote homeownership through the market was the deepening of the housing finance market. The Financial Institutions Act was enacted in 1993 which opened the door for private mortgage lenders to

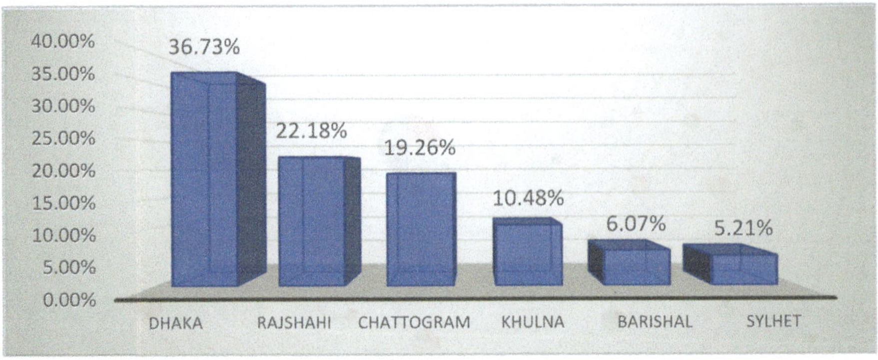

Fig. 5.3 Share of the aggregate budget by administrative divisions of Bangladesh *Source* Calculated by the Author from the National Budget of FY 2006/7 to FY 2008/9

operate and helped the housing market to expand. Currently, 23 private companies are active in the market and providing housing finance. The government of Bangladesh introduced the value-added tax (VAT) to increase public revenue, however, as the policy reforms for trade liberalization, in the early 1990s, the maximum tariff on imported goods was reduced from 250% to only 45%. On the one hand, the policy reforms encouraged the emergence of real estate developers to supply luxurious apartments using imported construction materials in the absence of local industries of construction materials, but on the other hand, the introduction of VAT caused an increase in property price (Sen & Tisdell, 2004).

5.4.1.1 Contradicting Market Enabling Initiative: Subsidized Home Loans

According to World Bank's market enabling prescriptions, the state should avoid subsidized and directed credit towards housing. In Bangladesh, however, the state-owned housing financer BHBFC was funded by the state Treasury. By 1992, the government provided BDT 1.1 billion to BHBFC as capital. Afterwards, it raised capital by selling government-guaranteed debentures of BDT 18.6 billion to different banks. In the budget of the fiscal year 2015–2016, BDT 5 billion was again allocated for credit-starved BHBFC as a loan at only a 3% interest rate. BHBFC used to provide mortgages below market rates where the loan disbursement was granted by the government. Due to an overly bureaucratic system, the mortgages were allocated through rationing but not through proper underwriting. Moreover, due to political influences, the allocation could never be an efficient financial process (Rahman, 2008). According to Hoek-Smith (1998), it mostly served the higher-income households. Moreover, such interest rate subsidy systems distorted the market which made it difficult for private mortgage financers to enter and operate in the market (Rahman,

2008). After a decade since the adoption of the enabling policy, there were only three specialized home loan providers in the market in 2003 (Farzana, 2009).

In the past year, the state took another initiative of providing housing loans through four public commercial banks and BHBFC at a subsidized rate to its employees. Since 2018, the government employees are eligible to get subsidized home loans at a rate of 5% while the current market rate is 10%. Home loan at a subsidized rate might be positive for the housing market as it increases the demand but simultaneously it helps to increase the property price too which affect the affordability of the limited income households who remain outside of such subsidized home loan schemes.

5.4.1.2 State Agencies as a Developer: Irrational Subsidization in the Provision of Plots and Flats

Despite the government's constitutional commitment to ensure housing for all, subsidized sites and services plots provided by state agencies turned into posh residential areas in Bangladesh. In majority cases, RAJUK (the Capital Development Authority) and National Housing Authority (NHA) provided residential plots at much below market prices to politically influential and higher-income groups (Chowdhury, 1992; Rahman et al., 2011; Islam et al., 2006). Besides sites and services schemes, recently RAJUK and NHA have also been providing flats. However, according to different studies, all of the projects of RAJUK and NHA, in the end, have served the higher middle, and high-income households only due to faulty allocation criteria, corruption and clientelism (Haque, 2012; Akter, 2013; Hossain, n.d.).

Despite the above-mentioned complying and contradicting market enabling initiatives to promote homeownership like most of the neoliberal cities in the world, except a few from the developmental states, the homeownership rate of Dhaka has declined. Despite the strategies adopted to increase homeownership, the share of owner-occupied houses reduced to 18.5% by 2011 (BBS, 2011), which was as high as 31.9% back in the middle of the 1990s (Westfall and de Villa, 2001). The strategies to expand homeownership rates could not make the market accessible for all. The market only served the high end of the population.

5.5 Unlocking Land Value and New Geographies of the City: Accumulation by Dispossession

The gentrification and redevelopment in Dhaka favour a very small portion of the urban population like many other neoliberal cities in the world. In a short time, the capital Dhaka has transformed into a global city with a landscape dominated by new establishments and advertisements of real estate projects offering lucrative land and housing deals speck the city. However, the majority of these projects are of high-end real estate mostly for the powerful and affluent classes.

As mentioned earlier, due to the privatization of vital sectors like health and education, hospitals, universities, and private schools have been mushrooming in the city, most of which are accessible only for the rich. The privatization of urban spaces restricts the accessibility of the urban poor and forced them to move to the peripheries. There have been numerous incidents of bulldozing squatters and evictions of the poor during the past three decades. The projects are taken for the beautification of Dhaka, as an attempt to make it a world-class neoliberal city, have also caused peripheralization of the poor from the city. For example, the government took the 'Hatirjheel' lakefront development project which has displaced numerous poor households living in the project area who have been bound to move to urban peripheries. Moreover, due to this development, the land prices of surrounding areas have been appreciated too and instigated more private sector gentrification there. Hence the poor and low-income households living adjacent to the area over the decades, have been displaced from or dispossessed of their land where high-income apartments are being erected (Hossain, 2013).

Particularly since the 1990s, the state has become reluctant about public housing programs. hence the task was transferred to the real estate developers based on a neoliberal strategy to unlock land values through market activities. Though the city was expanding through public and private land development projects, the renowned residential areas within the city never lost their attractiveness for gentrification. The owners of residential premises gradually allow the development of high-rise apartments by corporate developers demolishing their old homes in exchange for ownership of four or more new flats. It has become a popular way to arrange for long-term income as rents and to distribute properties among inheritors (Bertuzzo, 2014). Unregulated real estate activities have caused exponential price hikes of land through unhealthy competition. The increased land price instigated further gentrification and evolved new commercial characteristics of these areas accessible only by high-income households (Farzana, 2017).

5.5.1 Relaxation of Planning Regulations in Favour of Gentrification

It is evident from several studies (Farzana, 2017; Nahrin, 2008; Shumi, 2006) that, in the case of Dhaka, there are instances of modification of land use regulations, height zoning, etc. in favour of gentrification. High-rise development in residential areas was legalized by the modification of rules to fulfil the demand of the developers acting as gentrification agents. Though such policy support in favour of gentrification is recommended in neoliberalism, such market-operated densification and resulted in property price appreciation are benefitting the affluent only.

5.5.2 *Accumulation by Dispossession by State Agencies Under the Doctrine of Eminent Domain*

Both in the second part of Article 42 of the Constitution of Bangladesh and Acquisition and Requisition of Immovable Property Ordinance 1982 The Site and Services Schemes, the state has given the power of an eminent domain. Land for site and services schemes and apartments by RAJUK and NHA are carried out on acquired private lands mostly occupied by the poor, low-income people and peasant farmers (Morshed, 2013). The affected households rarely get the payments/compensations timely and most of the time the payments are not delivered in full due to well recognized unrestrained corruption (CARE, 2003). Therefore, the state agencies are causing the dispossession of the poorer section of the population by helping the richer group accumulate property at a subsidized rate.

5.6 Affordability Crisis

The right to adequate housing has been compromised by the market-based reforms and the structural reconfigurations that neoliberalism has entailed. Neoliberalism increases the income and wealth inequalities through 'accumulation by dispossession', where rich people accumulate capital dispossessing the poor (Harvey, 2004). In 2015, Dhaka was found as the most expensive among comparable cities in the subcontinent, and surprisingly, more expensive than many cities of developed countries too. The rank of Dhaka 71 in the list of cities worldwide based on the cost of living, while the ranks of New Delhi, Kathmandu, and Karachi were 128, 125 and 132 among 133 cities (Economic Intelligence Unit, 2015). Inequalities in income and wealth distribution are rising at an alarming rate in Bangladesh especially in Dhaka. According to recent estimates by the Centre for Policy Dialogue (CPD), wealth inequality in terms of the Gini coefficient stands at a staggering 74.00, whereas the Gini coefficient for income inequality is 48.00 in Dhaka (The Daily Star, May 2018).

In respect of housing wealth inequality, only 30% of households in Dhaka own housing property. The remaining 70% of households live in rental housing, a handful numbers of government quarters for employees or in informal houses (BIGD, 2017). Affordability crisis exists in respect of both owning and renting a decent home in Dhaka for the majority of its population. The Consumers Association of Bangladesh (CAB) has revealed that the rental inflation rate is higher than overall living costs inflation by an average of 1.7 during the five years from 2012 to 2016. According to a survey conducted in 2007 by the same organization, house rent in Dhaka increased by 250% during 17 years from 1990 to 2007.

In respect of homeownership affordability, the extremely expensive land and housing property in Dhaka have made homeownership unaffordable for most of its population. The emergence of the neoliberal real estate market in the early 90s resulted in an exponential price hike of land and apartments (Fig. 5.4). Surprisingly,

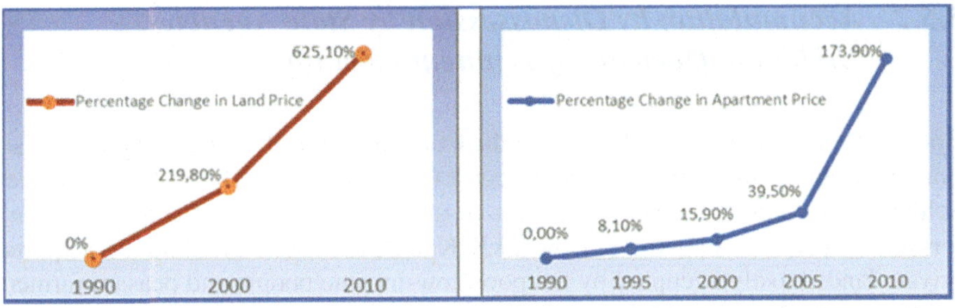

Fig. 5.4 Land and apartment price hike trend from 1990 to 2010 in the capital Dhaka. *Source* Statistical Yearbooks, BBS, Government of Bangladesh

the land prices of Dhaka and suburban New York are comparable, while the average income of the residents of Dhaka is a hundred times lower. The average land price in Dhaka increased by 625.1% within two decades since 1990. And the average price of apartments increased by 173.9% within the same timeframe (REHAB, 2012).

5.6.1 Legalizing the Use of Undeclared Money: Contributes to the Price Appreciation of Property

There was a Sect. 19B inserted in the year 1999 in the Income Tax Ordinance 1984. According to the new section of the ordinance, one can buy apartments with one's untaxed or undeclared money and convert this black money into white by paying the property transfer taxes. Section 19B also declared that the source of invested money would not be investigated by an anti-corruption agency or the National Bureau of Revenue. This law benefitted the black money holders from the high-income group and made the property market unstable. The decade from 2000 to 2010 witnessed a sharp increase in apartment prices, especially rising at an exponential rate from the year 2006 (Das, 2014). Such a sharp rise in property prices would be due to the increased demand from the sudden injection of black money into the market. Hence, such initiative of allowing undeclared money to be invested in property might be a stimulus for the market, but detrimental for the provision of affordable housing.

5.6.2 Public–Private Partnership (PPP): Corruption and Clientelism

PPP has been considered as the last resort in the provision of services in the neoliberal economy due to the dwindling financial capacity of the state and unaffordable services resulted from full privatization (Bult-Spiering and Dewulf, 2006; Savas,

2000). Hence, the latest role of the state as facilitator is to take initiative for housing provision through a public–private partnership which has also been recommended in the policy guidelines adopted in Bangladesh. Bhashantek Rehabilitation Project (BRP) was a PPP project initiated in 2004 in Mirpur for constructing 111 six-storied buildings for rehabilitating the evicted squatters.

The project was designed to deliver 13,000 flats within five years. However, the developer's contract was cancelled with only 10 buildings completed in October 2010 on the ground of corruption in the construction and distribution of flats and failure to deliver the flats on time. The project was handed over to the National Housing Authority and, abandoning the plan of rehabilitation, the land has been decided to be utilized for the provision of housing for government employees (Akter, 2013).

The first-ever PPP initiative for housing provision in Dhaka was not successful due to the lack of transparency in appointing the private developer which in turn resulted in mismanagement and corruption in the scheme. Moreover, the project failed to accommodate the demand and aspirations of the target group in designing affordable and sustainable dwelling units (Akter, 2013). There are many other PPP schemes of NHA and RAJUK in the pipeline. The outcome of the schemes depends on the implications of lessons learned from BRP.

5.7 Conclusion

The paper has discussed the adoption of neoliberal policies in Bangladesh and how neoliberalization and globalization have turned Dhaka into a megacity with the burden of mismatching between ever-increasing population and city services including housing provision. Neoliberal reforms in the housing sector of Dhaka are the non-existence of the application of any rent controls, deepening of the housing finance market and reforms in economic and planning regulations to promote the real estate market. Despite the reform policies, the housing of Dhaka has become unaffordable for the majority of its population. General economic reforms under neoliberalism contributed to immensely increased income inequalities and the Market enabling housing policies only cater to the interests of the high-income group and resulted in the unanticipated price appreciation of real estate properties.

References

Abdullah, A. (Ed.). (1991). *Modernization at Bay: Structure and change in Bangladesh.* University Press Ltd.

Afenah, A. (2009). *Conceptualizing the effects of neoliberal urban policies on housing rights: An analysis of the attempted unlawful forced eviction of an informal settlement in Accra, Ghana.* DPU Working Paper No. 139. London: UCL.

Ahmed, J. U., Sultana, H., & Faroque, A. R. (2017). Eastern housing limited: marketing strategies of a real estate company in Bangladesh. *Vision: The Journal of Business Perspective, 21*(1), 86–92.

Akhter, A. (2013). *A study on physical requirements of housing for low-middle income families in Dhaka City—An attempt towards affordability*. Unpublished Masters thesis, Department of Architecture, Bangladesh University of Engineering and Technology.
BBS. (2011). Bangladesh Population Census 2011. Bangladesh Bureau of Statistics, Government of Bangladesh, Dhaka.
Bertuzzo, E. (2014). During the urban revolution—Conjuncture on the streets of Dhaka. In L. Stanek, et al. (Eds.), *Urban revolution now* (pp.49–70). Ashgate Publishing.
BIGD. (2017). *The State of Cities 2017: Housing in Dhaka*. BRAC Institute of Governance and Development, BRAC University, Dhaka.
Brenner, N., & Theodore, N. (2002). Cities and the geographies of 'Actually Existing Neoliberalism.' *Antipode, 33*(3), 349–379.
Bult-Spiering, M., & Dewulf, G. (2006). *Strategic Issues in Public–Private Partnerships*. West Sussex, UK: Wiley, Blackwell.
CARE. (2003). *Land policy and administration in Bangladesh: A literature review*. CARE SDU Reports and Studies.
Chakrabarti, D. P. G. (2001). Urban crisis in India: New initiatives for sustainable cities. *Development in Practice, 11*(2–3), 260–272. https://doi.org/10.1080/09614520120056397
Choguill, C. L. (1993). Housing policy trends in Bangladesh: Meeting the needs of a low-income population. *Cities, 10*(4), 326–336.
Chowdhury, A. I. (1992). Urban land market in Bangladesh. In N. Islam, A. Islam (Eds.), Urban Land Management in Bangladesh (pp. 115–122). Dhaka: Ministry of Land, Government of Bangladesh.
Chowdhury, A. U. (2010). The Dhaka chamber of commerce and industry: Origin, development and role in the economy. In *Commercial history of Dhaka*, Dhaka, Bangladesh.
COHRE. (2006). *Government obligation on forced evictions*. http://www.cohre.org/view_page.php?page_id=101#article153.
Das, M. S. (2014). Easy credit and real estate bubble in Dhaka, Bangladesh—The Nexus and policy implications for Bangladesh Bank. *World Review of Business Research, 4*(3), 162–180.
Deshpande, S. (2004). Slums of Mumbai: Crying for bottoms-up approach. In Mumbai City development strategies (Eds.), Indian Merchants' Chamber Economic Research and Training Foundation, Mumbai (pp. 13–44).
Doling, J. (2002). The south and east Asia housing policy model. In M. R. Agus, J. Doling, & D.-S. Lee (Eds.), *Housing policy systems in South and East Asia* (pp. 178–188). Palgrave Macmillan.
Doling, J., & Ford, J. (2007). A union of home owners, editorial. *European Journal of Housing and Planning, 7*(2), 113–127.
Doling, J., & Ronald, R. (2010). Homeownership and asset-based welfare. *Journal of Housing and Built Environment, 25*, 165–173.
Dorling, D. (2014). *All that is solid: The great housing disaster*. Allen Lane.
Economic Intelligence Unit. (2015). *Worldwide Cost of Living Report*, London, United Kingdom.
Farzana, F. (2009). Shortages of middle-income owner-occupied housing in Dhaka—Failures of government or market? *Plan plus, 5*, 12–25.
Farzana, F. (2017). Dhaka: An example of landuse succession where market forces supersede planning regulations. *Jahangirnagar University Planning Review, 14*(June), 1–16.
Gough, J. (2002). Neoliberalism and socialisation in the contemporary city: Opposites, complements and instabilities. In N. Brenner & N. Theodore (Eds.), *Spaces of neoliberalism: Urban restructuring in North America and Western Europe* (pp. 58–79). Blackwell.
Haque, H. K. N. (2012). *The political economy of urban space: Land and real estate in Dhaka City*. IGS Working Paper Series No. 03/2012. Institute of Governance Studies, BRAC University, Bangladesh.
Harvey, D. (2004). The 'new' imperialism: Accumulation by dispossession. *Socialist Register, 40*, 63–87.
Harvey, D. (2005). *A short history of neoliberalism*. Oxford University Press.
Hodkinson, S. (2012). The new urban enclosures. *City, 16*(5), 500–518.

Hoek-Smit, M. C. (1998). Housing finance in Bangladesh—Improving access to housing finance by middle and lower income groups. Prepared for Ministry of Local Government, Rural Development and Co-operatives, GOB and UNDP/UNCHS (Habitat).

Hossain, K. H. (n.d.). *Public policies on urban and housing in Bangladesh—The context governance.* Ministry of Housing and Public Works, Bangladesh Secretariat, Dhaka. C:\DOCUME-1\ADMINI-1\LOCALS-1\Temp\Public-Policies-on-Urban-and-Housing-inBangladesh-Works-Secretary-l.doc.

Hossain, S. (2013). Migration, urbanization and poverty in Dhaka, Bangladesh. *The Journal of the Asiatic Society of Bangladesh (Humanities), 58*(2), 369–382.

Hundt, D. (2015). Neoliberalism, the developmental state and civil society in Korea. *Asian Studies Review, 39*(3), 466–482. https://doi.org/10.1080/10357823.2015.1052339

Islam, N., Mahbub, A., Nazem, N. I., Angeles, G., & Lance, P. (2006). *Slums of urban Bangladesh: Mapping and census, 2005.* Centre for Urban Studies.

Kabir, A. H. (2012). Neoliberal hegemony and the ideological transformation of higher education in Bangladesh. *Critical Literacy: Theories and Practice, 6*(2), 2–15.

Kadi, J., & Ronald, R. (2014). Market-based housing reforms and the 'right to the City': The variegated experiences of New York, Amsterdam and Tokyo. *International Journal of Housing Policy, 14*(3), 268–292. https://doi.org/10.1080/14616718.2014.928098

Lee, J., Forrest, R., & Tam, W. K. (2003). Home-ownership in East and South East Asia: Market, state and institutions. In R. Forrest & J. Lee (Eds.), *Housing and social change: East-west perspectives* (pp. 20–45). Routledge.

Logan, J., Fang, Y., & Zhang, Z. (2009). Access to housing in urban China. *International Journal of Urban and Regional Research, 33*(4), 914–935.

Morshed, M. M. (2013). Illegality of private subdivision and access to land for housing by the urban poor in Dhaka. *Habitat International, 44*, 386–393.

Nahrin, K. (2008). Violation of land use plan and its impact on community life in Dhaka City. *Jahangirnagar Planning Review, 6*, 37–47.

Nuruzzaman, M. (2004). Neoliberal economic reforms, the rich and the poor in Bangladesh. *Journal of Contemporary Asia, 34*(1), 33–54.

Peck, J., & Tickell, A. (2002). Neoliberalizing space. In N. Brenner & N. Theodore (Eds.), *Spaces of neoliberalism: Urban restructuring in Western Europe and North America* (pp. 33–57). Blackwell.

Quadir, F. (2000). The political economy of pro-market reforms in Bangladesh: Regime consolidation through economic liberalization. *Contemporary South Asia, 9*(2), 197–212.

Rahman, K. K. (2008). Development of housing finance and its impact on socio-economic uplift in the emerging economy in Bangladesh. In *Proceedings of the IFC Conference on "Measuring financial innovation and its impact"*, Basel, 26–27 August 2008.

Rahman, M. A. U., et al., (2011). Can an enabling approach promote the transformation for scaling-up pro-poor housing initiatives in Bangladesh?. In: *12th Naerus Conference 2011*, Madrid, Spain, 20–22 October 2011.

REHAB. (2012). *A comprehensive study on the real estate sector of Bangladesh.* Real Estate and Housing Association of Bangladesh.

Rolnik, R. (2013). Late neoliberalism: The financialization of homeownership and housing rights. *International Journal of Urban and Regional Research, 37*(3), 1058–1066. https://doi.org/10.1111/1468-2427.12062

Ronald, R. (2008). *The ideology of home ownership: Homeowner societies and the role of housing.* Palgrave Macmillan.

Ronald, R., Lennartz, C., & Kadi, J. (2016). What ever happened to asset-based welfare? Shifting approaches to housing wealth and welfare security. *Policies and Politics, 45*(2), 173–193.

Savas, E. S. (2000). *Privatization and public–private partnerships.* Chatam House.

Sen, R. K., & Tisdell, C. (Eds.). (2004). *Economic globalization: Social conflicts, labor and environmental issues.* Cheltenham, UK: Edward Elger Publishing Ltd.

Shin, H. B. (2009). Property-based redevelopment and gentrification: The case of Seoul. *Geoforum, 40*(5), 906–917.
Shumi, S. (2006). *Commercialization impact of Dhanmondi residential area.* Unpublished BURP Thesis, Department of Urban and Regional Planning, Jahangirnagar University, Dhaka.
Smith, N. (2002). New urbanism: Gentrification as global urban strategy. *Antipode, 34*(3), 427–450.
Sobhan, R. (1991). *The decade and stagnation: The state of the Bangladesh economy in 1980s.* University Press Ltd.
Songsore, J., McGranahan, G., & Kjellen, M. (2004). Tenure, housing and environmental management among families in the greater accra metropolitan area (ACCRA) of Ghana. *Research Review Supplement, 15*, 69–83.
The Daily Star. (2018, May 12). *Why Bangladesh's inequality is likely to rise.*
Tipple, A. G. (1994). The need for new urban housing in sub-Saharan Africa: Problem or opportunity. *Journal of African Affairs, 93*, 587–608.
Wang, Y. P., Shao, L., Murie, A., & Cheng, J. (2012). The maturation of the neo-liberal housing market in urban China. *Housing Studies, 27*(3), 343–359. https://doi.org/10.1080/02673037.2012.651106
Watson, M. (2009). Planning for the future of asset-based welfare? New Labour, Financialized economic agency and the housing market. *Planning, Practice and Research, 24*(1), 41–56. https://doi.org/10.1080/02697450902742148.
Westfall, M. S., & de Villa, V. A. (2001). Urban indicators for managing cities. © Asian Development Bank. http://hdl.handle.net/11540/276. License: CC BY 3.0 IGO.
Wong, T.-C. (2006). Revitalizing Singapore's Central City through gentrification: The role of waterfront housing. *Urban Policy and Research, 24*(2), 181–199.
World Bank. (2005). *End of MFA quotas: Key issues and strategic options for Bangladesh readymade garment industry.* The World Bank Poverty Reduction and Economic Management Unit.
Wu, F. (2015). Commodification and housing market cycles in Chinese cities. *International Journal of Housing Policy, 15*(1), 6–26. https://doi.org/10.1080/14616718.2014.925255

Chapter 6
Increasing Housing Demand in Pakistan

Anwar Hussain, Ateeq Ahmed, and Wajahat Hussain

Abstract Although the increasing population is the key source of human capital, but it also has many socio-economic and environmental implications for any country. The population explosion along with other factors such as urbanization, foreign remittances, migration, conflicts, real estate business and government policies drastically impacts the housing market dynamics. It is the responsibility of the government to provide housing facilities at affordable prices to accommodate the poor masses. The government should intervene in the housing sector to manage the house rents, construction and land prices. This chapter highlighted the trends in the population, housing units at the rural and urban levels in Pakistan. Moreover, it also highlighted the key challenges facing the housing sector in Pakistan.

Keywords Urbanization · Housing policy · Pakistan

6.1 Introduction

An adequate and comfortable dwelling is not possible without basic human needs such as food, clothing, and shelter. The developing nations are facing a huge shortage of housing problems. According to the UN-Habitat survey (2016), in the year 2010, about 980 million people in the cities do not have proper homes and there will be a further 600 million demand for new houses by 2030. Globally, by 2025, an additional 1 billion new homes will be required for the rising population with an estimated cost of $650 million per annum. Although over time, more colonies and houses have been established but still there is a shortage of accommodation in cities. During 2014 more than 30% of urban households were living in slums in developing countries (Ahmad et al., 2018).

A. Hussain (✉) · A. Ahmed
Department of Economics and Development Studies, University of Swat, Swat, Khyber Pakhtunkhwa, Pakistan
e-mail: anwar@uswat.edu.pk

W. Hussain
School of Economics, Quaid-i-Azam University, Islamabad, Pakistan

A. Kundu et al. (eds.), *Accessible Housing for South Asia*,
https://doi.org/10.1007/978-3-030-88881-7_6

Pakistan is one of the populous countries with a current population of 207.78 million. The annual growth rate of the population is 2.40% (Pakistan Bureau of Statistics, 2020). It has been estimated that Pakistan will cross 250 million by 2025, and more than 50% population will live in urban areas of Pakistan (Government of Pakistan, 2015).

Since independence, Pakistan conducted 6 national wide population censuses till now. These are known as 1961, 1972, 1981, 1998, and 2017 censuses. The total population was 207.77 million in the year 2017 as compared to 132.35 million in the year 1998 showing an increase of 57% in the total population. The annual average national growth rate of the population is 2.4%. Similarly, the average annual growth rate of the urban population is 2.70 which is higher than the rural population growth rate of 2.23%. The data shows that the population growth rate of Khyber Pakhtunkhwa and Baluchistan is higher than the growth rate of Punjab and Sindh provinces. The population of Khyber Pakhtunkhwa grew from 17.7 million to 30.5 million with an annual growth rate of 2.9% during 1998 and 2017 (Table 6.1).

The trends of District-wise population show that Peshawar District has the highest population growth rate (3.39%) than other districts during 1998 and 2017. The population of Federally Administered Tribal Areas (FATA) also increased by 1.8 million during 1998–2017 with an annual growth rate of 2.4% (Table 6.2). The annual average population growth rate of Baluchistan is 3.37%, which is higher than the national average population growth rate of 2.4% and other Punjab and Sindh provinces. In Baluchistan province, the Quetta District is the most populous district with an average annual growth rate of 4.79% in the year 2017 (Table 6.3).

The total population of Punjab increased by 33% between 1998 and 2017. The population growth rate of Rajanpur is 3.16%, which is higher than the population growth rate of other districts. Jhelum has the lowest population growth rate (1.41%) than other districts. The percentage increase of population in Rajanpur and Jhelum Districts was 80.86 and 30.49%, respectively, during 1998 and 2017 (Table 6.4).

The total population of province Sindh was 47,886,051 in the year 2017 as compared to 30,439,893 in the year 1998 showing an increase of 57.31% during 1998–2017. The population increased over time in all the districts of Sindh with different growth rates. The Malir District was recorded with the highest population growth of 105.78% while the lowest population increase was observed in Karachi South District (21.22%). The average annual population growth rate of Malir District was 3.86% and Karachi South District was 1.02%. The population of Tharparkar District has increased by 80.43% during 1998–2017 with an average annual growth rate of Tharparkar is 3.15 (Table 6.5).

The statistics of population and housing units in Pakistan during 1998 and 2017 show that these have increasing trends over time and across provinces in Pakistan. With the rise in population, Pakistan will face multiple socio-economic challenges including lack of sufficient housing facilities. The housing shortage of 1.07 million in the year 2020 will be increased to about 6.9 million housing units by 2025 (Iqbal, 2020).

The rate of urbanization has been recorded highest in South Asian countries (UNDP, 2019). According to the statuesque, the population grows by 2.3 million per

Table 6.1 Provincial-wise population in Pakistan

Name of the administrative unit		Population						Average annual growth rate
		1951	1961	1972	1981	1998	2017	1998–2107
Pakistan		33,740,167	42,880,378	65,309,340	84,253,644	132,352,279	207,774,520	2.4
	Rural	27,754,670	33,225,806	48,715,689	60,412,173	89,315,875	132,189,531	2.23
	Urban	5,985,497	9,654,572	16,593,651	23,841,471	43,036,404	75,584,989	2.7
Khyber Pakhtunkhwa Province		4,556,545	5,730,991	8,388,551	11,061,328	17,743,645	30,523,371	2.89
	Rural	4,051,800	4,972,475	7,192,896	9,395,675	14,749,561	24,793,737	2.87
	Urban	504,745	758,516	1,195,655	1,665,653	2,994,084	5,729,634	2.96
FATA		1,332,005	1,847,195	2,491,230	2,198,547	3,176,331	5,001,676	2.41
	Rural	1,332,005	1,822,547	2,477,930	2,198,547	3,090,858	4,859,778	2.41
	Urban	–	24,648	13,300	–	85,473	141,898	2.7
Punjab Province		20,540,762	25,463,974	37,607,423	47,292,441	73,621,290	110,012,442	2.13
	Rural	16,972,686	19,988,052	28,424,728	34,240,795	50,602,265	69,625,144	1.81
	Urban	3,568,076	5,475,922	9,182,695	13,051,646	23,019,025	40,387,298	2.74
Sindh Province		6,047,748	8,367,065	14,155,909	19,028,666	30,439,893	47,886,051	2.41
	Rural	4,279,621	5,200,047	8,430,133	10,785,630	15,600,031	22,975,593	2.36
	Urban	1,768,127	3,167,018	5,725,776	8,243,036	14,839,862	24,910,458	2.46
Baluchistan Province		1,167,167	1,353,484	2,428,678	4,332,376	6,565,885	12,344,408	3.37
	Rural	1,022,618	1,125,016	2,029,094	3,655,604	4,997,105	8,943,532	3.33
	Urban	144,549	228,468	399,584	676,772	1,568,780	3,400,876	3.49
ICT		95,940	117,669	237,549	340,286	805,235	2,006,572	4.91
	Rural	95,940	117,669	160,908	135,922	276,055	991,747	6.95
	Urban	–	–	76,641	204,364	529,180	1,014,825	3.48

Source Population Census 2017 (Pakistan Bureau Statistics)

Table 6.2 District-wise population in the year 1998 and 2017 in Khyber Pakhtunkhwa province

Administrative units (Province/Districts)		Population 1998	Population 2017	Number of households 2017	Average annual growth rate
Khyber Pakhtunkhwa		17,743,645	30,523,371	3,845,168	2.89
	Rural	14,456,435	24,793,737	3,104,154	2.87
	Urban	3,287,210	5,729,634	741,014	2.96
Bannu		675,667	1,167,892	119,993	2.92
	Rural	627,991	1,117,927	113,735	3.08
	Urban	47,676	49,965	6,258	0.25
Lakki marwat		490,025	876,182	98,051	3.1
	Rural	443,147	786,762	87,009	3.06
	Urban	46,878	89,420	11,042	3.45
Dera Ismail khan Division		1,091,211	2,019,017	244,372	3.29
	Rural	836,921	1,609,621	187,537	3.5
	Urban	254,290	409,396	56,835	2.53
Dera Ismail Khan		852,995	1,627,132	201,301	3.45
	Rural	634,446	1,264,901	150,220	3.69
	Urban	218,549	362,231	51,081	2.69
Tank		238,216	391,885	43,071	2.65
	Rural	202,475	344,720	37,317	2.83
	Urban	35,741	47,165	5,754	1.47
Abbottabad		880,666	1,332,912	216,534	2.2
	Rural	722,762	1,039,775	171,369	1.93
	Urban	157,904	293,137	45,165	3.3
Batagram		307,278	476,612	69,525	2.33
	Rural	307,278	476,612	69,525	2.33
	Urban				
Haripur		692,228	1,003,031	163,490	1.97
	Rural	609,493	876,454	143,167	1.93
	Urban	82,735	126,577	20,323	2.26
Mansehra		978,157	1,556,460	239,275	2.47
	Rural	916,781	1,411,605	217,494	2.29
	Urban	61,376	144,855	21,781	4.61
Torghar		174,682	171,395	26,464	−0.1
	Rural	174,682	171,395	26,464	−0.1
	Urban				
Stan		472,570	784,711	101,911	2.7

(continued)

Table 6.2 (continued)

Administrative units (Province/Districts)		Population 1998	Population 2017	Number of households 2017	Average annual growth rate
	Rural	472,570	784,711	101,911	2.7
	Urban				
Hangu		314,529	518,798	48,270	2.66
	Rural	250,312	416,358	38,155	2.71
	Urban	64,217	102,440	10,115	2.48
Karak		430,796	706,299	73,144	2.63
	Rural	402,903	655,150	67,784	2.59
	Urban	27,893	51,149	5,360	3.24
Kohat		562,644	993,874	121,344	3.03
	Rural	410,731	723,728	85,581	3.02
	Urban	151,913	270,146	35,763	3.07
Mardan		1,460,100	2,373,061	311,868	2.58
	Rural	1,164,972	1,933,736	252,486	2.7
	Urban	295,128	439,325	59,382	2.11
Swabi		1,026,804	1,624,616	214,209	2.44
	Rural	847,590	1,348,691	177,254	2.47
	Urban	179,214	275,925	36,955	2.29
Charsadda		1,022,364	1,616,198	221,058	2.44
	Rural	829,513	1,346,023	183,437	2.58
	Urban	192,851	270,175	37,621	1.79
Nowshera		874,373	1,518,540	198,808	2.94
	Rural	647,343	1,179,890	152,066	3.2
	Urban	227,030	338,650	46,742	2.12
Peshawar		2,026,851	4,269,079	489,843	3.99
	Rural	1,044,035	2,299,037	253,787	4.23
	Urban	982,816	1,970,042	236,056	3.72
Buner		506,048	897,319	94,095	3.05
	Rural	506,048	897,319	94,095	3.05
	Urban				
Chitral		318,689	447,362	61,619	1.8
	Rural	288,067	397,568	54,556	1.71
	Urban	30,622	49,794	7,063	2.59
Shangla		434,563	757,810	89,695	2.96
	Rural	434,563	757,810	89,695	2.96

(continued)

Table 6.2 (continued)

Administrative units (Province/Districts)		Population 1998	Population 2017	Number of households 2017	Average annual growth rate
	Urban				
Swat		1,257,602	2,309,570	274,620	3.24
	Rural	883,350	1,613,670	189,173	3.22
	Urban	374,252	695,900	85,447	3.31
Lower dir		717,649	1,435,917	155,338	3.71
	Rural	673,314	1,395,544	150,723	3.9
	Urban	44,335	40,373	4,615	−0.49
Upper dir		575,858	946,421	120,228	2.64
	Rural	552,957	902,256	114,259	2.61
	Urban	22,901	44,165	5,969	3.51
Malakand Protected Area		452,291	720,295	91,414	2.47
	Rural	409,112	652,095	82,892	2.48
	Urban	43,179	68,200	8,522	2.43
FATA (Overall)		3,176,331	5,001,676	558,379	2.41
	Rural	3,090,858	4,859,778	542,255	2.4
	Urban	85,473	141,898	16,124	2.7
Khyber Agency		546,730	986,973	111,558	3.15
	Rural	492,367	889,433	99,799	3.15
	Urban	54,363	97,540	11,759	3.12
Kurram Agency		448,310	619,553	67,244	1.71
	Rural	423,165	579,556	63,235	1.67
	Urban	25,145	39,997	4,009	2.47
Mohmand agency		334,453	466,984	48,118	1.77
	Rural	334,453	466,984	48,118	1.77
	Urban				
North Waziristan Agency		361,246	543,254	59,003	2.17
	Rural	355,281	538,893	58,647	2.21
	Urban	5,965	4,361	356	−1.63
Orakzai Agency		225,441	254,356	31,253	0.64
	Rural	225,441	254,356	31,253	0.64
	Urban				
South Waziristan Agency		429,841	679,185	80,717	2.43
	Rural	429,841	679,185	80,717	2.43
Bajaur Agency		595,227	1,093,684	120,457	3.25

(continued)

Table 6.2 (continued)

Administrative units (Province/Districts)		Population 1998	Population 2017	Number of households 2017	Average annual growth rate
	Rural	595,227	1,093,684	120,457	3.25
	Urban				
FR Bannu		19,593	43,114	4,188	4.23
	Rural	19,593	43,114	4,188	4.23
	Urban				
FR D.I. Khan		38,990	68,556	6,924	3.01
	Rural	38,990	68,556	6,924	3.01
	Urban				
FR Kohat		88,456	118,578	14,339	1.55
	Rural	88,456	118,578	14,339	1.55
	Urban				
FR Lakki Marwat		6,987	26,359	3,348	7.22
	Rural	6,987	26,359	3,348	7.22
	Urban				
FR Peshawar		53,841	64,691	7,065	0.97
	Rural	53,841	64,691	7,065	0.97
	Urban				
FR tank		27,216	36,389	4,165	1.54
	Rural	27,216	36,389	4,165	1.54
	Urban				

Source Population Census 2017 by Pakistan Bureau Statistics (2017)

year. This huge influx of inhabitants will lead to high housing demand during the next 20 years (World Bank, 2018).

The demand for urban housing is about 3 million and the total shortfall in Pakistan for housing is 10 million (Hassan et al., 2019). Certain factors are leading to housing demand in Pakistan. The rapid growth in population, urbanization of cities, changing social patterns, and migration from rural to developed areas caused housing shortages. These factors are discussed in detail in subsequent sections.

6.2 Rapid Growth in Population

Before independence, the population of Pakistan in the united subcontinent was about 16.6 million during 1901 while after independence it grew up to 32.5 million (Rukhanuddin and Ahmed, nd). Baluchistan is the largest province of Pakistan area-wise having a share of 44% with the least populated province of Pakistan. While

Table 6.3 District-wise population in the year 1998 and 2017 in Baluchistan province

Administrative units (Province/Districts)		Population 1998	Population 2017	Number of households 2017	Average annual growth rate
Baluchistan		6,565,885	12,344,408	1,775,937	3.37
	Rural	4,797,055	8,943,532	1,301,212	3.33
	Urban	1,768,830	3,400,876	474,725	3.49
Awaran		118,173	121,680	18,094	0.15
	Rural	93,320	87,436	13,881	−0.34
	Urban	24,853	34,244	4,213	1.7
Kalat		237,834	412,232	55,497	2.93
	Rural	204,040	339,774	45,654	2.71
	Urban	33,794	72,458	9,843	4.09
Kharan		96,900	156,152	24,035	2.54
	Rural	69,094	111,497	18,370	2.54
	Urban	27,806	44,655	5,665	2.52
Khuzdar		417,466	802,207	120,405	3.49
	Rural	287,884	525,071	81,296	3.21
	Urban	129,582	277,136	39,109	4.07
Lasbela		312,695	574,292	93,165	3.24
	Rural	186,113	295,048	53,904	2.45
	Urban	126,582	279,244	39,261	4.24
Mastung		150,650	266,461	38,801	3.04
	Rural	126,519	231,332	33,781	3.22
	Urban	24,131	35,129	5,020	1.99
Washuk		110,009	176,206	31,540	2.5
	Rural	92,826	154,334	27,517	2.71
	Urban	17,183	21,872	4,023	1.27
Gwadar		185,498	263,514	39,922	1.86
	Rural	85,346	101,915	17,275	0.94
	Urban	100,152	161,599	22,647	2.55
Kech		413,204	909,116	138,403	4.23
	Rural	303,728	606,980	91,658	3.7
	Urban	109,476	302,136	46,745	5.48
Panjgur		234,051	316,385	42,628	1.6
	Rural	197,535	236,061	31,590	0.94
	Urban	36,516	80,324	11,038	4.23
Jaffarabad		291,290	513,813	79,273	3.02
	Rural	213,973	355,808	56,023	2.71

(continued)

Table 6.3 (continued)

Administrative units (Province/Districts)		Population 1998	Population 2017	Number of households 2017	Average annual growth rate
	Urban	77,317	158,005	23,250	3.82
Jhal Magsi		109,941	149,225	25,047	1.62
	Rural	101,844	141,400	23,791	1.74
	Urban	8,097	7,825	1,256	−0.18
Kachhi		199,457	237,030	30,140	0.91
	Rural	172,151	202,598	25,868	0.86
	Urban	27,306	34,432	4,272	1.22
Nasirabad		245,894	490,538	66,681	3.69
	Rural	207,463	393,947	53,999	3.42
	Urban	38,431	96,591	12,682	4.96
Sohbatpur		141,527	200,538	30,523	1.85
	Rural	133,321	187,671	28,359	1.81
	Urban	8,206	12,867	2,164	2.39
Chagai		104,534	226,008	31,081	4.13
	Rural	92,586	209,689	29,060	4.39
	Urban	11,948	16,319	2,021	1.65
Killa Abdullah		360,724	757,578	97,210	3.97
	Rural	286,975	608,236	77,919	4.02
	Urban	73,749	149,342	19,291	3.77
Nushki		98,030	178,796	22,662	3.21
	Rural	74,082	132,410	17,023	3.1
	Urban	23,948	46,386	5,639	3.53
Pishin		376,728	736,481	128,080	3.58
	Rural	326,532	593,339	102,304	3.19
	Urban	50,196	143,142	25,776	5.66
Quetta		773,936	2,275,699	276,711	5.83
	Rural	208,799	1,274,494	148,093	9.96
	Urban	565,137	1,001,205	128,618	3.05
Sibi Division		630,901	1,038,010	158,643	2.65
	Rural	499,866	812,288	125,748	2.58
	Urban	131,035	225,722	32,895	2.9
Harnai		76,652	97,017	17,353	1.24
	Rural	60,637	72,463	13,031	0.94
	Urban	16,015	24,554	4,322	2.27
Kohlu		99,846	214,350	26,827	4.09

(continued)

Table 6.3 (continued)

Administrative units (Province/Districts)		Population 1998	Population 2017	Number of households 2017	Average annual growth rate
	Rural	90,181	196,924	24,676	4.19
	Urban	9,665	17,426	2,151	3.14
Lehri		88,599	118,046	18,651	1.52
	Rural	76,418	101,438	16,143	1.5
	Urban	12,181	16,608	2,508	1.64
Sibi		103,746	135,572	20,228	1.41
	Rural	55,279	71,145	11,278	1.33
	Urban	48,467	64,427	8,950	1.51
Ziarat		80,748	160,422	28,999	3.67
	Rural	80,112	157,016	28,308	3.6
	Urban	636	3,406	691	9.21
Barkhan		103,545	171,556	26,041	2.69
	Rural	95,875	159,380	24,347	2.7
	Urban	7,670	12,176	1,694	2.46
Killa Saifullah		193,553	342,814	53,478	3.05
	Rural	168,254	280,071	43,574	2.71
	Urban	25,299	62,743	9,904	4.88

Source Population Census 2017 (Pakistan Bureau Statistics)

Punjab is the most populated province about 56% of the total country and share of land country-wise is about 26%. Even though in 1998 the urban populations were only 32% in a few major urban areas. But currently, this ratio is increasing with rapid growth and migration towards urban areas. During the past two decades, this trend of urbanization in Karachi, Rawalpindi-Islamabad, Lahore, Faisalabad, and Peshawar is growing at an alarming level (Pakistan Social and Living Standards Measurement Survey, 2010).

Pakistan conducted the sixth census population in 2017 after the 20 years of the long-term gap. The purpose of the population census is to collect data for government and policymakers to analyse the needs of public demands (Abid, 2018). According to the census survey, the population growth during the past 19 years is 57% while the urban-rural population is 37 and 67%, respectively. The male–female ratio is 52.2 and 48.8%, respectively. The total population of the country according to the recent census is 207.8 million. During the last census of 1998, the population of Pakistan was 130 million which reveals that the growth rate of the population is 2.4%. The province wise the share of Punjab is 55.62% whereas the population increased by 36.4 during the past two decades. The urban segment. Nevertheless, Punjab is the largest urbanized region and still, 63.9% of people live in rural areas. While the share of the female ratio is 49% as compared to 1998 as it was 48.2%. Sindh is the second

Table 6.4 District-wise population in the year 1998 and 2017 in Punjab province

Administrative units (Province/Districts)		Population 1998	Population 2017	Number of households 2017	Average annual growth rate
Punjab		73,621,290	110,012,442	17,103,835	2.13
	Rural	49,490,394	69,625,144	10,714,102	1.81
	Urban	24,130,896	40,387,298	6,389,733	2.74
Attock		1,274,935	1,883,556	306,649	2.07
	Rural	990,756	1,393,550	228,435	1.81
	Urban	284,179	490,006	78,214	2.9
Chakwal		1,083,725	1,495,982	266,109	1.71
	Rural	909,935	1,212,042	217,585	1.52
	Urban	173,790	283,940	48,524	2.61
Jhelum		936,957	1,222,650	204,792	1.41
	Rural	665,893	868,448	145,783	1.4
	Urban	271,064	354,202	59,009	1.41
Rawalpindi		3,363,911	5,405,633	888,765	2.52
	Rural	1,455,240	2,530,117	418,177	2.95
	Urban	1,908,671	2,875,516	470,588	2.18
Bhakkar		1,051,456	1,650,518	268,244	2.4
	Rural	875,214	1,390,404	226,306	2.46
	Urban	176,242	260,114	41,938	2.06
Khushab		905,711	1,281,299	211,686	1.84
	Rural	676,742	928,469	153,048	1.67
	Urban	228,969	352,830	58,638	2.3
Sargodha		2,665,979	3,703,588	600,224	1.74
	Rural	1,911,287	2,612,543	420,867	1.65
	Urban	754,692	1,091,045	179,357	1.95
Mianwal		1,056,620	1,546,094	238,006	2.02
	Rural	836,610	1,217,699	186,770	1.99
	Urban	220,010	328,395	51,236	2.13
Gujranwala		3,400,940	5,014,196	747,214	2.06
	Rural	1,523,106	2,065,260	301,072	1.61
	Urban	1,877,834	2,948,936	446,142	2.4
Gujrat		2,048,008	2,756,110	442,399	1.57
	Rural	1,456,342	1,928,714	308,668	1.49
	Urban	591,666	827,396	133,731	1.78
Hafizabad		832,980	1,156,957	175,180	1.74
	Rural	605,865	754,106	114,058	1.16

(continued)

Table 6.4 (continued)

Administrative units (Province/Districts)		Population 1998	Population 2017	Number of households 2017	Average annual growth rate
	Urban	227,115	402,851	61,122	3.05
Mandi Bahauddin		1,160,552	1,593,292	252,120	1.68
	Rural	943,983	1,266,892	199,336	1.56
	Urban	216,569	326,400	52,784	2.18
Narowal		1,265,097	1,709,757	239,916	1.59
	Rural	1,110,711	1,452,509	200,434	1.42
	Urban	154,386	257,248	39,482	2.72
Sialkot		2,723,481	3,893,672	574,143	1.89
	Rural	1,938,758	2,750,310	400,653	1.85
	Urban	784,723	1,143,362	173,490	2
Lahore		6,340,114	11,126,285	1,757,691	3
	Rural	1,131,026	0	0	
	Urban	5,209,088	11,126,285	1,757,691	4.07
Kasur		2,354,506	3,454,996	526,166	2.03
	Rural	1,781,918	2,564,161	385,537	1.93
	Urban	572,588	890,835	140,629	2.35
Nankana Sahib		1,044,865	1,356,374	215,934	1.38
	Rural	886,714	1,110,321	176,003	1.19
	Urban	158,151	246,053	39,931	2.35
Sheikhupura		2,276,164	3,460,426	517,850	2.22
	Rural	1,561,422	2,258,636	334,617	1.96
	Urban	714,742	1,201,790	183,233	2.77
Faisalabad		5,429,547	7,873,910	1,225,266	1.97
	Rural	3,111,114	4,113,582	631,434	1.48
	Urban	2,318,433	3,760,328	593,832	2.57
Chiniot		965,124	1,369,740	218,607	1.86
	Rural	694,707	947,202	150,625	1.64
	Urban	270,417	422,538	67,982	2.37
Jhang		1,869,421	2,743,416	427,390	2.04
	Rural	1,448,038	2,145,226	332,134	2.09
	Urban	421,383	598,190	95,256	1.86
Toba Tek Singh		1,621,593	2,190,015	338,469	1.59
	Rural	1,307,901	1,748,085	267,821	1.54
	Urban	313,692	441,930	70,648	1.82
Sahiwal		1,843,194	2,517,560	392,509	1.65

(continued)

Table 6.4 (continued)

Administrative units (Province/Districts)		Population 1998	Population 2017	Number of households 2017	Average annual growth rate
	Rural	1,481,284	2,000,440	309,865	1.59
	Urban	361,910	517,120	82,644	1.89
Okara		2,232,992	3,039,139	493,180	1.63
	Rural	1,692,787	2,207,349	360,592	1.4
	Urban	540,205	831,790	132,588	2.29
Pakpattan		1,286,680	1,823,687	304,405	1.85
	Rural	1,094,936	1,535,591	256,016	1.79
	Urban	191,744	288,096	48,389	2.16
Bahawalnagar		2,061,447	2,981,919	481,276	1.96
	Rural	1,653,998	2,360,823	379,449	1.89
	Urban	407,449	621,096	101,827	2.24
Bahawalpur		2,433,091	3,668,106	584,864	2.18
	Rural	1,685,327	2,496,848	392,678	2.09
	Urban	747,764	1,171,258	192,186	2.38
Rahim Yar Khan		3,141,053	4,814,006	701,520	2.27
	Rural	2,524,103	3,781,370	537,401	2.15
	Urban	616,950	1,032,636	164,119	2.74
Dera Ghazi Khan		1,643,118	2,872,201	343,361	2.98
	Rural	1,356,519	2,324,346	270,524	2.87
	Urban	286,599	547,855	72,837	3.46
Rajanpur		1,103,618	1,995,958	262,490	3.16
	Rural	917,221	1,658,756	215,883	3.16
	Urban	186,397	337,202	46,607	3.16
Layyah		1,120,951	1,824,230	281,929	2.59
	Rural	925,937	1,502,725	232,310	2.58
	Urban	195,014	321,505	49,619	2.66
Muzaffargarh		2,635,903	4,322,009	667,515	2.63
	Rural	2,209,824	3,627,238	557,112	2.64
	Urban	426,079	694,771	110,403	2.6
Multan		3,116,851	4,745,109	760,858	2.23
	Rural	1,688,376	2,686,819	429,984	2.47
	Urban	1,428,475	2,058,290	330,874	1.94
Khanewal		2,068,490	2,921,986	466,390	1.83
	Rural	1,680,104	2,357,910	375,349	1.8
	Urban	388,386	564,076	91,041	1.98

(continued)

Table 6.4 (continued)

Administrative units (Province/Districts)		Population 1998	Population 2017	Number of households 2017	Average annual growth rate
Lodhran		1,171,800	1,700,620	262,650	1.97
	Rural	1,001,712	1,434,910	220,432	1.9
	Urban	170,088	265,710	42,218	2.37
Vehari		2,090,416	2,897,446	458,068	1.73
	Rural	1,754,984	2,391,743	377,144	1.64
	Urban	335,432	505,703	80,924	2.18

Source Population Census 2017 (Pakistan Bureau Statistics)

largest province. The population growth rate 57.3% or 17.44 million during the past 19 years (Rana, 2017). The province-wise population trend since 1998 is reported in Table 6.6.

Pakistan's population is predicted to be 227 million by 2025. If the existing population growth rate remain persisted then the population of Pakistan would be approximately 230.7 million in 2027 and yet 63% of the total population is younger generations below 30 years. This will lead to certain socio-economic issues most particularly the alarming issue of food, cloth, and shelter (Pakistan vision 2025) (Zakria & Muhammad, 2009). There will additionally burden on the government for housing demand in Pakistan. Whereas the government doesn't have any proper initiatives for housing in Pakistan. With the current situation, Pakistan will be facing an acute shortage of new affordable houses. As the Pakistan social living standard shows that most people don't have even an adequate place and shelter for satisfactory living. The population growth inserts the pressure on the urban areas particularly face great challenges because of rapid urbanization and migration.

6.3 Rapid Urbanization

During the past two decades, the urban population of the world increased to 80 million in 2015–2020. From 2010 to 2015, the Asian region observed 77 million growth in urban regions. While the global population grew during the past three decades to 1 billion while by 2050 two-thirds of the population will be living in cities (United Nations, 2019).

Pakistan is one of the urbanized countries among the south Asian countries. The size of the urban population across provinces and big cities increase over time (Tables 6.7 and 6.8). The huge influx of people from rural in search of better social life is increasing the unban status in Pakistan. In the year 2015, the housing demand for new housing units was 4.4 million in major cities of Pakistan. The major cities

Table 6.5 District-wise population in the year 1998 and 2017 in Sindh province

Administrative units (Province/Districts)		Population 1998	Population 2017	Number of households 2017	Average annual growth rate
Sindh		30,439,893	47,886,051	8,585,610	2.41
	Rural	14,744,436	22,975,593	4,185,828	2.36
	Urban	15,695,457	24,910,458	4,399,782	2.46
Jacobabad		727,190	1,006,297	177,867	1.72
	Rural	536,883	709,170	125,341	1.47
	Urban	190,307	297,127	52,526	2.37
Kashmor		677,120	1,089,169	185,143	2.53
	Rural	509,199	835,556	140,872	2.64
	Urban	167,921	253,613	44,271	2.19
Kambar Shahdad Kot		924,294	1,341,042	223,154	1.97
	Rural	690,371	943,478	155,051	1.65
	Urban	233,923	397,564	68,103	2.83
Larkana		1,001,608	1,524,391	261,331	2.23
	Rural	596,129	822,754	140,795	1.71
	Urban	405,479	701,637	120,536	2.92
Shikarpur		880,438	1,231,481	207,555	1.78
	Rural	668,459	928,232	155,902	1.74
	Urban	211,979	303,249	51,653	1.9
Ghotki		968,797	1,646,318	296,670	2.82
	Rural	764,799	1,242,780	223,706	2.58
	Urban	203,998	403,538	72,964	3.65
Khairpur		1,547,751	2,404,334	412,857	2.34
	Rural	1,042,543	1,628,484	280,079	2.37
	Urban	505,208	775,850	132,778	2.28
Sukkur		931,387	1,487,903	263,042	2.49
	Rural	449,102	767,788	135,906	2.86
	Urban	482,285	720,115	127,136	2.13
Badin		1,106,272	1,804,516	359,376	2.6
	Rural	872,490	1,414,138	282,574	2.57
	Urban	233,782	390,378	76,802	2.73
Dadu		1,106,717	1,550,266	286,810	1.79
	Rural	871,600	1,167,097	217,340	1.55
	Urban	235,117	383,169	69,470	2.6
Hyderabad		1,494,866	2,199,463	434,869	2.05
	Rural	233,568	366,708	71,523	2.4

(continued)

Table 6.5 (continued)

Administrative units (Province/Districts)		Population 1998	Population 2017	Number of households 2017	Average annual growth rate
	Urban	1,261,298	1,832,755	363,346	1.98
Jamshoro		582,094	993,142	180,922	2.85
	Rural	437,282	558,955	103,199	1.3
	Urban	144,812	434,187	77,723	5.94
Matiari		494,244	769,349	143,023	2.35
	Rural	380,934	586,759	110,382	2.29
	Urban	113,310	182,590	32,641	2.54
Sujawal		513,702	781,967	153,018	2.23
	Rural	452,667	696,262	136,397	2.29
	Urban	61,035	85,705	16,621	1.8
Tando Allahyar		493,526	836,887	165,503	2.81
	Rural	344,944	575,094	114,105	2.72
	Urban	148,582	261,793	51,398	3.02
Tando Muhammad Khan		438,624	677,228	131,565	2.31
	Rural	338,254	535,178	103,853	2.44
	Urban	100,370	142,050	27,712	1.84
Thatta		599,492	979,817	184,868	2.61
	Rural	508,214	803,759	152,881	2.44
	Urban	91,278	176,058	31,987	3.51
Karachi Central		2,277,931	2,971,626	538,983	1.41
	Rural				
	Urban	2,277,931	2,971,626	538,983	1.41
Karachi East		1,472,896	2,907,467	509,239	3.64
	Rural				
	Urban	1,472,896	2,907,467	509,239	3.64
Karachi South		1,478,047	1,791,751	327,518	1.02
	Rural				
	Urban	1,478,047	1,791,751	327,518	1.02
Karachi West		2,089,509	3,914,757	634,459	3.35
	Rural	73,568	283,247	44,051	7.34
	Urban	2,015,941	3,631,510	590,408	3.14
Korangi		1,561,742	2,457,019	421,618	2.41
	Rural				
	Urban	1,561,742	2,457,019	421,618	2.41
Malir		976,193	2,008,901	338,257	3.86

(continued)

Table 6.5 (continued)

Administrative units (Province/Districts)		Population 1998	Population 2017	Number of households 2017	Average annual growth rate
	Rural	333,942	857,922	149,820	5.08
	Urban	642,251	1,150,979	188,437	3.11
Mirpur Khas		1,006,329	1,505,876	286,547	2.14
	Rural	683,876	1,080,124	209,861	2.43
	Urban	322,453	425,752	76,686	1.47
Tharparkar		914,291	1,649,661	301,625	3.15
	Rural	868,146	1,517,590	274,691	2.98
	Urban	46,145	132,071	26,934	5.68
Umer Kot		664,797	1,073,146	212,356	2.55
	Rural	535,375	829,785	163,551	2.33
	Urban	129,422	243,361	48,805	3.37
Sanghar		1,319,881	2,057,057	374,609	2.36
	Rural	920,185	1,468,652	270,891	2.49
	Urban	399,696	588,405	103,718	2.05
Naushahro Feroze		1,087,571	1,612,373	275,693	2.09
	Rural	855,746	1,232,571	212,073	1.94
	Urban	231,825	379,802	63,620	2.63
Shaheed Benazirabad		1,102,584	1,612,847	297,133	2.02
	Rural	776,160	1,123,510	210,984	1.96
	Urban	326,424	489,337	86,149	2.15

Source Population Census 2017 (Pakistan Bureau Statistics)

Table 6.6 Trends in the population and housing units during 1998 and 2017

Area	Census 1998				Census 2017		
	Region	Population	Number of Households	Number of housing units	Population	Number of Households	Number of housing units
Khyber Pakhtunkhwa	Rural	14,456,435	1,928,668	1,842,488	24,793,737	3,104,154	3092260[a]
	Urban	3,287,210	406,158	368,748	5,729,634	741,014	742325
Punjab	Rural	49,490,394	7,381,698	7,336,193	69,625,144	10,714,102	10687778
	Urban	24,130,896	4,214,660	3,200,934	40,387,298	6,389,733	6420175
Sindh	Rural	14,744,436	2,579,230	2,850,989	22,975,593	4,185,828	4188464
	Urban	15,695,457	2,136,069	2,171,403	24,910,458	4,399,782	4382508
Baluchistan	Rural	4,797,055	887,246	775,954	8,943,532	1,301,212	1297723
	Urban	1,768,830	221,312	195,162	3,400,876	474,725	472342

Source Pakistan Bureau of Statistics

Table 6.7 Present and future of urbanization in Pakistan

S. no	City	Year 1998 (% Urban)	Year 2005 (% Urban)	Year 2010 (% Urban)	Year 2015 (% Urban)	Year 2020 (% Urban)	Year 2025 (% Urban)	Year 2030 (% Urban)
1	Pakistan	32.52	36.99	39.89	42.56	45.04	47.33	49.45
2	Punjab	31.27	36.31	39.56	42.54	45.27	47.78	50.07
3	Sindh	48.75	52.00	54.07	55.97	57.70	59.28	60.73
4	KPK	16.87	23.40	27.62	31.50	35.07	38.34	41.36
5	Baluchistan	23.89	29.70	33.44	36.87	40.02	42.91	45.56

Source Jan and Iqbal (2008)

(Karachi, Lahore, Peshawar, Rawalpindi, and Faisalabad) will need a further 78% of houses in the year 2035 to meet the challenges housing crisis.

Even the changing patterns from joint families' system to nuclear families will increase the burden on housing (Hina & Ijaz, 2017). Pakistan has more than one million population in 10 big cities in the year 2011, (Karachi 13.8 million, Lahore 7.3 million, Faisal Abad 3.1 million, Islamabad and Rawalpindi 3.8 million) and by 2025 these population of these cities will rise from 45–56%. Karachi alone will be crossing 20 million and Lahore 11 million. The countrywide demand for new housing units increases by 270,000 units each year (Kugelman, 2014).

Rapid urbanization has created a shortage of houses. The poor urban planning, and inefficient land and housing markets have all played a role in intensifying the demand for housing. Thus the shortage of housing units created an additional burden for the government and community resources.

6.4 Migration and Housing Shortage

Migration plays a significant role in shaping the housing market. The influx of local migrants from rural to urban inclines the elasticity of housing demand and supply. This rural-urban shifts upward the demand for housing. The continuous flow of migrants creates certain problems related to clean drinking water, infrastructure, and high housing prices, and less greenery (Haque & Nayab, 2007). The migration in the country started with the independence and bifurcation of the Subcontinent into two separate entities Pakistan and India in 1947. The cold war in 1979 in Afghanistan was another setback for our country where more than 3 million refugees migrated to Pakistan. Meanwhile, the recent internal civil-military conflict also led to internal migration in various regions of Khyber Pakhtunkhwa and FATA. The seasonal migration and rural-urban movement inside the country is another influencing factor of migration. Thus, these factors are responsible for migration which causes the housing shortage alongside other than socioeconomic and cultural factors (Ahmad et al., 2018).

Table 6.8 Population trends in big cities of Pakistan

S. no	City	Year 1941 (%)	Year 1961 (%)	Year 1981 (%)	Year 1998 (%)	Increase during 1941–1961 (%)	Increase during 1961–1981 (%)	Increase during 1981–1998 (%)	1998–2017 Average Annual Growth Rate (%)
1	Rawalpindi	0.185	0.340	0.795	1.410	1.84	2.34	2.29	2.16
2	Lahore	0.672	1.296	2.953	5.443	1.93	2.28	2.51	2.55
3	Gujranwala	0.085	0.196	0.601	1.133	2.31	3.07	3.50	1.82
4	Multan	0.143	0.358	0.732	1.197	2.50	2.04	2.22	1.98
5	Hyderabad	0.135	0.435	0.752	1.167	3.22	1.73	1.86	2.23
6	Karachi	0.387	1.913	5.208	9.339	4.94	2.72	2.66	2.60
7	Sialkot	0.139	0.167	0.302	0.422	1.20 t	1.81	2.07	1.89
8	Peshawar	0.173	0.218	0.566	0.983	1.26	2.60	3.60	3.39
9	Quetta	0.065	0.107	0.286	0.565	1.65	2.67	3.58	5.83

Source Jan and Iqbal (2008), Pakistan Bureau of Statistics (2017)

According to the census of 1980 and 1998, the housing shortage due to this informal migration was 570,000 housing units and the availability was only 300,000 new house units. This data shows that only 50% of the rural and urban needs were met. On the other hand, the requirement for new house units in 2005 was 6 million units and 8 million in 2010. Another important dimension of internal migration is conflict. The number of families left their households owing to war amid Pakistani forces and militant groups. The operation of the Pakistan military against terrorist groups in FATA and Khyber Pakhtunkhwa led to the mass exodus from their homelands. About 94% of the population was internally displaced during the various operations in the above areas. Although most of the regions are now free from terrorist groups most of the families decided to be settled in cities and urban regions (Siyal et al., 2018).

The remittances and flow of money from outside the country play a key role in the economic development of countries. The remittances of the Pakistani workers working abroad are mainly utilized in the housing sector and businesses of real estate. These resources are used for the rents, purchasing, and construction of houses. This is the reason that the current economic oil crisis in the gulf countries followed by COVID-19 impacted the income of millions and therefore affected the housing market in Pakistan. In Pakistan, the ownership of houses increased in urban areas from 78 to 85%. Similarly, in the rural areas, it increased from 96 to 98%. The other foremost changes that were observed in investment in the old house to a new house were from 42 to 62%. Thus there is a greater impact of remittances on the living standard and housing investment in Pakistan (Ahmed, Iqbal and Mustafa, 2020).

6.5 Real Estate Investment in Pakistan

The real estate includes areas such as commercial markets, plots, hoteling, retailing and renting, leasing of spaces for trading and official purposes. The real estate sector contributes 9% to the total GDP in Pakistan (Elaan Marketing, 2021). The estimated cost of Pakistan's investment and expenditures on real estate is about $5.2 billion per annum (Safawat, 2016). Similarly with buying and selling of this real estate sector has spill-over effects on other industrial sectors such cement, steel, wood, cable, etc. The gap between supply and demand is increasing over the time and the real estate market is unable to meet the demand thus put pressure on the prices of the real estate.

The big investors prefer to invest in real estate because of high-profit and low-risk. The rapid expansion in the real estate business is due to the migration of people from rural to urban regions.

6.6 Government Policies for the Housing Sector

It is the responsibility of the government to provide basic human needs including food, cloth, and shelter to its citizens. That's why most of the developed states such as England, the USA, Singapore, Malaysia, have adopted certain policy measures to meet the required housing demand. The British government, planned for 2015–20 to provide 1 million house units in five years. Chile adopted a policy to reduce housing shortage owing to that the demand and shortage of housing dropped from 242,000 house units to 126,000 in just four years. While the government also aims to achieve 75% affordable housing for all during 2002. Similarly, the USA adopted certain policy outlines for their citizens to ensure minimum housing for all, increasing housing supply and encouraging new construction. The government achieves the goals by reducing the new housing demand to only 18% in 2012 (Tariq et al., 2018).

Pakistans government also adopted certain policies and projects to meet the housing challenges in Pakistan. Though in 1960 Pakistan adopted a policy for the settlement of katchi abadis huge public housing program (Korangi). The government of Punjab took a good initiative namely "Ashiana Housing scheme" to provide feasible houses at affordable prices for the middle class but the project failed due to certain obstacles and irregularities (Khali & Nadeem, 2019). The first-ever, National Housing Policy (NHP) 2001 focused on providing a constructive atmosphere to boost the housing sector. The policy is anticipated to provide a basic housing unit for all. The policy aims to plan various land in urban and rural areas for housing construction irrespective of private and public land. The government in 2008 provided a detailed framework for the construction of one million new housing units on yearly basis to meet the housing demands (Tariq et al., 2018).

The current government of Pakistan Tehreek-i-Insaf in 2018 has adopted the "Naya Pakistan Housing Programme". The State Bank of Pakistan will advance the loans for the housing sector at affordable rates. Therefore, the government initiated to provide PKR 250 billion loans at easy instalments. The government targeted providing loans to 200,000 people in the first stage. The government through this program aims to provide five million housing units with an affordable price of PKR 3 million for the next 5 years. The details of the government program are given in Table 6.9. The government projected to provide 650,000 housing units in the first year of planning (Khali & Nadeem, 2019).

The government still is facing severe housing challenges and requires to work on many fronts. The income and housing price ratio in Pakistan is 20:1 compared to the global average of 5:1 (Global Village Space, 2021). The gap between housing prices and income is increasing for instance between 2012 and 2017 the housing cost in Pakistan exceeded with a ratio of 180% to a growing income of just 15%. The land price during the last decades increased by 152% (Ammar, 2019). Moreover, the government still failed to adjust the persistent scenario of katchi abadis and proper planning to deliver satisfactory housing to low-wage workers and their families. In Karachi only, approximately 60% of the city's inhabitants reside in informal settlements. Even though the current government has taken a good initiative to deliver basic housing facilities for lower-middle-income groups. The government still has a lot of potentials to improve and implement housing policie (Saleem, Tauheed and Arif, 2020).

6.7 Conclusion and Recommendation

The population of Pakistan increased over time at district, provincial and national levels. The population explosion along with other factors such as urbanization, foreign remittances, migration, conflicts, real estate business, and government policies which drastically impact the housing market dynamics. It is the responsibility of the government to provide housing facilities at affordable prices to accommodate the poor masses. The government should intervene in the housing sector to manage the house rents, construction, and land prices.

References

Abid, N. (2018). Islamic Republic of Pakistan Pakistan Population and Housing Census 2017 monitoring/Observation Mission National Report ER.

Ahmad, A., Iqbal, N., & Siddiqui, R. (2018). Determinants of housing demand in urban areas of Pakistan: Evidence from the PSLM. *The Pakistan Development Review, 57*(1), 1–25.

Ahmed, A., Iqbal, N., & Mustafa, G. (2020). Measuring the impact of remittances on housing demand: Evidence from large cities in Pakistan (No. 2020: 10). Pakistan Institute of Development Economics.

Ammar, R. (2019, March 23). Will PTI's housing programme address the root causes of the housing crisis? *Dawn* https://www.dawn.com/news/1439813.

DHS. (2020). Demographic Household Survey.

Elaan Marketing. (2021). Economic factors affecting real estate in Pakistan.

Government of Pakistan. (2015). National report of Pakistan for HABITAT III. Ministry of climate change. Islamabad.

Global Village Space. (2021). Pakistan's housing market is leading the economy: What has changed?

Haque, U., & Nayab, D. E. (2007). Engine of Growth. Pakistan Institute of Development Economics.

Hassan, S. Z., Naeem, M. A., Waheed, A., & Thaheem, M. J. (2019). Assessment of socio-economic profile and residents' satisfaction living in apartments and single-unit houses in Islamabad, Pakistan. *International Journal of Strategic Property Management, 23*(5), 284–297.

Hina, S., & Ijaz, N. (2017, January 16). *The six biggest challenges facing Pakistan's urban future.* IGC International Growth centre. https://www.theigc.org/blog/the-six-biggest-challenges-facing-pakistans-urban-future/.

Iqbal, N (2020). Sustainable housing, Pakistan Institute of Development Economics (PIDE).

Jan, B., & Iqbal, M. (2008). Urbanization trend and urban population projections of Pakistan using weighted approach. *Sarhad Journal of Agriculture, Pakistan, 24*(1), 173–180.

Khali, I., & Nadeem, U. (2019). *Optimising the Naya Pakistan housing policy opportunity* (No. 1). Working Paper.

Kugelman, M. (Ed.). (2014). *Pakistan's runaway urbanization: What can be done?* Asia Program.

Naseer, I. (2020, March 18). *Sustainable housing the news.* https://www.thenews.com.pk/.

Pakistan, Ministry of Statistics, Pakistan Bureau of Statistics. (n.d.). Press Release of Provisional Summary Results of 6th Population and Housing Census- 2017. Retrieved March 20/10/2020, from http://www.statistics.gov.pk/assets/publications/Population_Results.pdf.

Pakistan Demographic Household Survey chapter 1: Introduction.

Rana, S. (2017, August 25). 6th census findings: 207 million and counting. *The expresstribune*. Pakistan vision 2025 www.pc.gov.pk.

Rukhanuddin, A.R., & Ahmed, T. (nd). Pakistan Chapter 1: the DHS program United Nations (2019). World Urbanization Prospects The 2018 Revisions. Department of Economic and Social Affairs.

Safawat, Z.V. (2016). Real estate of Pakistan spends $5.2 billion on construction in a year says the Pakistan Bureau of Statistics, Linkdin (2016).

Saleem, A., et al. (2020). Karachi—housing without a future? The News International, Newspaper (2020).

Siyal, G. E. A., Khalid, I., & Qaisrani, A. (2018). Internal migration and urbanization: A case study from semi-arid regions of Pakistan.

Tariq, F., Salman, M., Hasan, J., Zafar, Z., Malik, S., Nawaz, M., ... & Sheikh, N. B. (2018). Appraisal of national housing policy-a case of Pakistan. *Technical Journal, 23*(3), 1–8.

UN Habitat. (2016). Urbanization and development: Emerging futures world cities report 2016.

UNDP. (2019). Sustainable urbanization, sustainable development goals.

World Bank. (2018). Project appraisal document on a proposed credit in the amount of SDR99.6 million US$145 million equivalent to the Islamic Republic of Pakistan for a Pakistan housing finance project. World Bank.

Zaki, S. (2016). Real estate of Pakistan spends $5.2 billion on construction in a year says the Pakistan Bureau of Statistics.

Zakria, M., & Muhammad, F. (2009). Forecasting the population of Pakistan using ARIMA models. *Pakistan Journal of Agricultural Sciences, 46*(3), 214–223.

Chapter 7
A Review of Rural Housing Schemes in India for Sustainable Habitats

Asraful Alam, Lakshminarayan Satpati, and Ishita Mandal

Abstract Specialization in economic activities, production of goods and services, and changes in nature of consumption have created and widened the distinction between urban and rural areas over time. These variations are embedded within the settlement morphologies to exhibit various types of settlement patterns. Every geographical region is unique in terms of its environmental characteristics and therefore, the settlements and housing associated with it have distinctiveness of their own which is an important input, for sustainable human habitation. The present scenario of rural housing in India is conditioned by several policies like the National Housing Policy, and the National Housing and Habitat Policy and various Government schemes are implemented mainly to meet the demand for a growing population without proper regard to the nature of the households. Over time, the gap between housing stock and the number of households has been decreasing, which is a positive sign no doubt but the dwelling units often do not do justice to the nature of requirements of the rural society. As per different estimates, the rural housing shortage is still quite high and on many occasions, the quality of housing is highly compromised due to a lack of sufficient funds and allegedly corrupt practices in the implementation of the schemes. Proper identification of beneficiaries, allotment of the required fund, a judicious mix of modern technology with traditional knowledge system, provisioning of related amenities and community participation in project implementation and maintenance could make the schemes more cost-effective and viable in terms of the creation of local employment opportunities too, which have been critically analysed in this paper.

A. Alam (✉)
Department of Geography, Serampore Girls' College, University of Calcutta, Hooghly, West Bengal, India

L. Satpati
Department of Geography & Director, UGC-HRDC, University of Calcutta, Kolkata, India

I. Mandal
Department of Geography, University of Calcutta, Kolkata, India

A. Kundu et al. (eds.), *Accessible Housing for South Asia*,
https://doi.org/10.1007/978-3-030-88881-7_7

Keywords Sustainable human habitation · Requirements of the rural society · Housing shortage · Quality of housing · Community participation · Local employment opportunities

7.1 Introduction

The man realized from the very beginning of human civilization, the need for shelter to safeguard himself from elements of nature as well as other threats. The history of the evolution of human civilization bears testimony to the fact that shelter has evolved over time and gone through many changes. The economic activities, services, specialities provided by different places define their identity as urban and rural areas. This variability has contributed to the evolution of settlement patterns differing in their morphology and essence. Although every region with its situation is unique, there is a similarity in every rural area. In rural areas, people are very close to Mother Nature. Generally, they do not disturb or modify nature as such to bring catastrophic consequences. The naturally available materials are used to build houses. In this man-nature relationship, nature plays important role in shaping rural houses, though modernization takes place everywhere. The topographic expression, climatic pattern and socio-economic determinants like income, occupation, religion, etc. create different moulds for rural landscape (Adeyekun, 2019; Kumar & Venkataramana, 2008; Sen, 2010).

The housing needs correspond to the growth of the population. Higher the growth of population more will be the need for dwelling units. Besides the population growth, fragmentation of land holdings and houses in a rural environment created more demand in this context. In countries that are suffering from huge population overload with high population density, the situations are worst. Better opportunities in urban areas often attracted the deprived rural people and forced them for leaving behind unmanageable properties. Without proper maintenance, a large section of the housing stock is reduced to dilapidated houses that are most vulnerable to natural disasters. The rural households in India also face a similar situation. The vicious cycle of poverty and debt compels rural people to live in misery.

Addressing the issue of the absolute housing shortage is not the only challenge to solve the housing issues in rural India. Often, while meeting the target of number of houses the quality of the houses is compromised. If low-poor quality materials are used, then the durability of the houses will be shorter and would require regular repairs and maintenance or a complete reconstruction. This cycle will go on repeating itself leading to enormous demand for investment in housing recurrently. Rural houses were originally built in complete harmony with nature. The traditional architectures, designs helped the households to live according to the climate and topography of a region. In contrast, building of concrete boxes like those in urban areas impacts the environs in ways that are not desirable. However, to upscale the housing supply to achieve "housing for all", modern technology and materials are introduced and implemented at the cost and total negligence of the traditional mechanism of building a house that is specific to the geo-environmental realities of the area.

Rural housing comprises a house with all its amenities and facilities like water supply, electricity, toilet, etc. Though India is trying to put efforts for betterment, the unavailability of these facilities in most of the places are still evident as reflected in housing statistics and reports to investing in rural housing could attract some employment opportunities and that would help rural people to earn a livelihood as well as to enhance the lifestyle (Albrecht et al., 2017). The overarching objective of this article is to analyse how the housing policies and schemes have impacted the requirements of better housing and what are the shortfalls.

7.2 National Policies

Since Independence India has faced many challenges regarding rural housing. Partition of India in 1947 resulted in an unprecedented scale of in-migration from the neighbouring country of then Pakistan. In that context, India formulated policies to develop urban areas keeping the need of the migrants and their resettlement in urban areas. While the central approach was the development of urban areas, some small initiatives were also taken by the government to provide housing sites, fund, and technical assistance, basic amenities to the rural poor and marginalized people. The first Rural Housing Policy was outlined by the then Union Ministry of Works, Housing and Supply in 1985. According to it, the Government will work based on aided self-help for the betterment of the housing sector for the rural poor (Singh, 2008). The Draft National Housing Policy came into being during the 8th Five-Year plan, which called for investment in housing to provide shelters, improve the conditions of existing houses and provide the basic amenities to the rural people (Kumar et al., 2016). The policy was placed before parliament in 1988 and aimed to eradicate houselessness by 2001. It comprised of several different agendas like provision of housing sites for rural SC/ST population with special reference to women, eradication of poverty, rural employment, sustainable living, skill development, technological development, access to funding through loan cum subsidy mechanism, etc.

In 1994, another National Housing Policy was adopted. The role of the Government was defined to be that of a facilitator for the people belonging to medium and higher income groups and for the poor and marginalized people Government would be a "provider". Two aspects were taken into consideration. Firstly, encouraging the judicious use of locally available building materials for different geo-climatic regions; secondly, creating a sustainable living environment by constructing and improving the condition of houses with making provision of more housing sites (Kumar & Venkataramana, 2008). In this policy, the government encouraged investment coming from the private sector. As per the policy, the Reserve Bank of India issued guidelines to allocate 1.5% of the incremental deposit of some scheduled commercial banks to the housing sector out of which 30% would be going to the beneficiaries directly and 70% would be going to the agencies to construct and supply houses to people (Tiwari & Rao, 2016). It also assured minimum displacement of rural people due to developmental projects (Bose, 1999).

The National Housing Policy, 1994, was continued as the National Housing and Habitat Policy in 1998. The policy set the target of making 2 million houses annually out of which 1.3 million would be constructed in rural areas with adequate amenities. Keeping in mind, that the population growth would demand more shelters, the policy allowed a provision for making surplus houses appropriate quality at affordable cost. It gave impetus to the poor and marginalized section of the society including women, elders, and physically handicapped persons. The private sector and cooperative societies were given incentives to construct houses and for the rural areas and especially for the rural poor. Provisions were also made for rural people to get a chance to gain knowledge and skills to build sustainable houses with local materials.

To implement these policies, several programmes and schemes were launched such as Indira Awas Yojana, Pradhan Mantri Gramodaya Yojana (Gramin Awas), Bharat Nirman Programme, Pradhan Mantri Awas Yojana (Grameen) (Kumar, 2017; Kumar et al., 2016).

7.3 National Schemes and Programmes

The most important scheme or programme for rural housing was Indira Awas Yojana. It was first launched during the 6th five-year plan as a sub-scheme of RLEGP (Rural Landless Employment Guarantee Programme) and later it was connected to JRY (Jawahar Rozgar Yojana). It is a subsidy (a joint venture of centre and state government) based programme targeted to rural BPL (Below Poverty Line) households and also the family members of defence personnel who died in duty, retired people of armed forces and people of minority groups. It provided the freedom to the beneficiaries to choose their design and technology. The local authorities were responsible for the identification of beneficiaries and disbursement of funds.

Pradhan Mantri Gramodaya Yojana (Gramin Awas) was launched in 2000–01 to provide basic amenities and services like rural electrification, pure drinking water, etc. in rural India. The primary aim of the scheme was to make the habitations sustainable and less polluted by providing latrine facilities, LPG service, plantation with community participation, etc. In 2005, it was replaced by Bharat Nirman Programme to carry forward the above-mentioned aims and objectives. It put several programmes tied with IAY to fulfil all the targets (Kumar et al., 2016).

In 2016, the Government of India renamed and restructured the IAY as Pradhan Mantri Awas Yojana (Grameen) which included certain changes to plug the loopholes and make the programme more efficient and productive. It addressed the drawbacks and increased the allocation per house to Rs. 1.2 lakh in plains and Rs.1.3 lakhs for the hilly region. It was also mandated that the funds will be directly credited to the bank account of the beneficiaries with a proper tracking mechanism of its utilization. Also, the quality of the houses was assured to be taken care of by National Technical Support Agency. Under this flagship programme of the Government of India, several rural programmes were converged for creating a habitat equipped with all required facilities, promoting rural employment for alleviation of poverty and so on (Rao,

2019). As per the recent report, out of the 15 million targets set by MoRD (Ministry of Rural Development), 88 lakh houses have been completed and ready for handing over to the targeted beneficiaries of this programme. MoRD with the help of the National Informatics Centre (NIC) launched AwaasSoft to review the housing quality from a remote distance through captured Geotagged photographs of houses. To provide housing for all by 2022, the Government launched Rural Housing Interest Subsidy Scheme (RHISS) for the households who are covered under the PMAY-G scheme to avail resources (MoRD, 2020).

7.4 State-Run Schemes and Programmes

There are some state-run schemes and programs to impact development at the grass-roots level in the rural areas. There are 15 states/UTs that have their rural housing schemes (Sinha & Biswas, 2008). Some of which are described below.

The Government of Kerala formulated several schemes, viz. EMS Total Housing Scheme for landless and houseless BPL families, Tribal Housing Scheme for tribal people in Wayanad district, Suraksha Housing Scheme for EWS people New Suraksha Housing Scheme with increased construction cost per dwelling, Tsunami Rehabilitation Programme, M.N. Laksham Veedu Punarnirmana Padhathi scheme to reconstruct the dilapidated houses, Housing scheme for women and so on (Government of Kerala, n.d.-a, n.d.-b, n.d.-c, n.d.-d; Stuff reporter, 2016). Tamil Nadu Government put forward the Tamil Nadu Village Habitations Improvement (THAI) Scheme (2011–2016) to solve the issues of resource and infrastructure inequality to all habitations(Government of Tamil Nadu, n.d.-d), Chief Minister Solar Powered Green House Scheme (CMSPGHS) for rural poor people at free of cost (Government of Tamil Nadu, n.d.-a), Rural Buildings Maintenance and Renovation Scheme (RBMRS) for the renovation of institutional buildings (Government of Tamil Nadu, n.d.-c), Clean Village Campaign (2003) to make villages visually pleasing through sanitary revolution (Government of Tamil Nadu, n.d.-b). Similarly, Basava Housing Scheme, Devraj URS Housing Scheme-Rural Scheme, Dr. B.R. Ambedkar Nivasa Yojana-Rural Scheme, etc. in Karnataka (Government of Karnataka, n.d.), Environmental balanced prosperous village development scheme provides eco-friendly development approach with a focus on human and natural resource development in Maharashtra are devoted in the rural housing sector (Government of Maharashtra, n.d.). The Government of West Bengal also provides free-of-cost shelters to the poor backward people under the scheme of 'Gitanjali' and 'Amar Thikana' (Government of West Bengal, n.d.). The Government of Odisha initiated some schemes which are Biju Pucca Ghar Yojana, launched in 2014 to convert all kutcha houses to pucca houses to withstand the climatic challenges and natural disasters. The traditional forest dwellers, ST population and those who needed to be rehabilitated due to natural, cultural, developmental and political issues are covered under the scheme (Government of Odisha, 2017). Pucca Ghar Yojana (Mining) scheme covers the mining areas especially the nine districts of the state (Government of Odisha,

2018a). To provide houses for construction workers, the Nirman Shramik Pucca Ghar Yojana scheme has been launched (Government of Odisha, n.d.). The government of Andhra Pradesh launched various schemes in this regard such as Rural Permanent Housing, Rajiv Gruha Kalpa, Rajiv Swagruha, etc. In 2005, most of the state-run schemes were merged to form subsidy-based Integrated Novel Development in Rural Areas and Model Municipal Areas (INDIRAMMA) housing scheme, which was launched in 2006 and was renamed as NTR housing scheme later on (Rajeev 2016). The scheme was focused on BPL households without pucca houses to cover within a certain time frame (Government of Andhra Pradesh, 2013). This scheme also includes the facilities like drinking water supply, individual sanitary latrines, drainage, power supply to every household,etc.The other States having their schemes include Gujarat, Jammu & Kashmir, Himachal Pradesh, Daman and Diu, Pondicherry, Punjab, Sikkim, Jharkhand, etc. (Sinha & Biswas, 2008).

7.5 Technology Transfer

The Central Building Research Institute (CBRI) initiated various cost-effective building materials and technologies. The Centre for Application of Science and Technology to Rural Areas (ASTRA) and the Indian Institute of Science (Bangalore) has developed energy-efficient technologies for sustainable rural habitats. The institutions that have been working in this context are Housing and Urban Development Corporation Ltd. (HUDCO), Building Materials and Technology Promotion Council (BMTPC) and several Rural Building Centres (RBCs). Not only Government agencies but other organizations and freelancers regarding scientific technologies have been devoted to rural housing. The common objective of all these is the transfer of innovations, eco-friendly materials from research centres to where needed and also to help in enhancing skill development of the artisans. MoRD also constituted the National Mission for Rural Housing and Habitat for this purpose so that the sustainable and affordable housing facility specifically for certain locations can be provided within a specific time frame with the participation of the community itself. It also focused on technology and bylaws for construction. In the context of bylaws, the Ministry of Home Affairs (MHA) Government of India formed some guidelines for making the houses earthquake resistant. For this purpose, the Bureau of Indian Standards (BIS) seismic codes were introduced in the guidelines. The National Innovation Foundation, an autonomous institution of the department of science and technology provides support to the grass root innovators to implement it on the rural landscape (Kumar, 2014b; Kumar et al., 2009). Technological innovation with scientific temperament in harmony with the environment, human welfare and behaviour, etc. is needed. Some innovations like using flurogypsum plaster to stand in rain, portable C-brick machine for making durable bricks using sand, fly ash and cement, etc. Low-cost materials like bamboo, rice husk are used to make the earthquake-resistant structure (Gore, 2016).

Few technologies for passive cooling of the houses have been used, among them 'Sky therm cooling' technique is quite common, which is also a cost-efficient mechanism. In this method, the flat roof is used to make a pond like a container which is covered in the daytime with a movable insulating cover. The roof pond will absorb heat from the building throughout the day and at night after removal of the insulating cover it will radiate out the stored heat. The mechanism can be used for winter days also (Prasad et al., 1979).

India is known for the courtyard type of dwellings in rural areas. The courtyard in low-rise buildings can efficiently condition the indoor climate with the outer environment and enhance the airflow for better ventilation (Aldawoud & Clark, 2008). In addition, green technologies (Liu et al., 2014) will reduce the carbon emission from houses. The expanded thickness of the walls may also be used as a passive cooling technique (Kang et al., 2016; Khosla, 1983). The passive cooling techniques with insulating walls and low use of fossil fuel can effectively reduce the energy consumption of a household (Yang et al., 2010). To lower down the use of fossil fuel for kitchen purpose, the Government initiated the programme for providing subsidized LPG connections for poor people.

Based on different climatic conditions and geomorphologic hazards, some recommendations for construction are made under Pradhan Mantri Awaas Yojana-Gramin. The resources available in any specific region are highly considered in these recommendations. Although all states are not covered under one catalogue (UNDP, 2016).

Housing is undisputedly a core basic need of human beings (Kumar, 2014b). Globalization and the process of increasing economic integration have limited the capacity of States to provide adequate resources for fulfilling the economic, social and cultural rights of their citizens, including housing and essential social services. Numerous macroeconomic aspects control the availability of resources for social spending. Globalization or global neoliberalism is diverse, many of its elements are having an important impact on housing systems, and consequently in housing law, policy and especially housing rights. The growth and power of globalized corporations concerned with housing; The globalization of property rights, housing finance markets and the promotion by owner-occupied; globalized real estate investment in housing; the reordering of cities and slums; new responsibility for the state about housing; and the effect of globalized migrants and refugees all present new and undetermined challenges (Warner 2010).

7.6 Housing Conditions

India is a country of different types of people settling in either rural or urban areas. According to the recent census report (2011), 833 million people out of 1.21 billion live in rural areas. But there is a decline in the rural population from 72.19% in 2001 to 68.84% in 2011 in terms of rural-urban distribution. The rural population of non-EAG (Empowered Action Group) states decreased more than that of EAG states. The loss of rural population can be attributed to the migration and inclusion to urban (Census, 2011d).

About 168 million people reside in 207 million census houses in rural India for residential or non-residential or for both purposes. Most of the rural populations (39.4%) have one room dwellings followed by two rooms, three rooms and so on. Where a very low share of total rural populations (4.8%) have five and more than five rooms in a house, 4.3% of households do not have a regular room to stay. The rural areas of the Indo-Gangetic Plain showed a reduction in a house with five rooms or more than that, whereas Kerala showed opposite conditions (Census, 2011c). It can be elucidated that the houses were getting fragmented and that increased number of households—from 138 million in 2001 the number of households increased to 168 million in 2011). The increase in the number of household and population increased in rural India has been steady and consistent since 1971.

From Table 7.1, a housing trend can be observed. Since the year 1981, the housing stocks with the number of households have increased. With time the gap between housing stock and household has been decreasing. From the decreasing gap and decadal growth rate of both categories, it may seem like most of the households possess their dwelling units outwardly. But the estimation of the working group on rural housing (MoRD) revealed a different scenario. Besides the gap between the housing stock and the number of households, the number of houses in the category of obsolescence, congestion and others was vital factors affecting fulfilment of the requirement. The total shortage in 2012–17 was 43.6 million (Table 7.2). Another working group estimated the shortage to be around 48.8 million for the 12th plan out

Table 7.1 Trends in rural housing stock and households, 1981–2011 and estimates for 2012

	1981	1991	2001	2011	2012[a]
Housing stock (in millions)	81.9	108.5	135.1	166.2	169.6
Households (in millions)	89.9	111.5	138.3	167.8	171.1
Households – housing stock (in millions)	−8.1	−3	−3.2	−1.7	−1.5
Decadal Growth (in %)					
Housing stock	—	32.5	24.6	23	—
Households	—	24	24	21.4	—
Annual exponential growth (in %)					
Housing stock	—	2.8	2.2	2.1	—
Households	—	2.2	2.2	1.9	—

Source Kumar (2014a)
Note [a]Forecasted using annual exponential growth rates between 2001 and 2011; housing stock includes occupied census houses used as residences and residences-cum-other uses.

Table 7.2 Estimation of the rural housing shortage by working group on rural housing for the 12th Five-Year Plan

Factors taken into account for assessing housing shortages	Shortage (in millions)
Number of households not having houses in 2012	4.15
Number of temporary houses in 2012	20.21
Shortage due to congestion in 2012	11.3
Shortage due to obsolescence in 2012	7.5
Additional housing shortage arising between 2012 and 2017	0.5
Total rural housing shortage during 2012–2017	43.6

Source Singh et al. (2013)
Note All numbers for 2012 were projections based on intercensal growth rates between the Censuses of 1991 and 2001

of which 90% belonged to BPL families (Kumar et al., 2016). Several studies estimated housing shortage using different approaches and presented differing scenarios, for example, Singh calculated it around 140 million where Kumar (2014a) found it about 62 million.

In 2001, the average rural household size was 5.4, which means a five-member houschold size was at the centre of focus and 32.4% of normal households had five members. The increased number of households created a demand for more houses. About 2.59 lakh households having 4.5 mean size were homeless at that time (Census, 2001b). The scenario is almost the same for the census year 2011. In this decade also about 1.92 lakh households with a 4.3 average size remain unsheltered (Census, 2011b).

Pucca houses were less in rural areas (65.8%) amongst which SC's and ST's account for 43.8 and 63% respectively. In contrast, Kutcha houses were in higher proportion in SC's and ST's with 13.8% and 11.3%, respectively (Ghosh, et al., 2021; Kumar et al. 2016).

In the case of the housing conditions in rural areas in 2011, most of the houses are in liveable conditions (47.5%) followed by good ones (45.9%). But overall there is 6.5% of houses that are in decaying conditions across the country. The more or less same situation prevailed since 2001 (Census, 2001a). People in the Union Territories have houses in good conditions, even in mountainous regions of the Himalayas and Deccan trap, people live in good houses. But in the northern plain, which is supposed to be the best site for housing, the houses are in mere liveable condition. Out of the 6.5% decaying houses, West Bengal, Assam, Odisha (Orissa), etc. ranks high with more than 10% dilapidated households (Census, 2011a).

Houses without basic facilities are not so liveable for people, because they have to fetch those facilities from far outside the premises or habitation areas of the village. Only 35% of households have a water facility in their premises; 36% and 18% of them have to bring water from about 500 m and more than that distance respectively.

Around 55% are electrified and 43% use kerosene for lighting the house. Proper sanitation facilities are very important for a healthy environment whether it is a rural or urban area. Unlike an urban area, rural India is far behind in terms of drainage facility, only about 36.8% of households are covered under this and 63.3% are left behind. After many attempts to develop the housing sector, there is a lack of latrines in rural areas. People use firewood, crop residue or cow dung cake in the kitchen within or outside the premises (Census, 2011c).

7.7 Critical Analysis Regarding Housing Policies and Schemes

There were several efforts made through policy and programmes by states as well as central government to limit the housing problems in India, but most of them affected had a partial impact. Though the housing sector was mentioned as a productive investment in the policies, due to the non-liability of the Government, the fund allotted could not be utilized. Moreover, it could not generate economic resources. To provide the fund and other services to the dwellings, the proper identification of beneficiaries was needed. As the identification process at the grass-root level was not so organized in rural areas, the benefits did not accrue to the targeted section of the society (Kumar et al., 2016). The financial help, building materials, technologies and infrastructure were also inadequate to improve the conditions (Singh, 2008). The engaged architects in rural housing schemes were unaware of the needs of rural landscapes and rural people (Khosla, 1983).

Concurrent evaluation of housing programmes was done for corrective action and course correction. An evaluation study revealed that the rural houselessness or in other words house shortages decreased from 0.47% in 1981 to 0.28% in 1991 in India, (excluding Assam and Jammu & Kashmir). Together with Maharashtra (highest rural house shortage in 1991) Gujarat and Madhya Pradesh accounted for more than 60% of the total housing shortages. In the case of basic amenities specifically safe drinking water, more households were covered under this facility but about one-third of the rural households were left behind in 1991. Tube wells are considered as a source of safe drinking water instead of a supply of treated water through the pipeline. Only about 9% of the household had a toilet facility. State-wise the percentages show different situations (Sundaram & Tendulkar, 1995).

There is still a substantial backlog, and the root cause can be attributed to the rapid population increase and continuous demand for housing. The housing stock created through various programmes has deteriorated in quality over time due to a lack of maintenance. Besides that, the materials used for these were of average to poor quality that resulted in their dilapidated condition sooner than expected. In census 2001, it is reported that about 6.2% of census houses (residence and residence cum other uses purpose) were in dilapidated condition and about 18% were temporary (Majumder, 2011). Also, the funds allocated by National Housing Bank and HUDCO was proved lucrative for a few states only and as there were no directive criteria mentioned to identify the beneficiaries, many of the poor sections were deprived of (Kumar et al., 2016).

Only the scheme Indira Awas Yojana was succeeded with a fluctuating target and achievement value. According to a government report, the IAY scheme had some loopholes like unevaluated state of housing, the discrepancy in the selection of beneficiaries, failed monitoring system and worst quality of houses in terms of design suitability and materials used. It provided unsustainable housing which was not the aim. The quality degradation lowers the average lifespan of houses from 30 to mere 10 years (Sharma, 2018b). It is evident in a study that the women population was neglected in places which may increase the resentment. In many areas of the Kashmir valley, the identified and selected beneficiaries are forged as they are from the above BPL category. This raises the question of the role of PRI, on what criteria that population is getting enlisted (Hussain & Yaseen, 2017).

As per the report of the Ministry of Rural Development in 2020, there are 62 lakhs of backlog present under the Pradhan Mantri Awas Yojana (Grameen) scheme (MoRD, 2020). Also, the allocations of funds are mostly in few states like Madhya Pradesh, West Bengal, Odisha and Uttar Pradesh. Arunachal Pradesh, Goa, Nagaland and Daman and Diu are the states/ UTs with nominal development under this scheme. The dwindling amount of funds in recent years leads to a slow pace of development (Radha & Mary, 2020; Sharma, 2017). The common people are less aware and lack of participation in the habitation development creates problems at the people's end (Mathi & Jerin Rose, 2020). The scheme preserves the dignity of women (Dash, 2018; Sharma, 2018a).

More than 10 million households live in dilapidated houses, and 29 million live in temporary houses (Census of India, 2011) and 67% of households cannot access adequate housing in India (Ghosh, et al., 2021; Tiwari & Rao, 2016). Besides the backlog, the condition of temporary houses is troublesome because these houses need to repair in almost every year which is beyond the means of many households. There are 25.7% (2011–12) people on average who are below the poverty line across the country in rural areas (RBI, 2012) and at present in India, near to 300 million people are still below the poverty line (Alok, 2020). It was reported that policies on housing are currently focused on providing houses for all, but the quality is being neglected. More than 90% of people under the EWS and LIG category are facing such shortages and quality issues. If urban areas are facing such problems despite having high priority than rural areas, then the condition can be assumed (Anonymous, 2016; Jain, 2014). Where 77% of the Indian population is struggling to earn livelihood every day (Tewari, 2015), people cannot opt to repair the houses every year. So the quality can be an issue in this regard (Kumar & Venkataramana, 2008). To solve this problem, semi-permanent houses are built. This kind of architecture helps in lowering down the cost of constructing pucca houses and on the other hand, gives strength to the houses to withstand any calamity. With the limited budget for each dwelling unit, single-room houses can be made within which the whole family have to reside. If the rural areas will convert to areas with several single rooms like boxes, then it is time to rethink. Even private sectors emphasized urban areas (Khosla, 1983) on the other than less interest in rural areas because of the high concentration of poor in rural area and their affordable capacity is low as compared to urban area.

In the case of state policies, there are some critical observations. In Odisha, the beneficiaries have the opportunity to choose house design and corresponding technology among various options. The state and district authorities act as a nodal point in all steps. The houses are sanctioned in the name of the woman head of the household that will empower the women in the society. To make the schemes transparent, no contractors are included and the funds are directly credited to the bank account of the beneficiaries. The progress of housing is verified through uploaded images of houses in the Awaas App developed by the Central or State Government (Government of Odisha, 2017, 2018a, b). The scheme INDIRAMMA, in Andhra Pradesh, encouraged microfinance institutions to give loans for building houses to the beneficiaries. However, the report suggests many poor households were exploited by the high rate of interest and further pushed them into debt cycle and poverty. Though the authority tried to control the situation by enabling people to get loans at a cheaper rate, the casualties that occurred due to this could not be corrected (PTI, 2010). The attempt by the Kerala Government to meet the requirement of adequate and affordable housing with the cooperation of the public and private sector and community in Kerala is noteworthy, but the overpopulated places with kutcha and semi-pucca houses are out of maintenance (TNN, 2018). Tamil Nadu is the first state to focus on habitation as a unit of development in rural areas and also to provide free solar-powered housing with 300 square foot area (Government of Tamil Nadu, n.d.-a, n.d.-d).

7.8 Prospect of Indian Rural Housing

The Government has constructed millions of pucca houses over the years and the remaining kutcha houses are expected to be converted to the pucca structure over a period. It is observed that the building material for pucca house is increasing the indoor temperature. The thermal lag of conventional mud houses (Chel & Tiwari, 2009; Madhumathi et al., 2014)houses that helped in maintaining the indoor comfort are missing here to some extent. India, have various rural housing problems and their multidimensional complexity, both in terms of economic development and sufficient provision of housing and support services (Kumar, 2014b). The services of the skilled professional, development authority, engineers, financial supporters and cooperative societies are not accessible in rural villages in India. In this respect, housing construction is a people's process in rural areas (Shah, 2000). It is needed to create a demand-based market for technological advancement in this sector. Through public procurement or in general through the convergence of public schemes, technologies, vernacular materials and local human resources a demanding market can be built. This will encourage the private enterprises to make a venture in the rural sector which will, in turn, will embolden the research and development institutes to be more innovative (Sinha & Biswas, 2008). In the complex relationship of man and nature, both are influencing and modifying each other. But with the view of sustainable housing, it is assumed to have balance with nature. The determinant of occupation can be overlooked as the Government took the responsibility for its poor citizens. Access to adequate, safe and affordable housing is the first indicator of the 11th Sustainable Development Goal. Housing is necessary because it allows people to lead healthy, secure, productive and dignified lives and because it is a durable asset that provides owners with a way to save and gain access to credit (Gillard et al., 2018).

7.9 Conclusion

From the above discussion, it is evident that rural houses in any country are largely dependent on nature. Be it nature or socio-economic factors, rural houses are like mirrors reflecting their influence. With the functioning of democratic and socialist governments, the occupational determinant is becoming inadmissible. For the successful running of the taken policies and schemes in this regard need a proper public–private forum. But the quality may be a questionable loophole in this regard. The self-governance at grass roots level should be empowered enough to solve the problems related to identification of the needy people and the disbursement of funds. People are unaware of the technical assistance for housing development. Moreover, there is a vast continuum of rural housing typologies across the country for which different technologies and awareness is needed as well as the rural housing schemes with differential financial assistance (Dutt, 2008). Architects who are employed for rural housing schemes are not very much acquainted with the needs of rural landscapes (Khosla, 1983). Energy-intensive materials are being used instead of keeping the conventional knowledge (Tiwari, 2001). That brings employment on one hand and modifies the indoor climate on the other hand (Kumar & Venkataramana, 2008; Madhumathi et al., 2014). New technologies like passive cooling mechanisms should be encouraged in the global warming concern (Kumar et al., 1994; Tiwari et al., 1994). The economic and social status of the households often determines the acquisition and deprivation of basic amenities. In most cases, poor people have to comprise with the situations (Pal et al., 2015). If there is a never-ending demand for housing for increasing population pressure, quality also cannot be maintained so far as funding is concerned. However, this problem cannot be tackled without a robust population policy on the one hand and a planned intervention in improving the housing stock in the rural sector, on the other. Not only the shortages of houses but also the availability of basic services and amenities to the households are very important because the mere housing structure does not suffice in attaining a healthy and sustainable life. More extensive studies in all the states are required to come up with a solution on this matter. Sustainable housing strategies should address not only the environmental impacts of the site but also the emissions/pollution embedded in construction (Rubenstein, 2012). Transparent Government policies and involvement of public–private partnerships are likely to improve rural housing management and sustainability.

References

Adeyekun, A. J. (2019). *effective advocacy for rural housing in India: A village survey in Dadri Toy, Haryana* (A Practical Solution to Improve the Quality of Life in Rural Communities) (P. K. Patel (Ed.), 1st ed.). P. K. Patel Publications.

Albrecht, D. E., Loveridge, S., Goetz, S., & Welborn, R. (Eds.). (2017). *Rural housing and economic development* (Illustrate, p. 1). Routledge Advances in Regional Economics, Science and Policy. In Rural Housing and Economic Development, Routledge.

Aldawoud, A., & Clark, R. (2008). Comparative analysis of energy performance between courtyard and atrium in buildings. *Energy and Buildings, 40*(3), 209–214. https://doi.org/10.1016/j.enbuild.2007.02.017

Alok, A. (2020). Problem of Poverty in India. *International Journal of Research and Review, 7*(1), 174–181.

Anonymous. (2016, March 7). Housing shortfall for EWS, LIG segments at 95%: CSE. The Economic Times.

Bose, C. V. A. (1999). Blueprint to march towards shelter for all by 2010 AD. In R. C. Choudhary & P. D. Prasad (Eds.), *Basic rural infrastructure and services for improved quality of life* (Vol. 2). National Institute of Rural Development.

Census. (2001a) Condition of Census houses used as residence and residence-cum-other use. In Census of India. Retrieved April 30, 2020.

Census. (2001b). Data highlights. Retrieved April 30, 2020.

Census. (2011a). Households by the condition of Census houses occupied by them. Census of India. Retrieved April 30, 2020, from http://censusindia.gov.in/2011census/Hlo-series/Hl-data/DDW-HH0101-0000.xls.

Census. (2011b). Houseless Households by Household Size. Retrieved April 30, 2020.

Census. (2011c). Houses, household amenities and assets data 2001–2011-Visualizing through maps. Retrieved April 30, 2020.

Census. (2011d). Rural-urban distribution of population: Census 2011 (Issue July). Retrieved April 30, 2020.

Chel, A., & Tiwari, G. N. (2009). Thermal performance and embodied energy analysis of a passive house-Case study of vault roof mud-house in India. *Applied Energy, 86*(10), 1956–1969. https://doi.org/10.1016/j.apenergy.2008.12.033

Dash, D. K. (2018, June 6). Majority of houses sanctioned under PMAY scheme in the name of women: PM Read more at: https://economictimes.indiatimes.com/wealth/personal-finance-news/majority-of-houses-sanctioned-under-pmay-scheme-in-the-name-of-women-pm/articleshow/64474213.cms?utm_s. The Economic Times. Retrieved June 04, 2020.

Dutt, C. (2008). Rural housing: Agenda for future action. In S. B. Verma (Ed.), *Rural infrastructure: Sanitation, housing, health care* (pp. 181–197). Sarup & Sons.

Ghosh, P., Alam, A., Ghosal, N., & Saha, D. (2021). A Geospatial Analysis of Temporary Housing Inequality among Socially Marginalized and Privileged Groups in India. Regional Science Policy & Practice.

Gillard, R., Datey, A., Sudmant, A., Oates. L., & Gouldson, A. (2018). Resilient and affordable housing for all: Lessons on house building from Kochi and Trivandrum, India. Coalition for Urban Transitions. London and Washington, DC. http://newclimateeconomy.net/content/citiesworking-papers.

Gore, M. M. (2016). Rational use of science & technology: Key to development of Rural India. *Kurukshetra A Journal on Rural Development Science & Technology for Rural India, 64*(09), 5–7.

Government of Andhra Pradesh. (2013). Performance Audit of Implementation of INDIRAMMA Housing Scheme. *Accessed, 03*(06), 2020.

Government of Karnataka. (n.d.). Rural Schemes. Rajiv Gandhi Housing Corporation Limited. Retrieved June 3, 2020, from https://ashraya.karnataka.gov.in/index.aspx.

Government of Kerala. (n.d.-a). Housing. Retrieved June 3, 2020, from https://kerala.gov.in/housing-department.

Government of Kerala. (n.d.-b). Suraksha Housing Scheme. Retrieved June 3, 2020, from http://www.kshb.kerala.gov.in/index.php?option=com_content&view=article&id=28&Itemid=58.

Government of Kerala. (n.d.-c). Tribal houses In Wayanad District. Retrieved June 3, 2020, from http://www.kshb.kerala.gov.in/index.php?option=com_content&view=article&id=14&Itemid=71.

Government of Kerala. (n.d.-d). Tsunami Housing. Retrieved June 3, 2020, from http://www.kshb.kerala.gov.in/index.php?option=com_content&view=article&id=27:tsunami-housing-scheme&catid=22:tsunami-housing-scheme&Itemid=38.

Government of Maharashtra. (n.d.). Environmental balanced prosperous village development scheme. Rural Development & Panchayat Raj Department. Retrieved June 3, 2020, from https://rdd.maharashtra.gov.in/en/Environment-Village-Development.

Government of Odisha. (n.d.). Rural Housing Odisha. Retrieved June 3, 2020, from https://rhodisha.gov.in/.

Government of Odisha. (2017). Guidelines of Biju Pucca Ghar Yojana. Retrieved June 3, 2020.

Government of Odisha. (2018a). Guidelines for Pucca Ghar Yojana (Mining). Retrieved June 3, 2020.

Government of Odisha. (2018b). Modified Guidelines of "Nirman Shramik Pucca Ghar Yojana(NSPGY)." Retrieved June 3, 2020.

Government of Tamil Nadu. (n.d.-a). Schemes: State Schemes: Chief Minister Solar Powered Green House Scheme (CMSPGHS). Retrieved June 3, 2020, from https://tnrd.gov.in/schemes/st_cmspghs.php.

Government of Tamil Nadu. (n.d.-b). Schemes: State Schemes: Clean Village Campaign. Retrieved June 3, 2020, from https://tnrd.gov.in/schemes/st_cvc.html.

Government of Tamil Nadu. (n.d.-c). Schemes: State Schemes: Rural Buildings Maintenance and Renovation Scheme (RBMRS). Retrieved June 3, 2020, from https://tnrd.gov.in/schemes/st_rbrms_13.php.

Government of Tamil Nadu. (n.d.-d). Schemes: State Schemes: Tamil Nadu Village Habitations Improvement (THAI) Scheme. Retrieved June 3, 2020, from https://tnrd.gov.in/schemes/st_thai.php.

Government of West Bengal. (n.d.). Scheme Details. Housing Department. Retrieved June 3, 2020, from https://www.wbhousing.gov.in/pages/display/7-scheme.

Hussain, M., & Yaseen, G. (2017). A study of loopholes in selection criteria of Indira Awaas Yojana (IAY) scheme in district Anantnag of Kashmir valley. *International Journal of Research in Economics and Social Sciences (IJRESS), 7*(6), 472–483.

Jain, A. K. (2014, December). Housing for all: Will the economically weaker sections of the society continue to live in slums and squatter settlements? Is it possible to redevelop existing areas and open up new avenues for social housing? Architecture-Time Space & People, 38–44.

Kang, J., Yoon, H., Kim, W., Kodur, V., Shin, Y., & Kim, H. (2016). Effect of wall thickness on thermal behaviors of RC walls under fire conditions. *International Journal of Concrete Structures and Materials, 10*(3), 19–31. https://doi.org/10.1007/s40069-016-0164-5

Khosla, R. (1983). Architecture of rural housing: Some issues in India. *Social Scientist, 11*(4), 56. https://doi.org/10.2307/3517024

Kumar, A. (2017). Policy imperatives for rural housing in India. *Shelter, 18*(2), 20–26.

Kumar, A., Deka, A., & Sinha, R. (2016). Rural housing in India: Status and policy challenges (Issue August 2017). https://doi.org/10.13140/RG.2.2.16047.43687.

Kumar, A. (2014a). Estimating rural housing shortage. *Economic and Political Weekly, XLIX*(26–27), 74–79.

Kumar, N. (2014b). Technological solution for sustainable rural housing by 2022. *International Journal of Combined Research & Development, 3*(3), 7–15.

Kumar, N., Prasad, R., Shankar, R., & Iyer, K. C. (2009). Technology transfer for rural housing an interpretive structural modeling approach. *Journal of Advances in Management Research, 6*(2), 188–205. https://doi.org/10.1108/09727980911007208
Kumar, S., Tiwari, G. N., & Bhagat, N. C. (1994). Amalgamation of traditional and modern cooling techniques in a passive solar house: A design analysis. *Energy Conversion and Management, 35*(8), 671–682. https://doi.org/10.1016/0196-8904(94)90050-7
Kumar, S. V., & Venkataramana, M. (2008). Rural housing: An overview. In S. B. Verma (Ed.), *Rural infrastructure: sanitation, housing, health care* (pp. 172–180). Sarup & Sons.
Liu, W., Spaargaren, G., Mol, A. P. J., Heerink, N., & Wang, C. (2014). Low carbon rural housing provision in China: Participation and decision making. *Journal of Rural Studies, 35*, 80–90. https://doi.org/10.1016/j.jrurstud.2014.04.005
Madhumathi, A., Vishnupriya, J., & Vignesh, S. (2014). Sustainability of traditional rural mud houses in Tamilnadu, India: An analysis related to thermal comfort. *Journal of Multidisciplinary Engineering Science and Technology (JMEST), 1*(5), 3159–3199.
Majumder, B. (2011). *Housing on the hills in India.* Concept Publishing Company.
Mathi, P. S., & Jerin Rose, G. (2020). Rural development through Pradhan Mantri Awaas Yojana (PMAY) in Kanyakumari District. *Studies in Indian Place Names (UGC Care Journal), 40*(18), 2298–2308.
MoRD. (2020). Annual report 2019–20. Ministry of Rural Development. https://rural.nic.in/sites/default/files/AnnualReport2019_20_English.pdf.
Pal, R., Aneja, N., & Nagpal, D. (2015). Inequality in housing and Basic Amenities in India. Munich Personal RePEc Archive, 61994.
Prasad, C. R., Dutt, G. S., Sathyanarayan, S. R. C., & Rao, V. K. (1979). Studies on sky-therm cooling. *Proceedings of the Indian Academy of Sciences, 2*(3), 339–356. https://doi.org/10.1007/BF02848931
PTI. (2010, November 1). AP Indiramma housing scheme exposing poor to unscrupulous MFIs. THE HINDU. Retrieved June 03, 2020.
Radha, K., & Mary, J. F. (2020). Progress and prospects of PMAY scheme in India. *The International Journal of Analytical and Experimental Modal Analysis, XII*(I), 1887–1895.
Rajeev, M. (2016, May 23). Govt. rechristens Indiramma as NTR Housing scheme. THE HINDU. Retrieved June 04, 2020.
Rao, P. S. (2019). Rural development schemes in India–A study. *IJRAR, 06*(1), 1072–1076.
RBI. (2012). Number and percentage of population below poverty line. Retrieved April 28, 2020, from https://www.rbi.org.in/scripts/PublicationsView.aspx?id=18621.
Rubenstein, M. (2012). Emissions from the Cement Industry. http://blogs.ei.columbia.edu/2012/05/09/emissions-fromthe-cement-industry/.
Sen, J. (2010). Janobasati Bhugol (Second). PaschimBango Rajyo Pustak Parshad.
Shah, K. (2000), Workshop 21, "Urban-Rural-Linkage-Infrastructure and Transport", July2000 (p. 3). www.Zef.de/gdialogue/program/papers_Day_3/ws-infrastructure-shah.pdf.
Sharma, J. (2017, October 5). Dream Project PMAY(G) of power-packed PM at snail's pace in Rajasthan. DNA. Retrieved June 02, 2020
Sharma, A. (2018a). Not enough takers for Pradhan Mantri Awas Yojana (Grameen): Kerala to Centre The Economic times. Retrieved June 03, 2020.
Sharma, A. (2018b, June 27). Scheme named after former PM Indira Gandhi to be closed. The Economic Times. Retrieved June 02, 2020.
Singh, M. (2008). Housing for rural poor. In S. B. Verma (Ed.), *Rural infrastructure: Sanitation, housing, health care* (pp. 162–171). Sarup & Sons.
Singh, S., Swaminathan, M., & Ramachandran, V. K. (2013). Housing shortages in Rural India. *Review of Agrarian Studies*, 54–72.
Sinha, B., & Biswas, I. (2008). Shelter: A big challenge for Rural India. *Accessed, 03*(06), 2020.
Stuff Reporter. (2016, May 18). Housing scheme for women. THE HINDU. Retrieved June 03, 2020.

Sundaram, K., & Tendulkar, S. D. (1995). On measuring shelter deprivation in India. *Indian Economic Review, 30*(2), 131–165.

Tewari, S. (2015, July 13). 75 percent of rural India survives on Rs 33 per day. India Today. Retrieved April 28, 2020

Tiwari, G. N., Upadhyay, M., & Rai, S. N. (1994). A comparison of passive cooling techniques. *Building and Environment, 29*(1), 21–31. https://doi.org/10.1016/0360-1323(94)90049-3

Tiwari, P. (2001). Energy efficiency and building construction in India. *Building and Environment, 36*(10), 1127–1135. https://doi.org/10.1016/S0360-1323(00)00056-1

Tiwari, P., & Rao, J. (2016). Housing policies in India. In N. Yoshino & M. Helble (Eds.), *The housing challenge in emerging Asia: Options and solutions* (pp. 262–302). Asian Development Bank Institute.

TNN. (2018, December 1). Laksham Veedu colonies undergo image makeover. THE TIMES OF INDIA. Retrieved June 03, 2020.

UNDP. (2016). A Compendium of Rural Housing Typologies Pahal-Volume-I. UNDP; PMAYG, MoRD. Retrieved April 27, 2020, from https://www.undp.org/content/dam/india/docs/pahal.pdf.

Warner, K. (2010). Global environmental change and migration: Governance challenges. *Global Environmental Change, 20*(3), 402–413.

Yang, X., Jiang, Y., Yang, M., & Shan, M. (2010). Energy and environment in Chinese rural housing: Current status and future perspective. *Frontiers of Energy and Power Engineering in China, 4*(1), 35–46. https://doi.org/10.1007/s11708-010-0001-5

Chapter 8
Sheltering Urban Poor: Looking for a New Approach

Dinabandhu Mondal and Joydeep Saha

Abstract Degree of urbanization varies spatiotemporally in India, and so also the levels of urban poverty. Taking examples of two states in India i.e. Bihar (less urbanized with a higher incidence of urban poverty) and Maharashtra (more urbanized with a lesser proportion of urban poverty), this paper aims to examine whether housing policies for the urban poor should only be geared towards slums, which are often considered as the spatial manifestation of urban poverty. Relying broadly on data drawn from Census of India (2011) and India Human Development Survey (2011–12), this paper attempts to put forward a point that town-level household asset data, along with the data on slums, could bring better insights in understanding the spatial manifestation of urban poverty, thereby making a case of policy attention and financial allocation not only for slums but for non-slum areas as well, both in large cities and small and medium towns. A critical review of recent urban housing programmes like IHSDP and PMAY HFA reveals that several associated issues like definition and identification of slums, individual's possession of BPL card and land ownership need to be readdressed, to provide a safe and secure shelter to inhabitants, living both in slums and non-slum areas across different size-categories of urban centres.

Keywords Urbanization · Urban Poverty · Asset · Slum · Housing

8.1 Introduction

India is experiencing rapid urbanization, making provisions of housing and associated amenities like potable water supply and standard sanitation a key challenge. Urban poor, in particular, needs access to such provisions, as their low income mostly generated out of employment in informal activities cannot sustain the higher cost of urban living. Therefore, it is imperative that the 'urban poor' has to be properly

D. Mondal
Centre for the Study of Regional Development, School of Social Sciences, Jawaharlal Nehru University, New Delhi 110067, India

J. Saha (✉)
Department of Geography, Bijoy Krishna Girls' College, Howrah-1, West Bengal, India

A. Kundu et al. (eds.), *Accessible Housing for South Asia*,
https://doi.org/10.1007/978-3-030-88881-7_8

identified and then provided with access to aforesaid amenities. Since, reliable and time-series data on income and expenditure of households at town level, further disaggregated at ward level is not available, social scientists often tend to look at the data on 'slums', which are often considered as the spatial manifestation of urban poverty. Usually, housing and associated amenities are provided by Urban Local Bodies to 'Notified' and 'Recognized' slums, but, as Census of India (2011), identifies slum clusters, with a minimum of 60 households or 300 population criterion, many smaller pockets inhabited by urban poor remains excluded. Hence, it would be better to look at ward-level asset data, along with slum data, so that poor household can be properly identified and better served, even if they live in non-slum areas. One should note that Census collects a wide range of data on household assets, specifically consumer durables, which may be regarded as a proxy indicator of household income or expenditure. Needless to mention, the column on 'none of the assets specified' or say assetless households indicate the poor. Given this context, this paper aims to explore the dynamics of urban poverty across various size classes of urban centres, with a special focus on dwelling structures in slums and non-slums and to assess the efficacy of existing housing policies for the urban poor. The structured plan of this article is as follows. Following the introduction, the second section provides very brief glimpses of approaches of urban poverty measurement in India. The third section looks at the latest scenario of urbanization and urban poverty in India, to select the study area. The fourth section includes data sources and methodologies. The fifth and the most lengthy section has a few sub-sections, dealing with an overview of urbanization processes and patterns, assetless households and housing structure and condition across size-classes of urban centres in the study area. The sixth section reviews planning perspectives related to housing for the poor, while the seventh one attempts to make comments on the efficacy of housing schemes. The last section ends with summarizing the findings and arguing for inclusive schemes for better policy implications.

8.2 Glimpses of Urban Poverty Measurement

In 1962, a working group of Planning Commission concluded that the minimum monthly expenditure for each household of five persons (for adult consumption units) should not be less than Rs. 125 for urban at 1960–61 prices. Subsequently, a Planning Commission Task Force (1979) took up the job of poverty estimation based on average calorie norms, i.e. 2100 Kcals per capita per day in urban areas. Lakdawala Committee (1993) incorporated both 'consumption expenditure' and 'nutritional intake' based approaches into the poverty estimation exercise and also contributed to state-specific urban poverty lines subjected to inter-state price differentials. Unlike previous estimates, the original National Sample Survey household consumer expenditure data were used by this committee without any adjustment to the National Accounts Statistics (NAS) consumption. In 2011, Tendulkar Committee adopted the officially measured urban poverty line of the year 2004–05 estimated through

Lakdawala methodology and converted this Uniform Recall Period consumption-based poverty line into an Mixed Recall Period-consumption based poverty line. As far as the 'nutritional intake' approach is concerned, a household's consumption pattern and preference change over time and space. Lakdawala Committee itself noted that 'this way of deriving poverty line (linked to the calorie norms) while being anchored in a norm of calorie requirement, does not seek to measure the nutritional status, and more specifically the incidence of malnourishment or undernourishment' (Planning Commission, 2014: 35). Conventionally established money-metric measures of poverty through the 'consumption expenditure' approach also fails to capture the multidimensional nature of poverty, a substantial number of studies have used 'asset index' based on household's access to housing amenities and possession of durable goods. A series of Demographic and Health Surveys (DHS), across different countries, have used this index as a proxy of 'household income'—often obtained from multiple sources with transient or fluctuating nature. 'Wealth Index' used in India's National Family Health Survey and District Level Household and Facility Survey is an example of this point.

8.3 Urbanization and Urban Poverty—State Level Scenario

The latest Census figures of 2011 show that around 31% of the population lives in urban centres in India. If one carefully looks at the level of urbanization across states in this country, a broad geographical pattern emerges out. Southern and south-western states have a higher level of urbanization, for example, Kerala (47.7%) and Maharashtra (45.2%). On the other hand, north-eastern (except Mizoram: 52%) and northern states have relatively lower proportions of people living in urban centres, with glaring examples of Himachal Pradesh (10%) and Arunachal Pradesh (22.9%). Central and eastern states mostly depict an average picture, and in fact, few states like Bihar (11.3%) and Odisha (16.7%) show very low levels of urbanization. This geographical pattern of urbanization does not vary much from earlier decades. Even in between 1981–91 and 1991–2001, western and south-western states had relatively higher levels of urbanization mainly due to the growth of the industrial and service sector and resultant non-agricultural employment. Eastern and central states also had low levels of urbanization, mainly because of persistent dependence on agriculture vis-à-vis very limited industrial development. The states located in the northern and north-eastern parts of India had low levels of urbanization because of hilly terrain. One should note that between 2001 and 2011, few northeastern states like Sikkim, Nagaland and Tripura have experienced a spectacular increase in percentages of people living in urban areas. This is happening probably due to the expansion of non-agricultural activities like tourism. On two extremes, Punjab and West Bengal, show an opposite picture. Punjab, getting massive support of agricultural as well as industrial development, has seen an increase in level of urbanization from 27.7% (1981) to 37.5% (2011). On contrary, West Bengal, during the same period, is slowly improving (from 26.5 to 31.9%), due to limited industrial expansion. In between

1981 and 2011, only Goa, Mizoram, Tamil Nadu, Kerala, Maharashtra, Gujarat, Karnataka, Punjab, Haryana and West Bengal have been the top and consistently urbanized states. Geographical patterns of urban poverty show a mixed picture, with two extremes of central and eastern India on one hand and southern and northeastern states on the other.

States located in central India like Madhya Pradesh (18.1% below poverty line) and eastern India like Bihar (34.5%), Jharkhand (27.4%) and Odisha (17.1%) show a grim picture. But in the northeastern part of India, where Nagaland, Manipur and Mizoram do not report any sort of urban poverty. Again down South, a state like Kerala, with very high levels of human development, only reports 7.7% urban dwellers below the poverty line.

The urban poverty scenario varies when one starts looking at both agriculturally as well as industrially developed states. Punjab, a state which has achieved milestones in terms of agricultural development, reports only 5% of urban residents below the poverty line. Gujarat and Maharashtra, two well-known industrialized states, have 12 and 14.2% urban poor people, respectively. Middle-rung states like West Bengal (12.1) and Tamil Nadu (12.9), exhibit resemblance to the all-India figure (i.e. 13.4%). A minute look at the bi-variate map (Fig. 8.1) showing both levels of urbanization (2011) and urban poverty (2011–12) together reveals interesting patterns. Bihar and Jharkhand, although remain at lower levels of urbanization, consist of higher proportions of urban poor. Hilly states of Himachal Pradesh and Arunachal Pradesh show lower levels of urbanization vis-à-vis lower urban poverty. Highly urbanized states like Kerala, Maharashtra and Tamil Nadu depict an average level of urban poverty. States like Rajasthan, Uttar Pradesh and Chhattisgarh exhibit moderately lower levels of urbanization vis-à-vis moderately higher levels of urban poverty. After looking at the state-level scenario of degree of urbanization, levels of urban poverty and percentage of the population living in slums, two states, namely Bihar and Maharashtra have been chosen, which show an opposite reality. Bihar with a less degree of urbanization (11.3%), 34.5% urban poor and 10.5% of slum population, stands opposite to Maharashtra (45.2% urban dwellers) having 14.2% urban poor and 23.3% slum population.

8.4 Database and Methodology

This paper is entirely based on secondary data sources. Data drawn from the Primary Census Abstract and Household Tables on housing structure and condition as well as household assets published by Census of India in 2011 are used. "Non-slum" statistics as stated in this paper implies total city minus slum areas. The Census of India database is used for this. Data on the urban poor is collected from India Human Development Survey (IHDS-II: 2011–12) which uses Tendulkar Poverty Line. Apart from this, the latest National Sample Survey Report on Slums is used as a supporting database. To strengthen the interpretations made out of the database, suitable statistical methods (descriptive measures like cross-tabulation and analytical measures

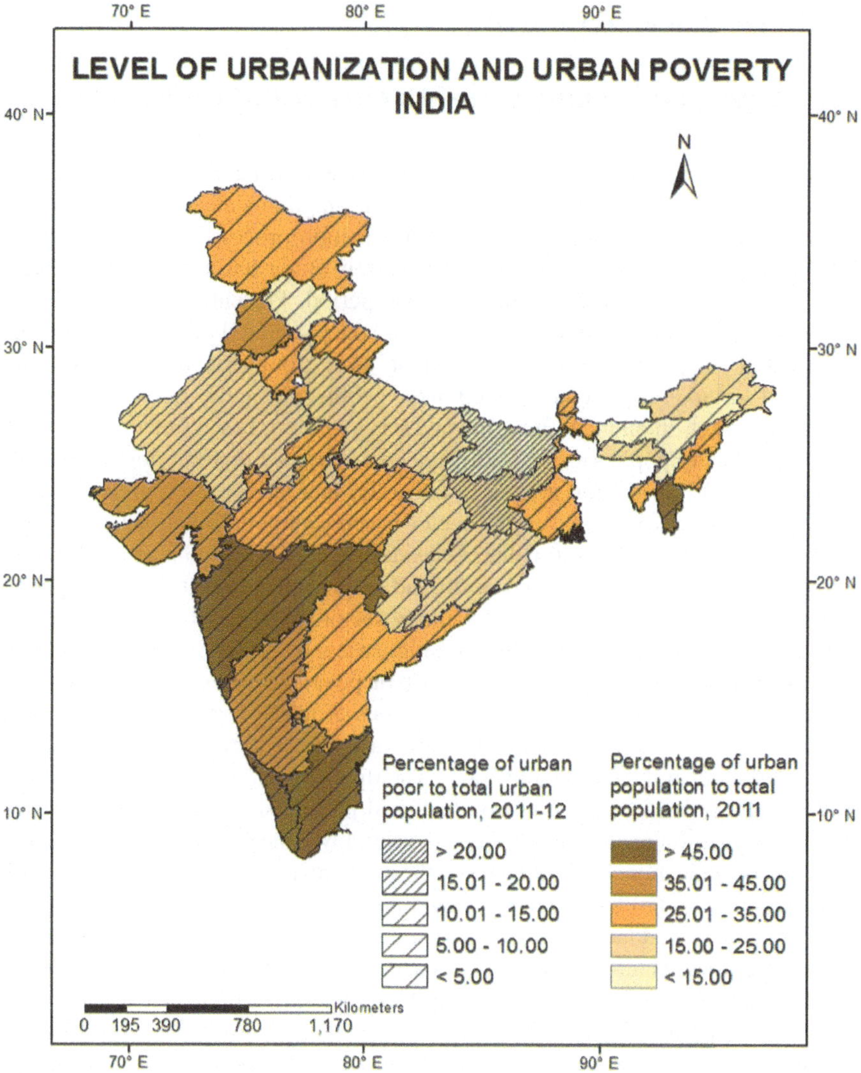

Fig. 8.1 Level of Urbanization and Urban Poverty, 2011–12

like Pearson's Product-Moment Correlation), as well as cartographic methods (like bivariate mapping through ArcGIS 10.2 version and Box-Plotting through SPSS 17.0 version), are applied here.

8.5 Discussion and Analysis

8.5.1 Bihar and Maharashtra—An Overview of Urbanization

Bihar has a rich history of urban settlement formation, starting from the establishment of *Mahajanapadas*[1] to capital cities by different kingdoms and a subsequent spurt of market and trade functions propelled urbanization processes (Kumar & Punia, 2014:35). But, in terms of population distribution, Bihar has always been more or less 'rural' in the pre and post-independence period. Presently, in few cities, the major share of the urban population has been concentrated. For example, the state capital Patna has grown up to a great extent, as it provides administrative, trade, market and service-sector related functions to people. Gaya, the second-largest city, also offers market, small manufacturing and service-sector based functions. Over the years, the growing popularity of Bodhgaya as a religious tourism hotspot has also contributed to the population growth of Gaya. By and large, agricultural prosperity and expansion of market and service-sector based economic functions have driven the progress of urbanization in Bihar. Considering the river of Ganga as a dividing line, one often tends to demarcate north and south Bihar, and it has been pointed out that persistent dependence on the primary sector of the economy and associated lower rates of growth have not unleashed higher levels of urbanization in north and central Bihar.[2] From Bihar, a large number of people out-migrate to more developed states like Maharashtra to avail themselves of job opportunities. Maharashtra is one of the most urbanized states in India and always reports a higher share of urban dwellers than the national average. The distribution of urban settlements and population in the state reports an asymmetrical pattern since 1961, where most of the urban population resides in few Class-I cities. Over the period, this asymmetrical pattern has become more intensified when the medium and small towns, though, large in number, are losing their share of population. Urbanization in pre-independence India has been shaped largely by colonialism and Maharashtra is no exception. The British government built port cities in coastal areas to handle trade relations and Bombay (now Mumbai) was one of them. Consequently, Mumbai still controls the financial, industrial and as well as entire urban scenario of Maharashtra and the surrounding region. After independence, the urban population in Maharashtra grew faster than the national average. Urban growth in India is generally attributed to the

[1] *Mahajanapadas* refer to 'large territorial units', total 16 in number, mostly came up in Gangetic valley during Century 600 BCE (see Roy and Lorge: *Chinese and Indian Warfare–From the Classical Age to 1870* Routledge: 2014:34).

[2] http://governancetoday.co.in/the-challenge-of-urbanizing-bihar, accessed on 14.12.2016—this web article highlights that the weak economic base, very limited efforts on poverty reduction strategies, legislative bottlenecks, governance hindrances are the root causes behind lower levels of urbanization in Bihar.

Table 8.1 Population distribution across size-classes of urban settlements, Bihar, 2011

	Size-class	Number of towns	Population	Towns (%)	Population (%)
Total	I	26	6,755,370	13.07	57.45
	II	28	1,829,820	14.07	15.56
	III	76	2,539,376	38.19	21.60
	IV	22	334,484	11.06	2.84
	V	38	264,276	19.10	2.25
	VI	9	34,690	4.52	0.30
	SUM	199	11,758,016	100	100
Slum	I	23	717,872	26.14	58.00
	II	20	227,053	22.73	18.35
	III	41	273,803	46.59	22.12
	IV	4	18,954	4.55	1.53
	V	0	0	0.00	0.00
	VI	0	0	0.00	0.00
	SUM	88	1,237,682	100	100

Source: Calculated from Primary Census Abstract, Census of India, 2011

rapid natural increase. In addition, Maharashtra has historically been the migrant-receiving state of other states as well as rural-urban intra-state migration which significantly contributes a lot to urban expansion in the state (Maharashtra State Development Report, 2002:279–310). Rapid industrialization in the post-independence era accelerates urban growth in Maharashtra as urbanization and industrialization are highly correlated. Industrial development attracts large-scale labour migration and also offers infrastructural facilities for further expansion of urban areas.

Bihar shows a lopsided urban system, where around 58% of residents concentrate in 26 Class-I cities, but only 15.6% reside in the almost same number of Class-II towns (Table 8.1). Class-III towns are also having a significant chunk of the urban population. But, Class-IV, V and VI towns, which means, small towns, have very low shares of urban population (only 6% in total). It seems that non-agricultural functions are somewhat stagnant in these small towns, and the industrial and service sector-led development has occurred in large cities only. Out of 199 urban settlements, 88 report slum population, and the size-class distribution of slum population is almost the same as general urban population. It suggests that poor people, spilling over from villages, have migrated into large cities for obtaining a livelihood, thereby increasing the proportion of slum dwellers. Such a process, operating all over the state for a certain period, has resulted in higher levels of urban poverty.

The urban system of Maharashtra reports a skewed distribution, where about 77% population resides in only 44 Class-I cities when 54 Class-II cities manage to get only 7% urban dwellers and Class-III (167) urban centres 10% (Table 8.2). However, in small towns i.e. Class-IV, V and VI only 7% of urbanites live. Therefore, it is observed that the urban scenario in the state is highly tilted towards large cities. Maharashtra

Table 8.2 Population distribution across size-classes of urban settlements, Maharashtra, 2011

	Size-class	Number of towns	Population	Towns (%)	Population (%)
Total	I	44	38,968,920	8.24	76.68
	II	54	3,747,639	10.11	7.37
	III	167	5,307,632	31.27	10.44
	IV	134	1,904,249	25.09	3.75
	V	109	786,358	20.41	1.55
	VI	26	103,461	4.87	0.20
	SUM	534	50,818,259	100.00	100.00
Slum	I	43	10,677,702	22.75	90.12
	II	43	712,513	22.75	6.01
	III	91	424,904	48.15	3.59
	IV	10	26,313	5.29	0.22
	V	2	6991	1.06	0.06
	VI	0	0	0.00	0.00
	SUM	189	11,848,423	100.00	100.00

Source: Calculated from Primary Census Abstract, Census of India, 2011

also records a higher chunk of slum dwellers as 23.3% urban population live in slums as per Census of India, 2011. 189 urban centres out of 534 in Maharashtra report slums. The size-class distribution of slums is also asymmetrical similar to the general urban population but the degree of asymmetry for slums is much larger, as about 90% of slum dwellers live in Class-I cities only. However, the medium and small urban centres exhibit a very low percentage of slum population.

8.5.2 Assetless Households

Household income or expenditure data is not available for urban centres. However, the Census of India gives a wide range of data on household assets like Radio, Television, Mobile, Computer, Bicycle, etc. Along with these assets, there is a column on 'none of the assets specified' or assetless households which indicate the poor. Here, in this paper, these assetless households are used as a proxy indicator of the urban poor. As far as assetless households are concerned, one can distinguish between slum and non-slum areas. In Class-I cities of Bihar (Fig. 8.2), the proportion of assetless households is quite higher, and in fact, non-slum areas have higher shares (64.5%) than slum areas (51.8%). On the other hand, in the case of Class-II and III towns, this gap between slum and non-slum areas is very less (around 2%). It indicates that people belonging to the assetless category are there in non-slum areas, maybe in very small clusters or even without a home. In the case of slum and non-slum areas of Maharashtra (Fig. 8.3), the difference is much less in Class-I cities, whereas it goes

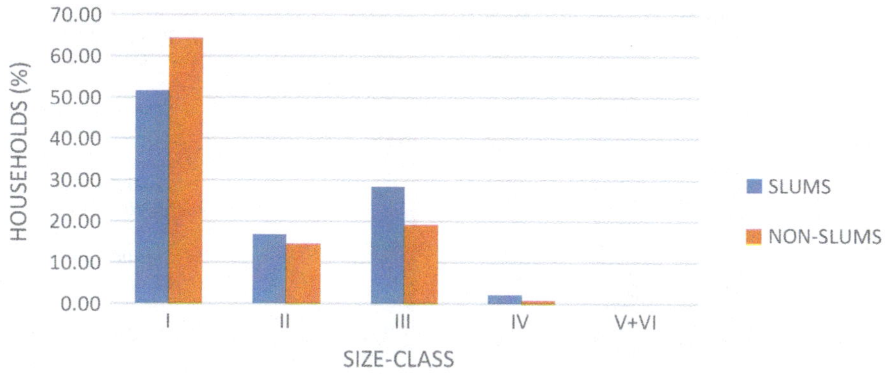

Fig. 8.2 Assetless Households in Slums and Non-Slums, Bihar, 2011 *Source Computed from Census of India, 2011*

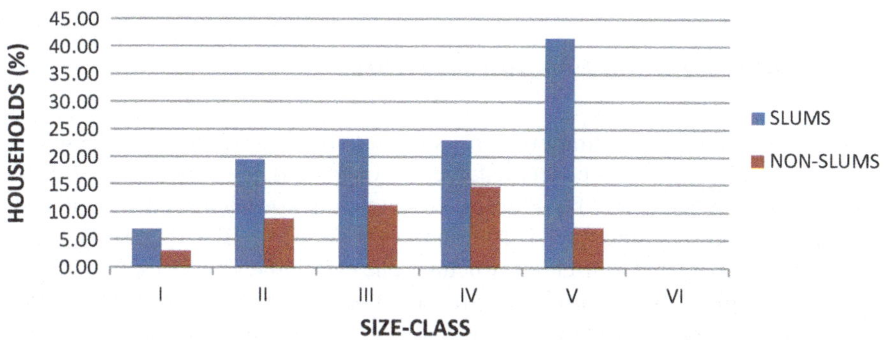

Fig. 8.3 Assetless Households in Slums and Non-Slums, Maharashtra, 2011 *Source Computed from Census of India, 2011*

very high for the medium and small urban centres. Class-I urban centres record 7% of slum households are assetless in slums while it is 3% for non-slum areas. Quite surprisingly, the higher shares of assetless households are observed in medium and small urban centres of Maharashtra, ranging from 19.6 to 41.7% in slums while in the non-slum areas, it varies from 7.3 to 14%. So, the size-class distribution suggests that the provision of affordable housing is a key challenge in large urban centres of Maharashtra and the non-poor people are compelled to live in slums as they cannot manage to access affordable housing.

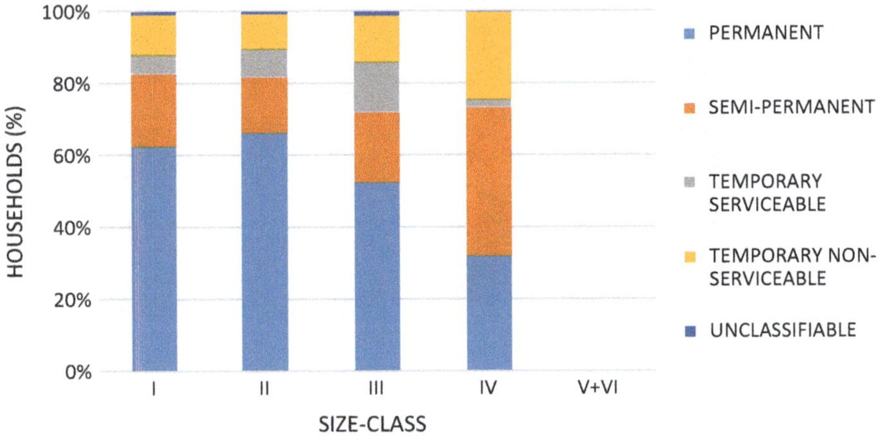

Fig. 8.4 Slum Housing Structure, Bihar, 2011. *Source Computed from Census of India, 2011*

8.5.3 Housing Condition and Structure

As far as the housing condition of census houses (both 'residence' and 'residence cum other use') in slums is concerned, there is only a slight gap between cities and smaller towns in Bihar. In Class-I cities, 9.7% of slum households are dilapidated,[3] whereas the corresponding value is 10.6 and 11.0% for Class-III and Class-IV towns. But, in the case of slum household structure, one can find a lot of variation. Class-I cities are having a lion's share of a permanent housing structure in slums, whereas this is exactly the opposite in the case of smaller towns. Semi-permanent slum houses show less variation among Class-I, II and III urban centres, however, this percentage is huge, i.e. almost double in Class-IV towns. Almost 26% of slum households are having a temporary structure in Class-III towns. In Class-IV towns, almost 25% of slum households are characterized by temporary non-serviceable structures. Even in Class-I and Class-II urban centres, this corresponding value is 11.2 and 9.8%, respectively (Fig. 8.4). This analysis suggests two things very clearly. Firstly, large urban centres with municipal corporations and municipalities have done well in the provisioning of housing to their slum residents. In slums of Class-I cities, as many as 51.8% households are assetless, but 62.6 and 20.1 slum households stay in permanent and semi-permanent structures respectively. Perhaps, better job opportunities with higher earnings have also slum dwellers to construct permanent/semi-permanent houses. Secondly, many residents of smaller urban centres do not have sufficient income to construct a permanent structure or to convert the temporary structure into permanent ones and coupled with the limited role of *Nagar Parishads*/Town Councils, housing has become a key challenge. In Class-IV towns, the share of

[3] Dilapidated census houses are those which show 'signs of decay or those breaking down and required major repairs and are far from being in condition that can be restored or repaired'.

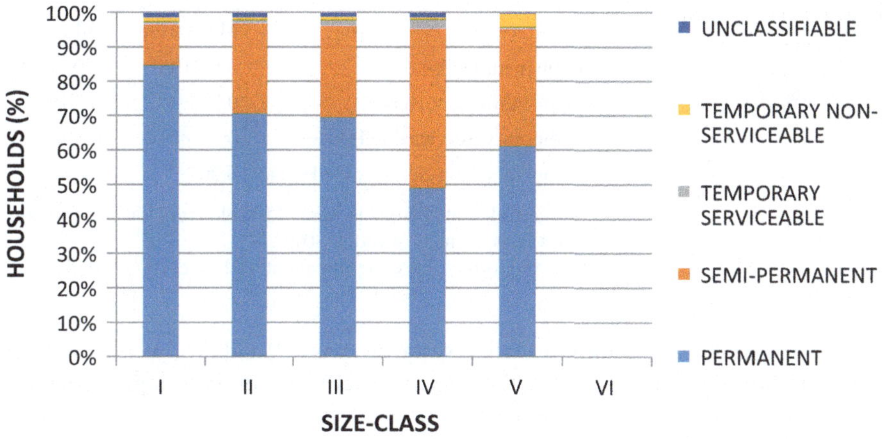

Fig. 8.5 Slum Housing Structure Maharashtra, 2011. *Source Computed from Census of India, 2011*

assetless households is not much (only 2.4%), but a sizeable chunk of households, having a range of assets, are still living in temporary non-serviceable structures.

In Maharashtra, the share of dilapidated households increase consistently from Class-I to Class-V urban centres, but here also the range is small, from 2.7 to 8.1%, respectively. In general, slums in Maharashtra represent a more or less average picture corresponding to India, as 803 out of 1000 notified and 484 out of 1000 non-notified slums report the majority of pucca houses (NSSO, 2013[4]). The slums in Class-I cities are in a better status where almost 85% and 12% of households reside in permanent and semi-permanent houses (Fig. 8.5), respectively. The share of assetless households in slums of Class-I cities reported as 7% only implies that the slum residents are in a position to access better shelter on their own through construction or renting. The cost of fetching and living in a house in non-slum areas of Maharashtra is so expensive that many residents cannot afford it and are thus compelled to live in slums.

Quite surprisingly, the shares of permanent housing in slums of Maharashtra decline consistently in medium and small urban centres. Class-II and III towns have 70% households with permanent houses when Class-IV manages to exhibit only 49 and 61% for Class-V. On the contrary, the semi-permanent houses are reported to have increased from larger to small urban centres, as does the assetless households. That suggests ULBs and parastatal bodies have neither done well to arrange permanent shelter for their residents nor have they been able to construct such houses. If one looks at the serviceable houses made of mud, un-burnt brick or wood and especially non-serviceable, i.e. houses made of grass, thatch, bamboo or polythene etc., which are not considered to be inhabitable, surprisingly cover a larger share in small urban settlements. Moreover, these temporary serviceable and non-serviceable housing are highly correlated with the assetless households, both of them have a larger chunk in

[4] NSSO does not conduct household surveys in slums, and that is why it reports information on majority of the houses present in slums.

Table 8.3 Correlation coefficients of housing structure with assetless households, 2011

	Maharashtra	Bihar
Permanent House	−0.419**	−0.582**
Semi-Permanent House	0.254**	0.203
Temporary Serviceable House	0.280**	0.590**
Temporary Non-Serviceable House	0.207**	0.045

Source Calculated from Household Tables on Housing Structure and Assets, Census of India, 2011
Note ** Correlation is significant at 0.01 level (two-tailed)

small towns in slums. In slums of Maharashtra, the class-III and IV towns show assetless households as high as 23.1 and 41.7%, respectively, similarly higher presence of the temporary houses as 3.2 and 4.5%.

To assess how the asset deprivation of the household is related to the accessible housing structure for the urban centres of Maharashtra and Bihar, Pearson's Product Moment Correlation has been used in this study. The percentage of assetless household and the percentage of household having permanent housing structure are negatively correlated for both the states as strong correlation coefficients are observed to be −0.419 and −0.582 for Maharashtra and Bihar respectively at a 0.01 level of significance (Table 8.3).

In the case of semi-permanent, temporary serviceable and temporary non-serviceable housing structure the relation with assetless household is found to be positive for both the states, though the degree of magnitude differs, as Maharashtra reports low to moderate figures (ranges 0.20–0.25) but highly statistically significant at 0.01 level of significance for all three categories. Likewise, for Bihar, the temporary serviceable housing is recorded strong significant relation (0.590) when the two other categories having low figure (0.203 and 0.045) and not significant. Therefore, one can infer that the assetless household is not only poor but also deprived to access affordable dwelling structure and are left to reside in houses made of temporary materials like mud, unburnt brick, wood, grass, thatch, bamboo, polythene, etc.

Here, using box plots, an attempt has been made to identify the urban centres, both in Maharashtra and Bihar, which are outliers in terms of the housing structure and asset deprivation, denoting that they are 'distant' from the main group of data set (Sidhwani, 2015). If one compares the average levels of housing structure and assetless households across these outlier urban centres with the overall condition of the state, a distinct pattern of discrepancy can be observed. Here is an attempt to understand how the selected housing structure, i.e. Permanent, Semi-Permanent, Temporary Serviceable and Temporary Non-Serviceable Houses and Assetless Households differ in these two states (Figs. 8.6 and 8.7).

The comparative analysis (Table 8.4 and Fig. 8.6 and 8.7) shows that there is a marked variation between the two states and the housing condition in Maharashtra is better compared to the state of Bihar. In Maharashtra, the share of household living in permanent and semi-permanent houses are quite larger (59.1 and 53.2%, respectively) as compared to Bihar (34.5% and 20.8%, respectively). However, 2

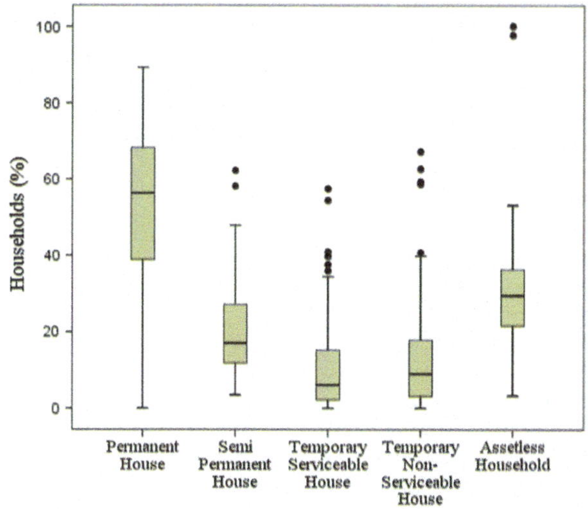

Fig. 8.6 Slum housing structure and asset deprivation, Bihar *Source Computed from Census of India, 2011*

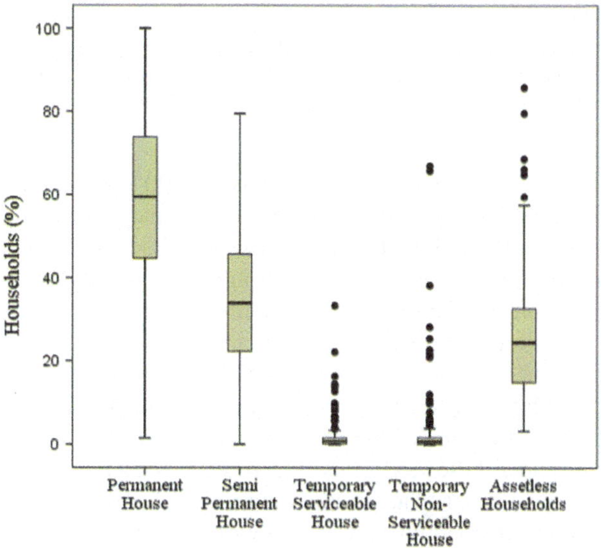

Fig. 8.7 Slum housing structure and asset deprivation, Maharashtra *Source Computed from Census of India, 2011*

Table 8.4 Comparison of outlier* Urban Centres with the Total Slum Condition

		Permanent house (%)	Semi-permanent house (%)	Temporary serviceable house (%)	Temporary non-serviceable house (%)	Assetless households (%)
Maharashtra	Number of Outlier Towns	0	0	20	22	6
	Outlier Urban Centre	0	0	10.5	18.0	70.7
	Total slum	59.1	34.5	1.9	2.9	25.6
Bihar	Number of Outlier Towns	0	2	6	5	2
	Outlier Urban Centre	0	60.2	44.3	57.7	98.9
	Total slum	53.2	20.8	11.5	13.8	30.7

Note * Outlier urban centres have been computed, as those with values greater than the thirrd quartile + 1.5* the interquartile range, or less than the first quartile –1.5* the interquartile range
Source: Computed from the Household Tables of Census of India, 2011

small outlier towns (Kasba with approximately 30,000 population and Murliganj 28,000 population, both Nagar Panchayats, having 36 and 21% permanent dwelling units, respectively) in Bihar did report as high as 60.2% semi-permanent houses that are because the coverage of permanent houses in these towns is lower. The shares of temporary serviceable and non-serviceable houses in Bihar which are in worst and uninhabitable condition, are observed as high as 11.5 and 13.8%, respectively, and for the outlier towns, it goes up to 44.3 and 57.7% in that order. Maharashtra, on the other hand, exhibits very low shares under these categories (1.9 and 2.9%), but what is a concern for the state is that there are many outlier urban centres that have very high figures under these categories. The presence of a large number of outliers in turn reflects a huge disparity across the towns in Maharashtra. It is discerned that most of these outliers are medium and small towns. Therefore, it is imperative to note that affordable housing is a serious challenge for this state. The assetless households for Maharashtra are reported as 25.6% while Bihar, not surprisingly, reports no less than 30.7% with two outlier towns more than 98.9%. But it is unexpected for these towns to have more than 98% of households living without any specified assets which pinpoints doubt about the credibility of the data.

8.5.4 *Housing and Slum Issues—Planning Perspectives in India*

Since the inception of five-year plans in India, Government has tried to address shelter issues inclusively. During first five-year plan (1951–56), in the housing policy, subsidies and soft loans were made provisional for low and middle-income group people. In the second five-year plan (1956–61), legal provisions of slum clearance and checking of new slums became important (Shaw, 1996). However, little efforts were present for improving slum conditions. The third five-year Plan (1961–66), assigned immediate priority to slum problems in six important cities like Delhi, Calcutta, Bombay, Madras, Kanpur and Ahmedabad. It also envisaged the formulation of minimum standards of housing facilities for urban residents (ibid.). The fourth five-year plan (1969–74) document recognized the importance of shelter in the context of increasing rural-urban migration. It advocated the formation of an apex cooperative society for disbursing loans. In April 1970, Housing and Urban Development Corporation (HUDCO) started working, to disburse loans and grants for the development of housing and provision of resources for technical assistance. Presently, it is spearheading this activity by granting loans for housing boards, development authorities, city improvement trusts, municipal corporations and Public Sector Undertakings. However, most of its grants were meant for larger cities to house industrial workers (ibid.). The sixth five-year plan (1980–85) can be regarded as a benchmark in urban planning. The plan document stated that HUDCO should emphasize loan disbursement to Economically Weaker Section (EWS) and Low Income Group (LIG) housing. HUDCO still claims to benefit EWS and LIG sections of society. Apart from this, the Integrated Development of Small and Medium Towns (IDSMT) scheme attempted to address housing and other infrastructural requirements in small and medium towns of the country. Seventh Plan document (1985–90) emphasized on Environmental Improvement of Slums (EIS) and the extension of IDSMT to towns having less than 3 lakh population. Eighth five-year plan document (1992–97) stated "the scope of the Environmental Improvement of Urban Slums (EIUS) is being widened to ensure that the EIUS, the Urban Basic Services Programme, the Nehru Rojgar Yojana (NRY) and the Scheme of Liberation of Scavengers form a coordinated whole". Assurance of providing tenurial rights and evolving feasible cost recovery mechanisms are important pre-conditions for the success of the programme in a longer-term context. Urban Basic Services for the Poor (UBSP) scheme was implemented to enable absolute improvement in the lives of slum dwellers and the formation of registered societies/cooperatives of slum dwellers at the community level. In 1996, National Slum Development Programme was launched. Centre provided fund based on urban slum population in states. It aimed at providing physical amenities (water supply, storm drainage, solid waste and garbage management, etc.), community centre (primary health check-up and education centre) as well as shelter up-gradation and construction. Ninth five-year plan document (1997–2002) estimated the up-gradation of 7 lakh slum housing units under NRY. This plan document reasserted its priority towards slum up-gradation in situ and environmental improvement of slums. Within the slum dwellers, people belonging to the BPL category got special attention in the document. National Housing Bank (NHB) was found instrumental in providing housing grants for slum dwellers. Apart from this, this plan document envisaged acceptance of international assistance for slum improvement. In 2001, Valmiki Ambedkar Awas Yojana (VAMBAY) was launched exclusively facilitating the construction and up-gradation of dwelling units of slum residents. It also tried to streamline the improvement of the living environment in slums. The financing pattern of this scheme was shared by the Union and state governments on 50:50 ratios. The eleventh five-year plan document (2007–12), however, observed that slum dwellers are largely deprived of basic urban facilities like water supply and sanitation. The existing scheme of Valmiki Ambedkar Awas Yojana (VAMBAY) and the discontinued scheme of the National Slum Development Programme (NSDP) have been subsumed into Integrated Housing and Slum Development Programme (IHSDP). It also aims at ameliorating the living conditions of slum dwellers as well as holistic slum development in terms of shelter and other physical amenities. The financing pattern of this scheme was shared by the Union and state governments on 80:20 ratios. An Approach to the twelfth five-year plan (2011) noted that urban poor still 'lack of access to basic amenities such as water supply, sanitation, health care, education, social security and decent housing' and are going through 'multiple deprivations and vulnerabilities'. It suggested that Government should use the land as leverage in the market and adopt the PPP model to 'improve the scope of affordable housing for weaker sections'.

A major finding from the above paragraphs is that despite various Government initiatives, a larger chunk of the urban poor is living in the squalor of slums and squatter settlements. They cannot access the basic physical amenities of urban life. One should note that there have only been mere changes in names and funding patterns for all these schemes, but the focus (i.e. amelioration of living environment in slums) and components (physical infrastructure like water supply and drainage system and social infrastructures like health centres and schools) have remained more or less same. Another thing appears clearly: The government is gradually moving towards slum-free cities to facilitate cities' beauty and economic growth or say to promote urban management. Scholars have argued that urban rich and poor live in a symbiotic socio-economic sphere and share common public space (Patel, 2011). However, urban poor have little to say in political decision-making. As evident in Delhi, preparation of the Commonwealth Games (2010) as part of a 'world-class city' has led to the demolition of several slums. Delhi's slum policy, being biased against poor residents, tends to create mushrooming of squatter settlements (Dupont, 2008).

8.5.5 Sheltering Urban Poor—(Only) in Slums and Cities?

One of the important findings, as emanating from the data analysis above, is the relatively poorer housing structure in slums belonging to small and medium towns of Bihar and Maharashtra. However, on the policy front, the Government has not focused much on these towns. Only the implementation of IDSMT, to a certain extent, helped such towns up to 2005. Although Jawaharlal Nehru Urban Renewal Mission (JNNURM), the major urban programme launched in 2005, had two attached schemes for Non-Mission small and medium towns: (1) Urban Infrastructure Development Scheme for Small and Medium Towns (UIDSSMT)—binding together the existing programmes of Integrated Development Scheme for Small and Medium Towns (IDSMT) and Accelerated Urban Water Supply Programme (AUWSP) and (2) Integrated Housing and Slum Development Programme (IHSDP)—subsumption of the existing programmes of Valmiki Ambedkar Awas Yojana (VAMBAY) and discontinued National Slum Development Programme (NSDP). Most of the projects undertaken in JNNURM were concentrated in relatively more developed states like Maharashtra, West Bengal, Tamil Nadu, Uttar Pradesh, Andhra Pradesh and Gujarat. Out of the total funding of JNNURM (approximately, Rs. 18,462 crores), Basic Service for the Urban Poor (BSUP) component received only 22.7% and Urban Infrastructure and Governance (UIG) received 77.3%. There was a systematic decline in the percentage of population covered by JNNURM with size-class of urban centres (Kundu & Samanta, 2011). Scholars have critically argued that through advocating neoliberal urban agenda, this scheme biased against poor people in several ways. Construction of flyovers and roads often relocated them from demolished slums, and some of the prescribed reforms like full cost recovery and user charge policies along with the participation of private agencies hit them hard. Another issue was the limited technical and financial capacity of small and medium towns (Chandran, 2010; Mahadevia, 2006; Mukhopadhay, 2006). IHSDP aimed to construct 'integrated' dwelling units with living rooms, kitchen and toilet together. But, due to cultural inhibitions, people might not prefer to use the toilet located under the same roof as attached to the living room. Rather, they might use it for storing utensils, furniture and other unused stuff. Rajiv Awas Yoana (RAY), launched in 2011, also aimed towards providing basic urban amenities to slum dwellers as well as finding suitable vacant land for rehabilitating them in affordable houses, finally to reach a goal of slum-free cities in the long run. It proposed that 22–25% of developed land of all housing projects should be earmarked for EWS/LIG category and reforms should come to enable the urban poor in possessing legal entitlement over dwelling space. This scheme envisaged states to make Plan of Action (POA) (including different stages like Identification of cities and slum pockets; spatial and non-spatial survey-based digital mapping) to formulate a model for slum development - both redevelopment of existing slums and relocation of slum dwellers in earmarked vacant land. This scheme included the development of own or rented houses in notified as well as non-notified slums. The basic objectives and conceptual framework of RAY say that it is no different from other slum development schemes. What is rather new and appreciable in RAY is its planned model, i.e. digitally mapped slums and database for chalking out slum redevelopment projects and provision of new land for slumdweller rehabilitation. However, one could also anticipate that the earmarking of vacant land for slum dwellers is meant for shifting poor people to a distant part of the city from the main focus of the socio-economic and political sphere. Apart from this, the policy of checking new slums also appear to be backed by elite politics-based notion of city cleaning and beautification. In a way, it reflects the exclusionary nature of large cities. Remote Sensing-GIS based approach of digital mapping of slums is also difficult to implement for municipal bodies of small and medium towns due to lack of technical manpower. These towns might have to depend on external agencies, which again might not thoroughly understand the socio-economic and ecological setting of these slums. Recently, Atal Mission for Rejuvenation and Urban Transformation (AMRUT) has also been implemented to facilitate infrastructure development in smaller cities, especially for basic service provisioning in areas of water supply, sewerage and transportation.

Another concern is the sole focus on 'slums' for benefitting the urban poor. The definition of 'slums' is itself questionable. As per Census of India, 'A Slum, for Census, has been defined as residential areas where dwellings are unfit for human habitation by reasons of dilapidation, overcrowding, faulty arrangements and design of such buildings, narrowness or faulty arrangement of the street, lack of ventilation, light, or sanitation facilities or any combination of these factors which are detrimental to the safety and health'. Census of India categorizes slums into three categories—notified, recognized and identified. The first category is 'notified' by state/local administration through legal acts; the second one is also 'recognized but not formally notified' by these bodies; and the last category is defined as 'A compact area of at least 300 population or about 60–70 households of poorly built congested tenements, in the unhygienic environment usually with inadequate infrastructure and lacking in proper sanitary and drinking water facilities'. However, NSSO considers the slum cluster cut-off as 20 or more households. It has been argued that with increasing events of slum eviction cycles and breakdown of large slums into smaller clusters in Indian cities, Census definition lacks inclusive nature (Bhan & Jana, 2013). Even non-slum areas can have poor and vulnerable people residing in small clusters, and that is why ward-level data on asset-less households may come in handy for the policymakers.

8.5.6 *Affordable Housing*

For the past few decades, with the increasing concentration of economic and commercial activities, Indian cities are experiencing rapid economic as well as population growth. But the supply of housing stock has not increased concomitantly with the pace of urbanization which results in a huge shortage of affordable housing in cities. Housing is a basic need for a human being. 'Affordable Housing' is a relative term and has different meanings in different contexts simply because the dynamics of the country vary with spaces and what may be affordable to one may not be to others. The Task Force of the Ministry of Housing and Urban Poverty Alleviation (MoHUA, GoI: 2008) defines based on income level, size of dwelling and Rent or EMI. Based on these three parameters, the standard norms vary across the sections of the society, from the Economically Weaker Section (EWS) to Higher Income Group (HIG). The housing shortage is now a key challenge in urban India. In states like Maharashtra, the problem is more alarming and pronounced. Increasing urbanization coupled with continuous in-migration from other states as well as the rural-urban trend accelerates the housing crisis especially in large cities like Mumbai etc. As Gandhi (2012) has observed, formal housing in Mumbai is so expensive that only 5–6% of the city's population can afford a house. So it is evident that the migrants, although somehow manage to get a job in informal or other sectors, income level cannot allow them to access formal housing rather they are left to the slums. Thus, the failure of formal housing markets to provide low-cost housing has led to the emergence of slums as informal market solutions for many poor households (Baker & McClain, 2009; Gandhi, 2012). This problem is more serious, given the fact that 75% of the estimated slums in Maharashtra are 'non-notified' (NSSO, 2012), which often lack attention from the policymakers, ULBs and parastatal bodies. The Central Government acknowledges the significance of housing problem in the country and has initiated various schemes and policies over time to address these issue of affordable housing and slums but have failed to achieve goals.

Very recently, Ministry of Housing and Urban Affairs (MoHUA) has attempted to implement *Pradhan Mantri Awas Yojana—Housing for All* (Urban) scheme, in which 'affordable housing project' i.e. a housing project where 35% of houses are constructed for people belonging to Economically Weaker Section (EWS), whose annual income is less than 3 lakhs of rupees. It should be kept in mind that although this scheme aims to cover all Statutory Towns, the 'focus' will be again on 500 Class-I cities. It should be applauded that as it plans to cover 'slum'" as well as 'non-slum' areas as well.

8.6 Conclusion

Mainly due to physiographic heterogeneity and differential levels of non-agricultural employment, the degree of urbanization varies across states, and it is not possible to draw its one-to-one correlation with levels of urban poverty. This paper attempts to focus on housing structure and condition in the context of assetlessness to identify genuine 'poor' at the ward level, both in 'slum' and 'non-slum' areas, who should be benefitted through urban housing schemes promoted by the government. In the context of Niti Aayog's avowed principle of 'cooperative federalism' in eliminating poverty, urban housing policies need to be more specifically geared towards the need of the respective states. While Maharashtra requires to develop affordable houses to sieve out middle-class urban dwellers from slums, Bihar should not only focus on building houses for slum dwellers in large urban centres but should also consider large numbers of poor people living in non-slum areas. As Maharashtra continues to act as a magnet for a huge number of job-seekers from other states, provisioning shelter for the existing poor and vulnerable population as well as making further shelter arrangements for new and temporary migrants should remain as a key policy agenda. It should also be noted that 'integrated housing' with provisions of living room-kitchen-toilet needs to re-emerge in urban housing policy ambit, and it requires proper implementation through continued efforts. While dovetailing recently floated schemes of Smart City Mission along with Swachh Bharat, an individual 'integrated house' and 'integrated housing cluster' must have a combined provision of living rooms-kitchen with clean fuel use-toilet-store rooms-garbage disposal space. Another policy agenda is sustained infrastructural development of small and medium towns, through AMRUT, so that they can offer diversified as well as specialized economic opportunities to people.

Acknowledgement An earlier version of this book chapter was presented at the National Conference on 'Making Cities Resilient: Post Habitat III', organized by Department of Geography, Shaheed Bhagat Singh College, University of Delhi, 3-4 February, 2017. We are thankful to the participants for their comments.

References

Baker, J. L. & McClain, K. (2009). Private sector initiatives in slum upgrading. World Bank, Working paper, 48928. Retrieved from https://documents1.worldbank.org/curated/en/926321468158372627/pdf/489280NWP0Box338934B01PUBLIC10UP18.pdf.

Bhan, G., & Jana, A. (2013). Of slums or poverty: Notes of caution from Census 2011. *Economic and Political Weekly, 48*(18), 13–16.

Chandran, D. (2010). An appraisal of Jawaharlal Nehru National Urban Renewal Mission (JNNURM): Case Studies of Thiruvananthapuram and Kochi. M.Phil Dissertation submitted in Centre for the Study of Regional Development, Jawaharlal Nehru University, New Delhi, India.

Dupont, V. (2008). Slum demolitions in Delhi since the 1990s: An appraisal. *Economic and Political Weekly, 43*(28), 79–87.

Gandhi, S. (2012). Economics of affordable housing in Indian cities: The case of Mumbai. *Environment and Urbanization Asia, 3*(1), 221–235.

Kumar, R., & Punia, M. (2014). Urbanisation in Bihar: Need to break stigma. *Journal of Asian Network for GIS-Based Historical Studies, 2*, 32–42.

Kundu, D., & Samanta, D. (2011). Redefining the inclusive urban agenda in India. *Economic and Political Weekly, 46*(5), 55–63.

Mahadevia, D. (2006). NURM and the poor in globalising mega cities. *Economic and Political Weekly, 41*(31), 3399–3403.

Ministry of Housing, & Urban Poverty Alleviation. (2008). Report of the High Level Task Force on Affordable Housing for All. Retrieved from http://www.naredco.in/pdfs/report-high-level-task.pdf.

Mukhopadhay, P. (2006). Whither urban renewal? *Economic and Political Weekly, 41*(10), 879–884.

National Sample Survey Organisation (2013). *Key Indicators of Urban Slums in India*, 69th Round July-December 2012. Retrieved from http://www.icssrdataservice.in/datarepository/index.php/catalog/94/related_materials.

Patel, S. B. (2011). Inclusionary housing. *Economic and Political Weekly, 46*(43), 13–14.

Planning Commission of India. (2014). *Report of the expert group to review the methodology for measurement of poverty.* Retrieved from https://niti.gov.in/planningcommission.gov.in/docs/reports/genrep/pov_rep0707.pdf.

Shaw, A. (1996). urban policy in post-independent India: An appraisal. *Economic and Political Weekly, 31*(4), 224–228.

Sidhwani, P. (2015). Spatial inequality in big Indian cities. *Economic & Political Weekly, 50*(22), 55–62.

Chapter 9
A Detailed Study on the Mud-Bonded Masonry Houses in Nepal Both Before and After 2015 Gorkha Earthquake

Binod Khadka

Abstract Being a developing country with the majority of rural settlements followed by historic settlements, Nepal has a large percentage of old and new unreinforced mud-bonded masonry (URMM) houses. Along with this fact, Nepal has a bitter reality of lying in a highly earthquake-prone region, which has led to huge structural damages (especially URMM houses) in each earthquake (including the recent 2015 Gorkha earthquake). This reveals the poor construction technique adopted in Nepal and shows the immediate need to make suitable improvements in the structural characteristics of URMM houses. However, the immediate introduction and implementation of new methodology and technology for sustainable improvement of structural characteristics might not be fruitful/effective until and unless the ways of the past are well understood. Hence, analysing the past and current ongoing construction technology is always necessary for future intervention to any structure. So, with an intention to present the entire common construction techniques (both good and bad) of mud-bonded masonry (MM) houses and contribute to its further improvement, a detailed reconnaissance survey (includes inspection of nearly 36,000 old and new MM houses), active group discussions and questionnaires with engineers, local people and masons were carried out in different geographical regions of Nepal for nearly 9 years (since early 2012). It was observed that the majority of the old houses (constructed before the 2015 earthquake) were lacking seismic consideration and had a huge variation in local construction techniques (influenced by the availability of building materials, housing purpose, economic condition, locality construction practices, climatic condition, caste system, etc.). But after the 2015 Gorkha earthquake, such variations were drastically reduced, and comparatively, there was an improvement in construction practices. The overall obtained findings (present and past status of MM houses, good and bad/deficiencies construction techniques, common structural elements, etc.) are expressed through the data and further verified using good quality pictures as evidence which has been the highlighting part of this paper and contributed to developing a clear concept for all the readers. This paper also presents the recommendation based on the management of old MM houses and improvements to be done in construction practices. (The author wants to thank his family, colleagues

B. Khadka (✉)
Government of Nepal, National Reconstruction Authority, MOUD, DLPIU, Okhaldhunga, Nepal, India

A. Kundu et al. (eds.), *Accessible Housing for South Asia*,
https://doi.org/10.1007/978-3-030-88881-7_9

and the entire technical staff of NRA, DLPIU, Okhaldhunga, for their support and encouragement during the overall detailed investigating phases).

Keywords Mud-bonded masonryhouses · Construction techniques · Deficiencies · 2015 Gorkha earthquake · Reconnaissance survey · Recommendations · Housing types

9.1 Introduction

Nepal is a beautiful landlocked country with great topographical and cultural diversity. Apart from its beauties, Nepal falls under a high seismic zone area and has a long history of earthquake hazards. During each earthquake, Nepal has to bear a massive loss in structural damage and casualties. Under such a risky scenario, being a developing country, most rural settlements and old historic cities of Nepal has a huge percentage (more than 40%) of URMM houses (Khadka & Shakya, 2021; Khadka, 2020; Khadka & Jiang, 2019; Khadka & Shakya, 2016). Inspite of the weak strength of mud mortar and brittle nature of URMM structure, they are found to be significant construction in Nepal for a long time and are still in practice in large numbers due to poverty, ignorance poor transportation facility, religious or cultural aspects and shortage in skilled manpower (Khadka & Shakya, 2021; Khadka, 2020; Khadka & Jiang, 2019; Khadka & Shakya, 2016).

Nepal consists of 83% rural population, and about 90% of total houses in Nepal are non-engineered construction (Central Bureau of Statistics, 2012). The significant number of mud masonry houses before the 2015 earthquake were unreinforced without any seismic consideration like lacking seismic bands, haphazard modification of house and increase in the storey number over old structure, mixed building materials, no periodic repair and maintenance and so on (Khadka & Shakya, 2021; Khadka, 2020; Khadka & Jiang, 2019; Khadka & Shakya, 2016). The majority of available old masonry houses (especially in historic cities) were constructed before the enforcement of the building code. Lack of awareness of the house-owner and local masons, and ignorance of implementation authority towards effective implementation of safe, economic earthquake–resistant structure, has been a significant factor in continuing non-engineered construction practices. In addition, the detailed damage assessment during the 7.8 Mw 2015 Gorkha earthquake showed that except for some severe but localized damages in Reinforced concrete (RC) buildings, massive structural damages were mainly concentrated in masonry structures (Khadka & Shakya, 2021; Khadka, 2020; Khadka & Jiang, 2019; Khadka & Shakya, 2016). This miserable scenario further confirmed the trend of poor construction and maintenance practices observed in Nepal's local masonry houses. Realizing this, the Government of Nepal (GoN) launched the National Reconstruction project under National Reconstruction Authority (NRA) in all 31 earthquake-affected districts targeting to improve local earthquake-resistant construction techniques. This project hired a large number of technical staff (Engineer, Sub-Engineer, and Assist. Sub-Engineer) in all earthquake-affected regions to efficiently proceed the reconstruction works and also conducted several earthquake-resistant construction training programs for both technical staff and local masons. Along with the NRA, several national and international non-governmental organizations (I/NGO) are involved in supporting this reconstruction project. Although the building materials like stone, brick, mud, timbers were quite similar to previous houses but after the 2015 earthquake, there is some drastic improvement in the construction practices like installation of seismic bands, interconnecting the wall wythes, use of light roofing materials, reducing the floor storey number, and so on.

It is always necessary to understand the past structure so that we can learn both good and bad construction practices from it and successfully implement it with necessary improvements required in our upcoming structures. In Nepal's case, many studies have been made related to the historical monuments, but few studies have been made about the residential MM buildings. So, with an intention to express Nepal's overall local MM houses in detail, this paper has mainly focused on the construction practices and made a comparative study between previous (before the 2015 earthquake) and current new MM housing. Along with this, some recommendations (based on the actual housing scenario, discussion with local people, masons, and engineers) are provided for further improvement in old existing and present new MM houses. This study acts as helpful (informative) material to establish baseline information for all groups of people about Nepal's local MM residential houses.

9.2 Seismicity of Nepal and the Recent 2015 Gorkha Earthquake

The entire territory of Nepal lies in a highly seismic hazard zone and is ranked as the 11th most earthquake-prone country in the world (UNDP, 2009) due to its location at the boundary of subduction between the Indian and Tibetan plate (arc length). Nepal has much evidence of the historical earthquake. The first human recorded was in 1255 A.D. of around 7.7 M_w and other recent recorded earthquakes like 1934's 8.1 M_w, 1980's 6.5 M_w, 1988's 6.6 M_w, 2011's 6.9 M_w, and 2015's 7.8M_w. The comprehensive study of all these recent and historic major earthquakes shows that the casualties were caused mainly due to the collapse of structures and those structures were mostly URMM houses.

On recent 25th April 2015, at 11:56 am local time, a devastating 7.8M_w earthquake hits Nepal (with a focal depth $\approx$ 8.2 km $\pm$ 2.9 km and epicentre $\approx$ 80 km NW from Kathmandu) (USGS, 2015), which affected 31 districts, killed around 8,896 people, 198 missing, 22,302 seriously injured, and rendered millions of people homeless (NPC, 2015; MoHA, 2015). The main shock was followed by 553 earthquakes of local magnitude greater than 4.0 within the first 45 days (Adhikari et al., 2015) among which 7.3M_w on 12th May was the major aftershock recorded.

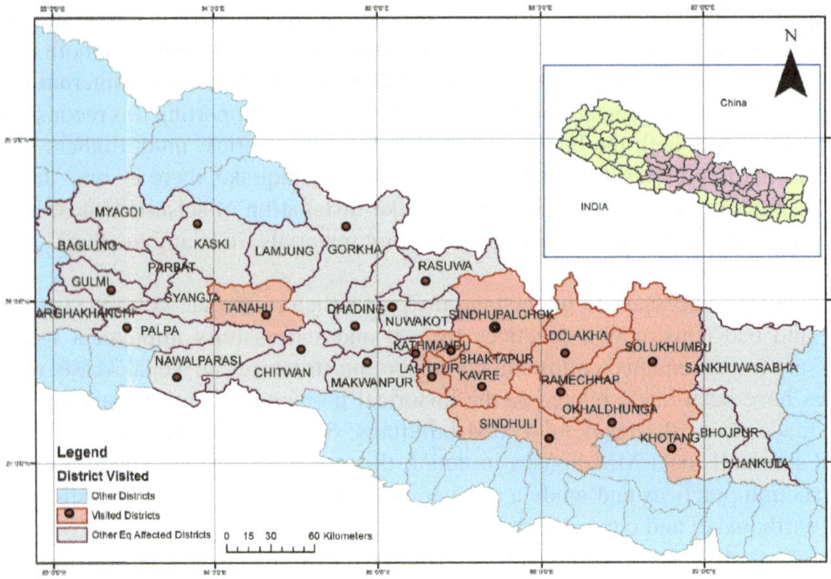

Fig. 9.1 Places visited before and after the 2015 Gorkha earthquake, Nepal

9.3 Methodology

Considering the necessity of detailed study on MM houses of Nepal, a reconnaissance survey was conducted visiting the majority of geographical regions (Himalayan, Hilly, and Terai) of Nepal, including several earthquake-affected districts like Kathmandu, Bhaktapur, Lalitpur, Kavrepalanchowk, Dolakha, Sindhupalchowk, Tanahu, Sindhuli, Ramechhap, Okhaldhunga, Solukhumbhu, Khotang, Rasuwa, Nuwakot, Makwanpur, Dhading, Gorkha, as shown in Fig. 9.1. This study was conducted from early 2012 till August 2021, which includes nearly 18,000 new MM houses and 17,500 old MM houses. In this chapter, the houses constructed before and after the 2015 earthquake are considered as old and new MM houses. In addition to a detailed reconnaissance survey, practical group discussions and questionnaires with engineers, local people, and masons were also conducted.

9.4 Mud-Bonded Masonry (MM) Houses in Nepal

In context to Nepal (accommodating a large percentage of rural settlements), MM houses are the popular housing type since long periods of time, which illustrates the religious or cultural aspects, traditional architecture, and construction practices adopted by our ancestors using locally available materials like mud, stone, brick, timber, bamboo, thatch, etc. According to the 2011 National Population and Housing

Census, mud-bonded brick/stone masonry buildings were the most common in all geographical regions of Nepal, i.e. 44.2% (Central Bureau of Statistics, 2012). Similarly, a recent study shows that more than 90% of the newly constructed houses in rural settlements are MM houses (Khadka, 2020). The selection of such houses in large proportion in the past and even now is influenced by several factors like the poor economic condition of people, lack of transportation facilities, unskilled manpower, unavailability of modern materials, etc.

9.4.1 Materials

In Nepal, MM houses commonly use the following materials for several structural and non-structural components:

- Stone or brick: These materials are used as wall material and foundation. Bricks (sun-dried and burnt bricks) are common in historic cities of Kathmandu valley, i.e. Kathmandu, Bhaktapur, and Lalitpur, but in the case of remote Hilly and Himalayan regions, more than 98% uses locally available stone (in the form of boulders, rubble, dressed and semi-dressed stone) without being specific towards standard size and quality. Generally, the main varieties of stone used in Nepal are limestone, sandstone, dolomite, granite, quartzite, and marble (Bonapace & Sestini, 2003). Although sun-dried bricks were found to be used in old houses but currently, due to their low strength and moisture susceptibility, it is not used.
- Mud: As mud is commonly available, so it is used as a mortar for binding the masonry units (mortar joints) and also as a plaster, flooring, and roofing material. It was observed that the majority of the local houses in the rural settlement were not caring about the quality of the mud and simply using the soil available near their house periphery. Apart from this, in the high altitude regions, the majority of the houses followed dry masonry (without any mud mortar) due to the lack of sufficient suitable quantity of suitable mud mortar.
- Timber and bamboo: These materials are used as a structural members for flexible floor and roof structures, openings (only timbers used), partition walls. After the 2015 earthquake, timber (some houses also adopted bamboo) is used as seismic bands and posts. Due to a lack of good quality timber, the majority of new houses were found to be using softwood without treatment, which has created a high risk of fast deterioration of timber.
- Corrugated Galvanised Iron (C.G.I.) sheet, roof clay tiles, stone tiles, and thatch: These materials were found to be used as a roof covering material in the different geographical regions as per the material availability, climatic condition, and economic condition of people. But currently, after the 2015 earthquake, majority of the local people are conscious of the overburden in structure and have replaced the heavy roofing material with a C.G.I sheet.
- Reinforced concrete (RC): Before the earthquake, only some brick masonry houses in the old settlement like Kathmandu valley adopted RC in the form of a

slab. But now (after the 2015 earthquake), RC is commonly used as seismic bands. Generally, concrete mix proportion of 1:2:4 or 1:1.5:3 (cement: sand: gravel) and steel rebar of size 6 mm, 8 mm, 10 mm, and 12 mm are commonly found to be adopted.

It was observed that the majority of old MM houses used these materials without seismic consideration, but currently, after the 2015 Gorkha earthquake, there is a drastic improvement in its use.

9.4.2 Common Types of Mud-Bonded Masonry Houses and Their Present Condition

Nepal mainly consists of three regions, i.e. the Hilly, Himalayan, and Terai region. As this study primarily focuses on local residential MM houses, so it was observed that the housing types and construction techniques were hugely varying in different regions before the 2015 earthquake, which made this sector a quite vague topic to study. The construction techniques and housing types were highly influenced by the availability of building materials, housing purpose, locality construction practices, climatic condition, caste system, economic condition, client and mason self-design, etc.

Generally, 3–5 storey unreinforced mud-bonded brick masonry houses with varying types were observed in the old settlement of Kathmandu valley, as shown in Fig. 9.2a. In addition, row housing and common sharing of walls, floor and roof structures were common in old settlements, as shown in Figs. 9.4b and c. Similarly, in rural regions, 2–5 storey unreinforced mud-bonded stone masonry houses with large attic storage were observed, as shown in Fig. 9.2. Considering the overall housing scenario before the 2015 earthquake, a very low percentage (less than 10%) considered a seismic-resistant feature, which resulted in massive damages in URMM houses during the earthquake, as shown in Figs. 9.3 and 9.4. But there are still some old existing URMM houses with some partial damages in the old settlement of Kathmandu valley and rural settlement, which needs immediate retrofitting (see Figs. 9.2a, 9.4). The majority of the old partial damaged MM houses in old settlement are simply provided with inclined support (normal type of raking shores), as shown in Fig. 9.4d. As there are frequent earthquakes and aftershocks in Nepal, so such valuable historic houses might further damage or collapse soon, causing more casualties if not retrofitted in time. Apart from this, some houses were in a vulnerable state (excess damage) after the 2015 earthquake and needed immediate dismantling and reconstruction, as shown in Figs. 9.2a, 9.4a and b.

But comparatively, after the 2015 earthquake, most houses were constructed based on NRA's guidance under the supervision of engineers, due to which there was an improvement in construction techniques and less variation were observed in construction techniques and housing types (see Fig. 9.5). Apart from this, there were some new masonry houses which were self-modified by the client and local masons without

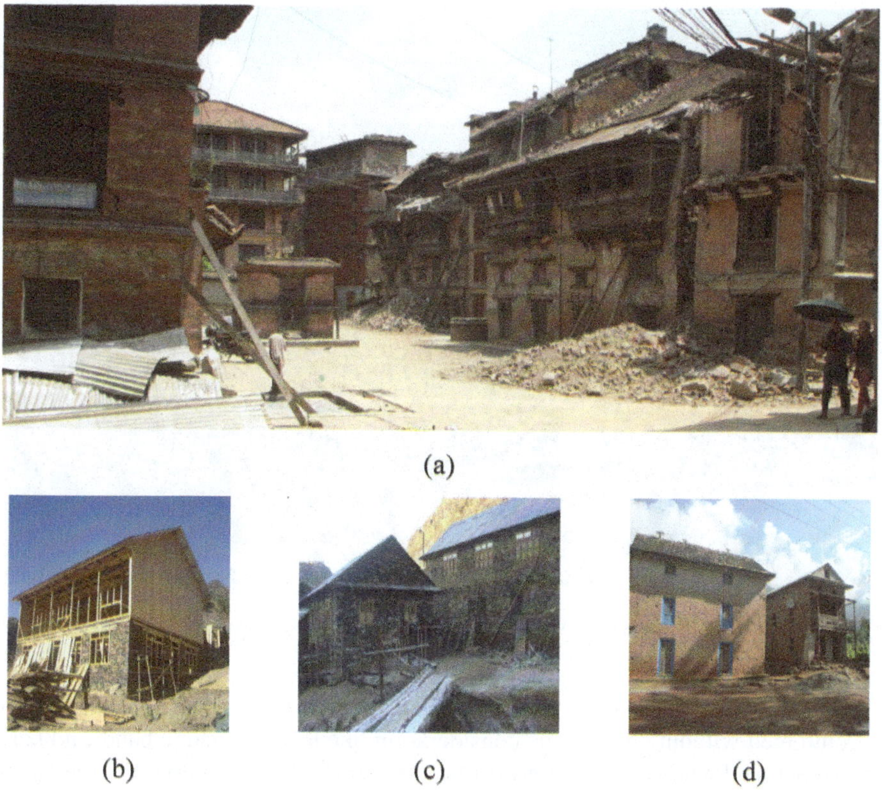

Fig. 9.2 Example of some common types of Mud-Bonded Masonry houses observed before the 2015 earthquake in different regions of Nepal: **a** brick masonry houses (Bhaktapur); **b** hybrid stone masonry houses (Dolakha); **c** dry stone masonry house (Dolakha); **d** stone masonry house with and without mud plaster (Sindhuli)

consulting Engineers like adding RC column in four corners of the masonry houses (see Fig. 9.5d), lower storey masonry and upper storey using light materials such as C.G.I sheet with timber framing (see Fig. 9.5e and f).

9.4.3 Common Structural Elements and Their Construction Techniques

This section discusses the common structural components of local residential MM houses like foundation, wall system, floor system, roof system, seismic bands and other miscellaneous system. As there were some differences observed in construction techniques both before and after the 2015 Gorkha earthquake, so such differences are also highlighted in this section.

Fig. 9.3 Structural damages observed during the 2015 Gorkha earthquake (Bhaktapur)

The study shows that most MM houses before the 2015 Gorkha earthquake were unreinforced without any seismic consideration like lack of seismic bands, no periodic repair and maintenance, improper tall structure (3–5-storey house), large-sized room, inappropriate hybrid structure and mixed masonry units, and so on. But after the earthquake, due to strict implementation of housing design rules by GoN followed by several earthquake-resistant training campaigns (for local masons and technical staff), and active involvement of technical staff in each earthquake-affected regions, more than 80% of newly built houses were better compared to past construction technique. New houses adopted earthquake-resistant features like interlocking masonry units, seismic bands, cornerstones, vertical reinforcement, light roofing materials, low storey, and small-sized rooms, which were hardly seen in old local houses before the earthquake.

9.4.3.1 Foundation and Damp Proof Course (DPC)

The majority of the foundation of old MM houses were shallow strip wall foundation (i.e. 300–915 mm in depth) and had no DPC or plinth band (>94% houses), which was a primary cause for excess dampness, fast deterioration of mud masonry joints, and weakening of structures from the base implying vulnerability even before the earthquake, as shown in Fig. 9.6c and d. Realizing this, after the recent 2015 earthquake, the new houses have followed minimum 915 mm depth criteria, including DPC or plinth band (60–100 mm thickness), either timber (see Fig. 9.7b) or RC (see

Fig. 9.4 Present condition of old URMM houses: **a** partially and extremely damaged brick masonry (Bhaktapur); **b** complete collapse of side attached house (Bhaktapur); **c** an example of damaged row housing with common sharing of walls and floor structure (Dhulikhel); **d** inclined support provided to several partial damaged houses (Bhaktapur); **e** unrepaired partially damaged stone masonry (Sindhupalchowk); **f** inappropriate repair and modification of partial damaged stone masonry (Okhaldhunga)

Fig. 9.5 Example of some common types of mud-bonded stone masonry houses observed after 2015 earthquake (Okhaldhunga): **a** one-storey house with timber bands and small attic storage; **b** one-storey house with RC bands and attic storage; **c** two-storey house; **d** hybrid structure (RC column in four corners and load-bearing walls; **e** two-storey hybrid house (first storey—stone masonry with timber bands and second storey—installation of timber framing for fixing C.G.I sheet); **f** two-storey hybrid house (1st storey—stone masonry with RC bands and 2nd storey—C.G.I sheet with timber fixing)

Fig. 9.6 Foundation details and dampness observed before 2015 earthquake: **a** typical foundation in old MM house; **b** excavation for foundation (Okhaldhunga); **c** dampness and brick deterioration observed due to lack of DPC (Dhulikhel); **d** deterioration of masonry joints (Tanahun); **e** typical stone foundation using flat through stone as DPC; **f** thick plastic layer installed as DPC (Sindhuli)

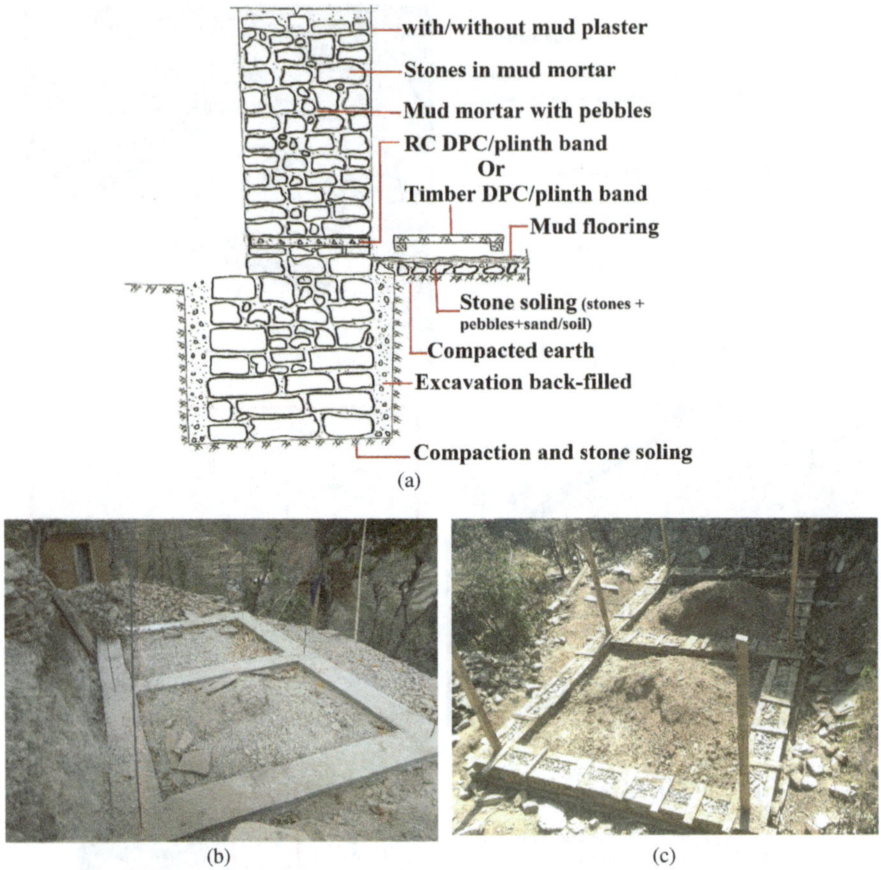

Fig. 9.7 Foundation and DPC band details of new MM houses after 2015 earthquake: **a** typical foundation including plinth band; **b** RC plinth or DPC band (Okhaldhunga); **c** timber plinth or DPC band (Okhaldhunga)

Fig. 9.7c) as a compulsion under supervision of technical staff. In some old MM houses, the use of thick plastic sheets, flat through stones were found to be adopted at plinth level as a DPC, as shown in Fig. 9.6e and f.

9.4.3.2 Wall System

Stone, brick and mud mortar (see Fig. 9.8) are the primary wall materials used, with thickness ranging from 350 mm to 600 mm both before and after the 2015 earthquake. Comparatively, most of the houses adopted 450 mm wall thickness both before and after earthquake. The mud used as mortar for wall construction is typically sourced from nearby construction site and manually prepared using local tools, as shown in Fig. 9.8.

Before the 2015 earthquake, the absence of seismic bands (see Figs. 9.2, 9.4, 9.9a and b), insufficient connection among masonry units (see Fig. 9.9c), use of bulky mass of mud mortar and small stone pieces as a filler material between wall wythes (see Fig. 9.9d), etc. were common in the majority of the walls. As a result, delamination, severe cracks, wall collapse in the form of out-of-plane and in-plane failure were common failures during an earthquake (see Figs. 9.2a, 9.3 and 9.4b). In addition to this, common sharing of walls and other structures were commonly observed in row housing of old settlement which lead towards weakness of entire structure and increased possibilities of collapse during lateral loading, as shown in Fig. 9.2a, 9.4a, b and c, and 9.9b. Similarly, inappropriate use of composite wall materials (like burnt and sun-dried bricks, bricks and stones, stones and timber, etc.) in different floor storey or same storey was also observed, as shown in Fig. 9.6c, 9.9a and b. Apart from this, there were some good examples of masonry structures that maintained structural integrity installing floor bands, good interlocking among masonry units, light-weight roofing, low floor height, etc. and survived during the 2015 Gorkha earthquake, as shown in Fig. 9.10.

But after the earthquake, seismic bands were typical in new MM houses constructed under the National Reconstruction Project. Several experimental results, numerical simulation, lessons learned from past earthquakes, and engineering judgments, have shown the importance of seismic band and vertical elements (RC or timber) towards improvement in seismic performance of masonry buildings (Khadka & Shakya, 2021; Khadka 2020; Khadka & Jiang, 2019; Endo et al. 2020; IS 1993; Ali et al. 2013). The past study showed that about 87% of the new houses were found to adopt bands (sill and lintel bands) but among those, around 22% of houses had adopted thickness lower ($\leq$50 mm) than the minimum required (75 mm) (Khadka, 2020). The horizontal bands either RC (75 to 100 mm) or timber (65 to 75 mm $\times$ 45 mm) were installed at a vertical interval of about 915 mm. Similarly, the

Fig. 9.8 Worker preparing mud mortar

Fig. 9.9 Wall construction and seismic consideration before 2015 earthquake: **a** tall hybrid brick masonry without any seismic bands (Bhaktapur); **b** old brick masonry without any seismic bands (Bhaktapur); **c** insufficient connection among masonry units (Sindhuli); **d** use of bulky mass of mud mortar and excess small stone or pebbles between wall wythes (Sindhuli)

Fig. 9.10 Masonry houses survived during the 2015 earthquake: **a** stone masonry (Okhaldhunga); **b** brick masonry (Kavre); **c** lower height one-storey stone masonry with light-weight roofing, and few openings (Sindhuli)

Fig. 9.11 Wall construction and seismic consideration after 2015 earthquake: **a** Vertical timber post (Okhaldhunga); **b** vertical rebar (Okhaldhunga)

vertical reinforcements in the form of timber posts (75 × 75 mm to 100 mm) or rebar (12 mm) were installed at different locations of the walls like corners, junctions, and also at the edges of the opening, as shown in Fig. 9.11. Along with seismic bands, interlocking among masonry units was observed, which has overall held the masonry buildings into a single unit (structural integrity), provided ductility and crack proof. Apart from this, some of the houses, as shown in Fig. 9.5d, e and f were also found which was self-modified by house owner and local masons.

9.4.3.3 Floor and Roofing System

Like in the past, flexible floor systems are still in practice, i.e. timber/bamboo (see Fig. 9.12a, b, c and d) used as a structural member with mud laid over it (see Fig. 9.12c). In the case of a roofing system, a sloped roof with timber or bamboo as a structural member (see Fig. 9.12e and f) is used. But compared to the past, new houses are trying to reduce unwanted weight due to flooring and roof coverings for better seismic performance, like reducing the use of mud laying in the floor and replacing it with timber plank or bamboo strips. Similarly, reducing the use of heavy roof coverings like stone tiles and replacing it with C.G.I sheets. The study shows that the majority of newly constructed MM houses (i.e., more than 98%) have adopted C.G.I sheets as a roofing system.

9.4.3.4 Gable Wall System

Usually, past gable wall systems used thick mud masonry without gable bands and height more than 1.2 m (see Fig. 9.13a); as a result, gable failure was common in the 2015 Gorkha earthquake (see Fig. 9.13b). Compared to the past, current MM gable wall systems are of low height and include bands. Similarly, considering easiness,

Fig. 9.12 Flooring (a, b, c and d) and roofing (e and f) system after 2015 earthquake: a timber arrangement for flooring (Okhaldhunga); b bamboo strips fixed above timber structure (Okhaldhunga); c mud laid over floor structure (Sindhuli); d lower view of floor structure (Sindhuli); e timber arrangement for roofing (Okhaldhunga); f lower view of roof structure (Sindhuli)

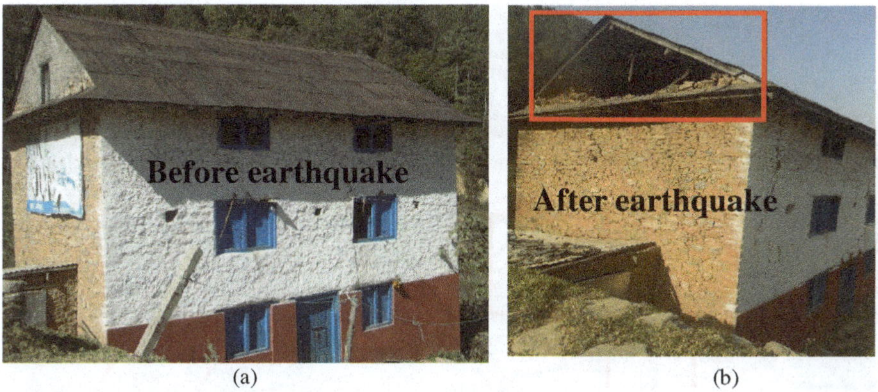

Fig. 9.13 Condition of gable wall system before and after 2015 Gorkha earthquake (Thankot): **a** high and thick-walled masonry; **b** gable failure after the earthquake

safety, and cheapness, the most recent gable system has replaced masonry gable walls with light materials like timber and C.G.I. sheet (see Fig. 9.5a and b).

9.4.3.5 House Storey and Room Size

Before the 2015 earthquake, the local people haphazardly modified their houses (adding new storey over previous old structures) using different mixed building materials compared to the lower storey (Khadka & Shakya, 2021; Khadka, 2020; Khadka & Jiang, 2019; Khadka & Shakya, 2016). Usually, two to five storeys with huge attic space (increase building weight) and no seismic bands (see Figs. 9.2, 9.3, and 9.4) were found. Such construction practices have automatically increased building weight (Newton's second law of motion, force = mass*acceleration, i.e. higher the mass, higher the internal inertial force generated), ultimately leading to a sudden collapse of structure and created a miserable scenario all over during the 2015 earthquake. Along with this, there was a trend of constructing a lengthy room (especially in rural region houses) with or without non-structural partition, as shown in Fig. 9.14a.

But after the 2015 earthquake, due to the strict implementation of the available guidelines and design provided by the Department of Urban Development and Building Construction (DUDBC) for MM houses, the majority of houses in rural settlement are one storey with small attic space (see Fig. 9.5a and b), which has automatically reduced building weight and developed the ability to perform better during the earthquake. The detailed study showed that around 10% of new houses had a single medium to large sized room, and more than 70% had only medium-sized rooms with low height attic space (see Fig. 9.7 and 9.11).

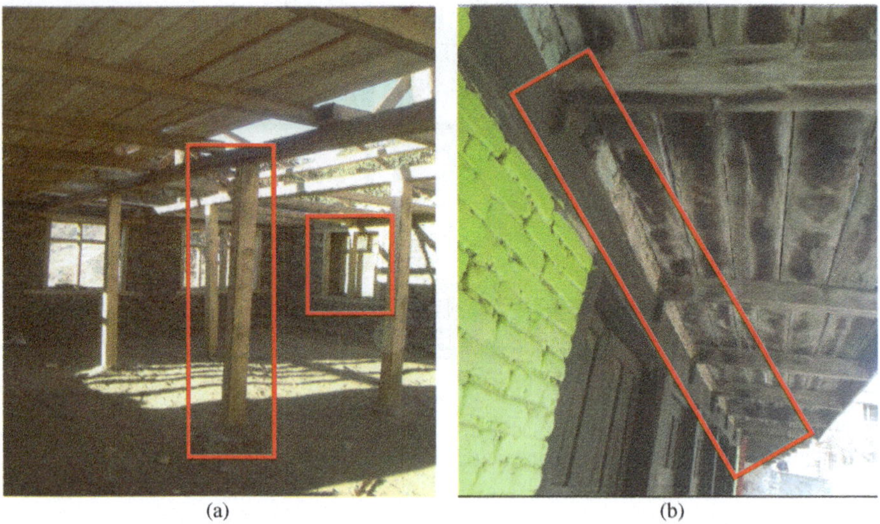

Fig. 9.14 Miscellaneous system followed before earthquake contributing additional support: **a** Vertical timber post and double frame opening before earthquake (Dolakha); **b** wooden locks used to fix or anchor the floor battens with the wall (Tanahun)

9.4.3.6 Miscellaneous System

As the majority of the old MM houses had lengthy room, so to avoid the issue of overburden in the wall, failure of flooring structure and the entire structure, vertical timber posts were installed at a certain span of timber beams in the form of additional support, as shown in Fig. 9.14a. Along with this, a double frame for doors and windows was also common in both old and new MM houses of Nepal (see Fig. 9.14a). In addition to these traditional techniques, the use of timber pegs or locks was also observed (see Fig. 9.14b) in old and new MM houses (about 15% of the investigated houses) to fix or connect building elements like timber floor battens and wall, roofing elements, etc.

9.5 Research-Based Recommendations

In addition to detailed house investigation, close interaction with local people, masons, and technical staff have further helped to understand the good and bad aspects observed in local housing.

- It was observed that still, the local people from rural settlements are ignorant regarding the actual drawbacks observed in old MM houses and the importance of earthquake-resistant construction techniques. As a result, local people are unable to play an active role in the reconstruction process. There is a need for an effective awareness campaign launched in all rural regions through the support of technical staff allocated in those particular regions. Along with this, the important highlighting awareness information can be circulated through the help of social media like newspaper, radio, television, etc. in the form of programs, advertisements, animations, and so on.

- Non-uniform mason training and public awareness campaigns were observed in poor accessibility areas. So there is a necessity of implementation of strict rules and better provision for uniform training in all regions, so that concrete knowledge and decision can be spread all over and safe structures are prepared in upcoming days.
- The issue regarding the quality of building materials was observed in both new and old MM houses, which might trigger structural damage in the upcoming days prior to earthquake. There should be a necessary awareness campaign for local people and local masons regarding the importance of good quality materials and the possibility of material treatment through locally available methods.
- The condition of old MM houses was miserable (no periodic assessment and maintenance) before the 2015 Gorkha earthquake, as shown in Fig. 9.15, which led to huge structural damages. Inspite of this, there are still some old historic MM houses existing after the 2015 earthquake with or without partial damages (see Figs. 9.4, 9.9a and b). But due to delays in retrofitting works and the frequent occurrence of the earthquake and aftershocks, these houses are about to collapse and diminish.

There is a need for active and strict efforts to preserve such houses. Skilled manpower should be prepared through effective training to lead and successfully retrofit the houses at a low cost using local materials. In addition to this, there is a need for periodic assessment and necessary maintenance works to preserve our existing old historic houses, which are the valuable gifts provided by our ancestors.

Similarly, some excess damaged houses (see Figs. 9.2a, 9.4a and b)were still available in earthquake-affected areas, which need immediate dismantling to avoid further casualties in upcoming earthquakes.

- Although the single or double medium room size and single-storey housing practices observed in new houses (see Figs. 9.5a and b) are comparatively safer than old multi-storied MM houses. But these small spaces seems to be insufficient for the rural people for their daily life, which has arisen dissatisfaction among several local people. This dissatisfaction may lead to haphazard modification of houses in upcoming days. So, the government should seriously focus on local people's general housing space requirements and provide suitable housing design and effective modification alternatives as per that.
- Still after 2015 earthquake, some client and local mason self-modified new houses were observed like inappropriate use of available materials, combining load-bearing masonry and RC columns (see Fig. 9.5d), and other several hybrid

Fig. 9.15 Miserable unmaintained condition of MM houses before 2015 earthquake: **a** cracks, dampness, erosion of wall materials and lacking maintenance (Bhaktapur); **b** cracks, erosion of mud mortar joints (Thankot); **c** unmaintained roof: leakage, haphazard roofing materials (Sanga); **d** decay in timber structural elements (Sindhuli)

structure, so such houses should be carefully investigated and necessary guidance should be provided for possible structural maintenance and improvements or correction.

- Still, the socio-economically backward population couldn't return to their normal life, so there should be certain provisions to support those people in reconstructing their houses.
- Nepal consists of higher percentage of hilly and Himalayan region, so there is challenging topography. In such cases, the poor transportation facilities observed in majority of these regions has triggered several difficulties like unable to transport the construction materials from one place to another, etc. So, GoN and several related authorities should focus in improving the stability of the road in these regions and facilitate local people with good transportation facilities.

9.6 Conclusion

This paper has highlighted the important aspects of the Mud-Bonded Masonry houses of Nepal in terms of materials used, common types of MM housing type and their condition, common structural system, and their construction practices. This study covers nearly 9 years of detailed investigation, so carefully analysing the entire construction practices, differentiable changes were observed in the MM houses constructed before and after the 2015 Gorkha earthquake.

In this modernized world where construction technology and safety methods has no boundary, in such scenario, a developing country like Nepal has been suffering a lot in terms of massive structural damages (mainly MM houses) and casualties in each earthquake since the past. The recent earthquake has revealed several bitter realities regarding the poor local construction techniques, and haphazard modification of old URMM structures adopted in our locality . The main reasons behind the partial and complete collapse of MM houses were the shallow foundation, haphazard composite use of building materials, no seismic bands, increasing floor storey beyond the capacity of the house structure, inadequate connection among the masonry units, and also among different structural system (wall to the roof, wall to floor, and so on). In addition to this, some additional issues like old aged building materials (unrepaired old aged house), unrepaired minor to extreme cracks in a wall surface, inappropriate mixed floor system, common sharing of structures like wall, floor structure, roof, etc. were especially observed in the old mud-bonded brick masonry houses of old settlement areas of Kathmandu, Lalitpur, Bhaktapur, Kavrepalanchowk, etc. Lack of adoption of engineering techniques and proper building materials, and misconception of local people and masons about the use and working phenomenon of structural components were observed in the majority of the URMM houses all over Nepal. But comparatively, after the 2015 Gorkha earthquake, there is drastic improvement been made in the construction practices through the active participation of the government, technical staff, several national and international organizations.

Analysing the entire housing scenario, some recommendations are presented highlighting the necessity of conducting effective uniform mason training (relating the importance of material quality and its treatment, seismic-resistant construction, and retrofitting) in all regions, immediate retrofitting of the old existing (with or without partial damages) MM houses and conduct periodic assessment and repair, implement strict rules and regulations regarding material quality and earthquake-resistant practices, maintain uniform distribution of resources, improve transportation facilities in all regions, and so on.

It was observed that many people only have basic information about MM houses in Nepal. Finally, this chapter has played a valuable role in visualizing the entire MM housing scenario in Nepal both before and after the 2015 earthquake. This information can be used as a baseline by several sectors to conduct new researches (related to the upliftment of social, economic, and structure sectors) focusing on MM houses.

References

Adhikari, L., Gautam, U., Koirala, B., Bhattarai, M., Kandel, T., Gupta, R., et al. (2015). The aftershock sequence of the 2015 April 25 Gorkha-Nepal earthquake. *Geophys Suppl Monthly Not R Astron Soc, 203*(3), 2119–2124.

Ali, Q., Khan, A.N., Ashraf, M., Ahmed, A., Alam, B., Ahmad, N., et al. (2013). Seismic performance of stone masonry buildings used in the Himalayan Belt. *Earthquake spectra, 29*(4), 1159–1181.

Bureau of Indian Standards. (1993). Improving Earthquake Resistance of Low Strength Masonry Buildings: Guidelines.

Bonapace, C., & Sestini, V. (2003). Traditional materials and construction technologies used in the Kathmandu valley. United Nations Educational, Scientific and Cultural Organization Paris; 2003.

Central Bureau of Statistics. (2012). Nepal housing and population census, Government of Nepal. National Planning Commission, Editor; 2012.

Endo, Y., Yamaguchi, K., Hanazato, T., Mishra, C. (2020). Characterisation of mechanical behaviour of masonry composed of fired bricks and earthen mortar. *Engineering Failure Analysis, 109*, 104280.

Khadka, B. (2020). Mud masonry houses in Nepal: A detailed study based on entire reconstruction scenario in 31 earthquake-affected districts. *Structures, 25*, 816–838. (Elsevier).

Khadka, B., & Shakya, M. (2016). Seismic characteristics of un-reinforced mud masonry buildings in Nepal. In *International Conference on Earthquake Engineering and Post Disaster Reconstruction Planning. 2016*. Bhaktapur, pp. 135–144.

Khadka, B., & Jiang, H. (2019). Mud Masonry houses in Nepal: A study based on reconstruction work after 2015 Gorkha Earthquake. In *2nd International Conference on Earthquake Engineering and Post Disaster Reconstruction Planning* (pp. 282–291). Nepal: Bhaktapur.

Khadka, B., & Shakya, M. (2021). Seismic characteristics of unreinforced mud masonry houses in Nepal: A miserable scenario before and after 2015 Gorkha (Nepal) earthquake. *Engineering Failure Analysis, 124*, 105308. https://doi.org/10.1016/j.engfailanal.2021.105308

NPC. (2015). Post Disaster Need Assessment (PDNA) Government of Nepal. National Planning Commission, Editor, Kathmandu.

MoHA. (2015). Situation Report of NRCS, Ministry of Home Affairs.

USGS. (2015). M 7.8-36km E of Khudi, Nepal. 2015. https://earthquake.usgs.gov/earthquakes/eventpage/us20002926/origin/detail.

UNDP. (2009). Nepal Country Report-Global Assessment of Risk. ISDR Global Assessment Report on Poverty and Disaster Risk 2009. United Nations Development Programme: Kathmandu, Nepal.

Chapter 10
A Road to Recovery: Housing Reconstruction in Bhaktapur Nepal Post the 2015 Gorkha Earthquake

Krittika Uniyal and Lila Nyaichyai

Abstract The 2015 Gorkha Earthquake in Nepal caused tremendous economic and social loss to Nepal, the mortalities and the widespread damage and devastation is believed to have been the most disastrous event in Nepal's recent history. It has been half a decade since this earthquake and even today Nepal struggles to cope with its socio-economic implications and damages. This paper takes the example of the severely impacted city of Bhaktapur in the Kathmandu Valley to understand the prevalent vernacular housing structures in Nepal and the current housing problems in the Kathmandu Valley. This paper analyses the current policy recommendations put in place by the Government of Nepal post the 2015 Gorkha Earthquake to address these challenges and the shortcomings of these policies.

Keywords 2015 Gorkha Earthquake · Traditional Nepali house · Post-earthquake reconstruction · Bhaktapur · Nepal

10.1 Introduction

Recent large earthquakes in the Himalayan region have resulted in tens of thousands of fatalities, and evidence suggests that multiple events throughout the Himalayas in the last 1000 years have had $M > 8.0$ and at least two have had $M > 8.5$, despite this, understanding of earthquake risk in the region is poorly constrained (Robinson, 2020; Wyss, 2005).

Nepal in particular is located in a highly active seismic zone (Manandhar, 2016), it is along the active main Himalayan Thrust arc, where the subducting Indian plate and the overriding Eurasian plate interact (Ader et al., 2012; Goda et al., 2015), and it is exposed to many natural and human-induced hazards (UNDRR, 2019). In the global

K. Uniyal (✉)
The Environmental Governance and Territorial Development Institute, University of Geneva, Geneva, Switzerland
e-mail: KrittikaUniyal@etu.unige.ch

L. Nyaichyai
Central Department of Library and Information Science, Tribhuvan University, Kathmandu, Nepal

A. Kundu et al. (eds.), *Accessible Housing for South Asia*,
https://doi.org/10.1007/978-3-030-88881-7_10

context, Nepal ranks 4th in terms of climate risk according to the Global Climate Risk Index which assesses the impacts of meteorological events about economic losses and human fatalities and more people are killed by disasters in Nepal than in any other country in South Asia (Eckstein et al., 2018; Shakya, 2016; UNDRR, 2019). This exposes more than 80% of Nepal's population to the risk of natural hazards, which includes not only earthquakes but also droughts, floods, landslides, extreme temperature, and glacier lake outburst floods (MoHA, 2017).

At present Nepal's population has surpassed 29 million people (Central Bureau of Statistics, 2018),[1] of which almost 80% depend on agriculture-based livelihoods. Limited domestic economy, geographically dispersed, unconnected population, as well as diverse groups belonging to various castes and ethnic groups contribute to the compounding social vulnerability to disasters. Contributing to the problem, Nepal occupies a noticeable place in global narratives of inadequate shelter. UN-HABITAT's (2003) recent inventory of *Slums of the World*, for example, lists Nepal fourth—just below Ethiopia, Chad, and Afghanistan—among the countries with the world's highest percentage of slum dwellers[2] (Rademacher, 2009).

With this socio-economic background the 2015 Gorkha Earthquake left hundreds of thousands homeless, and with the impending monsoon season and winter afterwards, in the first few months after the earthquake, the shelter became a high priority to most of the disaster-hit populations. This disaster exposed the soft spot of the growing housing challenge in Nepal's most populated urban space, the Kathmandu Valley. The 2015 Gorkha Earthquake has questioned the current construction techniques in Nepal, and has exposed the haphazard modification of the old structures (Khadka & Shakya, 2016) Post this the Government of Nepal (GoN) and the wider civil society acknowledged that there is a need to build a more earthquake-resistant housing in Nepal. This chapter takes the example of Bhakthapur city in the Kathmandu Valley to understand the prevalent vernacular housing structures in Nepal, and summarises the key findings and learnings from this disaster vis-a-vis the general housing style in the valley.

10.2 Methods

Baseline data for this chapter was collected through structured individual interviews, and personal observations in the Kathmandu Valley during and post the 2015 Gorkha Earthquake. It is supported by evidence that is gathered from a literature review and other secondary information as published by different sources on housing pre and post this earthquake in Nepal.

---

[1] https://cbs.gov.np/.

[2] UN-HABITAT, "Slums of the world: The face of urban poverty in the new millenium?" working paper (2003), Nairobi; cited by Davis (2006, 23).

10.3 The 2015 Gorkha Earthquake

On April 25, 2015, an earthquake of magnitude Mw 7.8 on the Richter scale struck mid-western Nepal. It was followed by hundreds of aftershocks, of which the most significant one occurred in the early afternoon of May 12, 2015, (Bothara et al., 2015; Yadav et al., 2018). The hypocentre of magnitude Mw 7.3 was located about 80 km northwest of the Kathmandu Valley in the Gorkha region oh Nepal (Ader et al., 2012; Goda et al., 2015) and was hence called the 2015 Gorkha Earthquake (as addressed hereafter). Intense shaking, casualties, and infrastructural damages from this earthquake were experienced in India, China, and Bangladesh as well (Lizundia et al., 2016; NPC, 2015a).

This earthquake caused tremendous damage and loss to Nepal, the fatalities, injuries and extensive damage and devastation makes it by far the most destructive earthquake ever to have occurred in Nepal (Bothara et al., 2015). It affected an area of approximately 30,000 square kilometres across fourteen districts, and according to the Post Disaster Needs Assessment (PDNA)Report published by the National Planning Commission of Nepal in June 2015, there were over 8,790 casualties and 22,300 injuries (NPC, 2015a). Thirty-one of the country's 75 districts were affected, out of which 14 were declared 'crisis-hit' to prioritize rescue and relief operations (OCHA, 2015) and another 17 neighbouring districts were partially affected (Fig. 10.1) (Lizundia et al., 2016; NPC, 2015a).

The total direct economic loss due to the earthquake was estimated to be US$7billion (NPC, 2015b; Bothara et al., 2015; Subedi & Bahadur Poudyal Chhetri, 2019). The mainshock triggered numerous landslides and rock/boulder falls in the mountain areas, blocking roads, and hampering rescue and recovery activities (Goda et al., 2015). Rural areas in the central and western regions were further isolated due to road damage, road obstructions from landslides, and destabilized slopes, which also left them more susceptible to flooding and landslides during the subsequent monsoon season. Areas in the high Himalayas and along the Mount Everest route were also impacted by landslides and avalanches triggered by the earthquakes (NPC, 2015a, b).

The destruction was widespread covering residential and government buildings, heritage sites, health posts, rural roads, bridges, water supply systems, agricultural land, trekking routes, hydropower plants, sports facilities, and around 7000 schools were either completely or significantly damaged (NPC, 2015b; Bothara et al., 2015; Subedi & Bahadur Poudyal Chhetri, 2019). Also, hundreds of historical and cultural monuments including the Kathmandu Durbar Square, a UNESCO World Heritage site, was severely damaged (Goda et al., 2015). Among all of this the private housing sector suffered the most devastating blow, the earthquake destroyed around half a million homes and damaged another quarter-million (Bothara et al., 2015; NPC, 2015a).

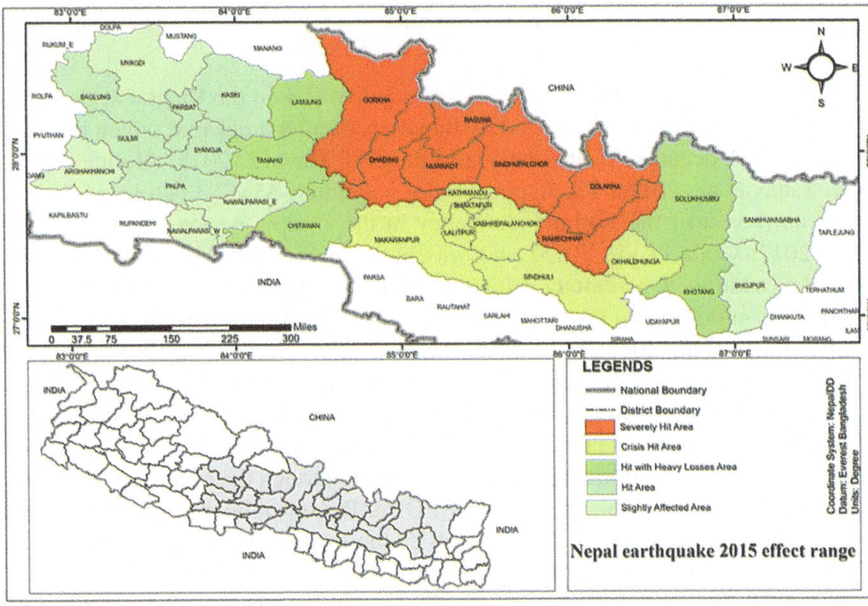

Fig. 10.1 Categories of the district affected in the 2015 Gorkha Earthquake published by the Ministry of Home Affairs (MoHA), Government of Nepal as of 21 May 2015. *Source* Government of Nepal (NPC, 2015a)

10.4 Nepal's Response to the 2015 Gorkha Earthquake

Immediately following this disaster an earthquake damage investigation team was set up (within May 1-7, 2015) to investigate the first-hand earthquake damages, meanwhile the Nepal Army set in motion a rescue and relief operation named 'Operation Sankatmochan'. They rescued and provided medical treatment to individuals affected by the disaster (NPC, 2015a; Shrestha & Pathranarakul, 2018). Also, the Government of Nepal carried out a massive household survey using mobile technology[3] to assess building damage in earthquake affected districts. Although the primary goal of this survey was to identify beneficiaries eligible for government assistance for housing reconstruction, it also collected other useful census-level socio-economic information. Since then the data is collected for a total of 11earthquake affected districts, impacting 762,106 buildings and 3,677,173 individuals, data addressing the socio-economic information (Fig. 10.2).

Nepal's institutional setup for disaster management was founded in 1982 by then the country also had the Natural Calamity Relief Act in place. In terms of disaster

[3] The Kathmandu Living Labs designed and developed an Open Data Portal post the 2015 Gorkha Earthquake, with the data from Central Bureau of Statistics and National Planning Commission, Nepal. It is a part of the Evidence for Development Programme implemented by The Asia Foundation and Development Initiatives.

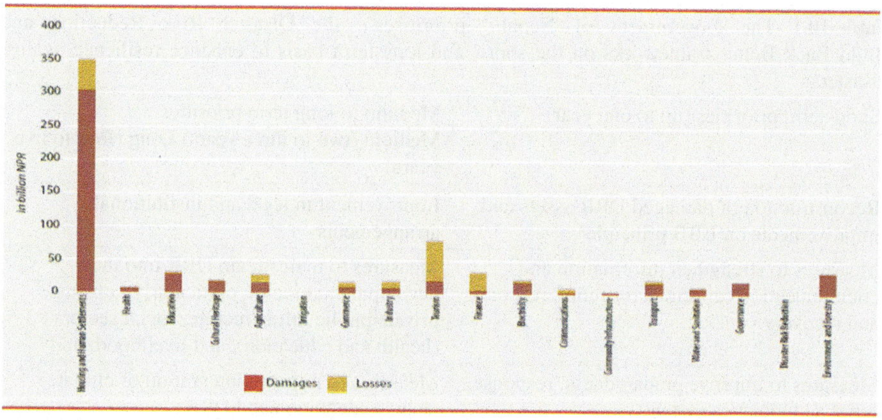

Fig. 10.2 The impact of the 2015 Gorkha Earthquake across sectors. *Source* Estimations by PDNA Team (NPC, 2015a)

response, the latest policy paper pre-2015 was the National Disaster Response Framework (NDRF), enacted in 2013 (Bisri & Beniya, 2016). Post the 2015 Gorkha Earthquake, the GoN promulgated the Reconstruction Act 2015 and established the National Reconstruction Authority (NRA). The NRA subsequently introduced various reconstruction policies and provisions to facilitate 'owner-driven' reconstruction under the 'Build Back Better' (BBB) approach (NPC, 2015a). For this purpose, 3000 engineers were deployed by the government to assist earthquake-affected households to build 'earthquake-resistant houses'—a process incentivized by the provision of the Private Housing Reconstruction Grant of USD 2750 (approx.). In doing so, homeowners at the ground level—who were previously accustomed to designing and building their own houses with little to no regulatory oversight—came to interact with new forms of regulations (building codes, permits, approved designs) for the first time (Limbu et al., 2019).

10.4.1 Steps to Build Back Better

In the recovery and reconstruction phase, the GoN acknowledged that it was critical to prevent actions that end up creating disaster risks, and this could be achieved first by increasing public awareness and second by investing the principle of Build Back Better. Noting the limited priority and resources given to Disaster Risk Reduction (DRR) before the earthquake, the government aimed to mitigate these challenges in the DRR system in Nepal on a short- and long-term priority basis (NPC, 2015a, b) (Table 10.1).

After the earthquake, modifications in the National Building Code, building by-laws, development of technical guidelines for construction, and retrofitting have been made for good construction changes in the entire nation. Along with which

Table 10.1 The Government of Nepal prioritises the Disaster Risk Reduction and Build Back Better frameworks on the short- and long-term basis to enhance resilience against disasters

Short-term priorities (up to one year)	Medium to long term priorities Medium (two to three years) Long (four to five years)
Reconstruction of damaged DRR assets and improvements on BBB principle	Improvement in legal and institutional arrangements
Measures to strengthen information and communication capacities for relief, response and recovery	Measures to mainstream DRR into the developmental sector, particularly housing, private public infrastructure, social sectors (health and education), and livelihood; and
Measures to improve preparedness, response, relief and logistics systems	Measures to improve integration of climate change adaptation and DRR
Measures to enhance multi-hazard risk monitoring, vulnerability assessment, risk information dissemination and awareness	

Source Government of Nepal (NPC, 2015a)

many non-governmental organizations have facilitated local people by providing appropriate guidance for constructing safe structures, train masons, and organizing public awareness campaigns (Khadka & Jiang, 2019). To make Nepal more earthquake resistant, the government decided to develop a seismic policy and set up a network for seismic monitoring throughout the country to promote seismological research (NPC, 2015a, b; Shrestha & Taniguchi, 2003).

This policy will include the revision of building codes, development of building by-laws for all municipal areas , and development of risk-sensitive land use plans for all the municipalities of the country. Along with seismic policies, the government implemented several DRR measures targeting secondary disasters to undertake risk assessment that will provide a basis for mitigation measures at the community level (NPC, 2015a; Bisri & Beniya, 2016; Peppercorn, 2016). As part of the recovery programme, the government will support early warning and preparedness measures and support strengthening and retrofitting of schools and hospitals that are critical to risk reduction in Nepal (NPC, 2015a, b).

The entire cost of rebuilding post the earthquake was estimated at around USD5 billion. All this in a country with economic growth that was already expected to slow, with an unemployment rate of more than 40%, and a reliance on agriculture, tourism and remittances to support its USD19 billion economy. Since then the Nepali government has scaled back GDP growth forecasts, it has been evaluated that the country's economic growth slumped back eight years due to the catastrophic earthquake followed by poor monsoon (Shakya, 2016; USAID, 2020). Thus, the slowdown in growth has resulted in a great setback to the country's plan of graduating to a developing country by 2022 from the current least developed status (Shrestha & Pathranarakul, 2018).

The Nepali government through the National Disaster Response Framework 2013 did manage to call for international assistance and partially coordinated the emergency response operational activities (Bisri & Beniya, 2016). In response to the Nepali government's international appeal for assistance, 34 countries rallied with 18 military and 16 non-military teams with a total force of 4521 people. The effort comprised an urban search-and-rescue team, engineers, air support personnel, and medical professionals (NPC, 2015a; Shrestha & Pathranarakul, 2018). India responded in <12 h and was the first international team to arrive in Nepal, China, Sri Lanka, Bangladesh, and Bhutan as close neighbours followed (Cook et al., 2016). The international media's extensive coverage of the earthquake was instrumental in generating all the financial help to Nepal (Shrestha & Pathranarakul, 2018).

10.5 The Case of Bhaktapur

Housing as the basic human need has become a complex problem for the low-income urban dwellers in Nepal, and to be able to afford a modest home in the Kathmandu Valley has become out of reach for most (Shrestha & Taniguchi, 2003). Housing in Nepal is largely a private matter; although government bodies exercise decrees of laws and regulations, Nepalese however built homes uniquely as per their ability and desire. Since there are numerous ethnic groups in Nepal, the traditional vernacular houses are uniquely designed and are reflective of different communities. These difference are primarily shaped by ecological and climatic conditions.[4] Also, the construction techniques of house building vary in different regions depending on the availability of building materials, housing purpose, locality construction practices, climatic condition, caste system, and so on (Khadka & Shakya, 2016). The apartment system of housing is a newly introduced concept in Nepal, and is still observed as a less common practice among low and middle income families.

The Kathmandu Valley (includes three big cities of Kathmandu, Lalitapur, and Bhaktapur) is in a hilly zone that has temporal climatic characteristics. The population of the valley has been rapidly increasing because of migration from different parts of the country. The absence of government intervention on the land market and housing has caused an ever-increasing price for the house and land property for construction in the Kathmandu Valley (Mathema, 1999). Buildings in Nepal are vulnerable to seismic actions, the majority of houses and buildings are not seismically designed and constructed (Mathema, 1999). During the 2015 Gorkha Earthquake, the poor performance of the buildings was to take the major share of the blame for the scale of the damage, these buildings performed poorly because they were made of very weak construction materials (such as dry stone, stone in mud mortar) or were constructed very poorly despite being of good materials (such as fired brick or stone in cement mortar, confined masonry, and reinforced concrete) (Bothara et al., 2015).

[4] The low land (*Terai*), and inner terai (*Chure*), Hill, Himalayas and trans-Himalayas are five climatic zones of Nepal.

The Newar community resides in the urban areas of the Kathmandu Valley, and they have a cultural history of living in compact settlements (Mathema, 1999; Scheibler, 1982), a step to conserve their cultivable fertile land. Recently, this notion has been greatly altered due to urbanization and new sources of livelihood other than agriculture. Bhaktapur (or Khwopa) is one of the historical old towns in the Kathmandu Valley (also known as living heritage), it is a source of heritage tourism and may families in the valley depend on it for their sustenance (Kunwar & Chand, 2016).

Bhaktapur municipality was hit with the highest damage and casualties in the 2015 Gorkha Earthquake, 18,900 buildings were fully destroyed and 9054 buildings were partially damaged (Shakya et al., 2016). Just after the earthquake, the compact settlement of Bhaktapur was like a 'ghost hunted' place for the whole first year. One of the research showed that locals of Bhaktapur, due to less financial capacity, felt that it would take them more than a decade to rebuild their homes (Welton-Mitchell et al., 2017). Post the earthquake, households were forced to clear the debris without any financial assistance from the government. Later the government announced grants to be given in period wise instalments,. the first phase grant amounted to USD 417, that was added by USD 1253 after assuring the owner has built the foundation and the final phase grant was of USD 835 (National Reconstruction Authority, 2017).

In Bhaktapur, local government bodies were in discussion on rebuilding the destroyed homes into better ones. Since, the private property and individual rights on people's private property were the most sensitive fundamental rights secured in Nepal's Constitution from long ago, the social culture and social psychology also dictated that homes fell under people's private matter. Hence, the fragmented land properties of every household even after the devastating earthquake could not incept new changes into practice. The new changes preferred combination of houses of tiny area ($<32\ m^2$) with more comfortable and seismic resilience houses, but this was seens as a problematic choice with the still prevalent joint family system in Nepal. People's dogmatic concept of a house as a private familial space proved stronger than the worst experiences of the earthquake hit. At present, although life inside the earthquake-hit area has started to resume, deplorable house construction-renovation remain a prevalent practice as money prioritises over safety. In may cases the house owners who rebuilt their homes had to sell off their land property or managed bank debt, as the income source of house owners is seldom enough to rebuild another house (Limbu et al., 2019; Mathema, 1999).

10.5.1 A Traditional Nepali House

In the case of Bhaktapur (and also the Kathmandu Valley at large), the main reasons for the partial and complete collapse of brick masonry houses were old aged building materials and various forms of major to extreme cracks on the surface of the walls, shallow foundation, haphazard composite use of building materials, increasing building's height beyond the capacity of the structural system of the building, mixed floor system, and lack of sufficient bands. In context to stone masonry outside the valley, the main reasons behind their partial or total collapse were inadequate connection in wall's corner/intersection, inadequate roof-to-wall and wall-to-floor connection, use of improper stone and filling of lots of haphazard small sizes stone without proper filling of voids, use of bulky/thick mud mortar, lack of sufficient bands, improper interlocking/bonding between entire thickness and length of the wall (Khadka & Shakya, 2016). Most of the damaged buildings were stone/brick masonry structures with no seismic detailing, whereas most reinforced cement concrete (RCC) buildings were undamaged. Hence it was understood that an adequate structural design was the key to reduce the earthquake risk in Nepal (Goda et al., 2015).

In order to foresee and minimise the damages form such disasters, it is essential to understand the construction of the traditional homes. Mountain homes largely in the Himalayan region and especially in Nepal were traditionally built with brick, mud, and stone with thatch roofs 'Khar' grass. In Nepal, many masonry buildings even today use the same knowledge and are constructed with walls made of sun-dried/fired bricks or stone with mud mortar, with building frames made of wood. These types of buildings generally have flexible floors and roofs and are more prevalent in rural areas (Gautam & Rodrigues, 2015; Goda et al., 2015).

One of the noticeable shifts in this pattern of vernacular house construction in Nepal was documented by Japanese scholars, Hanaoka and colleagues in a study carried out in 1996 for a period of 10 years (between 1996 and 2006) , in which they observed that during this time period Nepalese houses' roofing were largely changed from thatched roof and slate roofs to corrugated Iron roofs. The study found many people being satisfied with corrugated Iron roofs due to their durability, easy installation, cheaper cost, however, the study proclaimed that it caused the loss of beauty and loss of in-house thermal balance. This change in used materials was seen as the first changes to the traditional vernacular housing structure in Nepal (Hanaoka et al., 2009) (Fig. 10.3).

Types of roof used	
Roof	Percentage
Galvanized sheet	28.26
Tile/Slate	26.68
RCC	22.48
Thatched/straw	19.03

Types of the outer wall	
Outer wall	Percentage
Mud bonded bricks/ stone	41.38
Cement bonded bricks/ stone	28.74
Bamboo wall	20.23
Wood/Plank	5.31

Types of Foundation	
Foundation	Percentage
Mud bonded bricks	44.21
Wooden Pillar	24.9
Cement bonded bricks	17.57
RCC Pillar	9.94
Another type of foundation	2.33

Fig. 10.3 According to the latest National census, the statistics of housing in Nepal depicted that the foundation of houses in Nepal was built with these materials. *Source* National Population and Housing Census 2011 (National Population and Housing Census 2011, 2012)

The masonry materials are of low strength and thus are seismically vulnerable (Gautam & Rodrigues, 2015; Goda et al., 2015). Mud, brick, stone, wood, bamboo, slate and corrugated iron roof (*Jasta Pata*) are local construction materials in Nepal, which even today are used traditionally for construction as most of the housing are still rural construction in Nepal. The census statistics showed that 9.94% of houses were founded on RCC, but 22.48% of houses had RCC roofing. The burdened roofing and mixed kinds of materials were used in the housing. Although the quality of housing is low for a vast majority of the population, the incidence of extremely poor living conditions is limited. Even more impressive is the fact that there are virtually no public sector housing programs or comprehensive/consolidated land development schemes that have facilitated access to housing or land to any class of people, rich or poor (Mathema, 1999). According to the 2011 Census of Nepal, around 10% (9.94%) of total households live in houses with the foundation having RCC pillars, 17.57% households in a house with a foundation made up of cement-bonded bricks, 24.9% in the wooden pillar, 44.21% in mud-bonded bricks and 2.33 in another type of foundations. In urban areas, 28.42% of the households live in houses with the foundation having RCC pillars (GoN, 2011). Although the advancement and the change in the construction pattern has been quite rapid in the recent years, still the traditional constructions practices are commonly observed. In many cases these traditional and modern construction practices are combined which is governed largely by economic constraints.

10.6 Post-earthquake Reconstruction and its Challenges

The GoN has a longstanding experience of developing community infrastructure. At present several ongoing projects and programmes address the challenges of Building Back Better, with NGOs and development partners working with the government in a spirit of collaboration aimed at resilient reconstruction and rehabilitation. The existing system of governance and implementation needs to be strengthened. Planning and prioritizing for rehabilitation needs to be accomplished in a participative manner, formalizing community platforms alongside assessment by local bodies (village development committee/district development committees/ municipalities). Moreover local bodies should lead community infrastructure reconstruction, supported by the Ministry of Federal Affairs and Local Development.

Technical support should be provided by the Department of Local Infrastructure Development and Agricultural Roads and the District Technical Offices, which also needs to be strengthened (NPC, 2015b). With all the issues and challenges stated above it can be learnt that in the case of Nepal, poorly constructed homes can have the potential to increase the impact of disasters multifold. It is acknowledged by the GoN that, had the 2015 Gorkha Earthquake struck at night, and not in the middle of a Saturday, there may have been greater casualties as more people would have been inside vulnerable buildings that suffered damage or collapse (NPC, 2015a, b). The PDNA report stated that this disaster highlighted aspects of inequities in Nepali society spanning geography, income, and gender (NPC, 2015a), and poor rural areas were more adversely affected than towns or cities (UNICGTF, 2015). Following the earthquake reconstruction, by the GoN and with the support of several non-governmental organizations, there were numerous challenges that the government faced in regards to the implementation of its set frameworks, and the government identified challenges for Nepal during the post-earthquake reconstruction work.

First of which was the lack of and in certain cases inaccessibility of certified construction material such as reinforced concrete forced people to go back to using the traditional construction material hence compromising the overall quality of construction. Regarding socio-economic challenges, Nepalese households have been left by young male family members for foreign jobs, hence, the families rely on women family members, who are already under burden with household tasks. Also, since most of the families' occupation is agriculture, they lack liquid cash, which impacts all the decisions of an individual and of their family, as Oliver-Smith (1990) correctly thought up that 'the study of disaster is the study of poverty in the third world', holds true for Nepal too.

The heavier challenge in Nepalese housing is also the lack of 'techno-regime', that is the lack of building standards. Up until 1995, there were no building standards, what Nepalese engineers followed was Indian building standards. Even the house-owners were less aware of the need for engineering for building houses. 95% of rural houses were built without any engineering design and even in Kathmandu 55% of houses were built in absence of proper engineering design (Peppercorn, 2016). Even after the earthquake, the government announced a house-owner-driven approac,. the government limited technical assistance and fixed subsidy to each family, regardless of the amount of loss (The Asia Foundation, 2016).

The biggest challenge still remains the lack of adoption of proper engineering techniques and good quality building materials. There is a need for a detailed study about the old construction practices and ways to make necessary changes (Khadka & Shakya, 2016; Shakya, 2016) and to integrate them with the new ones. Furthermore, there is the general practice of building houses consulting local craftsmen hence these craftsmen must be well trained too about the earthquake-resistant construction methods. Also there is a need for a stricter implementation of the guidelines for building rules and regulations, meanwhile the conditions of the old masonry houses remains miserable both before and after the 2015 Gorkha Earthquake, so necessary planning must be made concerning that as well (Khadka & Shakya, 2016).

10.7 Conclusion

Since April 2015 Nepal has witnessed a substantial shift in its policies about disaster mitigation, yet there is a long way to cover regarding the efficient implementation to maximize the benefits of these policies. More work is needed to ensure the security of such vulnerable communities to prevent future devastation (Tallett-Williams et al., 2016). Insights and lessons will likely continue to emerge, especially since rehabilitation and reconstruction phases are still ongoing in Nepal (Cook et al., 2016).

References

Ader, T., Avouac, J.-P., Liu-Zeng, J., Lyon-Caen, H., Bollinger, L., Galetzka, J., Genrich, J., Thomas, M., Chanard, K., Sapkota, S. N., Rajaure, S., Shrestha, P., Ding, L., & Flouzat, M. (2012). Convergence rate across the Nepal Himalaya and interseismic coupling on the Main Himalayan Thrust: Implications for seismic hazard: COUPLING ON THE MHT. *Journal of Geophysical Research: Solid Earth, 117*(B4), n/a–n/a. https://doi.org/10.1029/2011JB009071.

Bisri, M. B. F., & Beniya, S. (2016). Analyzing the national disaster response framework and inter-organizational network of the 2015 Nepal/Gorkha earthquake. *Procedia Engineering, 159*, 19–26. https://doi.org/10.1016/j.proeng.2016.08.059

Bothara, J. K., Dhakal, R. P., Ingham, J. M., & Dizhor, D. (2015). *The challenges of housing reconstruction after the April 2015 Gorkha, Nepal earthquake* (p. 15).

Cook, A., Shrestha, M., & Zin Bo Htet. (2016). *International response to 2015 Nepal earthquake: Lessons and observations*. https://doi.org/10.13140/RG.2.2.35305.90722.

Eckstein, D., Hutfils, M.-L., Winges, M., & Germanwatch. (2018). *Global climate risk index 2019 who suffers most from extreme weather events? Weather-related Loss Events in 2017 and 1998 to 2017*.

Gautam, D., & Rodrigues, H. (2015). *Architectural and structural characteristics of indigenous Newari Chhen: Study of seismic risk and resilience in the historic urban nucleus of Bhaktapur City*, Nepal (p. 8).

Goda, K., Kiyota, T., Pokhrel, R. M., Chiaro, G., Katagiri, T., Sharma, K., & Wilkinson, S. (2015). The 2015 Gorkha Nepal earthquake: Insights from earthquake damage survey. *Frontiers in Built Environment, 1*. https://doi.org/10.3389/fbuil.2015.00008.

GoN. (2011). *National Population and Housing Census 2011*. https://unstats.un.org/unsd/demographic-social/census/documents/Nepal/Nepal-Census-2011-Vol1.pdf.

Hanaoka, S., Rijal, H. B., & Hata, S. (2009). Changes and improvements to traditional vernacular houses in a mountain area of Nepal. In *Proceedings of the 3rd International Conference on Environmentally Sustainable Development* (pp. 8–20). https://www.researchgate.net/publication/285719357_Changes_and_improvements_to_traditional_vernacular_houses_in_a_mountain_area_of_Nepal.

Khadka, B., & Jiang, H. (2019). *Mud masonry houses in Nepal: A study based on reconstruction Work after 2015 Gorkha earthquake* (p. 11).

Khadka, B., & Shakya, M. (2016). *Seismic characteristics of un-reinforced mud masonry buildings in Nepal* (p. 11).

Kunwar, R. R., & Chand, U. (2016). Natural disaster and heritage tourism: A study on the impacts of earthquake in Bhaktapur Nepal. *Journal of Tourism and Hospitality Education, 6*, 1–39. https://doi.org/10.3126/jthe.v6i0.14766

Limbu, B., Rawal, N., Suji, M., Subedi, P. C., & Baniya, J. (2019). *Reconstructing Nepal: Post-earthquake experiences from Bhaktapur, Dhading and Sindhupalchowk*.

Lizundia, B., Shrestha, S. N., Bevington, J., Davidson, R. A., Jaiswal, K., Jimee, G. K., Kaushik, H. B., Kumar, H., Kupec, J., Mitrani-Reiser, J., Poland, C. D., Shrestha, S., Welton-Mitchell, C., Tremayne, H., & Ortiz-Milan, M. (2016). *EERI earthquake reconnaissance team report: M7.8 Gorkha, Nepal earthquake on April 25, 2015 and its aftershocks*. Earthquake Engineering Research Institute.

Manandhar, B. (2016). Remittance and earthquake preparedness. *International Journal of Disaster Risk Reduction, 15*, 52–60. https://doi.org/10.1016/j.ijdrr.2015.12.003

Mathema, A. S. (1999). *Housing and land markets in Kathmandu*, Nepal.

MoHA. (2017). *Nepal Disaster Report 2017 The road to Sendai*. http://drrportal.gov.np/uploads/document/1321.pdf.

National population and housing census 2011. (2012). Central Bureau of Statistics (p. 263). https://www.google.com/search?q=national+population+and+housing+census+2011&oq=national+populationo&aqs=chrome.1.69i57j0l7.17348j0j7&sourceid=chrome&ie=UTF-8.

National Reconstruction Authority. (2017). National Reconstruction Authority. http://www.nra.gov.np/en/pages/view/fk2lRwucsHVwn9q-LAxpTW9mGJgIRz25rUWNDHdbkYk.

NPC. (2015a). *Nepal Earthquake 2015 Post disaster needs assessment Vol. B: sector reports* [Annual Report]. Government of Nepal, National Planning Commission. https://www.worldbank.org/content/dam/Worldbank/document/SAR/nepal/PDNA%20Volume%20A%20Final.pdf.

NPC. (2015b). *Sustainable Development Goals 2016–2030 National (Preliminary) Report*. Government of Nepal, National Planning Commission. file:///C:/Users/uniyal9/Downloads/SDG%20final%20report-nepal%20(1).pdf.

OCHA. (2015). *Disasters affect thousands across Asia-Pacific*.

Oliver-Smith, A. (1990). Post-disaster housing reconstruction and social inequality: A challenge to policy and practice. *Disasters, 14*(1), 7–19. https://doi.org/10.1111/j.1467-7717.1990.tb00968.x

Peppercorn, I. (2016). *Building better and safely: Stimulating the private sector for sustainable solutions in Nepal*. Evidence on Demand. https://doi.org/10.12774/eod_hd.marchr2016.pepperconi.

Rademacher, A. (2009). When is housing an environmental problem? Reforming informality in Kathmandu. *Current Anthropology, 50*(4), 513–533. https://doi.org/10.1086/604707.

Robinson, T. R. (2020). Scenario ensemble modelling of possible future earthquake impacts in Bhutan. *Natural Hazards*. https://doi.org/10.1007/s11069-020-04138-x

Scheibler, G. (1982). *Building today in a historical context Bhaktapur, Nepal*. Ratna Pustak Bhandar.

Shakya, K. (2016). Earthquake: Impact on Nepalese economy and women. *Lowland Technology International, 8*.

Shakya, M., Duwal, S., & Kawan, C. K. (2016). Rapid visual damage assessment of masonry buildings after 2015 Gorkha earthquake: A case study of Bhaktapur Municipality. In *International Conference on Earthquake Engineering and Post Disaster Reconstruction Planning*, Bhaktapur. https://www.researchgate.net/publication/301895500_Rapid_Visual_Damage_Assessment_of_Masonry_Buildings_after_2015_Gorkha_Earthquake_A_Case_Study_of_Bhaktapur_Municipality.

Shrestha, B., & Pathranarakul, P. (2018). Nepal government's emergency response to the 2015 earthquake: A case study. *Social Sciences, 7*(8), 127. https://doi.org/10.3390/socsci7080127

Shrestha, S. B., & Taniguchi, O. (2003). A holistic approach for providing affordable housing to the urban poor of Nepal. *Journal of Asian Architecture and Building Engineering, 2*(1), 153–160. https://doi.org/10.3130/jaabe.2.153

Subedi, S., & Bahadur Poudyal Chhetri, M. (2019). Impacts of the 2015 Gorkha earthquake: Lessons learnt from Nepal. In J. Santos-Reyes (Ed.), *Earthquakes—Impact, community vulnerability and resilience*. IntechOpen. https://doi.org/10.5772/intechopen.85322.

Tallett-Williams, S., Gosh, B., Wilkinson, S., Fenton, C., Burton, P., Whitworth, M., Datla, S., Franco, G., Trieu, A., Dejong, M., Novellis, V., White, T., & Lloyd, T. (2016). Site amplification in the Kathmandu Valley during the 2015 M7.6 Gorkha, Nepal earthquake. *Bulletin of Earthquake Engineering, 14*(12), 3301–3315. https://doi.org/10.1007/s10518-016-0003-8.

The Asia Foundation. (2016). *Nepal government distribution of earthquake reconstruction cash grants for private houses* (p. 48).

UNDRR. (2019). *Disaster risk reduction in Nepal: Status Report 2019* [Status Report]. https://reliefweb.int/sites/reliefweb.int/files/resources/68230_6nepaldrmstatusreport.pdf.

USAID. (2020). *Country development cooperation strategy summary fiscal years 2014–2020*. https://www.usaid.gov/sites/default/files/documents/1861/CDCS_summary_Final_nepal_updated20202.pdf.

Welton-Mitchell, C., Awale, R., James, L., & Khanal, S. (2017). Investigating community resilience in Bhaktapur district and surrounding areas in Nepal following the 2015 earthquake. In *16th World Conference on Earthquake Engineering*.
Wyss, M. (2005). Human losses expected in Himalayan earthquakes. *Natural Hazards, 34*(3), 305–314. https://doi.org/10.1007/s11069-004-2073-1
Yadav, S., Sieffert, Y., Crété, E., Vieux-Champagne, F., & Garnier, P. (2018). Mechanical behaviour of different type of shear band connections being used in reconstruction housing in Nepal. *Construction and Building Materials, 174*, 701–712. https://doi.org/10.1016/j.conbuildmat.2018.04.121

Chapter 11
Housing in Smart City—The Emperor has No Clothes

Darshini Mahadevia

Abstract The idea of 'smart cities' is being implemented in India through Smart Cities Mission (SCM). This paper, taking an example of Ahmedabad, critically assesses as to whether smart city, as conceptualised in global literature, would be achieved amidst lack of necessary data and land governance system necessary for planned city development on one hand and state support to rent-seeking and speculative real estate interests on the other. The case study is of Ahmedabad city, declared a smart city, essentially has only a small pocket of 2 km^2 of area under the SCM, wherein the In-Situ Slum Redevelopment (ISSR) component of the Prime Minister's Awaas Yojana (PMAY) is being implemented. This paper, therefore, presents the dynamics of smart cities in India, and how this global idea, is being implemented on one hand and how the PMAY's ISSR component is being implemented on the other.

Keywords Smart cities · Slum redevelopment · Land tenure · Ahmedabad · India

11.1 Introduction

In the Smart Cities panning out in India, there are three broad dynamics; picking up of the global idea of 'smart cities' rooted within a fascination for technology and its potential to solve all the problems or even malaises of urbanization in the country, its adaptation at the local level and superimposition of the idea of smart urbanism on the unknown local terrains, one of which is informality. The Smart Cities Mission (SCM) in India envisioned on comprehensive and inter-connected approach to urban development with public participation is packaged as a technocratic project of urban development. Smart Cities has been proposed as a 'Mission'; mission meaning having "a strong commitment and sense of duty to do or achieve something".[1] One hundred

[1] Retrieved on 10 September 2018 from https://www.collinsdictionary.com/dictionary/english/mission.

D. Mahadevia (✉)
School of Arts and Sciences, Ahmedabad University, Ahmedabad, India
e-mail: darshini.mahadevia@ahduni.edu.in

A. Kundu et al. (eds.), *Accessible Housing for South Asia*,
https://doi.org/10.1007/978-3-030-88881-7_11

cities, of the 4041[2] statutory[3] urban areas are included in the SCM, to achieve various development goals of the cities, which would otherwise have been pursued with or without the SCM or were being pursued under a former programme called the Jawaharlal Nehru National Urban Renewal Mission (JNNURM).

In parallel operate another major urban development programmes, many of them as missions; Atal Mission for Rejuvenation and Urban Transformation (AMRUT[4]), with nearly the same components as that of SCM, but benefitting 500 cities[5] of the total statutory urban areas,[6] Swachchh Bharat Mission (Clean India Mission), etc. Other sectoral programmes of the Government of India (GoI) have overlapped with the contents of the SCM.[7]

This paper attempts two analyses: (i) presents the changing idea of Smart City and (ii) assesses the progress of the housing component in the city of Ahmedabad, which is one of the 100 smart cities. The housing component of the Smart City Mission in Ahmedabad is the In-Situ Slum Redevelopment (ISSR) component of the Prime Minister's Awaas Yojana (PMAY). To note is the convergence of other programmes with the SCM in the selected Smart Cities.

The broad global narratives around 'smart cities' are; ideas embedded in the software-enabled technologies for urban management (Kitchin, 2014, 2015) and planning 'smart growth'. The latter has emerged to promote an urban planning idea to mitigate urban sprawl through land-use—transportation linkages, inner-city (brownfield sites) redevelopment, mixed land uses, Transit-Oriented-Development (TOD) to reduce personal automobile dependency for mobility, walkable neighbourhoods, creation of a strong sense of place (Ewing, 1997; Gordon & Richardson, 1997; Litman, 2003; Raparthi, 2015), and increasing densities in infill development (Balta et al., 2012). Smart growth is an idea rooted in the New Urbanism of the 1980s in the North American context (Hollands, 2008; Vanolo, 2016). The smart growth idea in a sense is not quite relevant for cities in India with high densities and mixed land uses (Munshi, 2013), although sprawl on 'greenfield sites' is seen around cities capture in the literature of frontier urbanisation (Gururani & Daspgupta, 2018; Denis et al., 2012).

The term 'smart' is more user-friendly than intelligent, as the latter refers to a quick mind while the former to quick response (Nam & Pardo, 2011). In policy and planning, the assumption is that the smart policies would lead to judicious base investment and fiscal measures along with smart human capital and technological

[2] From population census, 2011, retrieved on September 10, 2018 from http://censusindia.gov.in/2011-prov-results/paper2/data_files/India2/1.%20Data%20Highlight.pdf.

[3] Declared as urban through a statute. In the Indian federal structure, state governments declare settlements classified by as urban by population census, as urban governments through statutory process.

[4] 'Amrut' in Hindi, Sanskrit and many other Indian languages means 'nectar' for immortality.

[5] Retrieved on 10 September 2018 from http://mohua.gov.in/cms/amrut.php.

[6] Authors' surmise from the programmes announced on the national government's website http://mohua.gov.in/, retrieved on 10 September 2018.

[7] Based on the information retrieved on 17 September 2018 from http://mohua.gov.in/cms/schemes-or-programmes.php.

infrastructure for efficient productivity and attracting businesses (Caragliu et al., 2009). Smart city has also meant big data system for simulating future urban policies and programmes (Batty et al., 2012). The adjective 'smart' is linked to the concept of 'intelligent city' (Castells & Hall, 1994; Hollands, 2008; Komninos, 2002), mainly involving the relationship between the urban space and technology; i.e. the transition to forms of e-governance, innovations in urban areas; provision of ICT infrastructure (Vanolo, 2016). There is the big argument of dependence on technology for collecting big data for everyday urban management such as efficient public transport system, congestion monitoring, enforcement of public safety and security (Graham, 2012; Townsend, 2013), and response to environmental shocks (Townsend, 2013). Information and Communication Technology (ICT) use in everyday city governance (Castelnovo et al., 2016), is argued that it will enable citizens and communities to participate in the knowledge societies.

Smart city initiatives have excited the global Information and Communication Technology (ICT) players such as Cisco, IBM and others initially as in other contexts as well (Batty et al., 2012; Vilajosana et al., 2013). This has also been the case in India (Hoelscher, 2016). Dholera Smart City was marketed by Cisco (Datta, 2015).

The available voluminous critical literature on Indian 'smart cities' is either outrightly critical or recommends making them successful. Harris (2015) calls the available literature as 'promotional bombast' stating that Dholera (investigated by Datta, 2015) is an example of hyperbolic and unsubstantiated rhetoric (Datta, 2015: 25) as Dholera would be twice the size of present-day Mumbai by 2040 (Datta, 2015: 4). Datta (2015) herself calls Dholera an extension of the post-colonial modernization project, which earlier was through 'new towns'. In the contemporary times, the Dholera, Datta (2015) states is an extension of ongoing new-city making project; the new cities being the Ambani City (knowledge city near Navi Mumbai), Hitech City in Hyderabad (also called Cyberabad), eco-cities (such as Lavasa), Amravati (the new state capital of Andhra Pradesh marketed as having Singapore model of development and indeed planned by a Singapore firm[8]), etc. to extend the global project of the neoliberal state, but a more digitally led city-making of the recent years. Dholera is in the Delhi-Mumbai Industrial Corridor (DMIC) wherein 24 smart cities (Hoelscher, 2016: 32), mainly industrial ones[9] are proposed. Sampat (2015) calls Dholera an example of 'rentier growth', the predominant interests being that of real estate for private capital accumulation while forcing the state to invest in infrastructure. On this count, smart cities' agenda is also called elitist or exclusive (Hoelscher, 2016). The more mundane research suggests improvement in technology such as the Internet of Things and Artificial Intelligence for the success of Smart Cities in India (Chatterjee et al., 2018).

Smart cities in India are considered to have splintered vision (Hoelscher, 2016: 37) on account of the mission failing to conceptualize and develop an integrated set of

[8] Retrieved on 17 September 2018 from https://economictimes.indiatimes.com/news/politics-and-nation/how-andhra-pradesh-plans-to-make-its-new-capital-amaravati-a-world-class-city/articleshow/58767503.cms.

[9] Retrieved on 29 March 2018 from http://www.makeinindia.com/policy/national-manufacturing.

policies. Praharaj et al. (2018) suggest that the SCM, rather than being a stand-alone initiative should be integrated within the overall city development visions and their plans, such as the Master Plans and the former City Development Plans[10] (CDPs). The complex planning and governance mechanisms, illustrated through the study of the Bhubaneshwar Smart City Plan, argue that 'realigning policy, planning and institutional frameworks are critical' (Praharaj et al., 2018: 42) for the successful implementation of smart cities. While the general notion of smart cities assume that the citizens would participate in e-governance, taking the example of Indian cities, Praharaj et al., (2017: 1431) find that this was not the case and that engagement of citizens has been high only in the small and medium-sized cities due to civic intimacy. We pick up from the broader issues raised about the city governance (Nam and Prado, 2011) - something that has not received any great attention -) we investigate them in detail using the case study of one housing project within the Smart City projects taking the case of Ahmedabad. We critically view this housing project through interviewing existing occupants and the real estate developers in the Ahmedabad Smart City case study, accompanied by personal observations during the field visit. We have selected a critical assessment of a housing project because, a total of 73 projects 'affordable housing projects have been approved in 60 selected Smart Cities by the Ministry of Housing and Urban Affairs (MoHUA), Government of India for central assistance'.[11]

The 'smart cities' as an idea and SCM as an agenda is still unfolding; but is it that or increasingly looking like any former as well as concurrent urban development programme, is it a plain hyperbole (a *jumla*), is what is discussed in Sect. 11.2. The unravelling of the smart city projects in Ahmedabad and the governance challenges that emerge are discussed in Sect. 11.3. In Sect. 11.4 we discuss the tribulations of the SCM in the Indian context when any such global idea is propelled upon informal terrain and complex legal mesh of land legislation, arguing that like other urban development programmes unmindful of Indian ground reality and hence fated to fail, the SCM in India too would be another empty promise of rapid urban transformation.

11.2 Smart Cities Mission India

Indian Smart Cities Mission (SCM) is for 100 cities to improve conditions in the cities through harnessing technology and local area development have been identified through a competition held in three stages. The smart cities agenda and contents have changed over time. The agenda has come very close to any other urban development

[10] These were prepared under the now discontinued JNNURM for prioritising development projects in a city.

[11] See http://smartcities.gov.in/upload/uploadfiles/files/Housing%20Projects%20in%20SCP-%2060%20Cities.pdf (accessed on 7 February 2021). The site was last updated on 5 April 2017. The later data is not available.

programme except for a requirement of 10% of the city's electricity supply to be guaranteed through solar energy for maintaining a focus on harnessing renewable energy in the smart cities (HLRN, 2017: 11).

The first interest in smart cities in India was to build greenfield cities that could be linked with the Indian government's development of industrial settlements and Special Economic Zones (SEZs) to both promote industry-led urban growth and provide new urban spaces to address the population challenges in existing cities (Anand & Sami, 2015). The early smart cities were seen more than incremental improvements in service delivery and as means to build on state's and private sector's interest in infrastructure-led urbanization and the SCM was a logical extension of the earlier policy initiatives to promote urban industrialization—SEZs and industrial townships (Hoelscher, 2016: 32). Notably, the first two smart cities, fully greenfield, proposed much before the SCM, were in Gujarat, one Dholera, which has been mentioned and another Gujarat International Finance Tec-City (GIFT) City (to the north of Ahmedabad, adjoining Gandhinagar, the state capital). The Chief Minister of Gujarat[12] when ascended as the Prime Minister of India, took the idea of 'smart city' to the nation and announced the SCM at the national level, however, with the initial proclamations to build 'new cities', much like the Dholera and GIFT of Gujarat, but later on downplaying the idea of 'greenfield' cities when the guidelines were announced (Hoelscher, 2016: 34). Instead, focus shifted to 'brownfield' sites with the multi-sectoral and multi-institutional approach in such a way that almost all development projects could fall within the SCM ambit and increasingly looking like any other urban development programme (Srivathsan, 2015), with a minor difference of the city qualifying for the SCM were selected through a competition. In response to the allegation of 'corporate urbanism' (Sood, 2015) and elite accumulation where the citizens were largely absent (Burte, 2014), the national government introduced the idea of participation; however, through the use of ICT tools and no specification about how to go about it (Hoelscher, 2016: 35). The greenfield site development was not occurring due to problems of agriculture land acquisition blamed on the Right to Fair Compensation and Transparency in Land Acquisition, Rehabilitation and Resettlement (RFCTLARR) Act, 2013, which the national government attempted to modify in December 2014 through an executive order, which could not be adopted in the Parliament due to lack of a majority of the ruling party. This could be one of the reasons for giving up on the idea of 'greenfield' smart cities and instead, the focus shifted to redevelopment in the existing cities (Hoelscher, 2016: 36).

> Needing to bend to challenging political and economic realities, principally concerning financing and land acquisition, the current SCM has shifted focus towards a more grounded approach involving brownfield reconstruction and retrofitting in existing cities; with an increasing focus on participation in its vision, language and process. (Hoelscher, 2016: 29).

---

[12] In the federal and parliamentary system of governance in India, the states are headed by a Chief Minister and the nation by a Prime Minister. Both are elected by the elected members of the dominant political party of the state legislature and parliament, respectively.

In all proposals from 100 cities have been selected for central government funding under the SCM through competition declared in five rounds [13] towards promoting 'sustainable and inclusive cities that provide core infrastructure and give a decent quality of life to its citizens, a clean and sustainable environment and application of 'Smart' Solutions'".[14] Furthermore, the 'focus is on sustainable and inclusive development and the idea is to look at compact areas, create a replicable model which will act as a lighthouse to other aspiring cities. The Smart Cities Mission is meant to set examples that can be replicated both within and outside the smart city, catalyzing the creation of similar Smart Cities in various regions and parts of the country'.[15] The smart city features include mixed land use, inclusive housing, walkable localities, preserving and developing open spaces, promoting and developing a variety of transport options, citizen-friendly and cost-effective governance and eventually creating identity (to be read as branding) of the city.

The SCM has two components, Area-Based Development (ABD), which focusses on development in a small area of the city through projects related to infrastructure, housing, waste management and heritage development and Pan-city projects, by name for the whole city under which digital infrastructure is laid throughout the city. The ABD component has three models namely retrofitting of existing areas for a land parcel of above 500 acres (approximately 2 km^2), redevelopment for a land parcel of above 50 acres (0.20 km^2) and Greenfield development of above 250 acres (approximately 1 km^2) (MoUD, 2015).

The SCM has taken a project-based approach, that is, each project under the ABD or Pan City is approved by the central mission. The SCM at the area level also converges funds available from other national missions such as AMRUT, Swachchh Bharat Mission (Clean India Mission), etc. There is already confusion here as to which project is of the SCM and which of the other missions! Under the SCM, on the whole, 2884 projects have been approved of which 148 were completed (5.2% of the total approved) at the cost of Indian Rupee (INR) 18,720 million (USD 275 million[16]) (just 1.4% of the total envisaged investment) in mid-2018 and another 72% of them were at the stage when Detailed Project Report (DPR) was being prepared (Jadhav 2018[17]). Only 31 out of 90 cities have completed at least one project. NDMC[18] leads with 23 completed projects, Varanasi with 16 projects and Raipur with 10 projects. Among the total approved projects, 73 (2.5%) are for affordable housing and 159 (5.5%) for open spaces/riverfront projects and 73 cities have proposed app-based

[13] National Institute of Urban Affairs (NIUA) (2017): SMARTNET. Retrieved on 2 March 2018 from smartnet.niua.org: https://smartnet.niua.org/smart-cities-network.

[14] Retrieved on 14 September 2018 from http://mohua.gov.in/cms/smart-cities.php.

[15] Retrieved on 14 September 2018 from http://mohua.gov.in/cms/smart-cities.php.

[16] Considering 1 USD = INR 68 (rate in mid-2018).

[17] Jadhav, R. (2018): '2.5 Years into Smart City Plan, Only 5% of Projects Finished', The Times of India. 10 January. Retrieved on 25 May 2018 from, https://timesofindia.indiatimes.com/india/2–5-years-into-smart-city-plan-only-5-of-projects-finished/articleshow/62436408.cms.

[18] New Delhi Municipal Council (NDMC) is the municipal council of the city of New Delhi, India, and the area under its administration is referred to as the NDMC area. NDMC, covering an area of 43.7 km^2.

Pan-city solutions [19]. The funding for the SCM projects is from multiple sources: 23% as central government share, 22% as state government share, another 21% as a contribution from other central and state government missions (as convergence), 22% from the private sector for the Public–Private Partnership (PPPs), 5% as loans and 7% as the contribution of the city itself from its resources or mobilized through Corporate Social Responsibility (CSR) funds[20,21].

In all 73 'affordable housing projects' of total project cost of INR 17,035.95 crores[22] have been approved. The full list is available in Annexure 11.1. This list also includes projects for the informal sector other than housing, such as the development of hawkers' zone in Kochi and two market redevelopments in Ernakulum, as well as Middle Income Group (MIG) housing in Aurangabad. The MIG housing is also considered as 'affordable housing', but for the MIG segment.

The SCM agenda and projects have morphed from greenfield to brownfield developments. The projects are regular urban development projects and not even hi-tech. Only 11 cities have inclusive planning, including disabled-based, gender-based, safety and security approaches and inclusion of urban poor in their ABD/PAN city proposals[23]. Thus, on the whole, the SCM has remained a hyperbole than any significant move towards either 'smart growth' or 'smart city' as envisaged in the literature.

11.3 Smart City Ahmedabad

11.3.1 Description of Smart City Ahmedabad

The Ahmedabad Smart City Plan (SCP) has multiple proposals totalling INR 24,920 million, of which INR 6040 million are for Area Based Development (ABD) in a locality named Wadaj over about 2 kms^2 of the area which has very large slum pockets spread over the entire delineated area. The smart features included in the Wadaj ABD are solar energy, waste segregation, rainwater harvesting, Wi-Fi hotspots, intelligent traffic management, smart parking, energy-efficient street lighting and surveillance cameras (see Table 11.1 for their fund allocations for each). It defies logic as to how intelligent traffic management in the area selected for ABD would work in

[19] National Institute of Urban Affairs (NIUA) (2017): SMARTNET. Retrieved on 2 March 2018 from smartnet.niua.org: https://smartnet.niua.org/smart-cities-network.

[20] This data excludes that of nine cities selected in the last round.

[21] National Institute of Urban Affairs (NIUA) (2017): SMARTNET. Retrieved on 2 March 2018 from smartnet.niua.org: https://smartnet.niua.org/smart-cities-network.

[22] See http://smartcities.gov.in/upload/uploadfiles/files/Housing%20Projects%20in%20SCP-%2060%20Cities.pdf (accessed on 7 February 2021). The site was last updated on 5 April 2017. The later data is not available.

[23] National Institute of Urban Affairs (NIUA) (2017): SMARTNET. Retrieved on 2 March 2018 from smartnet.niua.org: https://smartnet.niua.org/smart-cities-network.

Table 11.1 List of projects in Ahmedabad SCP

S. no	Projects in SCP	Cost (in million)
Area-Based Development (ABD)		
Retrofitting Wadaj TOZ		
1	Intermodal hub	12.5
2	Utility Network (Water, sewerage, drainage, roads, street lighting, etc.)	38.5
Redevelopment Wadaj		
3	External Utility Network (Water, sewerage, drainage, roads, etc.)	2.8
4	Wastewater Treatment Plant	12.5
5	Residential and Allied Development (including internal utility network)	45.1
Smart features		
6	Solar Energy	2.2
7	Waste Segregation	0.1
8	Rain Water Harvesting	1.5
9	Smart Metering	2.6
10	OFC Network	0.2
11	Wi-Fi Hotspots	0.1
12	NMT Tracks / Cycle Tracks	0.2
13	Intelligent Traffic Management	0.6
14	Smart Parking	1.1
15	Energy Efficient Street Lighting	0.2
16	Surveillance Cameras	0.1
17	Others	54.8
Pan City		
Smart Transit Integrated Transit Management Platform + CCPS		
18	Integrated Transit Management Platform (GPS and AVLS, PIS, etc.)	9.0
19	Common Card Payment System (Smart Cards, readers, software, etc.)	10.4
	Command & Control Centre, OFC Network, and Integration of Services	
20	Command & Control Centre + OFC Network Connectivity	20.3
21	Surveillance Equipment & Integration, Intelligent Traffic Management	10.7
22	Integration with other services & Real-Time Tracking/Monitoring	3.5

Source Ahmedabad SCP Annexure (NIUA, 2017[24])

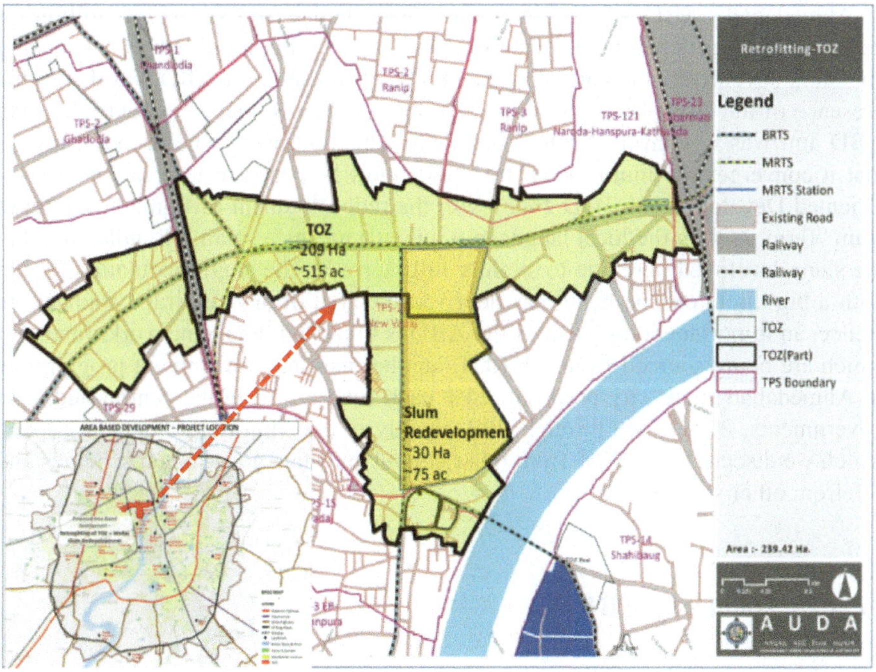

Fig. 11.1 ABD, Ahmedabad.[25]

absence of intelligent/smart traffic management at the city level. In addition, the Wadaj ABD (Fig. 11.1) will also have an intermodal transport hub of the existing Bus Rapid Transit (BRT) station, existing city-bus system[26] station and upcoming metro system's station. The city has also proposed Pan-city projects, such as an integrated transit platform with the primary aim to provide citizens access to public transport within 400 m of every household and a common card system for payment; and a command and control centre for surveillance as well as smart traffic control. The ABD component's important part is the redevelopment of a slum named Ramapir tekra in Public–Private Partnership (PPP) mode (see Annexure 11.1). The slum redevelopment is based on the In-situ Slum Redevelopment (ISSR) approach of the PMAY—Urban (for details of the ISSR see Mahadevia et al., 2018). Here we discuss the governance challenges; the land governance and identifying beneficiaries for the slum redevelopment.

[24] National Institute of Urban Affairs (NIUA) (2017): SMARTNET. Retrieved on 2 March 2018 from smartnet.niua.org: https://smartnet.niua.org/smart-cities-network.

[25] National Institute of Urban Affairs (NIUA) (2017): SMARTNET. Retrieved on 2 March 2018 from smartnet.niua.org: https://smartnet.niua.org/smart-cities-network.

[26] Ahmedabad, besides BRTS, has also city-bus system called Ahmedabad Municipal Transport Services (AMTS).

Ahmedabad's ABD is 2 km^2 in area and has a budget of INR 16,740 million for its development. As per the Ahmedabad Municipal Corporation's (AMC's) housing and slum development department, the choice of this area for ABD was due to the presence of the city's largest slum pocket here (named Ramapir no Tekro) and the ABD aim was to convert it into a habitable neighbourhood. The proposal argues that it converges the multi-modal transport hub t(he proposal to create a Transit-Oriented Development - TOD zone) with the redevelopment of Ramapir no Tekro slum. Term *tekro* in the local language (Gujarati) means a small hill indicating that the slum developed here due to slightly hilly terrain. The slight undulating terrain with a big ditch, on one hand, has deprived the area of any sewerage connection. Hence, an important component of the ABD is to lay a drainage network, funds for which are being sourced from AMRUT, another national government programme. In Ahmedabad smart city proposal, 24% each fund are from the central and state governments, 24% raised through PPP (mainly in the slum redevelopment aspect, which we discuss later), 22% from other central and state government schemes and 6% from other sources[27]).

11.3.2 Details of ABD

The ABD is 208 ha, declared a TOD zone, and has a maximum permissible Floor Space Index (FSI) of 4 for the redevelopment. The TOD zone includes a multimodal hub, utility networks and green spaces with pedestrian facilities. The slum redevelopment site is on 30 ha (14% of the ABD area), through a programme called in-situ slum redevelopment (ISSR), one of the components of the national housing programme, the PMAY—Urban. The slum redevelopment would rehouse 8,000 households in the private sector built housing, each unit of the size 30 m^2 having an in-built kitchen, bath and water closet as well as tap water, while the site would have roads, water and sewerage systems, wastewater plant, parks, green and community spaces. The low-lying areas have been proposed to be developed as parks. Currently, the entire slum area in the Ramapir no tekro has multiple settlements, called *chalis* in the local language—a *chali* is single rooms laid in a row. Thus, the redevelopment of this area is to be in six sectors (Fig. 11.2).

In the ISSR approach, a developer redevelops the site using permissible FSI (which is 4) in such a way that all the existing households are given a free house in the redevelopment, while the private developer benefits from excess built-up space made available through high FSI. The developer sells the excess built-up space, which is called a free-sale component of the project, to make profits. Over and above, the developer also has the additional benefit of applying the equivalent FSI (of the one consumed on the slum site) on other of the firm's plots elsewhere in the city. The developers have been attracted to redevelop the slums due to this additional FSI

[27] National Institute of Urban Affairs (NIUA) (2017): SMARTNET. Retrieved on 2 March 2018 from smartnet.niua.org: https://smartnet.niua.org/smart-cities-network.

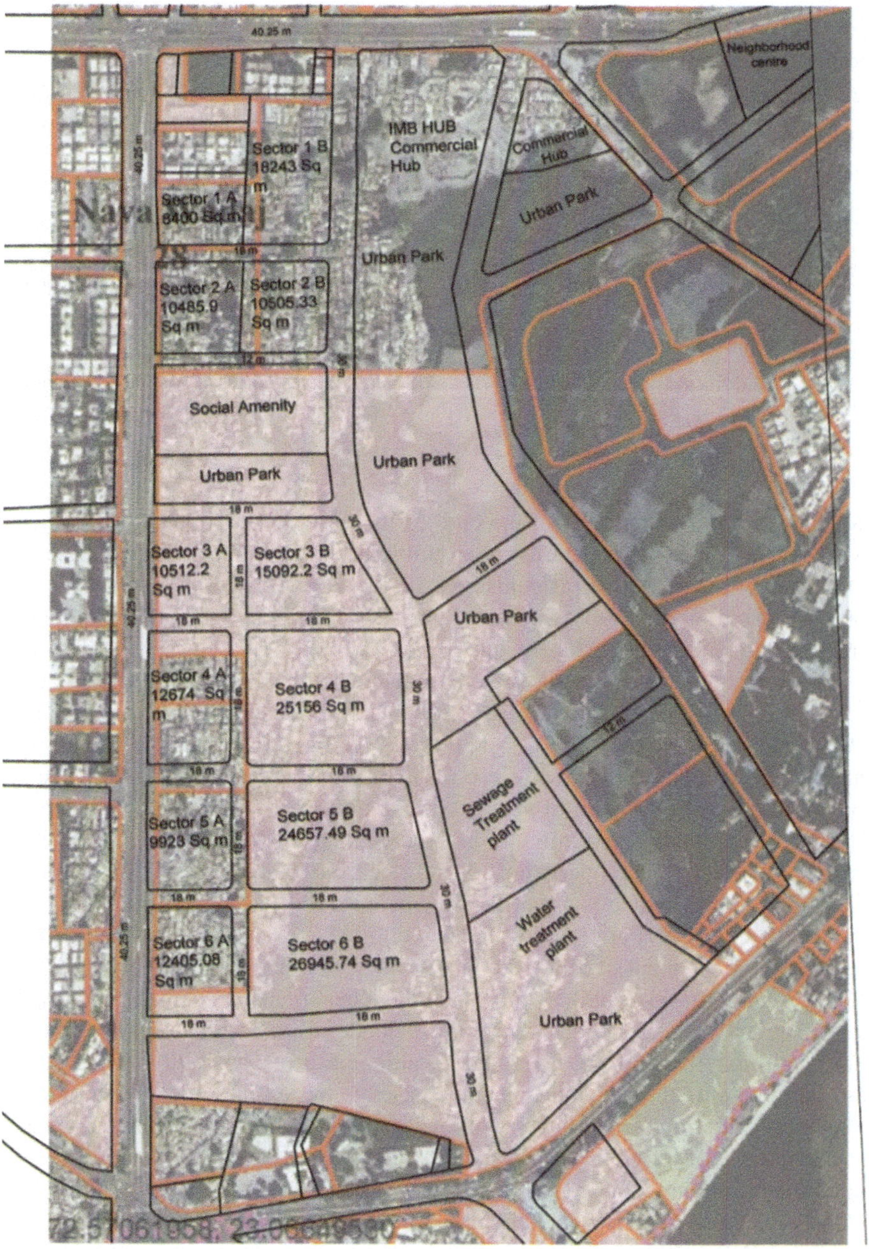

Fig. 11.2 Layout plan with Sectors of ABD Ahmedabad, Overlaid on the Town Planning Scheme

Table 11.2 Current status of work, Ramapir No Tekro

Sector no	Developer	Work stage
1	Cube Construction Engineering Ltd.	Numbering of houses complete, collection of documents ongoing
2	Shreeji Infracon	Status unclear
3	HN Safal	Document verification ongoing. 48 houses were cleared and a sample house has been constructed
4	Venus Builders (Nila infrastructure)	Numbering of houses complete, collection of documents ongoing
5	Cube Construction Engineering Ltd.	Document verification on going
6	RJP Infrastructure Pvt Ltd.	Numbering of houses complete, collection of documents ongoing

Source Primary survey conducted in June 2018

available for use in other parts of the city. At the onset of the project, the residents have raised a dispute with regards to several households living in the slums in the entire Ramapir no tekro; the residents give an estimate of 15,000 households versus 8,000 estimated by the AMC. Such disputes are endemic to any slum resettlement or redevelopment process (Mahadevia, 2014).

The redevelopment in the six sectors under the ISSR has been tendered out to five developers (Table 11.2). Under the in-situ slum redevelopment policy of 2013 of Gujarat,[28] the developers have to build, operate, maintain and then transfer the housing development to the AMC. The residents eligible for a dwelling unit in the scheme are ones who have proof of stay at Ramapir pre-2010 and can produce proof of their residency through a minimum of two among the following documents: an Aadhar card,[29] voter ID, property tax bill and electricity bill. Those unable to produce the eligibility proofs but are project-affected people (PAP) can pay INR 300,000 and obtain a dwelling unit. For preparing a list of eligible households for a dwelling unit, free or through payment of INR 300,000, some developers took the help of NGOs. After 3 rounds of verification which includes checking documents, photography and videography, the beneficiaries were provided with a card that approved them as the legitimate beneficiary. This listing, although a responsibility of the AMC, was undertaken by the developer in some cases to hasten the process. The project under the 'smart city' started even without an appropriate and adequate database. The governance of 'eligibility for resettlement' has been privatized, with a possible conflictual fallout in the near term.

On finalization of the list of beneficiaries, the developer paid a check of INR 72,000 at a rate of INR 6,000 per month as rent so that the current occupants vacated the

[28] For discussion on changes in the Slum Redevelopment Policies of Gujarat, see Mahadevia (2018).

[29] This is a Unique ID card given by the Government of India to all citizens.

site for a developer to start redevelopment works. The policy specifies the developer to give possession of the new dwelling units to the eligible beneficiaries within 24 months after evacuation. The new housing would be blocks of seven storeyed buildings. At the time of our survey, the various sectors were in different stages of redevelopment (Table 11.2).

11.3.3 Fuzziness in Land Ownership

The ISSR projects in Gujarat are to be developed only on government lands. A major portion of the Ramapir no Tekro is largely on land belonging to the district collector and the AMC. However, some parcels (we could not ascertain the exact area) in the south of the project were owned by charity trusts, mainly parts of sectors 4A, 5A and 6A. While the AMC officials informed us that these were acquired by the authority, this change did not reflect in the records of the Town Planning Scheme (the local level planning) document (see Fig. 11.2). Such an anomaly in land ownership is likely to create disputes in the coming years. Thus, this component of the 'smart city' does not even have an accurate land-related database for its implementation, leaving aside the use of technology for either planning or plan implementation.

One parcel in sector 1 belongs to the *Pashupalak Vikas Sahakari Mandli* having 42 dwelling units belonging to a particular community, namely the *Rabaris*, who are cattle-owning community and were given ownership of the land in the 1960s for grazing their cattle. Over time they have built big houses in these plots. The government initially notified their parcel also as a part of sector 1, stating that their houses were illegal as these were built on the grazing land. The residents filed a case in the Gujarat High Court in 2013, challenging the AMC's contention and demanding suitable compensation in money terms if they were to be moved. The area occupied by these contesting households has been post-plan excluded from sector 1, that is, from the 'smart city'. This small pocket of 'unsmart' would remain within the 'smart city' of Ahmedabad! Another contentious issue that would come up is with regards to the rights of tenants in sector 1, which has 75% of its occupants renting a house; these are colonies with small houses owned by Rabaris. The tenants are paying low rent of INR 1,500 per month and they would not find any equivalent house in the nearby localities if they were to be dispossessed of their current arrangement. Even on redevelopment, it is these powerful Rabaris who would get the houses and not targeted beneficiaries. The smart city project has conveniently bypassed this complexity.

11.3.4 Lack of People-Centric Approach

A main bottleneck in the project implementation is the lack of consent and cooperation of the existing residents. Each sector has specific problems, but some common issues emerged from discussions with residents, shop owners, NGOs and local leaders. The first one was the survey of eligibility conducted by the private developers in place of the local government, the AMC. The survey captured only 7,500–8.000 beneficiaries, whereas the residents claim that there are about 15,000 of them. The residents are demanding a fresh survey with a new cut-off date other than 2010 as per the policy mentioned above. Secondly, the incrementally built dwelling units of the residents, to accommodate expanding family size, are much larger than the 30 m^2 to be provided under the scheme. Thirdly, many residents conduct their livelihoods activities in the spill-over spaces on the ground, which would have to be given up in a multistoried building with a smaller living area of 30 m^2. Fourthly, the residents doubt the availability of rental housing in the nearby location at the cost of INR 6,000 (as mandated in the project) and that whether the development would be completed in the stated period or not; if not then they would be personally forced to bear the rents for time-overruns. The residents prefer to squat on the same site till the construction was completed to save the problem of finding rental housing, suggesting to the developers to take up phase-wise redevelopment. Fifthly, there is no scheme for 400 small shops in the locality. Lastly, the residents are unhappy that the AMC is not involved in any of the negotiations of the project leaving them at the mercy of the developers. The residents were even unaware that the redevelopment of the site was occurring under the Smart City Mission!

The residents' dissatisfaction has led to periodic protests and minor violence such as damaging and bringing down of the project announcement boards. The latter happened in sector 5 of the project area. An article in Sandesh, a vernacular newspaper, dated 16.3.2018 spoke about the agitations in sector 3, where checks were distributed after the evacuation of the 48 beneficiaries for the sample house. The people attacked the corporator as they were allegedly forced to accept the checks and some houses received multiple checks due to mismanaged beneficiary lists. The opposition leader commented that the slum dwellers were being scared into clearing their houses in the name of redevelopment. Some of the dwelling units have passed a notice above their doors that they would not cooperate till the AMC was directly involved in the project and took its responsibility.

The Area-Based Component (ABD) of the 'smart city' Ahmedabad has nothing 'smart' about it, in particular when it comes to formalizing the existing informal housing (the slums), as the city does not have an accurate database on the slums, which would include an estimate of a total number of households occupying each slum. The latest slum survey is of 2012 (AMC, 2014) when the survey should have been undertaken before the project implementation. The in-situ slum redevelopment through private developers began without a database, which the developers had to create, in a sense, out-sourcing the process of establishing citizenship to a private company, when this is squarely a state responsibility! Assessment of some of the developers involved in the project is that this slum redevelopment would remain incomplete and the 'smart city' ambition of improving living conditions of the urban poor would remain a mirage. What would a smart city be if just 8,000 dwelling units are to be constructed in the city under the SCM when 145,455 households are living in the slums in Ahmedabad city (AMC, 2014: 46)? Further, how can Ahmedabad be called a 'smart city' when just 2 km^2 of its 450 km^2 (AUDA, n.d.) would be covered and that too with the likelihood of only partial success?

11.4 The Emperor's Clothes

Smart cities, the contemporary global idea of urbanism that seeks an array of global strategies and ideas (Roy, 2011) of inter-referencing (North–South, North–North, South–South or increasingly South–North) that would produce a particular kind of urbanism through modernization, neoliberalism and its new form of governance (McCann et al., 2013; Roy, 2011) has become a new hubris in the Indian urbanization process. The nation is knocking at the global doors through her fantastic economic growth story[30] essentializing the need to have a remarkable urban story. 'Smart city' as an idea fits in well in the overall story of a nation modernizing, industrializing and urbanizing with the state-of-the-art infrastructure and technology-driven management. Much of the hubris in the SCM launching normalized when the city-level proposals came in that was very much in the same vein as they would have been under any other programme, the former JNNURM or the concurrent going AMRUT. The idea of Smart City, which is technology-driven, when implemented on the ground, without even the basic data, falls flat, as we see in the case of Ahmedabad.

In Ahmedabad 'smart city', the existing dwellers in the large informal settlement, which tends to have a complex land tenure system (as shown by Mahadevia, 2011, 2015). Fear of expulsion from their current living conditions of those not included in the beneficiary list has resulted in silent resilience. At the same time, lack of data about the slum households in the city, even incorrect land ownership data not in sync with the data used for planning, in Ahmedabad's case for TPS framing (Ballaney, 2013), has created a discrepancy in land ownership in parts of the area selected for 'smart city' implementation. In short, the smart city implementation has run into problems. At the national level, the SCM is nothing more than a regular programme addressing the urban development deficits, whichever way these are construed; as deficits of living conditions, housing or infrastructure. The case investigated, focused on improving housing conditions of the dwellers of the existing slum, that is, of intervention in a brown-field site, the complexities arising from the land regime and political process of defining urban citizenship (entitlement to the redevelopment) has stalled the process. That is 'Smart City', 'Housing for all', have become empty slogans, called 'jumla' in Hindi. That is, the Emperor has no clothes.

11.5 Annexure

See Table 11.3.

[30] http://blogs.worldbank.org/endpovertyinsouthasia/india-s-remarkably-robust-and-resilient-growth-story, accessed on September 18, 2018.

Table 11.3 Affordable Housing Projects in SCP-60 Smart Cities

S. no	State	City	Project name	Project cost (Rs. crores)
1	Gujarat	Ahmedabad	PPP Based Slum Rehabilitation in Junavadaj area	836.00
2	Karnataka	Belagavi	Development of Affordable Housing for EWS	84.00
3	Karnataka	Belagavi	EWS Housing in Approved BUDA Layout	43.52
4	Madhya Pradesh	Bhopal	Area-based development, TT Nagar—HFA	45.75
5	Madhya Pradesh	Bhopal	Development of Govt., Affordable, EWS and LIG housing, 15% affordable housing	876.25
6	Odisha	Bhubaneshwar	Janpath Government Housing Redevelopment	1260.00
7	Odisha	Bhubaneshwar	Mission Awaas	840.00
8	Odisha	Bhubaneswar	Rental Housing for Construction Workers	12.00
9	Odisha	Bhubaneswar	Project Kutumb- One stop Social Equity Centres	15.75
10	Tamilnadu	Coimbatore	Housing for all and Social Infrastructure	192.50
11	Madhya Pradesh	Indore	Slum Housing 131,716 m^2	158.06
12	Madhya Pradesh	Indore	Slum Housing Lodha Colony	74.70
13	Madhya Pradesh	Indore	Compensatory Housing 180,219 m^2	270.33
14	Madhya Pradesh	Indore	Free-Sale Housing 945,565 m^2	1418.35
15	Madhya Pradesh	Jabalpur	Affordable Houses (600)	83.72
16	Madhya Pradesh	Jabalpur	Compensatory Tenements Built-up	284.75
17	Madhya Pradesh	Jabalpur	Real-estate Sale Components Built-up	1228.54
18	Andhra Pradesh	Kakinada	Construction of 1560 pucca households which are Kutcha (weaker section)	74.88
19	Andhra Pradesh	Kakinada	Construction of 3200 Pucca Households which are Kutcha (weaker section)	153.60
20	Kerala	Kochi	Integrated redevelopment of Slum housing	141.40
21	Kerala	Kochi	Upgradation of infrastructure in Housing through Credit linked schemes	24.35

(continued)

Table 11.3 (continued)

S. no	State	City	Project name	Project cost (Rs. crores)
22	Kerala	Kochi	Construction & up-gradation of 755 DUs in Thuruthy, Kalvathy & Konchery colony	74.24
23	Kerala	Kochi	Broadway and Ernakulam market Redevelopment and Mattancherry spice market	110.00
24	Kerala	Kochi	Standard Hawker zones in Fort Kochi	5.00
25	Maharashtra	Pune	Affordable Housing	40.00
26	Maharashtra	Pune	Build affordable housing	40.00
27	Maharashtra	Solapur	Urban Infrastructure (Priority-2) (Project 7) Housing for urban poor	57.77
28	Maharashtra	Solapur	Housing for urban poor	116.22
29	Gujarat	Surat	Affordable Housing (PMAY) (1050 EWS/1950 LIG)	240.00
30	Gujarat	Surat	Affordable Housing (PPP) (5750 Units)	460.00
31	Andhra Pradesh	Visakhapatnam	Housing for all-1130 houses	54.24
32	Tripura	Agartala	Mixed Housing Development	295.00
33	UP	Agra	In-situ house upgradation	116.30
34	Maharashtra	Aurangabad	EWS Housing	90.2
35	Maharashtra	Aurangabad	LIG Housing	72.2
36	Maharashtra	Aurangabad	MIG Housing	198.5
37	Bihar	Bhagalpur	Urban Poor and Slums	51.50
38	UT	Chandigarh	Residential Affordable Housing	320.83
39	Uttarakhand	Dharamshala	Beneficiary led Housing, In-situ rehabilitation and Shelter for Urban Homeless	219.23
40	Madhya Pradesh	Gwalior	Development of 3686 Affordable Housing Unit on PPP under PMAY	294.88
41	Madhya Pradesh	Gwalior	Affordable Housing as Residental Component of Mixed-Use TOD Development in AHP- 1493 Units	
42	Madhya Pradesh	Gwalior	12 Housing Component in Gwalior Habitat and Trade Center-1984 Units	

(continued)

Table 11.3 (continued)

S. no	State	City	Project name	Project cost (Rs. crores)
43	Madhya Pradesh	Gwalior	13 Development of Rental Housing for Floating Population (600 Unit)	45.00
44	Karnataka	Hubli Dharwad	Affordable housing	103.32
45	Nagaland	Kohima	Slum rehabilitation and rejuvenation of the old houses	92.63
46	Rajasthan	Kota	Housing for all and Social Infrastructure	39.00
47	Uttar Pradesh	Lucknow	Infrastructure works & facilities etc. at slums	11.40
48	Tamil Nadu	Madurai	Housing for all	11.00
49	Karnataka	Mangaluru	EWS Housing	7.80
50	Maharashtra	Nagpur	Home Sweet Home	30.00
51	Maharashtra	Nagpur	Project "HOME SWEETHOME"	30.00
52	Sikkim	Namchi	Housing (Land of Building & Housing Deptt.)	50.00
53	Sikkim	Namchi	Infrastructure Works & Facilities at Slums	15.00
54	Maharashtra	Nashik	Project Niwaas—Slum Redevelopment	27.30
55	A & N	Port Blair	Housing & Slum Development Programme	4.84
56	Chattisgarh	Raipur	Affordable housing and EWS housing	74.18
57	Jharkhand	Ranchi	EWS Housing	38.84
58	Odisha	Rourkela	Vernacular architecture affordable housing (8000 units)	280.00
59	Karnataka	Shivamogga	Slum Redevelopment	81.00
60	Maharashtra	Thane	70 acre cluster redevelopment of Kisan Nagar	3974.00
61	Tamil Nadu	Thanjavur	Insitu slum rehabilitation for 335 HH	11.73
62	Tamil Nadu	Thanjavur	Housing along the proposed boulevard (mixed land use)	
63	Tamil Nadu	Thanjavur	Rehabilitation of 1824 slum HH-affordable housing	63.84
64	Andhra Pradesh	Tirupati	Housing at TMC Colony	88.5
65	Andhra Pradesh	Tirupati	Beneficiary linked Housing	15.36

(continued)

Table 11.3 (continued)

S. no	State	City	Project name	Project cost (Rs. crores)
66	Andhra Pradesh	Tumkur	Slum rehabilitation	17
67	Karnataka	Tumkur	EWS—Insitu Development	55
68	Madhya Pradesh	Ujjain	Ashray—Slum/Mill Workers/Affordable Housing	478.84
69	Gujarat	Vadodara	Slum free area	260.00
70	Uttar Pradesh	Varanasi	Affordable Housing	62.84
71	Tamilnadu	Vellore	Housing & Slum Development Programme	1.27
72	Andhra Pradesh	Warrangal	Housing for existing HHs living in Kachha & Semi Pucca Houses in a slum area	91.70
73	Andhra Pradesh	Warrangal	Non-slum Residential Areas Retrofitting	
	Total			17,035.95

Source http://smartcities.gov.in/upload/uploadfiles/files/Housing%20Projects%20in%20SCP-%2060%20Cities.pdf (accessed on February 7, 2021). The site was last updated on April 5, 2017. The later data is not available

References

Ahmedabad Municipal Corporation (AMC). (2014). *Ahmedabad slum free city action plan.* Ahmedabad: Ahmedabad Municipal Corporation. Retrieved May 28, 2018, from http://www.pas.org.in/Portal/document/PIP%20Application/Ahmedabad%20Slum%20Free%20City%20Action%20Plan%20RAY.pdf.

Anand, A., & Sami, N. (2015). *Urban corridors: Strategies for economic and urban development.* International Growth Centre Working Paper. Bangalore: Indian Institute of Human Settlements.

AUDA. (n.d.). *Revised Development Plan 2021*, Ahmedabad: Ahmedabad Urban Development Authority. Retrieved June 24, 2018, from http://deshgujarat.com/2013/02/07/audas-2nd-cty-draft-development-plan-2021-for-ahmedabad/.

Ballaney, S. (2013). *Supply of land for development—Land readjustment experience in Gujarat, India: Urban legal case studies.* Nairobi: UN-Habitat.

Balta, M., Tekel, A., & Tekel, H. (2012). Urban development process of built environments in metropolitan areas in Turkey: Case study of Angora settlement, Ankara. *Journal of Urban Planning and Development*. https://doi.org/10.1061/(ASCE)UP.1943-5444.0000101,pp.70-77

Batty, M., Axhausen, K. W., Giannotti, F., Pozdnoukhov, F., Bazzani, A., Wachowicz, M., Ouzounis, G., & Portugali, Y. (2012). Smart cities of the future. *European Physical Journal Special Topics, 214*, 481–518.

Burte, H. (2014). The 'Smart City' Card. *Economic and Political Weekly, 49*(46), 22–25.

Caragliu, A., Del Bo, C., & Nijkamp, P. (2009). *Smart cities in Europe.* Series Research Memoranda 0048. VU University Amsterdam, Amsterdam, Faculty of Economics, Business Administration and Econometrics.

Castells, M., & Hall, P. (1994). *Technopoles of the world.* Routledge.

Castelnovo, W., Misuraca, G., & Savoldelli, A. (2016). Smart cities governance: The need for a holistic approach to assessing urban participatory policy making. *Social Science Computer Review, 34*(6), 724–739.

Chatterjee, S., Kar, A. K., & Gupta, M. P. (2018). Success of IoT in smart cities of India: An empirical analysis. *Government Information Quarterly, 35*, 349–361.

Datta, A. (2015). Entrepreneurial urbanisation in Dholera Smart City, Gujarat. *Dialogues in Human Geography, 5*(1), 3–22.

Denis, E., Mukhopadhyay, P., & Zérah, M. H. (2012). Subaltern urbanisation in India. *Economic & Political Weekly, 47*(30), 52–62.

Ewing, R. (1997). Is Los Angeles-style sprawl desirable? *Journal of American Planning Association, 63*(1), 107–126.

Gordon, P., & Richardson, H. (1997). Are compact cities a desirable planning goal? *Journal of American Planning Association, 63*(1), 95–106.

Graham, S. (2012). Digital medieval. *Surveillance and Society, 9*(3), 321–327.

Gururani, S., & Dasgupta, R. (2018). Frontier urbanism—Urbanisation beyond cities in South Asia. *Economic and Political Weekly, 53*(12), 41–45.

Hoelscher, K. (2016). The evolution of the smart cities Agenda in India. *International Area Studies Review, 19*(1), 28–44.

Hollands, R. G. (2008). Will the real smart city please stand up? *City, 12*, 303–320.

Housing and Land Rights Network. (2017, June). *India's smart cities mission—Smart for whom? Cities for whom?* Working Paper. New Delhi: HLRN. Retrieved Aufgust 17, 2017, from http://hlrn.org.in/documents/Smart_Cities_Report_2017.pdf.

Kitchin, R. (2014). The real-time city? Big data and smart urbanism. *GeoJournal, 79*, 1–14.

Kitchin, R. (2015). Making sense of smart cities: Addressing present shortcomings. *Cambridge Journal of Regions, Economy and Society, 8*, 131–136. https://doi.org/10.1093/cjres/rsu027

Komninos, N. (2002). *Intelligent cities: Innovation, knowledge systems and digital spaces*. Routledge.

Litman, T. (2003). Measuring transportation: Traffic, mobility and accessibility. *ITE Journal, 73*(10), 28–32.

Mahadevia, D. (2011). *Tenure security and urban social protection in India*, CSP Research Report 05, Centre for Social Protection, Institute of Development Studies, Sussex.

Mahadevia, D. (2014). Institutionalising spaces for negotiations for the urban poor. In O. P. Mathur (Ed.), *Inclusive urban planning: State of the urban poor report*, 2013 (pp. 148–166). New Delhi: Ministry of Housing & Urban Poverty Alleviation, Government of India & Oxford University Press.

Mahadevia, D. (2015). Informality and shelter security in India. In D. Mahadevia (Ed.), *Shelter security in urban India—Pathways, barriers and outcomes* (pp. 1–31). New Delhi: Concept.

Mahadevia, D., Bhatia, N., & Bhatt, B. (2018). Private sector in affordable housing?—Case of slum rehabilitation scheme in Ahmedabad, India. *Environment and Urbanisation, Asia, 9*(1), 1–17.

McCann, E., Roy, A., & Ward, K. (2013). Assembling/worlding cities. *Urban Geography, 34*(5), 581–589. https://doi.org/10.1080/02723638.2013.793905

MoUD. (2015). *Smart city guidelines*. New Delhi: MoUD. Retrieved May 25, 2018, from https://smartnet.niua.org/sites/default/files/resources/smartcityguidelines.pdf.

Munshi, T. (2013). *Built form, travel behaviour and low carbon development in Ahmedabad*, India. Ph.D., University of Twente, Enschede, The Netherlands.

Nam, T., & Pardo, T. A. (2011). Conceptualizing smart city with dimensions of technology, people, and institutions. In *The Proceedings of the 12th Annual International Conference on Digital Government Research*, College Park, MD, USA, June 12–15, 2011.

Praharaj, S., Han, J. H., & Hawken, S. (2017). Innovative civic engagement and digital urban infrastructure: lessons from 100 smart cities mission in India. *Procedia Engineering, 180*, 1423–1432.

Praharaj, S., Han, J. H., & Hawken, S. (2018). Urban innovation through policy integration: Critical perspectives from 100 smart cities mission in India. *City, Culture and Society, 12*, 35–43.

Raparthi, K. (2015). Assessing smart-growth strategies in Indian cities: Grounded theory approach to planning practice. *Journal of Urban Planning and Development, 141*(4), 1–10.

Roy, A. (2011). Urbanisms, worlding practices and the theory of planning. *Planning Theory, 10*(1), 6–15. https://doi.org/10.1177/1473095210386065.

Sampat, P. (2015). *Dholera smart city: Urban infrastructure or rentier growth?* Policy Report No. 13. Chennai: The Hindu Centre for Politics and Public Policy.

Sood, A. (2015). Industrial townships and the policy facilitation of corporate urbanisation in India. *Urban Studies, 52*(8), 1359–1378.

Srivathsan, A. (2015, June 5). A trip down the rabbit hole of Modi's Smart Cities Wonderland. *The Wire*. Retrieved September 12, 2018, from https://thewire.in/economy/a-trip-down-the-rabbit-hole-of-modis-smart-cities-wonderland.

Townsend, A. (2013). Cities of data: Examining the new urban science. *Public Culture, 27*(2), 201–212. https://doi.org/10.1215/08992363-2841808.

Vanolo, A. (2016). Is there anybody out there? The place and role of citizens in tomorrow's smart cities. *Futures, 82*, 26–26.

Vilajosana, I., Jordi, L., Martinez, B., Marc, D. P., & Angles, A. (2013, June). Bootstrapping smart cities through a self-sustainable model based on big data flows. *IEEE Communications Magazine*, 128–134.

Chapter 12
Affordable Housing in Pakistan: The Policy and Institutional Imperatives

Nasir Javed and Syeda Sani-e-Zahra Naqvi

Abstract Several studies have been done on issues about the housing sector, and mostly have identified the policy and institutional constraints that negatively impact the provision of a balanced housing market. Unless the land and housing market sector are thoroughly reviewed and its policy and institutional imperatives addressed, the affordability gap would always be there. Some of the key policy issues that negatively impact the affordability index are lack of a sound system of urban land records, archaic city master plans, building regulations that favour sprawl and low-rise developments, incentives for investing in land and disincentives for rental housing, very low financing by the banks, lack of a mortgage market and ill capacitated regulators etc. This chapter looks at some of these key policy and institutional issues that impact the housing market, analyses with data and recommends key interventions that can lead to smart and dense cities with affordable housing for all sections of the society. It keeps in view the frameworks provided by the UNHABITAT, the World Bank and the recommendations made at several forums by the international development organizations in coming forward with several definitive recommendations.

Keywords Housing policy · Housing institutions · Pakistan

12.1 Introduction

Pakistan is the fastest urbanizing country in South Asia, with urban areas growing at a rate of 3%. The country is 36.91% (Economics, 2021) urbanized with a total population of around 220 million, where the urban population is concentrated in mostly eleven million-plus population cities. Urbanization in Pakistan gained momentum in the 1970s but has always been stuck with chronic urban issues including housing shortage, worsening every year, especially in the urban areas. Pakistan is facing an ever-escalating housing crisis, with a cumulative shortage of around 10–11 million housing units mostly in urban areas that too predominantly large, out of which 62% are required by the urban poor. The yearly demand of building 350,000 housing units

N. Javed (✉) · S. Sani-e-Zahra Naqvi
Urban Development Specialist, Lahore, Punjab, Pakistan

A. Kundu et al. (eds.), *Accessible Housing for South Asia*,
https://doi.org/10.1007/978-3-030-88881-7_12

in urban areas is only met 50% with housing supply further adding to the backlog, which resultantly gives rise to the continuous expansion of slums and squatters settlements, which are occupied by around 74% of urban inhabitants according to an estimate by the UN-HABITAT.

Unfortunately, most of the emphasis towards solving the housing problem has been towards the provision of subsidies and government-built housing units. Little emphasis has been given towards improving the housing market, which is by and large a private market, with the government acting as the regulator. Unless the land and housing market sector are thoroughly reviewed and its policy and institutional imperatives addressed, the affordability gap would always be there. Furthermore, deeper analysis and understanding is required regarding the factors affecting the provision of housing.

This chapter discusses some of these key policy and institutional issues that impact the housing market, analyses data and recommends key interventions that can lead towards the provision of affordable housing options.

12.2 Housing: Situational Analysis

The housing sector of Pakistan has several issues ranging from a housing shortage, supply and demand mismatch /gap, congestion, finance shortage, affordability aspects, high costs of construction, land speculation, etc. With regards to the quantitative housing shortage, huge disparities among housing supply and demand have been estimated to exist for various income groups. Hassan & Arif (2018) estimated that around 62% of the housing demand is for lower-income inhabitants earning up to PKR 12,000 monthly (Zainab Raza, 2020), represented in Fig. 12.1.

One of the qualitative shortage parameters is the '*congestion*' of the housing units. The average household size as per the Pakistan Population Census of 2017 is calculated to be 6.2 persons per unit nationally, and 5.97 for the urban areas, computed to be 3.1 persons per room and taken as an indicator of housing congestion based on the criteria by the UNHABITAT. Simple computations will not work here and would require disaggregated data with household income levels for estimating housing demand or formulating a housing policy or institutional framework correctly.

Karachi, the largest city of Pakistan houses around 700–800 katchi abadies with more than 7.5 million inhabitants, i.e. half of the population of the megacity (Choi, 2012). The contrasting side to the acute housing shortage for the low-income population is the availability of surplus housing options for the rich, e.g. 56% of available housing units for 12% of households in Lahore (Fig. 12.2). This surplus is not only available in the form of the built housing units, but also in the form of an estimated 1 million vacant serviced plots across the country either hoarded for investment purposes or waiting to be built because of lack of finances for construction. It is quite paradoxical that several new housing schemes are being approved for the city of Karachi and around 200,000 apartments under construction in high-rise buildings, where there are already around 300,000 plots and 68,000 apartments available in

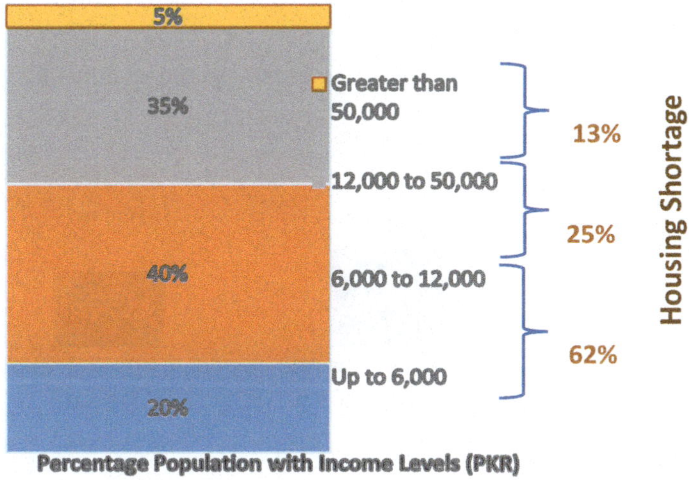

Fig. 12.1 Housing supply and demand gap across various income groups in Pakistan

Fig. 12.2 A mismatch between housing demand and availability in Lahore 2012

the city, not occupied for one reason or the other (Arif, 2018). A similar case is that of Lahore city where 231 schemes have been approved by the Lahore Development Authority between 1970 and 2010 and even those developed in the 1990s or later is still 90% vacant like jubilee town, LDA Avenue one and Mohlanwal (Khaliq-uz-Zaman (PERI), 2011).

12.3 The Real Challenge of Affordable Housing

12.3.1 Housing Affordability

Housing affordability, though a misleading term is a function of housing cost and household income for a particular area and is measured through affordability

Fig. 12.3 Housing costs 2018 versus 2012 (PKR)

indices/ratios as defined by various countries or international organizations. One of the most commonly used indicators is called the *Housing Affordability Ratio*, i.e. the ratio of monthly housing expenditure to the monthly household income. If the ratio doesn't exceed 30%, the housing is considered affordable. The other indicator is called Housing Price to Income Ratio, i.e. the ratio of median house price to annual median household income for an area, where the housing is considered to be affordable if the ratio is not greater than 3 (India, 2018).

Theoretically, housing cost comprises around 30% of land cost and 40% of construction cost, other components (design, permissions, connections and infrastructure etc.) contributing the remaining 30% of the cost, though land not being similar everywhere may contribute differently (Mumtaz, 2015). However, data shows that because of speculation, land prices increased by more than 100% between the years 2012 and 2018, accounting for as much as 70% of a single-storeyed unit cost in 2018 as compared to 57% in 2012, far exceeding the theoretical estimate of 30% (Fig. 12.3) (Ibrahim Khalil, 2019a).

12.3.2 Housing Solutions without a Holistic Approach

Realizing the crisis, almost every political government during the last 50 years, started its brand of '*housing for the poor*', starting with the slogan of '*Roti Kapra aur Makan*' (Bread, Clothing & Housing for all) by Z A Bhutto in the 70 s to the *Naya Pakistan Housing Scheme* of the current regime. However, none could deliver a mass scale solution or even a significant share. This is because all the efforts have been reactive and remedial and not preventive to identify real policy and institutional gaps leading to the housing crisis in the first place.

(a) **Regularization of Katchi Abadie's**:

After the elections of 1970, the Pakistan People's Party (PPP) initiated the 'Malikana Huqooq' or 'Ownership Rights Program' involving regularization of Katchi Abadies, followed by the Katchi Abadies Improvement Program in 1978, enacting a law that enabled the Provinces to promulgate their legislations and institutional arrangements.

(b) **Government-Sponsored Housing Projects:**

Political efforts for the poor other than the regularization of slums and squatters with limited sites and services programs have been very limited. Considering the government's job was to provide housing as a fundamental right, it has been misunderstood by both the government and the citizens that everything the government provides has to be free or heavily subsidized rather than cross-subsidizing or encouraging public–private partnerships. Another aspect is the top-down imposed planning approach without considering community participation, voice and ownership of the initiatives. To review a few examples:

- Prime Minister Muhammad Khan Junejo launched a 'Widow's Housing Project' in the mid-1980s after 3-Marla and 5-Marla schemes, which completed 20,000 two-room housing units in record time using Zakat Fund, but were never occupied by the widows because they refused to occupy those houses *because of social incompatibilities*
- In 2008, the Government announced another project for around 15,000 underprivileged families, but the promised 350 acres of land at various locations in Sindh was never transferred to the Housing Cell resulting in illegal occupying of land, *administrative issues between various government departments being the basic hurdle in the transfer of money and land.*
- In 2010–11, the Chief Minister Punjab announced the *Ashiana Housing Project* in Lahore, aiming to build more than six thousand housing units of 3 and 5 marlas of 500–600 sqft areas at a subsidized price. (Mumtaz, 2015). While only 500 houses have yet been constructed (DCC, 2021), the scheme *doesn't fulfil the purpose of inhabiting the poorest of the poor earning Rs. 20,000 or less monthly.*
- In 2018, the present government of Pakistan also announced the *Naya Pakistan Housing Program* to build 5 million housing units in five years.

Despite political commitments, all of the aforementioned projects failed for one or the other reason, either because of land issues, monetary challenges, institutional weaknesses or policy absence as well as incomplete homework on real housing demand, and the social and economic status of target beneficiaries. Moreover, a piecemeal curative approach was employed in these projects, rather than providing comprehensive preventive measures for both governance and market failure.

(c) **NGO-led Incremental Housing Projects:**

Several NGO-led initiatives for incremental housing, like *Orangi Pilot Project (OPP)* and *Khuda ki Basti* also gained some recognition yet remained just pilots. The OPP had been planned following the incremental housing approach that a common man follows from the low- or lowest-income segment. Whereas the Project resulted in benefitting the community with micro-credit facility, cheap construction material, technical skills and training in construction and mechanized building material, etc. it has its limitation of being replicated. The 'Khuda ki Basti' incremental housing scheme was first developed in Hyderabad, where the model of People; Land & Infrastructure was followed providing homeless people land against a small down payment and affordable monthly instalments covering the full cost of the plot.

Both the models are good experiments of housing for the poorest segment based on the principles of full cost recovery, affordability for low-income people, public participation, incremental houses and infrastructure development, public–private partnership and community organization, yet both the models have certain limitations, the most important being their inflexibility of replication for rapidly urbanizing cities, where a large number of rural migrants are entering for job opportunities in industrial and service economies and will not be in a position to own a housing unit unless their job location is fixed for ease of access.

12.3.3 Why Subsidized Housing Doesn't Reach the Lowest Income Population?

Although all political initiatives are announced for the lowest or low-income population, none of the housing initiatives reached the lowest segment for whom they were intended. This is because there has been no formal mechanism of determining housing affordability in Pakistan for various income groups or a method of classifying well-suited housing units for the same. These mechanisms are a prerequisite for housing provision through both supply-side measures such as social housing, and demand-side measures such as housing finance, involving processing of down payments, monthly instalments and subsidies.

The State Bank of Pakistan (SBP) has formulated a low-income financing policy for the Naya Pakistan Housing Program defining the low-cost housing to be starting with a minimum cost of Rs. 3 million, which when evaluated across the income quintiles reveals affordability only for the fifth quintile. Khalil (2019) even while modifying the SBP policy with a Shared Equity Model (SEM) analyzed affordability of low-cost housing units slightly improves it to the third quintile, but only for the smallest unit (Khalil, 2019), Table 12.2.

Even if all successes from all types of projects are summed up, they do not even have cumulatively provided housing for half a million families, since the independence, and the quantum of the problem before us is huge to be addressed in a piecemeal manner.

12.4 Market and Governance Failure: The Real Challenge and its Resolution

Pakistan has a weak spatial planning and urban governance system without holistic frameworks for land management, housing markets, legislation and taxation etc. Particularly, the housing sector in Pakistan does not have a holistic *Housing-for-All framework,* enabling housing provision for all segments of society. Resultantly, housing is only developed by commercial developers for the rich as free markets tend to develop for-profit maximization by providing options for high-income residents or investors. The responsibility lies with the government to correct such market failures through required policy and institutional reforms incentivizing developers to provide housing options suiting to all citizens socially, financially and culturally.

12.4.1 Policy and Institutional Imperatives

Some of the key policy and institutional issues that negatively impact the housing affordability index are discussed below under four key areas of *Land, Urban Planning, Finance and Institutional & Regulatory Improvements*, which need to be solved for an equitable housing market, for all sections of the society.

A. **Land Challenges**

   1. **A Distorted Land Market**:

      The land is not being treated as input material for housing in the Country, rather as a tradable commodity because of its speculative nature in the absence of any non-development taxes in keeping the vacant plots. The land and housing market in the absence of a comprehensive urban planning framework and a supporting real estate sector favours the rich and the speculators, where they have been using it as an alternative to investments in gold and bonds, because of its inflation-beating price appreciation. The result is a serious mismatch in supply and demand. Whereas hundreds of thousands of developed plots are lying vacant, waiting for the windfall dividends by investors and speculators, the poor are cramped into congested housing and informal settlements. Even middle-income families need lifelong savings to afford a decent or even less than decent accommodation.

2. **Urban Land (Mis)Management**:

   The most important of all is the **weak property rights** and **ineffective land titling and registration system,** which is not even designed for the urban areas in Pakistan. The procedures of property registration have several loopholes, where there is (1) institutional fragmentation; (2) lack of a central and shared database by all government authorities and real estate markets; (3) registration deed or transaction information without spatial information; and (4) the archaic system of manual records where tracking of property transactions is not possible. The development authorities have land record systems of their development schemes and so have some private developers as well as the Military controlled Cantonment Boards and Defence Housing Authorities.

   Furthermore, land acquisition and development regulations are considered a barrier to investment in Pakistan, where on average 140 days and 20 different documents are required in the case of government land, and 64 days and 10 documents for private land. Finally, unclear property rights result in the prohibition of mortgage finance, which is again essential for developing land given rapid urban expansion (David Dowall, 2007).

3. **High Public Land Ownership**:

   In well-functioning urban land markets, public ownership of land is usually kept lower than 5% while the remaining is privately owned. Cities in Pakistan, particularly development authorities own a large amount of land, which is often well located and serviced but is kept vacant and not placed on the market for potential residential, commercial and industrial development. In Lahore, 30% of land is owned by government entities whereas other cities in Pakistan in the range of 20–40%. Karachi has over 90% of publicly owned land but an extensive expansion of informal settlements as well. The public ownership of land is not an issue if the cities have clear land development policies putting the government land to its best use.

4. **Development Restrictions**

   A large proportion of serviced land either in the ownership of government authorities or under the control of professional land speculators is lying vacant, causing land scarcity, further pushing development and informal settlements at the periphery. The un-serviced land owned by the private sector has a lot of issues ranging from: seeking cumbersome and expensive planning permissions; need of trunk infrastructure to be available before implementation of their projects; following strict planning standards requiring as much as 50% of the site area to be dedicated for circulation and public spaces and to be transferred to the government authority. Thus, in the attempt to escape these scenarios, most of the developers end up developing informal and illegal settlements, which result in poorly planned communities, without proper sewerage and sanitation services, causing congestion and environmental degradation.

Solving the Land issues:

- *Develop a* ***GIS-based land records system*** for transparent land ownership record, and additionally the ease to identify and access land for developing affordable housing options.
- Map urban areas with the ***real estate purchase and rents rates*** for assessing their affordability or unaffordability for various income groups. Such information can be used in the allocation of low-income households at apparent unaffordable locations for making the housing market inclusive.
- Prevent land speculation by charging a ***non-development fee/tax*** from the developers that will unlock the land for housing development within the urban centres. South Korea in 1978 faced a 136% increase in land values due to land speculation with reduced land supply.
- In case, the developer doesn't want to develop the required housing options at his owned land parcel, allow '***Transfer of Development Rights (TDR***)' as a means to allow someone else to develop the same in that location.
- Allocate land at required locations for supply for mass housing at a rationalized and reasonable price. In the case of private land ownership, instead of compulsory land acquisition, adopt the ***public–private partnership*** model of housing development.
- For existing organic settlements, and slums up-gradation, promote regularization measures and introduce ***Land Consolidation/ Readjustment Tools***. These measures have been undertaken in several countries including India, where in-situ slum up-gradation and renewal has been carried out using land readjustment, by temporarily acquiring the entire slum area, providing basic services, and then returning a portion of the serviced area to the homeowners.

B. **Inadequate Urban Planning**

Pakistan lacks urban and regional planning legislation, a hierarchical institutional and regulatory framework complemented with a well-coordinated local government system for its implementation.

1. **Improving Housing Policy**:

There have been several attempts to develop policies to meet housing needs including the National Human Settlement Policy (1984), National Conservation Strategy (1988), National Housing Policy (1986), and lastly the National Housing Policy 2001. The National Housing Policy of Pakistan 2001, though with various excellent policy measures missed on providing answers to who, what and how of the housing provision, which is a primary function of a typical housing policy.

The policy framework needs to *classify housing concerning various occupancy structure* (single-family/multi-family, group or clustered housing), structural quality, tenure (owned, leased, rented, encroached etc.), and based on supply sources such as not-for-profit public/social housing (irrespective of government ownership) or for-profit/luxurious housing in the open market. In addition to the lack of a classification of housing, it is also important to realize that *housing is a social good* and is essential for developing healthy and functional communities.

The housing policy *must define the target beneficiaries* with regards to their socio-economic status for developing appropriate and affordable housing for all. For example, in India, the beneficiaries have been classified as four economic groups, such as High Income Group (HIG), Medium Income Group (MIG), Low-income Group (LIG), and Economically Weaker Sections (EWS), thus defining their income brackets and different housing models suiting to their habitation needs.

2. **Missing Strategic City Plans and Land Use Rules**:

Because of the lack of an urban planning framework, the cities of Pakistan do not have a single unified master/strategic plan for an entire city to be followed by all entities towards a collective vision. A few cities have valid master plans in place, and those who are exceptions have become outdated because of rapid urban growth and the inability of the cities to have kept their development pace matching to the population growth and physical expansion.

Another important factor is the poor quality of existing plans, based on the outdated static and rigid traditional planning concept, which fail to provide any strategic direction for future sustainable growth and economic development. This lack of spatial plans and poor quality of plans has resulted in a lack of developable and serviced land for the housing and economic needs as well as trunk infrastructure for the growing population, part of the reason being lack of sufficient funds to do so.

The planning instruments mostly propose residential zoning based on the linear population projections without considering the income level of the households, which is the most important factor in designating a housing area as affordable or not. Resultantly, most of the land and housing units developed is not affordable for the poor, pushing them towards the informal settlements within and at the city periphery, without adequate services and commute options.

Additionally, other spatial planning instruments like land-use rules also promote sprawling developments, which need a course correction towards developing complete communities, inclusive for all.

3. **Outdated Building Regulations**:

Building regulations, as adopted by most of the city authorities are inspired by the British suburban model of urban planning as exercised before the creation of Pakistan. They just offer one model of residential development with single-use zones with plots distributions, primarily supporting car-oriented development, rendering housing and other services unaffordable. Most houses are allowed to be developed maximum on the FAR of 1.5, with a spread-out layout along the roads and streets thus creating car-dependent residential schemes. The private housing schemes do not have any requirement of developing high-density high/low rise apartment buildings, suiting different income groups, thus allowing a greater number of households to share the high cost of infrastructure and services.

The building regulations/bylaws do not promote the housing nomenclature of clustered housing (low rise, high-density housing) developed around open courtyards or verandahs providing space for generating livelihood through crafting, sewing, stitching or small cottage industries.

Proposed Urban Planning Reforms:

- *Legislate Planning Obligations for all kinds of Developments*: Legislate the provision of low-cost housing options in all development initiatives by requiring mixed-use and mixed-income zoning, to promote vibrant, well-maintained localities for social cohesion (clustering of all low-income housing units at one location results in poverty intensification and poorly maintained spaces). The same practice has been used by several countries including Turkey and Singapore, to address housing shortages especially for low-income to middle-income households.
  - Introduce ***bonus or incentive zoning*** for developers in the form of increased building allowance (additional floors, additional number of housing units, economic options, parking spaces, etc.) for the provision of low-cost housing units as part of the planning obligations
  - Implement a compulsory provision of residential quarters for domestic servants for single-family, low rise housing zones, not only to provide them with affordable housing options but also to reduce their commuting needs.
- *Develop Social Housing Units for Low-income Households*: Government and community organizations need to develop and reserve housing units for low-income households for both selling and renting. Rental units are more important in social housing options as most of the low-income households need the flexibility to relocate to other areas as per their work needs.

- *Promote Several Housing Typologies*: Current planning rules in Pakistan only promote the plotting of land parcels in the name of housing. The housing policy needs to include several models of housing units to meet the need of various income groups.
  - One of the models could be low-rise, high density, multi-family clustered housing developments, with adjoining large land parcels for income generation such as waste segregation, treatment and disposal plant, or a compound with carpet weaving stations or handicrafts/products crafting, etc. The clustered housing is the most suited for those households who migrate from the villages with little or no education to be part of the labour class.
  - Another housing model for the low-income population is to provide low rise, high-density housing units developed on the model of precolonial multi-family dwellings with stacked private spaces, shared courtyards and verandahs, often with their ground floors dedicated for industrial and commercial use.
  - Naya Pakistan Housing Policy aims at developing only 9% of housing units as high rise and around 58% to be low-rise single-family housing units, which should be reviewed to address the housing need by mostly low to middle-income households.
- *Revise Building Regulations/Bylaws*: The building regulations and bylaws need to be revised to include more housing typologies as well as more a higher Floor-Area-Ratio to improve buildability, which will also result in a land saving.

C. **Missing Housing Finance**

The housing finance market, both in the form of mortgage finance or construction finance is almost non-existent in Pakistan. Pakistan's mortgage finance to GDP ratio is 0.23%, which is the lowest in the South Asia region, with Bangladesh at 3% and India at 7%. With yearly housing demand of as many as 350,000 housing units, only about 1,500 new mortgage loans are extended every year, where the average loan size in the year 2016 was only PKR 6.1 million and an average loan-to-value (LTV) ratio of 48% forcing the borrowers to arrange almost 52% from their savings.

Moreover, mortgage finance is only for the high-income group excluding the 70% population working in the informal sector because of having no documented credit transaction history or the ability to arrange down payment. Mortgage financing is also only available if a person owns a piece of land or can arrange collateral thus further depriving the low-income segment.

With a really small mortgage market, the builders in Pakistan do not have much access to construction finance, thus depending on the owners/buyers to arrange the instalment or to arrange loans from the speculators. This often results in delayed construction causing cost overrun as well, which affects housing affordability. Limited construction finance for the builders and developers is also because of their informal practice without getting registered with the regulators or achieving credit ratings.

One of the key reasons behind the limited availability of housing finance had been the absence of effective foreclosure laws providing security to the lenders for repossessing the defaulted property to recover its cost. The Financial Institutions (Recovery of Finances) Ordinance of 2001 although streamlined the foreclosure process of allowing financial institutions to repossess properties without taking cases to the superior courts, however, those non-judicial foreclosures were later rendered as 'exploitative practice', paralyzing the banking courts, leaving a huge backlog of cases and damaging the mortgage market.

The Naya Pakistan Housing Project with an over-ambitious target of constructing 5 million housing units has developed a Naya Pakistan Housing Authority (NHPA) taking a step towards the provision of non-judicial foreclosures by creating the position of an adjudicator for disputes resolution. In addition to this, an ordinance called the 'Recovery of Mortgage-backed Security Ordinance 2019' has been promulgated to facilitate financial institutions in granting those securities.

1. **Constrained Rental Housing**

   Rental legislation in Pakistan is also as fragmented as other urban sector legislation. Most of these instruments are based on the West Pakistan Urban Rent Restriction Ordinance 1959, thus posing several restrictions and discouraging rental properties across the Country. The weak legislative instruments have resulted in a skewed urban rental market with only a few housing units available for rental housing, and those too at a relatively high rental rate.

   Although the legislation in Punjab province has been replaced with a better Punjab Rented Premises Act 2009 allowing a written rent agreement, flexibility of determining the fair rent and controlling end of tenancy/eviction, however, most of the cities in Punjab province only have a maximum of 20% of rented housing units.

   Islamabad has a higher percentage of a rental housing unit at 40%, which is comparable to the cities in OECD countries with an average of 38%, the fair rent is still determined officially by the Controller of Rents, which is not allowed to be increased for a period of three years unless the landlord improves in the building. Similar restrictive measures continue in other provinces, thus discouraging rental properties.

   High taxation on rental income also discourages people from investing in rental housing units and encourage them to keep their plots vacant, waiting for the price escalation.

Table 12.1 Pakistan's Urban Household Incomes (PKR)

	Actual 2015–16
First Quintile (Lowest)	20,441
Second Quintile (Low-middle)	25,292
Third Quintile (Middle)	28,940
Fourth Quintile (High-Middle)	34,407
Fifth Quintile (Highest)	65,950

Housing Finance Resolution:

- Mortgage Finance:
  - *Improve mortgage financing policy to make housing affordable for low-income people:* The State Bank of Pakistan and Naya Pakistan Housing Project's mortgage financing policies, though devised for low-income borrowers, are not affordable for around 80% of the population (Tables 12.1 and 12.2). Moreover, if even all members of a low-income household combine their incomes to purchase a housing unit, there is a very low likelihood of their qualifying for a mortgage from commercial banks because of informal income sources.
  - *Introduce methods to subsidize land* for low-income households under both the State Bank and Naya Pakistan Housing Policies, as otherwise the housing units would be unaffordable for most of the low-middle income households, and would push the poor to slums and katchi abadies.
  - *Devise a mortgage policy for middle-income households*: The policies of the State Bank or Naya Pakistan Housing Project, need to be tweaked for middle-income households, who can afford a higher monthly instalment and are part of the formal economy such as the professionals, doctors, university professors, etc. (Ibrahim Khalil, 2019b). These limitations in the policies will make the middle-income household get into the housing units which are to be built for the low-income households, thus worsening their housing shortage.
  - *Promote Equity Loans* for credit-worthy, income constraint home buyers with characteristics of both equity and debt, and a margin of five years for interest-free repayment.
  - *Shared Equity Mortgages (SEM)* are proposed for the low-cost housing units in Pakistan as opposed to the State Bank Policy's self-liquidating fixed-rate mortgages, as the joint equity maximizing the initial down payment will reduce the amount to be financed by the banks, increasing affordability and limiting losses for the borrowers. Khalil. I (2019) analyses that the shared equity mortgaged financing can expand affordability of low-cost housing units to almost 60% of the households, i.e. up to the third quintile (Khalil, 2019).

Table 12.2 Affordability analysis of proposed SEM-Based mortgage financing in the SBP

	Unit type	Phase I prices	5% Down payment	SEM	Monthly mortgage installment	Percentage monthly household income				
	PKR					1^{st}Q (%)	2^{nd}Q (%)	3^{rd}Q (%)	4^{th}Q (%)	5^{th}Q (%)
3 Marla	1 Bed	1,600,000	80,000	320,000	9,663	47	38	33	28	15
	2 Bed	1,935,000	96,750	387,000	11,686	57	46	40	34	18
	3 Bed	2,354,000	117,700	470,800	14,216	70	56	49	41	22
	4 Bed	2,664,000	133,200	532,800	16,088	79	64	56	47	24
5 Marla	1 Bed	2,070,000	103,500	414,000	12,501	61	49	43	36	19
	2 Bed	2,525,000	126,250	505,000	15,249	75	60	53	44	23
	3 Bed	3,150,000	157,500	630,000	19,023	93	75	66	55	29
	4 Bed	3,550,000	177,500	710,000	21,439	105	85	74	62	33

  - *Expand Microfinance for Low-income Housing*: Around 72% of the employed population in Pakistan was part of the informal economy as per the Population Census of 2017, which implies their potential disqualification or unaffordability for a commercial loan or mortgage. Promote microfinance for low-income households who can afford small loans on easy terms and conditions for purchasing, constructing and maintaining their houses.

- Construction Finance:
  - Provide options for construction finance along with mortgage financing, enabling the developers to deliver housing units within a specified time, thus saving on inflation as well.

    Micromortgages: A model developed for an Indian company specializing in low-income mortgages can be developed for Pakistan, where the micro mortgage company could disburse loan payments to the developers on behalf of the borrowers, and those were required to pay some monthly instalments before actually living in the apartment.

- Subsidies:
  - *Introduce Cross-Subsidy*: Cross-subsidy in the housing sector has been employed by several countries, where some units are sold at higher prices because of size, use, location, etc. and a few are reserved for low-income households. Though, in the housing sector of Pakistan, this may not be very useful as there is a very small proportion of high-income households needing housing units as compared to huge low-income households.
  - *Interest or Mark-up Subsidy*: Introduce interest subsidies for low-income segments in the Naya Pakistan Housing Policy, where the currently proposed subsidy by the State Bank of Pakistan is not affordable for the bottom four quintiles. One way could be to provide such credit linked subsidy to the borrowers' account directly to the lending institution, reducing their monthly instalment.

D. **The Institutional and Regulatory Web**

Informal Development and Building Construction

Housing production in Pakistan has largely been an informal business where mostly individual landowners contract small and mostly informal builders for saving on the construction costs as well as to avoid lengthy administrative and regulatory procedures. Similarly, the builders and developers also do not want to be part of the formal construction market given the costs associated with regulations and taxes. As noted by a study by the World Bank, only about 270 of the 4000 members of the Pakistan Association of Builders and Developers (ABAD) had incorporated their businesses as companies (David Dowall, 2007).

12.4.2 Institutional and Regulatory Improvements

- Develop provincial and local wings of the Naya Pakistan Housing Authority for translation and implementation of the national policies, keeping in view the local conditions.
- Establish a Housing Facilitation Force (HFF) and recruit and train HFF to facilitate construction and housing area development (Mumtaz, 2018).
- Improve the functioning of government institutions involved in approvals or development of housing for preventing cost and time overrun for preventing housing price escalation.
- *Manpower and labour*: Develop regulatory mechanisms for providing skilled/trained labour and other professionals in the housing market for ensuring good quality and secure housing construction, needing lesser investments in repair and maintenance because of quality issues.

12.5 Conclusion

Pakistan is the fastest urbanizing country in South Asia, with its growth rate of urban population coming down to below 3% annually only over the past couple of decades, accounting for about 37% of its total population of around 225 million in 2021. The country is facing an ever-escalating housing crisis, with a cumulative shortage of around 10 million units, mostly in urban areas, restricted largely to eleven, million-plus cities. Only about 50% of the yearly demand of about 350,000 units is met through the regular supply system. This shortfall is met with congested multi-family living, informal settlements, slums and make-shift accommodations in old city quarters or informal housing emerging through subdivisions of agricultural land at the city peripheries.

Urbanization in Pakistan gained momentum in the 1970s, and since then the housing shortage has been a chronic issue, worsening every year. Almost 85–90% of the housing provision is in the private sector. The public sector caters to the needs of the employees of the government departments and state-owned enterprises. The land and housing market in Pakistan favour the rich and the speculators. Consequently, land has been used as an alternative to gold and savings and the private sector, being profit-oriented, has chosen to operate in the market segment for high income households and affluents. The result is a serious mismatch between supply and demand. Whereas hundreds of thousands of developed plots are lying vacant, waiting for the windfall dividends by investors and speculators, the poor are cramped into congested housing and informal settlements. Even middle-income families need lifelong savings to afford liveable accommodation with minimal basic services.

Realizing the crisis, almost every government during the past 50 years, came up with its brand of '*housing for the poor*', starting with the slogan of '*Roti Kapra aur Makan*' (Bread, Clothing & Housing for all) by Z A Bhutto in the 70 s to the *Naya Pakistan Housing Scheme* of the current regime. However, none could ensure mass production of dwelling units or even a sizable share. Unfortunately, all these projects have been based on providing subsidized housing for the poor but none addressed the real policy issues underlying the housing market failure. Several NGO led initiatives for incremental housing, like the *Orangi Pilot project* and *Khuda ki basti* gained some recognition but could not be anything other than just pilot projects. Government or NGO sponsored subsidized housing projects are not a sustainable solution because of their total dependence on state funds, and, more importantly, because they fail to correct the underlying issues that di the housing market.

References

Arif, A. H. H. (2018). Pakistan: The causes & repercussions of the housing crisis. *IIED.*
Choi, B. Y. S. (2012). *Making spatial change in Pakistan Cities growth enhancing*
David Dowall, P. E. (2007). *Urban land and housing markets in Punjab, Pakistan. IURD, Berkeley*
DCC. (2021). Ashiana housing scheme, Government of Punjab. https://dascon.com.pk/project/ashiana-housing-scheme-of-punjab-government/
Economics, T. (2021). Pakistan—urban population (% Of Total). https://tradingeconomics.com/pakistan/urban-population-percent-of-total-wb-data.html#:~:text=Urban%20population%20(%25%20of%20total%20population)%20in%20Pakistan%20was%20reported,compiled%20from%20officially%20recognized%20sources.
Ibrahim Khalil, U. N. (2019a). *Designing affordable housing plicy.*
Ibrahim Khalil, U. N. (2019b). *Optimizing Naya Pakistan Housing Policy Opportunity.*
India, R. B. o. (2018). Affordable Housing in India. *Reserve Bank of India Bulletin, Volume LXXII*(Number 1).
Khalil, I. (2019). *Mortgage Market Design for Low-Cost Housing Units in Pakistan.*
Khaliq-uz-Zaman (PERI), A. A. B. P. D. (2011). Urbanization of Arable Land in Lahore City in Pakistan: a Case-Study.
Mumtaz, B. K. (2015). Urban Gazette. In (Vol. Dec 2015): The Urban Unit.
Mumtaz, B. K. (2018) Resolving Pakistan's Housing Issues. In, *City Dialogue Series*: Urban Unit.
Zainab Raza, L. Q. N., T. (2010). *Policy brief: Urbanization in Pakistan: The availability of housing. Expanding housing fnance to the underserved in South Asia.* Washington DC: The World Bank.

Chapter 13
Multilocational Householding: Implications for Urban Development in Pakistan

Atif Bilal Aslam

Abstract Encouraged by this era of a globalized world, international migration is continuously increasing and is thus generating a complex of interconnected, multi-scaled spaces of varying influence spheres. This necessitates the investigation of much assumed local phenomena in a broader context. The broader context of globalisation also includes the processes partly formed by transnational networks of migrants. Such transnational migrant's networks and connections still need to be conceptualised to better analyse their implications for various multi-scaled spaces. This study, by employing a qualitative research approach, engaged Pakistani long-term migrants (in Germany) to investigate their transnational spatial practices in their respective origin places (in Pakistan) and the associated implications for the urban development in Pakistan. It has been found that Pakistani migrants, through the joint planning character of multilocational householding, mainly perform transnational spatial practices in the human capacity development sector and the housing market of Pakistan. It has been assessed through a constructed Urban Development Index (UDI) that the performed spatial practices had positive implications for the urban development sector in Pakistan, though at the micro-level. Moreover, the practices performed in the housing market exerted the largest positive impact within the constructed frame of UDI. Thus, the study concludes that the international migrants, through housing sector investments in the original places of developing countries, contribute significantly in shaping the urban places, particularly the built environment.

Keywords Globalization · Multilocality · Housing · Urban development · International migration · Pakistan

---

A. B. Aslam (✉)
Department of City and Regional Planning, University of Engineering and Technology, Lahore, Pakistan
e-mail: atif.aslam@uet.edu.pk

A. Kundu et al. (eds.), *Accessible Housing for South Asia*,
https://doi.org/10.1007/978-3-030-88881-7_13

13.1 Introduction

The world is currently going through a difficult phase due to the COVID-19 pandemic, which has disrupted life in almost all parts of the globe. Among many adverse effects, significantly reduced mobility and migration have also been observed due to the imposed restrictive measures by various nation-states in response to the COVID-19 outbreak (Takenaka, 2020; Yayboke, 2020). Some scholars (such as Musselwhite et al., 2020) are of the view that such COVID-19 effects and associated changes will be long lasting, while other scholars (such as Litman, 2020) believe that COVID-19-related transformations will be temporary and usual pre-COVID-19 mobility patterns will bounce back, once the socio-economic constraints posed by the COVID-19 will fade away. Pre-COVID-19 times have seen a continuous increase in international migration across the globe (Takenaka, 2020). The increased international migration in the pre-COVID-19 era has been explained through many theories in the literature, notably the theories of globalisation in general while livelihood strategies, transnationalism and multilocality in particular. These theories provide a conceptual framework to understand various transnational practices that are performed by the international migrants in their origin places. Continually increasing remittances back home by the international migrants has been seen as a manifestation of transnational connections that international migrants keep harbouring during their migration history. Many of the transnational practices by the international migrants at the origin places get operationalized through the instrument of remittances. Increased remittances to origin places have also been viewed as a strategy of international migrants to keep their transnational multilocational lifestyle intact (Dittrich-Wesbuer & Plöger, 2013).

There have been sufficient studies that cover the topic of transnational connections and practices of the international migrants, yet there exists a lack of understanding concerning the implications of such practices for the origin places (Schiller, 2014). The non-clarity of the subject matter has given rise to both optimistic and pessimistic views in the literature towards migration and development interaction debate. These conflicting theoretical perspectives have been explained as the outcome of the multi-disciplinary character of the topic, paradigm shifts in the social theory and the differing levels of analysis (De Haas, 2010). The relation of migration and development in origin places has mainly been viewed through the lens of remittances and their impacts on the development of the origin places. Many studies reported on the usage of remittances in generic terms of investment and consumption by the receiving communities and attempted to relate its implications for the change processes instigated at the origin places. Although the differentiation between the investment and consumptive usage of remittances is vague, a conflict exists among the scholars on the developmental (or non-developmental) character of its implications on the receiving communities. De Haas (2007), in line with the findings of Adelman et al. (1988) and Durand et al. (1996), argued that the remittances used even for consumptive purposes improve the life quality of the recipients and through multiplier effects, non-migrants also receive monetary gains. He further added, by referring to the work of Taylor et al. (1996) that the housing sector investments could trigger construction activity, employment opportunities and financial gains for non-migrants at the origin places and thus could also be regarded as developmental in character. Schmidt-Kallert (2009) pointed out that the international migrants maintain transnational connections with their origin places and thus by carrying out many transnational practices through these connections affect the development level in either positive or negative way at both origin and destination places.

The theory of transnationalism has given rise to the global or world city literature, which emphasizes the trans-border connections among the urban places which could be regarded as the migrants' origin and destination places. Thus, viewing the migrants' agency in the broader theoretical framework of transnationality poses another challenge of assessing mechanisms for the impacts of the transnational connections and multilocational householding on the overall development of the original urban places. This is partly because of having a non-consensus among the scholars over the definition of urban development. This study mainly investigates the transnational practices performed by Pakistani migrants through their multilocational household arrangements and devises an assessment mechanism to report on the implications of those practices for the urban development of origin places.

International migrants significantly affect urban life and through transnational connections, constitute a transnational social space between the origin and destination places (Schiller, 2014). However, urban studies have neglected migrants' agency, which is a significant aspect of urban life and agents of change for urban transformations (Ibid). Transnational multilocational householding has also been attributed as the global householding in the literature and has been viewed as the most significant social transformation in the twenty-first century (Douglass, 2006). Multilocality has also been attributed as the livelihood strategy of the migrants affiliated with the Global South (Baumgart, 2016). Despite having a strong role of migrants' agency, global forces have been observed as more powerful in shaping the urban places as compared to the local forces instigated through transnational connections (Pacione, 2009). Transnational connections among international migrants are maintained across three vital places of affiliations which are home, neighbourhood and city (Brickell & Datta, 2011). Figure 13.1 conceptualizes the presented theoretical debate for a better understanding of the multi-locational household arrangement of international migrants.

International migrants, mainly use remittances as the means to operationalize many of their transnational practices carried out in the origin places. Remittances are a source of household income from foreign economies sent back home by the temporary or permanent international migrants (International Monetary Fund, 2009). It includes cash and non-cash items sent through formal or informal channels across borders. The most challenging task is the estimation of remittances sent to origin places through informal channels (World Bank, 2011) as around 35–75% of the total remittance flows to developing countries through informal channels (Freund & Spatafora, 2005). To deal with this issue, The World Bank (2011) has recommended conducting deeper inquiries with the remittance senders and receivers both at the destination and origin places, thus highlighting the importance of multilocational household arrangements.

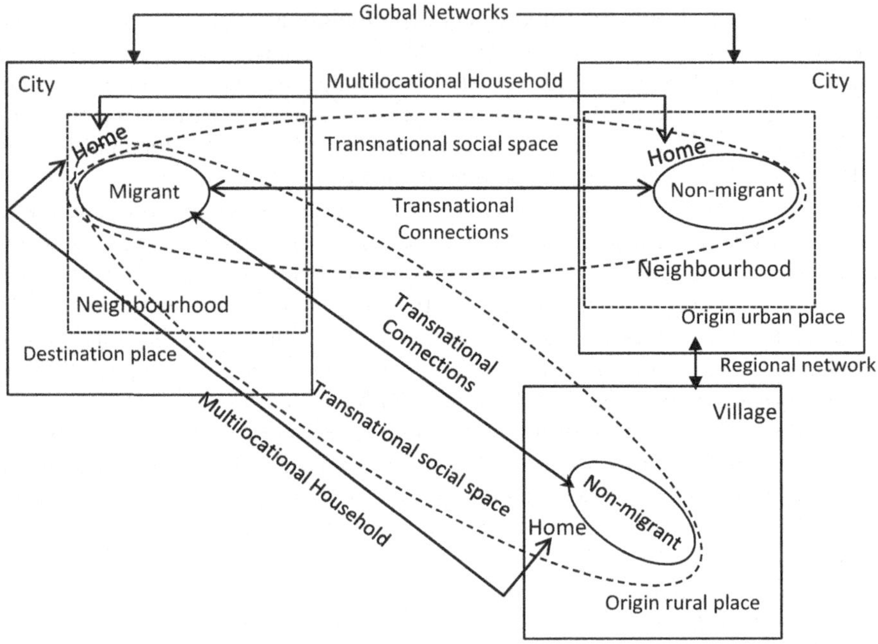

Fig. 13.1 Conceptualization of the transnational multilocational household arrangements. *Source* Adapted from Aslam (2015)

The term 'urban development' also requires a serious inquiry. The literature identifies a deficiency in prevalent conceptual understanding of 'urban development', which is ascribable to an underlying dilemma of missing consensus over the description of 'development' in the first place (Agunias, 2006; De Haas, 2007; Gasper, 2004; Global Migration Group, 2010; Njoh, 2006). This disagreement has led to the introduction of more subtle concepts of 'change' and 'transformation' in 'development theory'. Pacione (2009) pointed out seven global trigger forces—economic, social, demographic, technological, political, cultural, and environmental—which according to him have significant urban consequences. These global forces interact at different levels and contribute significantly to shaping urban places (Mieg, 2013). Thus, the practices performed within the identified urban dimensions eventually affect the development level of the place under inquiry. This provides a conceptual framework to understand the character of the various transnational practices performed by the international migrants at origin urban places. If such practices could be regarded as sustainable, it will affect the level of urban development positively, otherwise, such practices could be viewed as non-developmental to the origin places. Figure 13.2 combines the theories of 'urban', 'development' and 'sustainability' and attempts to provide a theoretical framework to understand urban development in a better way.

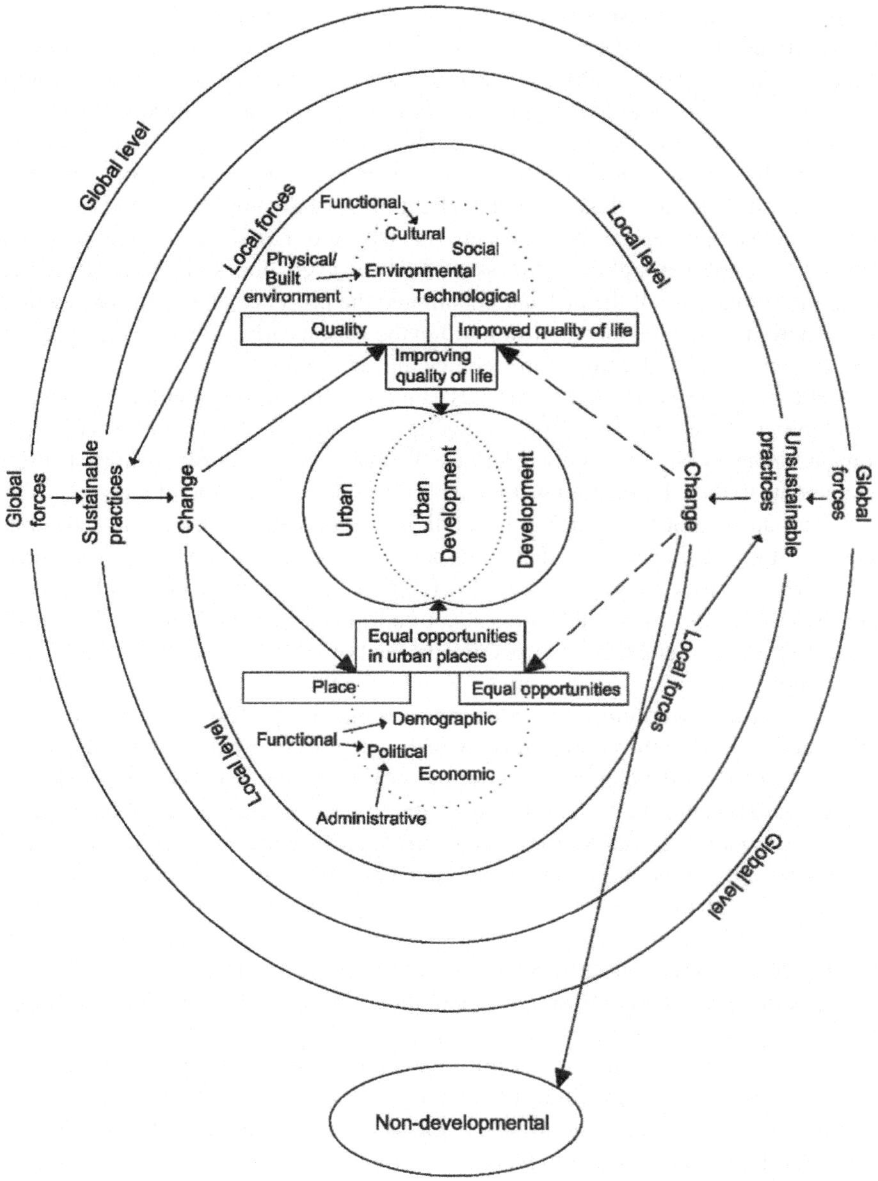

Fig. 13.2 A theoretical framework for understanding urban development. *Source* Aslam, 2015

Owing to a non-consensus over the definition of urban development, little is known about how to measure the level of urban development of any given local place. The World Bank (2020) has outlined a set of 19 indicators as urban development indicators. These indicators provide some understanding of the key dimensions of urban development, including demographic, socio-economic, and environmental characteristics of the relevant urban places. However, any indexing or composite method for determining the cumulative effect of the indicators on the measurement of urban development has not been provided by the World Bank. The identified deficiency is not a straightforward issue to be resolved. Jones et al. (2010) hinted about the complexity of the task and mentioned the presence of a series of potential contradictions and complementarities within the various urban forces which keep on strengthening, and at the same time, contesting each other.

Apart from the World Bank, the UN-Habitat introduced a method of the City Development Index (CDI) in 1997 for the measurement of the level of urban development for any urban place (Global Urban Observatory, n.d.). Further comprehensive refinements to the CDI method were made to include various other dimensions relevant to urban development, such as liveability, development level, poverty and equity (UN-Habitat, n.d.). The latest attempt to such effort is the 'Sustainable Development Index' which is a cumulative score of 231 (United Nations Department of Economic and Social Affairs, 2020) indicators identified under 17 broad sustainable development goals whereas Goal 11 specifically deals with sustainability of cities and communities.

However, all such composite indexing methods are performed at the scales of either the city level or the national level with the usage of relevant datasets. Measuring the level of urban development below the city scale has not been available yet. Due to that reason, it is difficult to assess the impacts of transnational practices of the international migrants on the level of urban development of the origin places. Nonetheless, it can be implied that such practices affect the urban development of any place, though the effect size of such impact might not be significant. Importantly, these indicators provide a clue concerning positive or negative changes which shape up urban places. It is required to investigate the implications of transnational practices of international migrants for urban development through selected urban indicators, though amended to adjust to the level of analysis.

Based on the theoretical departure points explained in the previous sections, this study inquires about the transnational practices performed by the international migrants and further attempts to assess the implications of such practices for the urban development of the origin places.

13.2 Research Methodology

This study involved long-term Pakistani migrants in the scientific investigation. Though any migrant who has resided abroad for at least a year is termed as a long term migrant according to the United Nations Statistics Division (1998) presented definition, however, this study included only those migrants who have lived in Germany for at least 5 years (study period) so that they could share an experience of their performed transnational practices in Pakistan.

The study was mainly an exploration of the transnational practices performed by the Pakistani migrants and the implications of such practices for urban development in the origin places which mainly required a qualitative research approach to be adopted. Face-to-face interviews was carried out with the members of the target population from the state of North-Rhine Westphalia (NRW), Germany. A single data collection instrument, i.e. an interview guide comprising of unstructured and semi-structured questions, was prepared. Employing a co-ethnic interviewing technique, all interviews were conducted in the native language of Pakistan, i.e. Urdu. Later, all the recorded interviews were then translated into English at the time of their transcription.

The unstructured questions generated a qualitative dataset that mainly inquired the nature and motives of transnational practices performed by the Pakistani migrants. The data generated from semi-structured questions were analysed to determine implications of performed transnational practices for urban changes in the origin places. The data was mainly analysed through frequency analysis, content analysis and index analysis. UN-Habitat (2000) urban indicators were mainly used to develop an Urban Development Index (UDI) and the implications of the performed transnational practices were assessed through the devised indexing method.

The Federal Office for Migration and Refugees (BAMF), Germany (2009) reported various demographic and socioeconomic characteristics of the Muslim migrants of South/Southeast Asian origin of which around one-third of migrants had Pakistani background. In the absence of any available sampling frame, the respondents from the target population were included in the sample to exhaust all the major types of migrants based on different demographic characteristics through snowball and convenience sampling. The carried out exercise gave a sample size of 20 respondents for detailed in-depth inquiry. The migration theory of households' livelihood strategies focuses mainly on households rather than migrants and views migrants as members of multilocational households. According to the theory, a joint planning character exists within such multilocational households facilitated through social space connections and mutual agreements. All these interviews were conducted with the head/one of the household's heads to grasp the performed transnational practices of the households instead of individuals during the study period.

13.3 Findings and Discussion

Regarding the socio-economic and demographic profile of the Pakistani migrants who took part in the study, around two-thirds of the respondents first entered Germany as students, while the entry status of one-fifth of the respondents was asylum seeker/refugee. Around one-third of the respondents belong to the age bracket of 16–29 and 40–49 each while about one-fourth of them were in their 30 s. The highest educational qualification attained by half of the respondents was a master's degree while one-fourth of them had a bachelor's degree. 38.9% of them were employees at the time of interview while 27.8% were either employers or self-employed. Only one-fifth of the respondents were single while the rest of the interviewees were married. Net monthly income of 37.5% respondents was within the range of 1,000–1,500 Euro while 18.8% respondents were earning monthly within the range of 2,000–2,500 and 2,501–3,000 each.

13.3.1 Urban Domains for Implications Assessment

The theoretical framework presented in Fig. 13.2 conceives urban development as an interaction of various urban dimensions. There exist complementarities and contradictions among these urban domains simultaneously. The key urban dimensions presented by the UN-Habitat (2000) can be grouped with the broader urban domains conceptualized in Fig. 13.2. For further analysis, those domains were selected where transnational migrants could have an impact due to the practices performed by them. These practices are often performed at the household level, or at times, neighbourhood level, whereas urban development is an interplay of the same parameters at the city level, which makes the task of implications assessment challenging. All the performed practices were envisaged within the broader urban domains to have a link at all the three tiers of the local level to address the issue of scale. The procedure is summarized in Table 13.1.

The exercise led to identifying the potential urban markets where Pakistani migrants were found to perform many of their transnational practices in their origin places. By considering the multifaceted implications of the performed practices within selected urban development domains, they were merged to identify potential urban development markets/sectors for transnational migrants. These were found to be the real estate markets, job markets, financial markets, business markets, and lastly the human capability development sector. The in-depth inquiry mainly revolved around exploring the transnational practices performed within the identified markets/sector whose findings are given below.

13.3.2 Transnational Practices of Pakistani Migrants

Mainly, non-migrant household members were assisting the Pakistani migrants (residing in Germany) to perform various transnational practices in Pakistan. Among these family members, fathers and brother/s were the key agents. This finding provides evidence of having a joint planning character among the migrant and non-migrant family members, thus making their living arrangement the multi-locational

Table 13.1 Selected urban development domains based on transnational practices

Urban development domains	Urban dimensions (UN-Habitat)	Envisaged performed practices/ associated aspects of performed practices
Physical/ built environment	Shelter	Improving access to facilities
		Investing in the housing market
		Investing in the real estate market
		Planning aspects
Economic	Economic development	Investing in business markets
		Remitting for general consumption
		Investing in financial markets/institutions
		Creating employment opportunity/ies
Environment	Environmental management	Investing in transportation modes
	Environmental sustainability	Locational aspects
Social	Social development and poverty eradication	Investing in social capital
		Gender aspects
		Maintaining social connections
Administrative	Governance	No link identified or visualized
Political		
Functional		
Demographic	–	Interacting labour market
		Causing internal migration
Technological	–	Transferring innovation
		Sending/carrying technology-related gifts
Cultural	–	Performing customary/religious practices
		Sending/carrying general gifts

Source: Aslam (2015)

householding. It is found that informal channels were used to send around 28–69% of the total remittances during the study period (5 years), which confirms the literature finding (Freund & Spatafora, 2005). Pakistani migrants were found to mainly perform the practice of taking care of the consumption needs of the non-migrant multilocational household members through remittances. After that, they were found making investments in the housing markets of the origin places. Table 13.2 provides

Table 13.2 Transnational practices of the Pakistani migrants during the study period

Sr. no	Transnational practices	Total (n = 20)
1	Meeting consumption needs of the household members	18
2	Investing in housing markets	9
3	Investing for the performance of cultural/ religious practices	6
4	Interacting with the labour market	6
5	Loan repayment	5
6	Investments in the businesses	4
7	Investing in financial institutions	3
8	Investing in social capital	3

Source Aslam (2015)

a summary of the practices performed by the respondents. It has also been found that the majority of them were performed in urban places.

Concerning frequency, remitting to multilocational household members was found to be the leading practice, however, considering the number of remittances sent for conducting different practices, investments in the urban housing markets of Pakistan came out as the leading practice (51.1% of all remittances). The sector, which attracted the second-largest remittance amount (35.9%) was human capacity development. Table 13.3 provides the remittances share to different identified urban markets/sectors.

Table 13.3 Summary of the performed practices and sent remittances during the study period

Domain/market/sector	Total		
	No. of respondents	No. of practices	Remittance (Euro)
General consumption	18	21	105,665 (35.9%)
Cultural	6	8	
Social capital	3	3	
Loan repayments	5	5	
Housing market	9	13	150,364 (51.1%)
Financial institutions	4	4	20,539 (7.0%)
Businesses	4	6	17,581 (6.0%)
Labour market	6	6	0
Total	–	66	294,149 (100.0%)

Source Aslam (2015)

13.3.3 *Implications of Performed Practices*

The practices performed by Pakistani migrants were found diverse and mainly carried out in four broad sectors. Complementarities and contradictions among the performed practices were found to have either positive or negative implications for the urban development of the origin places. For instance, investing in new house construction has many positive implicational aspects (De Haas, 2007; Taylor et al., 1996) for urban development, however, if the same house is constructed at a hazardous location and does not meet the local building bylaws, negative implicational aspects for the same practice are surfaced which are contradictory to the positive implicational aspects. The dual character of the aspects associated with the diversified practices makes the task difficult to determine the developmental (or non-developmental) status of the carried out practices. To tackle this issue, the associated aspects of the performed practices in line with the UN-Habitat urban indicators were identified, and then it was tried to ascertain their positive or negative implications for the urban development.

Pakistani migrants were mainly using remittances to carry out many of the transnational practices which had diversified implications for the urban development of the origin places. For instance, constructing a new house may have more implications for urban development due to various spinoff effects involved in comparison to the practice of saving money in local banks. Also, the same practice may have varying levels of implications due to its location (urban, suburban or rural) and the amount of remittance involved. Pacione (2009) identified the economic force as the leading one among other trigger forces to cause urban changes, and accordingly, it could be deduced that the more the remittances spent to carry out the practice, the more will be the implications of the practice for the urban development. Based on the number of remittances invested in different urban markets/ sector, weights for the practices performed in those sectors were calculated whose detail is given in Table 13.4.

Though the practice of sending or carrying gifts for the household members can be grouped with the practice of meeting the general consumption needs, it has been separately assessed for its implications for urban development as these are non-cash remittances. The estimated worth of the gifts was taken as the equivalent to the

Table 13.4 Weights for the performed practices in each sector

Sector/market	Remittances/worth (Euro)	No. of practices	Remittance /practice (Euro)	Weight
0	30,682	17	1,804.82	1
Human capability development	105,665	37	2,855.81	1.6
Housing market	150,364	12	12,530.33	6.9
Financial markets/ institutions	20,539	3	6,846.33	3.8
Business sector	17,581	4	4,395.25	2.4

Source Adapted from Aslam (2015)

remittance amount. Then the total remittance amount for every sector was divided by the number of practices performed within that sector to give remittance per practice value. Those practices for which the remittance amount was unknown or which did not need remittances for their operationalization were excluded from the calculations. It was the gift sector, which yielded the minimum value and hence was assigned a unit weight of 1. The weights for other sectors were derived by dividing the respective remittance per practice value by the same value for the gift sector. Based on the number of remittances invested in the housing sector, it carried the maximum weight, i.e. 6.9.

13.3.4 Urban Development Index (UDI)

Lastly, an Urban Development Index (UDI) was constructed to determine the implications of the aspects associated with the carried out practices. Though these practices were being performed at the household level, or in some cases, at the neighbourhood level, it is assumed that through the multiplier effect, these practices contributed towards the urban development at the city scale as well. Having no goalpost values derived through the past data, as in the case of the Human Development Index (HDI), the constructed UDI was not calibrated to give a value between a given range such as between 0 to 100, and hence it can yield a positive or negative value based on the nature of the implicational aspects of the performed practices. Despite having this inbuilt limitation of the UDI, it has been conceived as a useful tool to make comparative studies for different case study areas.

On the analogy of HDI and CDI, all the broad sectors where Pakistani migrants were performing transnational practices, were treated as sub-indices for computation of the UDI value. The score for every sub-index was calculated based on the implicational aspects of the performed practices. Quantitative values ranging from '−1' to ' +1' were assigned to the implicational aspects of the carried out practices. The aspects which were conceived as having positive implications for urban development were assigned a value of ' +1', which were conceived as negative, got '−1' value while the neutral aspects got a value of '0'. All the assigned values were then added up to get cumulative scores for every sub-index, and in that way, complementarities among the implicational aspects were added up while contradictions balanced out each other. Lastly, all the sub-indices values were summed up to give the UDI value. The UDI value can be interpreted as the direction (whether developmental or non-developmental) stimulated through the performed practices to assess their implications for the urban development of the origin places.

Table 13.5 presents the sub-indices values for every sector, which are summed up to have the cumulative UDI value. A positive UDI value simply tells the direction of the change element caused by the transnational practices performed by the Pakistani migrants during the study period. Without having an overall frame of city-level data for this study, the value, by no means can provide a contribution figure to overall development at the city scale. Still, these values provide some significant

Table 13.5 UDI of the performed practices

Index	Total
Gifts index	31.0 (7.2%)
Human capability index	56.0 (13.1%)
Housing market index	289.8 (67.6%)
Business markets index	21.6 (5.0%)
Financial markets index	30.4 (7.1%)
Urban Development Index (UDI)	428.8 (100.0%)

Source Aslam (2015)

insights. First, it provides a hint that the transnational practices performed by the Pakistani migrants during the study period contributed positively towards the urban development of the origin places, though it is unable to report on the question of 'how much'. Secondly, it shows the significance of the local housing markets as around two-thirds of the total score was caused by the practices performed in the housing market. Thirdly, around one-third of the total remittances were being consumed in the human capacity development sector, their positive contribution within the constructed UDI frame was found significantly less.

13.4 Conclusions

It is found that the transnational practices carried out by Pakistani migrants in the places of origin can be perceived as migrants' transnational lifestyles. The migrants maintain their transnational ties functional to enable them to perform various practices in the places of origin. Remittances to non-migrant family members are used as the main instrument to operationalize the intended practices. While doing so, they exhibit the character of joint planning and constitute multilocational households which are in line with Schmidt-Kallert's (2009) finding that multilocational household members avail themselves the opportunities of the concerned places of attachment. As the target population of this study was involved in cross-border interactions, this finding also lends its support to the literature on global householding in Pacific Asia (Douglass, 2006) an increasing trend of transnational interactions (Dittrich-Wesbuer & Plöger, 2013; Schiller, 2014).

The results reflect that these were mainly the transnational connections that enabled the migrants to perform a significant number of practices in the origin places, providing support to the findings of Brickell and Datta (2011). Dominantly, these transnational practices were being carried out in urban places. This shows the presence of a significant role being played by the migrants in bringing various changes to shape up the urban places. Thus, this study provides an important insight to address the literature deficiency of neglecting migrant's agency in urban studies

(Schiller, 2014). This study finds that, through transnational connections, migrants are significant contributors to urban life.

Other than sending money for meeting the consumption needs of the household members, investments in the housing markets of origin places remain a priority practice for almost half of the migrants. Assessing the implications of practices performed through remittances by the migrants is a complex task due to involved multifaceted complementary or contradictory aspects as pointed out by Jones et al. (2010). Though De Haas (2007) argued for the positive developmental status of such remittances for consumption and investment purposes, but to support his arguments, he did not provide any framework to address the issues of associated contradictions and scale. This study provides an important contribution in the shape of the Urban Development Index (UDI) which can deal with the mentioned issue. The results of the study provide an empirical base to provide support to De Haas (2007) arguments. Further, it also provides a method to determine the implications of the transnational practices for urban development at a scale below the city level. Currently, such composite indexing method to assess the impact of such transnational practices is hard to find, hence the study provides an important scientific contribution in this regard.

Finally, the study concludes that the performed transnational practices have overall positive implications for the urban development of origin places. Although contradictions within associated aspects of the carried out practices have been noted, the employed indexing method—UDI—balanced out such conflicting aspects as complementary dimensions were found more in number. Around two-thirds of the UDI, the score was caused by the practices performed in the local housing markets of Pakistan thus providing evidence for the significance of the housing sector investments for the migrant diaspora. It also reflects on the external dimension that exists beyond local or national borders (in line with the Cochrane, 2011 findings), which makes the migrants significant stakeholders for the urban development processes at the origin places. This reveals the significant role played by the international migrants in changing the urban landscape of the origin places. Though migrants play their part in bringing change within various other urban dimensions too, the study concludes that the most apparent change dimension is the built environment of the urban areas.

References

Adelman, I. et al. (1988) Life in a Mexican village: A SAM perspective, *The Journal of Development Studies, 25*(1), 5–24. Taylor & Francis

Agunias, D. R. (2006). *Remittance and development: Trends, impacts and policy options: A review of the literature*. Migration Policy Institute.

Aslam, A. B. (2015). *Implications of Return Migration Intentions of Pakistani Immigrants for Urban Development in Pakistan*. A Study of the Global Economic Crisis Period (2008–11) in Germany (Doctoral dissertation, Universitätsbibliothek Dortmund).

Baumgart, S. (2016). Multi-locality in the Global South–Observations of daily life in Bangladesh, Trialog, 116/117.

Brickell, K., & Datta, A. (2011). *Translocal geographies: Spaces*. Ashgate publishing.
Cochrane, A. (2011). Foreword. In E. McCann & K. Ward (Eds.), Mobile urbanism, cities and policymaking in the global age, University of Minnesota Press
De Haas, H. (2007). Remittances, migration and social development: A conceptual review of the literature, Social Policy and Development Programme (34), United Nations Research Institute for Social Development, Geneva, Switzerland
De Haas, H. (2010). Migration and development: A theoretical perspective. *International Migration Review 44*(1), 227–264. New York, Inc, Center for Migration Studies
Dittrich-Wesbuer, A., & Plöger, J. (2013). Multilokalität und Transnationalität – Neue Herausforderungen für Stadtentwicklung und Stadtpolitik (Multilocality and translocality: New challenges for urban development and urban policy), Raumforschung und Raumordnung 71(3), 195–205. Springer-Verlag Berlin
Douglass, M. (2006). Global householding and social reproduction in Pacific Asia, International Conference on Population and Development in Asia: Critical Issues for a Sustainable Future, Phuket, Thailand
Durand, J., et al. (1996). International migration and development in Mexican communities. *Demography, 33*(2), 249–264.
Federal Office for Migration and Refugees (2009) Muslim life in Germany: A study conducted on behalf of the German Conference on Islam, Research Report 6, 1st ed., Nürnberg
Freund, C., & Spatafora, N. (2005). Remittances: Transaction costs, determinants and informal flows, World Bank Policy Research Working Paper 3704
Gasper, D. (2004). *The ethics of development: From economism to human development*. Edinburgh University Press.
Global Migration Group (2010). Mainstreaming migration into development planning: A handbook for policy-makers and practitioners, International Organization for Migration (IOM), Denmark.
Global Urban Observatory (n.d.) Global Urban Indicators Database, Version 2, United Nations Human Settlements Programme, UN-Habitat.
International Monetary Fund (2009). Balance of payments and international investment position manual, 6th ed. (BPM6), IMF, Washington, D.C.
Jones, C., Jenks, M., & Bramley, G. (2010). Complementarities and contradictions. In M. Jenks, & C. Jones (Eds.), Dimensions of the sustainable city (2). Springer
Litman, T. (2020). Lessons from pandemics: Valuing public transportation. Planetizen. https://www.planetizen.com/blogs/109584-lessons-pandemics-valuing-public-transportation. Accessed 20 June 2020.
Mieg, H. A. (2013). *Institutional and social innovation for sustainable urban development*. Routledge.
Musselwhite, C., Avineri, E., & Susilo, Y. (2020). Editorial JTH 16–The Coronavirus Disease COVID-19 and implications for transport and health. *Journal of Transport & Health, 16*, 100853.
Njoh, A. J. (2006). Tradition, culture and development in Africa: Historical lessons for modern development planning, Ashgate.
Pacione, M. (2009). *Urban geography: A global perspective* (3rd ed.). Routledge.
Schiller, N. G. (2014). Transnationality: Transnationality and the city, A Companion to Urban Anthropology, 1st ed., edited by Nonini, Donald M., John Wiley & Sons, Ltd.
Schmidt-Kallert, E. (2009). A new paradigm of urban transition: Tracing the livelihood strategies of multi-locational households, Die Erde 140(3), pp. 319–336. Gesellschaft für Erdkunde zu Berlin
Takenaka, A. K., Villafuerte, J., & Gaspar, R. (2020). COVID-19 Impact on international migration, remittances, and recipient households in developing Asia. https://www.adb.org/publications/covid-19-impact-migration-remittances-asia. Accessed on 16 Sept 2020
Taylor, J. E. et al. (1996). International migration and community development. *Population Index, 62*(3), 397–418. Office of Population Research
United Nations Human Settlements Programme (UN-Habitat). (2000). Epilogue: The city development index (CDI), UN-Habitat.

United Nations Statistics Division. (1998). Recommendations on statistics of international migration, Revision 1, Statistical papers series M, No. 58, United Nations, New York.
United Nations Department of Economic and Social Affairs. (2020). The 17 Goals. https://sdgs.un.org/goals, and https://unstats.un.org/sdgs/indicators/indicators-list/. Accessed 19 Sept 2020.
World Bank. (2011). *Migration and remittances factbook 2011* (2nd ed.). The World Bank.
World Bank. (2020). Indicators, https://data.worldbank.org/indicator?tab=all. Accessed on 19 Sept 2020.
Yayboke, E. (2020). Five ways COVID-19 is changing global migration.". Center for Strategic and International Studies. https://www.csis.org/analysis/five-ways-covid-19-changing-global-migration. Accessed 16 Sept 2020.

Chapter 14
Naya Pakistan Housing Program: An Analytical Study of Mortgage-Backed Security Model and Legal Framework for Low-Cost Accessible Housing Scheme in Pakistan

Naureen Akhtar, Rao Imran Habib, and Attia Madni

Abstract Pakistan is currently facing an urban housing shortage of near four million mostly in low and lower-middle-income segments of the society. Almost every government has endeavoured to cope with this deficiency by introducing various models of conventional and Islamic financial products for home financing. Despite all the efforts of the state, the shortfall not only exists today but has increased manifolds, as the population is much inclined to urban life owing to various reasons. These products include, but are not limited to, home financing through the lease-based model, diminishing *mushārakah* and *murābahah* to the purchase order. Recently, the Government of Pakistan led by Chairman *Tehreek-e-Insaf* has also announced its pilot project of Naya Pakistan Housing Program (PHP) which claims to provide a low-cost and accessible housing facility to low and lower middle class of the society. This research work undertakes to analyse the existing models of financial products for home financing, including the proposed Mortgage-Backed Security Model, to check their propriety and suitability for NPHP. It also elaborates the legal framework for low-cost accessible housing in Pakistan under this pilot project of the PTI government. This paper finds that utilization of Mortgage-Backed *Sukuk* can represent an effective form of cheaper long-term financing. This study argues that effective foreclosure laws enhance the recovery rates from the borrower by the lender. Finally, this study suggests the establishment of a strong mortgage finance industry in Pakistan to achieve the undertaking of the PTI government of providing 5 million houses.

Keywords Housing finances · Mortgage-Backed Sukuk · Naya Pakistan Housing Program

---

N. Akhtar (✉) · R. I. Habib
University Gillani Law College, B.Z.U, Multan, Pakistan
e-mail: naureen.akhtar@bzu.edu.pk

A. Madni
Faculty of Shariah and Law, International Islamic University, Islamabad, Pakistan

A. Kundu et al. (eds.), *Accessible Housing for South Asia*,
https://doi.org/10.1007/978-3-030-88881-7_14

14.1 Introduction

Shelter is a necessity of life. Housing is one of the fundamental needs which provide a place of rest and peace of mind (Noonal & Watson, 2017). It is a place to reside in comfort with a family. Moreover, an adequate, and affordable standard of living is the basic requirement of every human being. Standard of living is one of the parameters of the Human Development Index. Human Development Index indicates the economic development of a nation (Vejzagic, 2014). Promoting a housing program is directly linked with the growth in the economy as it invites investment, engages unemployed citizens, and promotes entrepreneurship (Shirazi et al., 2012).

House financing is one of the four types of products of consumer financing. The other three products include personal loans, auto loans and credit cards. Housing finance includes the credit facility which is usually utilized in purchasing the residential land or improving it or it includes both purchasing and construction (Hassan, 2011). Usually, house financing involves four things, purchasing of land, construction of a house, purchasing of a constructed house and renovation (Shehzad, 2012).

Three important aspects of Housing programs/schemes include assessment of future needs, affordability and sustainability (Iqbal, 2020). The provision of affordable housing is essentially a state's responsibility in the modern era. Likewise, in Pakistan, it is the state's constitutional responsibility to ensure the availability of affordable housing to its citizens under Article 38 (d) of the Constitution of Pakistan, 1973 which provides that the state shall be responsible to provide the necessities of life for all the citizens, such as food, clothing, housing, education and medical relief, who are unable to earn their livelihood on account of infirmity, sickness or unemployment (GoP, 1973). Keeping in view this constitutional task every government, in Pakistan, tried to pay attention to the demand–supply housing balance in a country. However, the supply of housing has been not catching up with the ever-increasing demand for housing. In 2001, a National Housing Policy was devised to address the housing issues in Pakistan. This policy lacked proper implementation and failed to bring substantial improvement in the housing sector (Tariq et al., 2018). The government of PTI launched a housing scheme to address the issue of the availability of low-cost affordable residences.

Overall, Pakistan is facing a severe shortage of nearly 11–12 million housing units. The urban housing shortage is estimated to be around 4 million. On the other hand, rural and semi-urban housing shortfall is nearly 7–8 million (Rizvi, 2018). PTI national policy on affordable housing units declared that Pakistan is in dire need of 01 million housing units per year including 04 lacks housing units for rural and urban areas, respectively. It also includes 02 lakh housing units for semi-urban areas. The issue of house affordability has demanded the attention of policymakers, financial advisors and investors.

This study, in the first part, undertakes the analysis of different models of financial products for home financing introduced by various financial institutions in Pakistan at various times. The second part of this research undertakes the analysis of the proposed Mortgage Backed Security Model, to check their propriety and suitability for NPHP. It follows a discussion on the required legal framework for low-cost accessible housing in Pakistan under this pilot project of the PTI government.

14.2 Analytical Study of Different Models of Financial Products for Home Financing in Pakistan

The housing sector is too large for any financial institution or government to finance alone. Therefore, it usually involves the support of the private sector as investors and financial institutions along with the support of the public sector for the supply of housing. Several modes of financing for housing are in existence. Various financial products have been introduced by financial institutions in Pakistan for housing schemes. For this research work, the following three financial products, based on *Ijārah*, *Mushārakh* and *Murābahah*, are analysed to spotlight their basic structure of operation in Pakistan to provide housing facilities to the homeless section of the society.

14.2.1 Ijārah Housing Finance

This model of financing is designed based on a contract of *ijārah* primarily and a contract of *bay'* or sale is utilized in this model on a secondary basis at the time of its completion (Amin, 2018). The financial product called *ijārah wa iqtinā'* or *ijārah muntahīyyah biltamlīk* is designed in such a way that asset is given to the client by the financier at an agreed or pre-decided amount of money instead of rents. At the end of the lease period, the asset is sold to the lessee or client at an agreed price and the legal title of the asset is transferred to the lessee based on the pre-existence of the promise between the lessor and lessee (Vejzagic, 2014). This study argues that *Ijārah muntahīyyah biltamlīk* is a long-term contract, and therefore the fixed rental payment is susceptible to changes in market conditions. The investor demands a high return on the investment which is difficult for the low-income group. Figure 14.1 depicts the process involved in house financing by employing *ijārah muntahīyyah biltamlīk*.[1]

14.2.2 Mushārakah Housing Finance

Mushārakah Mutanāqisha or Diminishing *Mushārakah* is a financial product used commonly in Pakistan by financial institutions for house financing. Diminishing

[1] The diagram is developed by the researchers for providing better understanding of the financial product of Ijarah Muntahiyya Biltamleek.

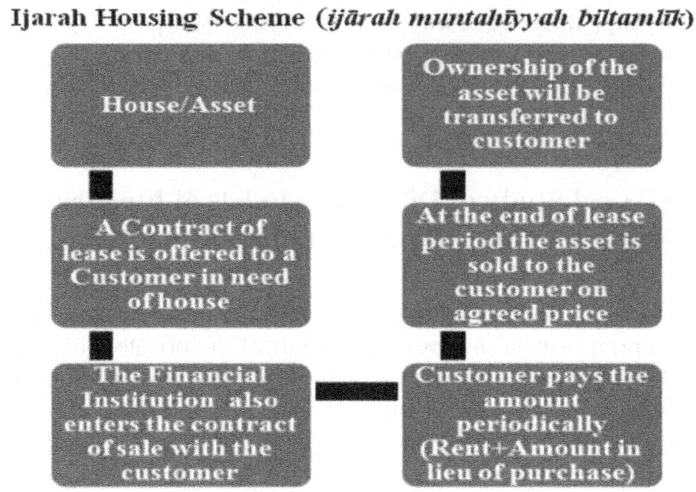

Fig. 14.1 Steps involved in the house financing through ijārah muntahīyyah biltamlīk

Mushārakah is a combination of three contracts, *Sharikah* (partnership), *ijārah* (lease) and *bay'* (Sale). In this model, the partnership comes into existence between the financial institution and the customer when the financial institution and the customer jointly purchased the asset. Therefore, the customer participates in the joint ownership of the asset with the financial institution based on *Sharikah al-Milk* (Shehzad, 2012). The share of the financial institution, the financier, is divided into small units. The customer pays the rent to the financial institution for using its resources based on the *ijārah* agreement. The customer purchases the share of the financial institution periodically until he becomes the sole owner of the property. As the customer purchases units of a financial institution, the payable amount instead of rent decreases. In the end, this payable amount becomes zero (Usmani, 2020). *Sharī'ah* issue in this contract is the leaseback agreement (Saeed, 2017). House Building Finance Corporation utilized this product in Pakistan for a long time. Figure 14.2 shows various steps involved in house financing through *Mushārakah Mutanāqisha*.[2]

14.2.3 *Murābahah Housing Finance*

Murābahah lil Āamir bil-shirā' or *Murābahah* to the purchase order is a sale of an asset at an agreed price between the parties to this contract. The agreed price covers the purchase price plus the profit margin. The financial institution purchases the asset on the demand of the customer and then sells it to the customer at a marked-up price on

[2] The diagram is developed by the researchers for providing better understanding of the financial product of *Mushārkah Mutanāqisha*.

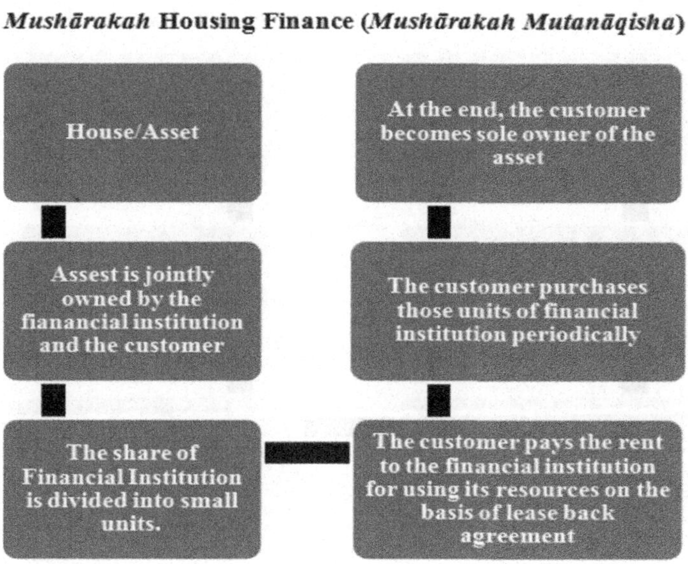

Fig. 14.2 Steps involved in the house financing through Mushārakah Mutanāqisha

a deferred payment basis (Ahmed, 2015). *Murābahah lil Āamir bil-shirā'* is a long-term contract and financial institutions cannot charge extra amount during the period of the contract, therefore, it becomes costly for the customers and doesn't suit them. *Murābahah lil Āamir bil-shirā'* is different from an instalment sale. In the contract of *Murābahah lil Āamir bil-shirā'*, the financier purchases the asset on the demand of the client. Later, the financial institution sells the asset to the client or customer on a deferred payment basis and the contract refers to the original cost along with the profit margin separately. In the contract of the instalment sale, the financier purchased the asset on the demand of the client and later sells the goods to the client on a deferred payment basis and the contract does not refer to the original cost along with the profit margin separately. The total cost of the financier is divided into instalments (Tameme, 2009). According to *Sharī'ah* scholars, this financial product is not suitable for house financing because of the issue in price. This financial product is not an ideal choice for a long-term financing project. This product is practised on a limited scale in industrial and agriculture sectors, respectively (GoP, 1988). Figure 14.3 depicts the process involved in house financing by employing *Murābahah lil Āamir bil-shirā'*.

The proceeding part of the article is designed to propose the model of financial product for the house financing for the pilot project of PTI.

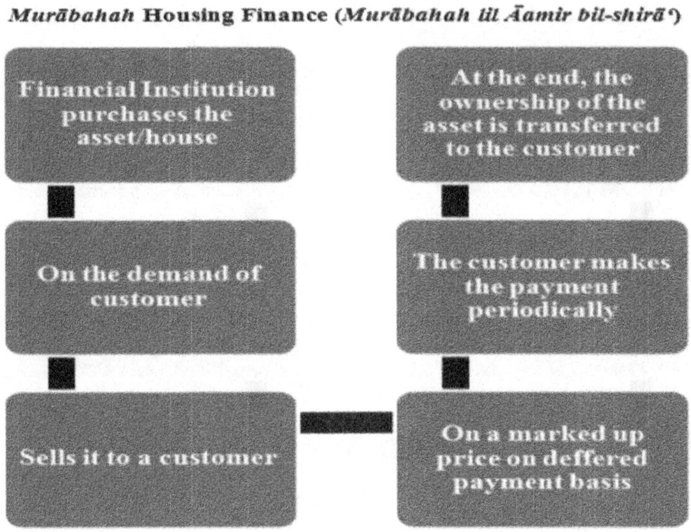

Fig. 14.3 The process involved in house financing by employing Murābahah lil Āamir bil-shirā'

14.3 Proposed Mortgage-Backed Security Model for House Financing in Pakistan

Sukuk are certificates of equal value evidencing ownership of the asset or its usufruct.[3] These certificates are asset-backed trust certificates based on *Mushārakah, Mudārbah, Ijārah, Istiṣnā'* and *Salam.* This study is aimed to propose Mortgage-Backed *Sukuk* for house financing in Pakistan for the pilot project of the Government of PTI. The proposed financial product must address key goals like *Sharī'ah* compliance, scalability and ease of implementation. Credit facilities available, through various models, previously addressed the high-income group of the society in Pakistan. Credit facilities available to the low-income group, in a state like Pakistan, is a challenge.

The prohibition of *ribā*, as a general rule, in Islamic Financial law prohibits the use of conventional bonds and debentures. *Sukuk* are the substitute to bonds and debentures issued by conventional financial institutions. *Sukuk* represents *Sharī'ah* compliant securities. They are securities having the dual features of both debt and equity financial instruments (Zolfaghari, 2017). This research work advocates the use of Mortgage-Backed *Sukuk* to meet the needs of financing for providing accommodation to the homeless people having low incomes. Mortgage-Backed *Sukuk* is asset-backed security and represents debt financing.

---

[3] Investment Sukuk, Sharī'ah Standard No. 17, Auditing and Accounting Organization for Islamic Financial Institutions (Bahrain: Accounting and Auditing Organization for Islamic Financial Institution, 2010), 468, retrieved from http://www.nbfi-modaraba.com.pk/Data/Sites/1/skins/nbfi/images/AAOIFI/ShariahStandard17.pdf, accessed on September 17, 2020.

The foremost parties concerned in Mortgage-Backed *Sukuk* are the customer or the client who is homeless, the government, credit institution, financial intermediary or Special Purpose Vehicle and investor. The client or customer will be the owner of the underlying asset, at the end of the transaction, upon the payment of all instalments to the credit financing institution. The government mortgages the underlying asset to the credit financing institution and, therefore, provides the security in the form of property in land for the repayment of the credit. The government proclaims the supervision of the whole process to maintain transparency and precision. Land or immovable property will be provided by the government for the project of NPHP. The government of Pakistan will mortgage the property inland to the financial institution which undertakes the availability of providing financing facility. Special purpose Vehicle (SPV) will be the issuing authority of Mortgage-Backed *Sukuk*. The investor will purchase the Mortgage-Backed *Sukuk* and becomes the *sukuk* holder (Akhtar et al., 2014). Financing through private mortgages remains small and does not meet the requirements of the customer or the client. Financing through public mortgages, involvement, and supervision of the government, is in the best interest of both the customer and the financier.

Various contracts are involved in the model of Mortgage-Backed *Sukuk*. For instance, the contract of sale on instalments between the customer or client and the government, the contract of mortgage between the government and the financial institution which provides the credit facility and to whom mortgagee rights have been assigned and the contract between SPV and investors. The proposed model of Mortgage-Backed *Sukuk* is presented in Fig. 14.4.

In the model of Mortgage-Backed *Sukuk*, the repayments made by the initial borrowers represent the liquidity flow that is received by the credit financing institution. SPV issues the Mortgage-Backed *Sukuk* to investors or lenders who supply funds to the financial markets. The mortgaged property forms a contingent receivable in the accounts of the credit financing institution (Rajapakse, 2011). It is pertinent to mention here that, because of the above-mentioned process; the loans will be converted into tradable securities in the capital market.

Credit financing through a mortgage for the construction of houses has better recovery rates than unsecured credit financing. History reveals that financing based on the underlying asset has low default risk. Therefore, this research work argues the utilization of Mortgage-Backed *Sukuk* for house financing because of reliability on an underlying asset which increases the chances of repayment of credit to the financier by the client. Moreover, this study argues for the redemption of the property in land by the government of PTI from the credit financing institution within a fixed time so that ownership of the house may be transferred to the customer in actuality at the end of the transaction.

This study suggests the issuance of Mortgage-Backed *Sukuk* instead of other financial products for housing schemes because of their high recovery rates than unsecured credit financing modes. Furthermore, this research work proposes the involvement of multilateral development banks which may play a significant role in financing the

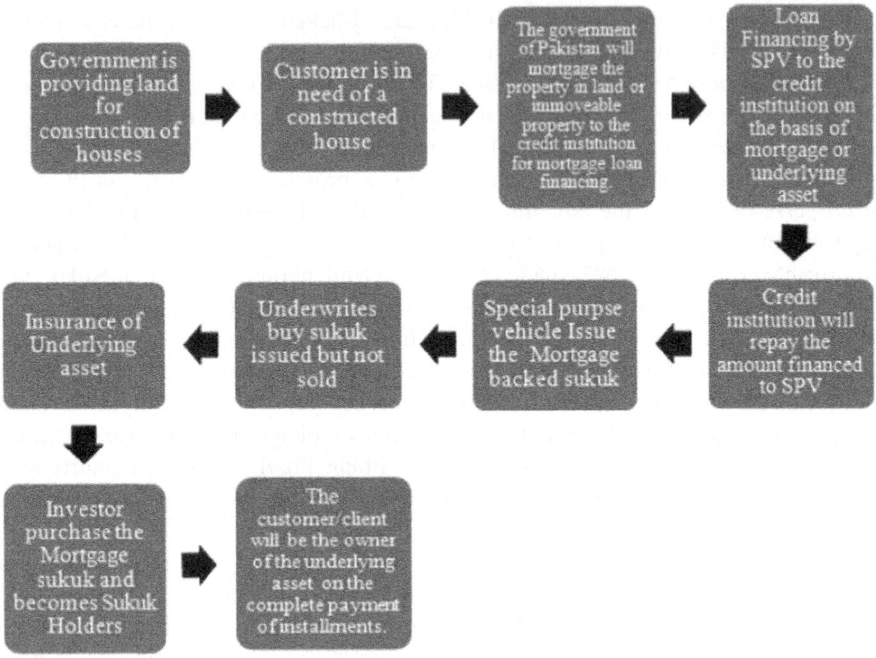

Fig. 14.4 Proposed model of Mortgage-Backed Sukuk

housing sector owing to their competencies in funding long-term projects. Allocation of sufficient financial resources is required to finance the construction and owning of the house.

The credit information is usually not available and becomes one of the restraints regarding investment in housing finance. The lenders or financiers are interested to get information about the borrowers in terms of their being progressive or creditworthiness to determine the risk associated with lending. Similarly, the borrowers are also interested in knowing the stipulations associated with the housing finance policy. This study suggests that the government of Pakistan must play role in developing the trust and confidence-based relationship between lenders or investors and borrowers or customers who will be the end-users of this housing finance scheme.

The ever-increasing demand for housing cannot be achieved without the establishment of a primary mortgage market. The long-term housing finance maturity and short-term deposits create liquidity risk for credit financing institutions. This disparity could be sorted out by establishing a secondary mortgage market. This article argues for the establishment of not only a strong primary mortgage market to finance the ever-increasing demand for housing but also the establishment of strong secondary market mortgage institutions. Furthermore, the establishment of refinancing companies for solving the liquidity problem of the primary mortgage market is required.

14.4 Analysis of Legal Framework for Naya Pakistan Housing Program

Housing finance needs a strong legal framework to provide low-cost accessible housing to the lower and lower–middle-class of the society. The core issue in credit financing by the financial institutions is the recovery of payment from the borrower by the creditor. The legislation provides remedies to the financial institution, the creditor or financier, for expeditious recovery of their outstanding payment in case of default of periodical payment by the borrower. A fragile and weak recovery system discourages the investors which consequently hinders the completion of the project. If customers are deterred from defaulting, this in turn would increase the confidence of the investor. To provide the legal framework for NPHP, the legal instrument promulgated is the Recovery of Mortgage-Backed Security Ordinance, 2019 (Hereinafter referred to as RMBSO, 2019). RMBSO, 2019 provides the mechanism for the recovery of credit in case the borrower commits a default in the payment of money due to him.

The issues in the implementation of the Financial Institutions (Recovery of Finances) Ordinance, 2001 have been addressed in RMBSO, 2019. One of the major hurdles that impeded the growth of mortgage financing in Pakistan was the non-availability of the option of pursuing non-judicial foreclosures by the financial institutions providing credit facilities. Efficient laws associated with foreclosure are required for the development of the mortgage market. Section 3 of RMBSO, 2019 provides that the legal right relating to a mortgaged property, created in favour of a secured creditor, can be enforced without the intervention of a court or tribunal. Furthermore, the RMBSO, 2019 allows the financial institution to proceed with foreclosure procedures under Section 3 (4) after the lapse of 60 days since the notice has been issued to the defaulter. This Ordinance allows the financial institutions to take possession of the asset mortgaged to them for the recovery of their due payments. This Ordinance also enables the financial institutions to approach the state to facilitate their control over the asset mortgaged.

Another impediment in the process of recovery of finances is the common practice of initiating frivolous cases in courts of law to avoid accountability on defaults by loan borrowers in Pakistan. The meticulous framework of RMBSO, 2019 provides the solution of the issue in the form of making mandatory the payment of 75% of the amount claimed in the notice of recovery sent to the borrower by the lender or financial institution if the borrower wants to avail the right to appeal against the action taken against him under Section 3 (4) of RMBSO, 2019.

An additional important development in RMBSO, 2019 is the mandatory registration of the creation of mortgage with the registering authority, the Central Depository Company, under Section 4 of RMBSO, 2019. The disbursement of credit shall not take place without the fulfilment of this mandatory provision. Such registration will provide a better *locus standi* to the secured creditor or financier in a court of competent jurisdiction against the default of the customer or borrower.

Section 6 of RMBSO, 2019 provides the authority to the government to intervene and help the creditor or financier for the recovery of mortgage money by taking possession of the secured asset and its related documents. Here, the government can play an effective role in the recovery of finances in case of default committed by the customer because the acts of designated state authority in this regard would not be challenged in any court of law or before any authority.

An overview of RMBSO, 2019 reveals that the ordinance contains all the relevant provisions to ensure the speedy and effective recovery of credit by the financial institutions from the borrowers or customers. The loopholes of previous recovery legislations have been tried to be covered in RMBSO, 2019. The current law is untested in the courts of law in Pakistan so far. It is anticipated to bring positive change in the process of recovery of credit. Moreover, legislation changing foreclosure laws in Pakistan is expected to facilitate PM Imran Khan's Naya Pakistan Housing Program to provide affordable housing to the lower-income group. The far-reaching impact of RMBSO, 2019 would help in changing the dynamics of the housing sector in Pakistan.

National Policy declares the development of the banking industry in Pakistan and the establishment of Pakistan Mortgage Refinance Company.[4] International Finance Corporation, a member of the World Bank Group, declares recently, in July this year, to invest 3.2 million dollars in Pakistan Mortgage Refinance Company Limited. This financial support will increase the overall availability of mortgage financing in Pakistan at present.

14.5 Conclusion and Recommendations

This research paper concludes that housing is of huge importance for families, society and the economy at large. A viable and sustainable housing program needs to address various housing activities like supply side, demand or finance side, planning and regulatory or legal framework.

This research paper, moreover, concludes that house financing through financial products of *ijārah muntahīyyah biltamlīk*, *Mushārakah Mutanāqisha* and *Murābahah lil Āamir bil-shirā'* by various financial institutions in Pakistan were more suitable for a high-income group of the society. The proposed model in this research work addresses the need for housing facilities by the low-income group in Pakistan. In addition to the above, this article concludes that a viable and sustainable model needs easier monetization by the credit institution and efficient recovery from the borrower. The proposed model has been designed to achieve the task so desired and needed. Utilization of Mortgage-Backed *Sukuk* can represent an effective form of cheaper long-term financing.

[4] National Affordable Housing Policy by the Government of Pakistan Tehreek-e-Insaf, retrieved from http://nphp.com.pk/government-policy-on-housing/, accessed on September 3, 2020.

The unavailability of mortgage finance in Pakistan, previously has posed a continuous challenge for the government to implement its plan for providing housing facilities to the low-income groups of the country. This unavailability was strongly linked with ineffective foreclosure laws in the state. This issue has been addressed in RMBS Ordinance, 2019. The mechanism provided in the said Ordinance aims to ensure efficient recoveries from the borrowers by the lenders or creditors. Though the statute is still untested in the courts of law in Pakistan, it is anticipated to bring positive change in the process of recovery of credit.

This paper, further, concludes that a suitable legal and institutional framework is required for the establishment of sound financial institutions and markets. A weak legal framework covering mortgages will provide an opportunity for the investor to control the real estate. Therefore, this paper argues for the establishment of a strong mortgage finance industry in Pakistan.

Legal framework having ineffective foreclosures laws, complicated land registration system and inadequate funds for long-term projects have been the key issues of the housing sector in Pakistan. This paper proposes electronic registration instead of manual registration, to allow the registration department to certify the documents instead of involving notaries. Moreover, this study proposes the empowerment of the financial institutions to foreclose the mortgaged property without the intervention of the court and the promotion of secondary mortgage market to enhance liquidity in the mortgage finance market.

References

Ahmad, R. (2015). A Critical Analysis of *Murābahah* Transaction in the Banking Sector of Pakistan. *Tahzīb Al-Afkār., 2015*, 17–28.

Akhtar, N., Habib, R. I., & Madni, A. (2019). Sharī'ah appraisal of mortgage backed Sukuk issued by financial institutions for house financing in Naya Pakistan housing program: Ana analytical study. *Review of Economic and Development Studies., 5*(1), 136–145.

Amin, H. (2018). Time to consider Al-Ijarah Muntahiya Bil Tamlik for Home Financing. May 28, 2018. Retrieved from https://www.iium.edu.my/news/time-to-consider-al-ijarah-muntahia-biltamleek-home-financing. Accessed on September 12, 2020.

Bilal, Q., & Rahim, M. (n.d.). Diminishing Musharakah: A model of financing in interest free banks. *Abysan Journal of Social Sciences, 7*(1), 150–157.

GoP. (1988). Council of Islamic Ideology, Government of Pakistan, Islamabad. *Bilasood Bankari*. Islamabad: Council of Islamic Ideology.

GoP. (1973). The Constitution of Pakistan.

Hassan, N. (2011). Issues and Challenges of Consumer Financing in Pakistan, Master thesis submitted at Department of Economics and Informatics, University West, Sweden, March 2011.

Hosen, M. (2020). The Pitfalls of the Malaysian Sukuk Industry: Issues and Challenges, Working Paper. Retrieved from https://www.researchgate.net/publication/317950429_The_Pitfalls_of_the_Malaysian_Sukuk_Industry_Issues_and_Challenges_in_practice. Accessed on September 19, 2020.

Iqbal, N. (2020). Sustainable Housing. *The News*. March 18, 2020. Retrieved from https://www.thenews.com.pk/print/630789-sustainable-housing. Accessed on September 09, 2020.

National Affordable Housing Policy by the Government of Pakistan Tehreek-e-Insaf. Retrieved from http://nphp.com.pk/government-policy-on-housing/. Accessed on September 3, 2020.

Noonan, J., & Watson, J. (2017). Against housing: homes as a human life requirement. *Alternate Routes: A Journal of Critical Social Research, 28*(1), 141–163. Retrieved from http://www.alternateroutes.ca/index.php/ar/article/view/22421. Accessed on September 07, 2020.

Rajapakse, P. J. (2011). Analysis of the concept of mortgage backed securities. *JLFM., 10*(1), 22–33.

Rizvi, Z. M. (2018). Pakistan Tehreek-e-Insaf National Housing Affordable Housing Policy. July 04, 2018. Retrieved from http://nphp.com.pk/government-policy-on-housing/. Accessed on September 13, 2020.

Saeed, M. (2017). Implementation Issues of Partnership (Musharka) and Diminishing Partnership (Muntiqa Musharaka) (December 31, 2017). Available at SSRN: https://ssrn.com/abstract=3276645or, https://doi.org/10.2139/ssrn.3276645.

Sharīʻah Standards for Islamic Financial Institutions. Bahrain: Accounting and Auditing Organization for Islamic Financial Institution, 2010.

Shehzad, M. A. (2012). Models of Islamic housing finance for the renovation of houses in Pakistan. *Housing Finance International.* (Winter 2012): 6–8.

Shirazi, N. S., Zulkhibri, M. A., & Syed, S. (2012). *Challenges of affordable housing finance in IDB member countries using Islamic modes.* Jeddah: Islamic Research & Training Institute.

Tameme, M. E. M. (2009). Demand and Supply Conditions of Islamic Housing Finance in the United Kingdom: Perceptions of Muslim Clients. Ph.D. thesis submitted at the School of Government and International Affairs, Durham University, 2009. Retrieved from https://core.ac.uk/download/pdf/84885.pdf. Accessed on September 12, 2020.

Tariq, F., Muhammad, S., & Javeria, H. (2018). Developing countries perspective on housing Affordability: Recommendations for Pakistan. *Technical Journal, University of Engineering and Technology, Texila, Pakistan., 23*(2), 1–10.

Usmani, M. I. A. (2020). *Meezan Bank's Guide to Islamic Banking.* 1st ed. Karachi: Dār Al-Ishāʻat, 2002. Retrieved from https://www.yumpu.com/en/document/read/43294470/diminishing-musharakah-meezan-bank. Accessed on September 10, 2020.

Vejzagic, M. (2014). Ijarah Muntahiyya Biltamleek: A Risk Management Perspective. *Merit Research Scholars., 2*(1), 1–7.

Zolfaghari, P. (2017). An Introduction to Islamic Securities. Working Paper presented at Uppsala University of Law. 2017.

Chapter 15
Rural Housing Programme (Indira Awaas Yojana) in West Bengal, India: Trends of Achievements

Saptarshi Mitra and Samrat Hore

Abstract Rural housing is one of the significant rural facets, as it represents the socio-economic conditions of an individual or the rural society as a whole. Indira Awaas Yojana (IAY) is one of the six mechanisms of 'Bharat Nirman' that tries to overcome the problems of shortage of housing shortage in rural India. This is an essential rural development scheme in India. The flagship programme for rural housing was launched in the year 1985–86, where the sole objective was to construct rural housing for the economically deprived rural people/families. The programme is being run by the rural local self-government institutions since its inception. The implementation of this programme is related to different factors. The paper analyses the district-wise performance of the state of West Bengal, which was one of the pioneer states of India in respect of the progress of rural development during the past decade of the twentieth century and early decade of the twenty-first century along with the related causes and consequences.

Keywords Rural housing scheme · Rural poverty · Rural self- government · Rural development

15.1 Introduction

The population is significantly higher in developing countries such as India, where about 67% of the total population lives in rural areas. The rural economy in India constitutes almost 46% of the national income, which is higher than in many other developed countries in the world (Chand et al., 2017). Ruminating the total habitable area of India (about 3.2 million km^2), the population density as a measure of the number of persons per square kilometre has increased from 324 in 2001 to 382 in 2011, nearly 17.90% rise over a decade (Sudhira & Gururaja, 2012).

S. Mitra (✉)
Department of Geography and Disaster Management, Tripura University, Agartala, Tripura 799022, India

S. Hore
Department of Statistics, Tripura University, Agartala, Tripura 799022, India

A. Kundu et al. (eds.), *Accessible Housing for South Asia*,
https://doi.org/10.1007/978-3-030-88881-7_15

By observing the overall statistics the rural population contributes to 68.84% of India's population, which is about 1250.3 million (Census of India, 2011). India faced the challenge of providing adequate shelter to 18.5 million citizens (Tiwari, 2001). Government of India lainched a scheme call Indira Awaas Yojana (IAY) to provide dwelling units free of cost to the rural poor (Planning Commission, 2013). The scheme is meant to provide support to the construction of dwelling units to members of Scheduled Castes (SCs), Scheduled Tribes (STs) and Freed Bonded Labourers (FBLs) and Non-Scheduled Castes (NSCs), Non-Scheduled Tribes (NSTs) living Below Poverty Line (BPL) in the rural areas (Hussain & Yaseen, 2018; Boruah, 2015). However, financial assistance for the IAY scheme is not equally distributed all over the country (International Environment Audit & Sustainable Development, 2013). A significant anomaly is found in the largest eastern Indian state, West Bengal, in terms of IAY, especially the northern and southern parts (Mitra, 2012). As one of India's largest populated states, rural housing is a chronic issue of West Bengal (Munsi, 2001).

No detailed district-wise study on IAY has been conducted in West Bengal to understand performance and financial support status in a combined manner. This chapter analyses the district-wise performance of the state of West Bengal, which was one of the pioneer states of India in respect of the progress of rural development during the past decade of the twentieth century and early decade of the twenty-first century along with the related factors. This study helps to understand the district pattern of rural development.

15.2 Location of the Study Area

West Bengal is one of the twenty-eight states of India, which extends between 21 degree 28′ North to 27 degree 13′ North latitudes and 85 degree 47′ East to 89 degree 51′ East longitudes. Located on the eastern margin of India, it is bounded on the north by the State of Sikkim, north and north-east by Bhutan which is on the lap of the Eastern Himalayas, on the west and north-west by Nepal, on the west by States of Bihar and Jharkhand, on the south and south-west by the Bay of Bengal and the State of Odisha, respectively, and the east by Bangladesh and the State of Assam respectively. The state has an area of 88,752.00 square kilometres, of which 85,427.26 square kilometres (96.25% to the total area) is the rural area (Census of India, 2001).

Administratively, the state was divided into three large tracts called Divisions, namely Presidency, Barddhaman and Jalpaiguri Divisions. The divisions comprise several districts. At that time, 19 districts in West Bengal including Kolkata, the capital city of the state, which is entirely urban districts. In all the districts, the maximum areas are demarcated as rural areas. Each of the other 18 districts has a separate three-tier rural local self-government other than general administration. This rural administration is structurally divided into the three-tier system which is known as Panchayati raj since its inception in 1978. Except for Darjeeling District, in all other 17 districts having rural area Panchayati structure is active. However, due to political conflict, Darjiling District has an actively two-tier Panchayati system; Darjiling, Kalimpong and Kurseong these three hill Subdivisions combinedly establish Darjiling Gorkha Hill Council (DGHC) and Siliguri Sub-division in Darjiling District creates Siliguri Mahakuma Parishad (SMP). Kolkata is the State capital of the state. Including Kolkata and all other head quarters of the district are generally located in the urban centers. It is mainly an alluvial plane area covered with different rivers and tributaries except norther Himalayan mountain region, western Chotonagpur plateau region and southern coastal regions.

15.3 Methodology

In the present analysis, we have considered all the 17 districts of state of West Bengal and the state itself, except Kolkata and Darjeeling. Kolkata has not been considered as it is an urban district. Further due to different administrative reasons, the data of Darjeeling District was not fully available. The available partial data of the district has, however, been considered.

To analyse the significant performance of each district based on the percentage of Physically achieved the target of IAY and percentage of financial utilization of IAY over one and a half decades (1996–97 to 2010–11), analysis of variance (ANOVA) test has been carried out. The level of significance is considered at 5%. Each district and different years are considered as two factors of the ANOVA and the findings on the percentage of physically achieved target of IAY (Table 15.1) and percentage of financial utilization (Table 15.2) are marked, respectively.

Both are the factors found significant at 5% level of significance, which implies significant effects are found among the districts and the years. To identify more significant districts and years, the Tukey HSD test has been performed which shows that Coochbehar, Jalpaiguri and Dakshin Dinajpur Districts are the top three significant districts. On the other hand, South 24-Parganas, Bankura and Malda Districts

Table 15.1 ANOVA on the percentage of physically achieved target of IAY of each district and overall state of West Bengal during 1996–97 to 2010–11

Factors	Degrees of freedom	Sum of square	Mean sum of square	Variance ratio (F value)	P-value (#Significant at 5%)
Year	14	67,150	4796	7.240	2.37e-12#
Districts	16	27,068	1692	2.554	0.00121#
Residuals	224	148,399	662		
Total	254	242,617			

Source Department of Panchayats and Rural Development, Govt. of West Bengal

Table 15.2 ANOVA on percentage of financial utilization of IAY of each district and overall state of West Bengal during 1996–97 to 2010–11

Factors	Degrees of freedom	Sum of square	Mean sum of square	Variance ratio (F value)	P-value (#Significant at 5%)
Year	14	22,941	1638.7	7.285	1.96e-12#
Districts	16	10,483	655.2	2.913	0.000225#
Residuals	224	50,388	224.9		
Total	254	83,812			

Source Department of Panchayats and Rural Development, Govt. of West Bengal

are the least three in respect of poor performance. Further, considering the performances, during the years under consideration, it was observed that a higher target was achieved during 2004–05, 2005–06 and 2010–11 years, wherever all districts have shown their least performance during 1996–97, 1998–99 and 2002–03.

A similar kind of test comparison is also carried out for the financial utilization of IAY as before, both the factors, districts and the years, are found significant at 5% level of significance. To identify more significant districts and years, the Tukey HSD test has been performed. Barddhaman, Coochbehar and Jalpaiguri Districts are the top three significant districts and Nadia, Howrah and Murshidabad Districts are the least three performers. On the other hand, considering the years, more financial utilisations are found during the years 1998–99, 1999–00, and 2004–05, whereas all districts had made least financial utilization during the years 1997–98, 2007–08 and 2008–09.

A correlation test has been also performed between the percentage of the physically achieved target of IAY and the percentage of financial utilization of IAY over the years (1996–97 to 2010–11) for each rural district and also the overall scenario of the state to find out the significant relationship between physical achievements and financial utilization of IAY (Table 15.3). The level of the test is considered at 5%, i.e. the p-value being lesser than 0.05 is considered as significant.

It has been observed that there is a significant correlation between the percentage of the Physically achieved target of IAY and the percentage of financial utilization of IAY over the years (1996–97 to 2010–11) of 11 districts out of 17. These districts are Jalpaiguri, Darjeeling*, Uttar Dinajpur, Dakshin Dinajpur, Nadia, North 24-Parganas, Hooghly, Midnapore, Bankura, Barddhaman and Birbhum. The performance of the remaining six districts Coochbehar, Malda, Murshidabad, South 24-Parganas, Howrah and Purulia, were not satisfactory. Though, no significant correlation has been found in respect of the overall state scenario among the physical achievement and financial utilization. Generally, well performance on physical achievement

Table 15.3 Correlation test outcomes of each district of West Bengal and overall state scenario

District	Correlation value	P-value (#Significant at 0.05)
Coochbehar	-0.3111792	0.2589
Jalpaiguri	0.528112	0.04301#
Darjeeling*	0.5472807	0.03473#
Uttar Dinajpur	0.5318503	0.04129#
Dakshin Dinajpur	0.6349734	0.01098#
Malda	0.2394446	0.3901
Murshidabad	0.474492	0.07392
Nadia	0.6845427	0.004874#
North 24-Parganas	0.6958016	0.003967#
South 24-Parganas	0.3919542	0.1485
Howrah	0.3924346	0.1479
Hooghly	0.8499829	0.00006#
Midnapore	0.6951025	0.004019#
Bankura	0.7488547	0.001316#
Purulia	0.3282945	0.2322
Barddhaman	0.5544707	0.03195#
Birbhum	0.7670584	0.0008463#
Total	0.2689339	0.3324

Source Department of Panchayats and Rural Development, Govt. of West Bengal

helps to utilize more funds for financial utilization. In other words, we may statistically emphasize that there is a significant correlation between physical achievement and fund utilization. Table 15.3 also shows that the highest positive correlation (0.8499) is observed in of Hooghly District and the least negative correlation (-0.3112) is in Coochbehar District.

15.4 Result and Discussion

Performance data summary of each district and overall state of West Bengal, based on (a) Physically achieved the target of IAY (in percentage) and (b) Financial utilization of IAY (in percentage) during the study period (1996–97 to 2010–11), is shown in Table 15.4.

The performance of each district of Indira Awaas Yojana (IAY) is mainly analyzed on these two above-mentioned characteristics of the study and reported in Fig. 15.1.

It has been noticed that the percentage of Physically achieved target of IAY of various districts in different years are more than 100%. The main reason behind

Table 15.4 Physical and financial data summary of each district and overall IAY of state of West Bengal during 1996–97 to 2010–11

District	Physically achieved the target of IAY (in percentage)	Financial utilization of IAY (in percentage)
	Mean ± S.D	Mean ± S.D
Coochbehar	96.91 ± 24.937	81.00 ± 12.724
Jalpaiguri	93.12 ± 22.332	77.13 ± 10.107
Darjeeling*	72.52 ± 20.788	71.14 ± 18.890
Uttar Dinajpur	84.04 ± 39.254	65.45 ± 15.383
Dakshin Dinajpur	86.91 ± 34.172	64.10 ± 23.788
Malda	69.63 ± 16.136	69.04 ± 12.285
Murshidabad	77.57 ± 26.438	61.79 ± 12.167
Nadia	72.40 ± 25.843	59.93 ± 16.972
North 24-Parganas	82.05 ± 30.841	67.56 ± 16.503
South 24-Parganas	55.38 ± 29.881	63.41 ± 22.562
Howrah	71.79 ± 23.904	60.71 ± 15.822
Hooghly	77.42 ± 35.029	69.83 ± 23.654
Medinipur	76.05 ± 32.258	71.29 ± 15.241
Bankura	64.82 ± 29.211	63.71 ± 16.792
Purulia	86.82 ± 49.898	64.43 ± 13.169
Bardhdhaman	89.72 ± 28.754	81.46 ± 25.173
Birbhum	74.36 ± 25.593	64.92 ± 17.783
Total	77.44 ± 13.002	89.99 ± 11.791

Source Department of Panchayats and Rural Development, Govt. of West Bengal

that unusual data is that some incomplete construction of housing works of the previous year was completed on the very next consecutive year. The process of making rural housing depends on multiple inter-related steps, like-beneficiary selection, land ownership, sanction order and sanction amount for the finally selected persons, 1st installment sanction amount, progress of work, local weather conditions, progress report based on 1st installment, the final instalment of the sanctioned amount, complete work with proper loge installation. Finally, this extensive work depends on the efficiency of the Rural Panchayati Raj management system.

The maximum percentage (232.53%) of the target was achieved by Purulia District in 2010–11 and the minimum (8.88%) target was attained by South 24-Parganas on 1999–00. Though the percentage of financial utilisation generally did not exceed 100% usually. In 1999–00, Darjeeling* District (specifically, Siliguri Sub-division) received the exact 100% for financial utilisation. On the other hand, the minimum percentage (22.19%) for financial utilisation was received by South 24-Parganas District in the year 1997–98. Based on such a wide range of data, we have classified the performance of the district for each year into three different groups-

(1) High Performance/Very Good (if the percentage of study characteristics is > 80%),
(2) Medium Performance/Satisfactory (if the percentage of study characteristics is 60–80%),
(3) Low Performance/Unsatisfactory (if percentage of study characteristic is < 60%).

Here, the study characteristic is either percentage of the Physically achieved target of IAY or the percentage of financial utilization of IAY.Heat-map index of physical performance has been carried out for each district and overall state of West Bengal and reported in Fig. 15.2; where low, medium and high performance is identified by three different colours white, yellow and green, respectively. For the percentage of the Physically achieved target of IAY, the Coochbehar District has been found highly performed among all the districts during the study period of one and half decades. Only in the year 1996–97 and 2006–07, the percentage of target achieved by the district has been found 'Unsatisfactory' and 'Satisfactory' level, respectively. For the remaining 13 years, the percentage of the target has been found 'Very Good'. Similarly, for Jalpaiguri District 'Unsatisfactory' has been observed only for 1999–00, 'Satisfactory' has been observed in 1996–97, 2002–03 and 2009–10; and for the remaining 11 years 'Very Good' performance has been observed.

A similar kind of classification analysis through heat-map index has been carried out to identify the percentage of financial utilization for each district and overall state of West Bengal, and reported in Fig. 15.3; where low, medium and high performance is identified by red, yellow and green colour, respectively. As a result, it has been found that Barddhaman District leads on the percentage of financial utilization. Among the 15 years, 11 years the district has received 'Very Good' amount financial utilization on 1999–00, 2000–01 and consecutive nine years from 2002–03 to 2010–11.

Different factors are associated with the varying performance of the implementation of the schemes in the state of West Bengal (Bandyopadhyay, 2003). Amongst few factors are common for almost all the rural areas of the state but few factors are very much localized (Singh, 1999). The spatiality of the districts is plays an important role in the implementation of the scheme.

Rural areas and their population share are not equally distributed all over the state of West Bengal (Census of India, 2011). Maximum rural areas of West Bengal are economically connected with agriculture and other primary activities (Fig. 15.4) except Kolkata and a few parts of Howrah, Hooghly, North and South 24-Paraganas Districts. Though gradually the percentage of urban areas is increasing day by day in all over the state but overall economy is greatly depends on primary activities like cultivation, fishing, hunting, agro-based industry, rural household-based industries and rural service sectors. The major trend of internal migration of India are following the urbanization process. And in a few cases, the counter migration towards the rural areas are happening primarily due to the government policies and extension of marketing processes.

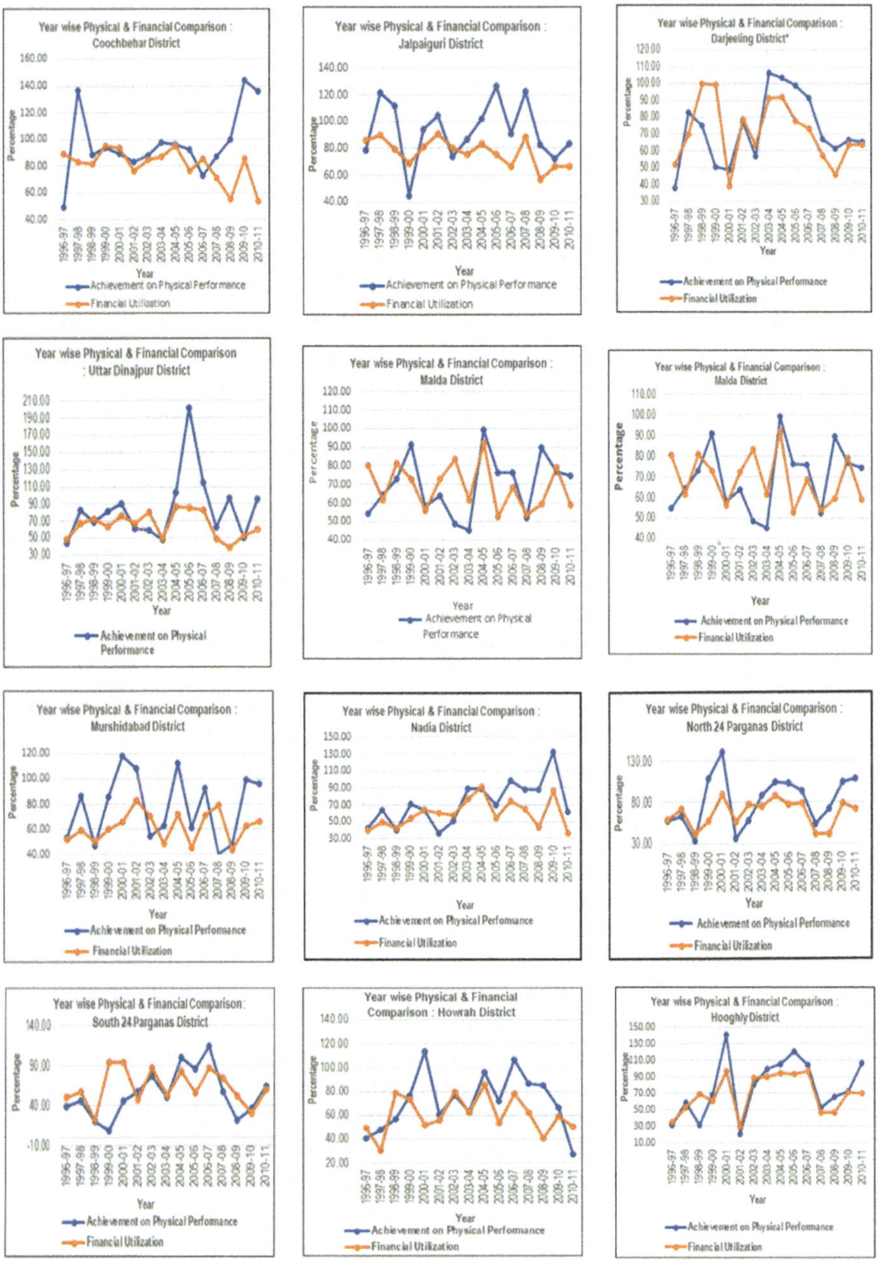

Fig. 15.1 District-wise physical and financial performance of IAY in the state of West Bengal during 1996–97 to 2010–11. *Source* Department of panchayats and rural development, Govt. of West Bengal

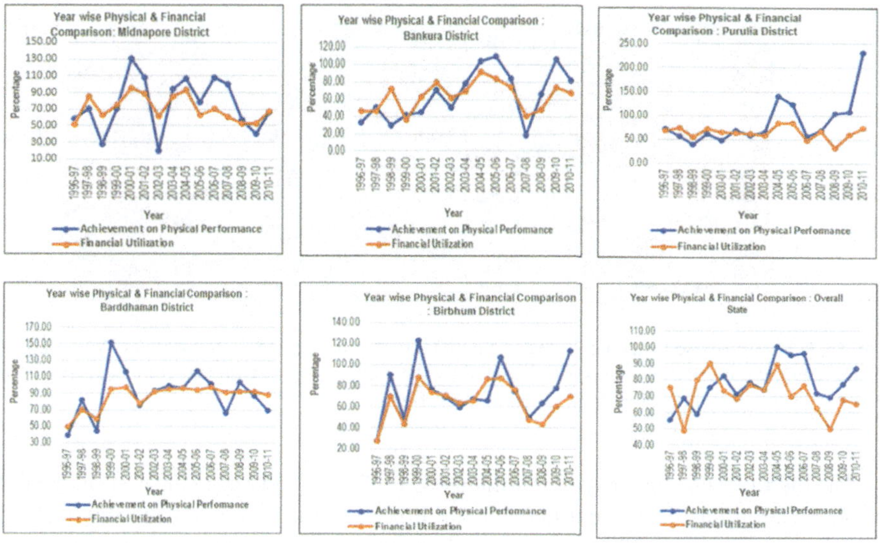

Fig. 15.1 (continued)

Districts	1996-97	1997-98	1998-99	1999-2000	2000-01	2001-02	20002-03	2003-04	2004-05	2005-06	2006-07	2007-08	2008-09	2009-10	2010-11
COOCH BEHAR	49.47	136.67	88.67	93.51	89.49	83.06	88.07	97.83	95.66	91.9	72.45	86.93	100	143.89	136
JALPAIGURI	78.39	121.59	112.23	44.67	93.76	104.46	74.02	87.19	102.4	126.71	90.82	122.21	82.64	71.93	83.72
SILSIGURI MP	37.89	82.80	74.65	50.21	48.85	77.22	56.92	106.33	103.18	99.02	91.74	66.89	60.98	66.2	64.97
U DINAJPUR	43.63	83.40	68.69	82.05	90.16	61.88	58.53	47.98	103.49	202.21	114.68	62.31	96.62	49.67	95.29
D DINAJPUR	67.50	78.05	50.11	81.69	117.38	60.37	106.95	48.41	112.29	116.8	104.91	55.7	75.71	56.54	171.24
MALDA	54.66	64.25	72.88	91.19	58.34	64.14	48.81	45.32	99.13	76.13	76.01	52.39	89.83	77.01	74.35
MURSHIDABAD	53.51	86.56	47.03	85.95	118.07	108.06	54.54	62.94	112.48	60.62	92.05	39.97	47.46	98.88	95.43
NADIA	42.04	64.09	40.28	71.52	64.30	35.94	50.60	89.31	89.2	70.31	98.92	87.6	88.11	132.28	61.55
NORTH 24 PGS	58.19	62.73	33.35	108.29	140.49	36.95	58.33	88.63	104.84	103.18	94.01	54.31	72.66	105.41	109.35
SOUTH 24 PGS	39.32	46.40	20.87	8.88	46.91	57.38	77.77	50.78	101.01	85.58	115.44	58.38	21.82	35.63	64.53
HOWRAH	40.83	48.32	56.67	76.90	113.97	60.39	76.39	62.82	96.21	71.66	107.084	86.75	85.15	66.09	27.65
HOOGHLY	31.59	58.41	32.07	68.55	140.57	21.34	81.35	99.17	105.59	120.77	103.83	53.12	65.94	72.52	106.45
MIDNAPORE	58.76	71.26	28.22	71.19	131.14	107.97	19.36	94.65	107.29	78.43	108.23	100.15	57.75	40.12	66.23
BANKURA	33.41	50.73	29.81	41.52	45.15	70.47	51.20	78.24	103.91	109.82	84.57	18.09	66.54	107.2	81.59
PURULIA	71.39	55.76	39.37	61.00	47.48	67.86	58.93	65.21	140.92	123.92	56.65	68.1	104.89	108.32	232.53
BARDDHAMAN	39.29	81.78	44.93	151.97	116.11	75.56	93.12	99.97	96.91	116.97	101.31	66.51	104.2	87.18	69.96
BIRBHUM	28.06	90.63	48.73	123.14	77.01	69.17	59.74	67.16	65.47	106.83	74.96	49.76	63.15	77.88	113.73
TOTAL	**55.33**	**68.53**	**59.06**	**75.18**	**82.36**	**71.41**	**78.62**	**73.87**	**100.22**	**95.35**	**96.27**	**71.78**	**69.47**	**77.21**	**86.94**
INDEX		**Low Performance**					**Medium Performance**					**High Performance**			

Fig. 15.2 District-wise heat-map index of physical performance IAY in state of West Bengal during 1996–97 to 2010–11. *Source* Computed by the authors. Data extracted from Department of Panchayats and Rural development, Govt. of West Bengal

The district-wise physical performance was not very regular. It has been found that 14 out of 17 districts and overall state physical performances were unsatisfactory in 1996–97. It is considered as the least performance year over the one and half decades. Whereas in 2004–05, 16 out of 17 districts and overall state physical performances were found very good, and this year may be considered the best performance of year during this 15 years study period.

Districts	1996-97	1997-98	1998-99	1999-2000	2000-01	2001-02	20002-03	2003-04	2004-05	2005-06	2006-07	2007-08	2008-09	2009-10	2010-11
COOCH BEHAR	89.60	82.98	81.84	95.00	93.80	76.20	84.52	87.16	95.59	76.7	85.67	71.07	55.56	85.4	53.86
JALPAIGURI	85.66	90.03	79.76	69.27	81.14	90.54	80.45	75.54	83.57	75.56	66.7	88.56	57.05	66.82	66.26
SILSIGURI MP	52.03	69.75	100.00	99.56	39.21	79.00	63.55	91.33	91.81	78.06	73.36	57.03	45.63	63.29	63.34
U DINAJPUR	48.64	67.20	73.30	64.18	76.69	67.55	80.45	48.67	86.81	85.12	82.78	48.35	38.9	52.48	60.51
D DINAJPUR	59.95	63.38	50.56	27.72	98.12	37.48	91.62	41.81	86.01	91.27	95.92	53.98	36.77	64.57	71.05
MALDA	80.49	61.56	81.17	73.14	56.03	72.70	83.50	61.73	91.95	52.76	68.58	53.94	59.49	79.36	59.15
MURSHIDABAD	51.47	59.17	50.30	59.86	66.13	83.04	69.91	48.10	71.71	45.52	70.58	79.18	43.42	62.62	65.59
NADIA	39.74	49.65	42.08	54.45	63.85	60.25	58.13	77.47	91.91	54.42	75.45	65.15	44.22	86.31	35.88
NORTH 24 PGS	58.79	72.17	41.33	58.57	90.01	56.98	78.11	75.04	89.19	78.22	79.01	42.28	42	78.73	73
SOUTH 24 PGS	50.07	57.32	22.19	94.41	94.27	47.94	87.49	52.89	83.27	56.31	87.02	75.27	51.87	30.54	60.31
HOWRAH	49.47	30.22	78.83	73.01	51.77	55.76	79.56	62.28	86.1	53.51	78.01	62.33	40.92	58.78	50.03
HOOGHLY	34.73	52.93	69.68	61.07	97.42	29.60	89.19	90.80	95.15	94.29	96.81	47.26	46.28	71.09	70.33
MIDNAPORE	51.98	86.00	63.30	75.73	95.65	88.38	61.52	85.41	93.74	63.01	71.08	60.52	52.27	53.02	67.75
BANKURA	46.47	45.73	71.91	36.67	63.54	79.71	61.63	69.98	91.78	84.42	73.79	40.39	48.16	74.22	67.33
PURULIA	68.44	74.11	55.23	71.62	65.61	63.32	62.08	57.61	83.75	83.41	47.21	67.07	33.11	59.93	73.96
BARDDHAMAN	49.66	70.90	59.12	95.07	97.49	7.79	92.16	95.95	96.47	94.97	97.53	91.02	92.49	92.75	88.5
BIRBHUM	27.49	69.65	43.81	88.12	73.52	70.74	63.38	65.80	86.54	87.58	75.92	47.76	43.39	60.1	69.99
TOTAL	**75.18**	**48.59**	**80.02**	**89.99**	**73.26**	**68.19**	**76.97**	**73.87**	**89.16**	**69.64**	**76.52**	**62.74**	**49.76**	**67.64**	**65.07**
INDEX				Low Performance				Midium Performance					High Performance		

Fig. 15.3 District-wise heat-map index of financial performance IAY in the state of West Bengal during 1996–97 to 2010–11. *Source* Computed by the authors. Data extracted from Department of Panchayats and Rural development, Govt. of West Bengal

The district-wise financial performance was also not very regular. A similar kind of observation has been identified for the financial utilization of each district and overall state. The year 2008–09 is considered the least performance year, where 16 out of 17 districts and overall state performances were found unsatisfactory. On the other hand, 2004–05 is considered the best performance year, where 16 out of 17 districts and overall state physical performances were found very good.

Different factors are associated with the varying performance of implementing the schemes in the state of West Bengal. Amongst few factors are common for almost all the state's rural areas, but few factors are very much localized. Share of Rural population also plays an important role in economic and financial achievements in IAY of the state (Fig. 15.5).

It has been found that the share of the rural population has a degree of association between financial assistance and physical performance. Where rural population share is higher, the financial assistance is also significantly high.

The three-tier Gram Panchayat mechanism is the driving force behind the implementation process of the rural housing programme. The beneficiary list of rural housing programme for the consecutive year of every village was prepared through the local-level rural administrative body (Gram-Sansad) which is clubbed and finalized at a higher level rural administrative body (Gram Sabha.). The final list of a Gram Panchayat was ultimately prepared based on the economic and social priority basis amongst rural communities. But the personal choice, political priority and many other interventions are there in selection, preparation, and execution processes. The state of West Bengal is advanced in terms of devolution of power, finances and functions of panchayats (Ghatak and Ghatak, 2002). Good governance is located at the core related to democratic decentralization and rural community participation, which is also extended towards corruption especially to political parties and increased the state's accountability to its citizens (Véron et al., 2006).

The availability of land in the name of the IAY beneficiary individually or in the joint name of wife and husband in a family is significant. The land law system and the family structure are very complex in the rural society of West Bengal. A minimum

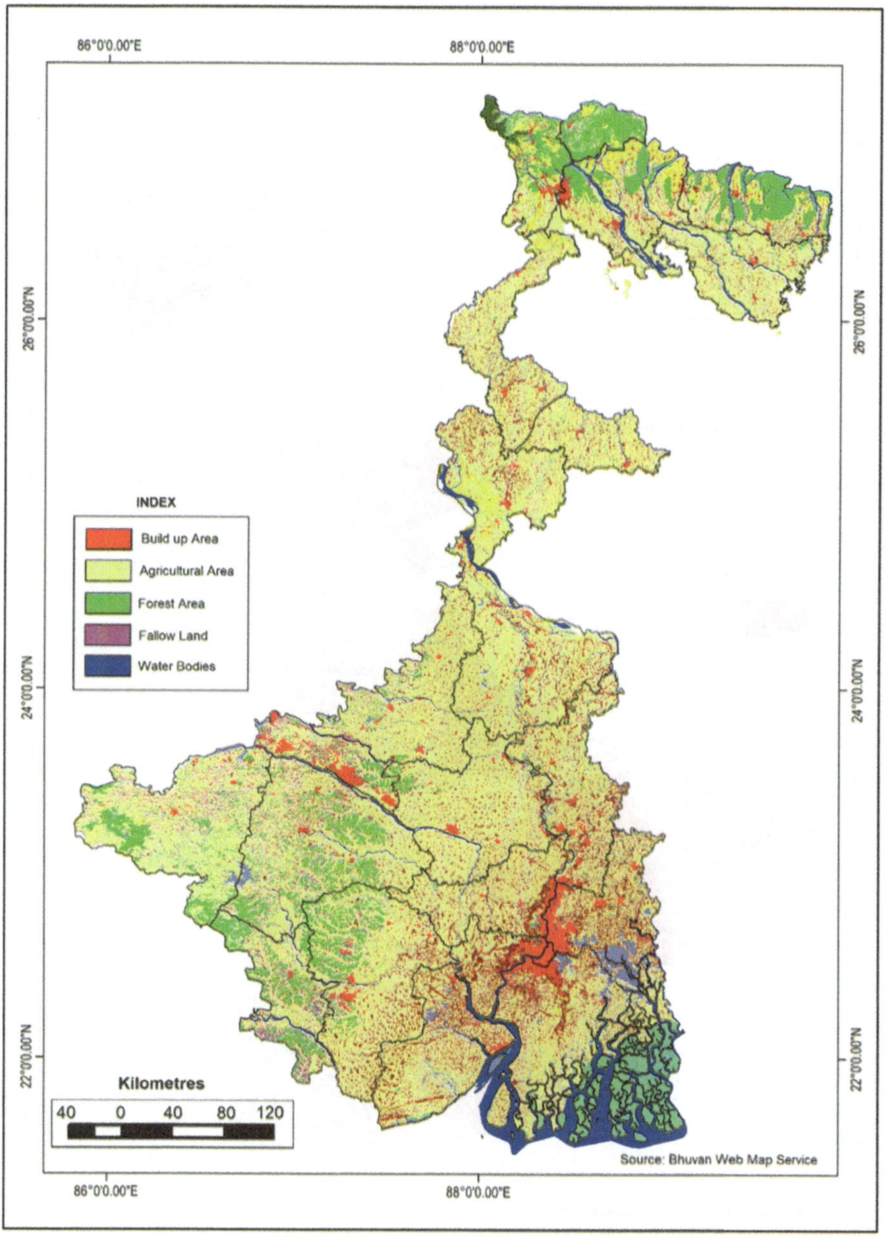

Fig. 15.4 Land-use pattern showing agriculture and allied activities dominate rural areas in the state of West Bengal

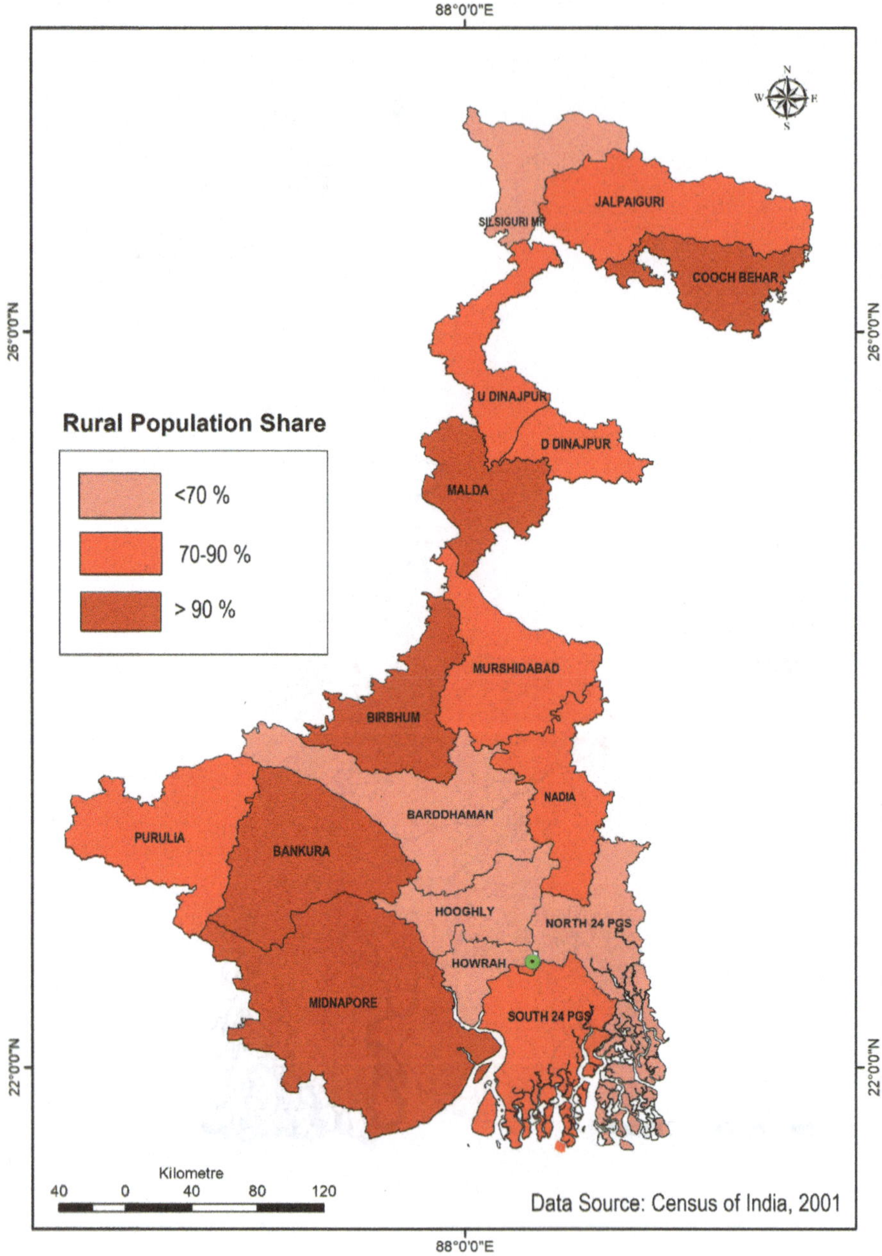

Fig. 15.5 District-wise percentage share of rural population distribution in the state of West Bengal

of 150–200 Square meters is required for the building of a new house. Therefore, the name transfer is not possible in many areas of the state within one financial year.

One of the significant factors which are related to the continuous demand for rural housing is different types of hazards with varying magnitudes. The different types of hazards are spatially associated with the state, like landslides, floods, river-bank erosion, cyclone, coastal surge, etc. Mainly in Darjeeling District due to the active earthquake and a few other geo-environmental reasons leads the landslides in different places. In Medinipur, Haora, Hoogli, Nadia, North and South 24-Parganas Districts extensive riverine flood incidents occurred frequently mainly in monsoonal season. The cyclonic disturbances and coastal surges are also frequent in coastal areas of the Districts of Medinipur and 24-Parganas. As a result, of these hazard phenomena, rural houses in different areas are demolished or partially converted into a dilapidated form, which turns ultimately again into the demand for new houses.

15.5 Conclusion

Indira Awaas Yojana (IAY) is the scheme for constructing permanent shelters for the rural poor where both Central and State Governments shared their contribution as aid. Districts wise variations in both the physical and financial performances of IAY are common throughout rural West Bengal. Rural local Self-governments, functioning through specialized mechanisms directly influences the overall progress of the scheme.

The districts of Coochbehar, Jalpaiguri and Dakshin Dinajpur are the top three significant districts and South 24-Parganas, Bankura and Malda are the least three districts in respect of physical performances of IAY in West Bengal considering the said period. On the contrary, Barddhaman, Coochbehar and Jalpaiguri Districts are the top three significant districts and Nadia, Howrah and Murshidabad Districts are the least three performers in respect of financial achievements.

References

Bandyopadhyay, D. (2003). Land reforms and agriculture: The West Bengal experience. *Economic and Political Weekly, 38*(9), 879–884.

Boruah, B. (2015). *Strategies of Rural Development: A Study of IAY SGSY and MGNREGA in the Golaghat District of Assam*. Dibrugarh University.

Chand, R., Srivastava, S. K., & Singh, J. (2017). Changing Structure of Rural Economy of India. New Delhi: National Institution for Transforming India. Retrieved from https://niti.gov.in/writereaddata/files/document_publication/Rural_Economy_DP_final.pdf.

Census of India. (2011). Census Report of India. New Delhi: Registrar General of India and Census Commissioner, India.

Ghatak, M., & Ghatak, M. (2002). Recent reforms in the panchayat system in West Bengal: Toward greater participatory governance? *Economic and Political Weekly, 37*(1), 45–58. Retrieved from https://www.jstor.org/stable/4411568.

Hussain, M., & Yaseen, G. (2018). Indira Awas Yojana: Concept, nature, objectives and role. *Scholars Journal of Arts, Humanities and Social Sciences, 6*(3), 720–728. https://doi.org/10.21276/sjahss.2018.6.3.33

International Environment Audit and Sustainable Development. (2013). Performance Audit on Indira Awaas Yojana. New Delhi: Government of India.

Mitra, S. (2012). Rural development programme in West Bengal A critical geographical appraisal. Kolkata: University of Calcutta. Retrieved from http://hdl.handle.net/10603/156740.

Munsi, A. (2001). Rural housing in West Bengal: Study of a backward region. *Journal of Rural Development, 20*(3), 425–445.

Planning Commission. (2013). Evaluation of Indira Awas Yojana. New Delhi: Government of India.

Singh, K. (1999). *Rural development: Principles, policies and management*. SAGE Publications.

Sudhira, H. S., & Gururaja, K. V. (2012). Population crunch in India: is it urban or still rural? *Current Science, 103*(1), 37–40. Retrieved from https://www.researchgate.net/publication/295634745_Population_crunch_in_India_is_it_urban_or_still_rural.

Tiwari, P. (2001). Housing and development objectives in India. *Habitat International, 25*(2), 229–253. https://doi.org/10.1016/S0197-3975(00)00019-9

Véron, R., Williams, G., Corbridge, S., & Srivastava, M. (2006). Decentralized corruption or corrupt decentralization? community monitoring of poverty-alleviation schemes in Eastern India. *World Development, 34*(11), 1922–1941. Retrieved from https://doi.org/10.1016/j.worlddev.2005.11.024.

Chapter 16
For the Urban Poor's Fairer Share in the Housing Process—Takeaways from People for Policy and Practice

Sangeeta Maunav

Abstract The Pradhan Mantri Awas Yojana–Housing for All (Urban) mission of the Government of India, with four mutually exclusive verticals, has been a commendable endeavour towards an inclusive program intervention that addresses the diverse nature and extent of Housing shortage with differential socio-economic, housing condition and tenure status across scales of urban demography. While the vertical-wise policy prescriptions have addressed the different dimensions of Housing Shortage to a measurable extent, a retrospective appreciation of the program as it is unfolding in the State of Karnataka suggests some design deficits in policy and implementation that has tempered the penultimate objective of reaching 'Housing for All' leaving a large section of the urban poor households waiting for their turn to avail the returns that the program is striving to offer. The paper draws upon a people-centred field level appreciation of PMAY (Urban) in 61 towns of Bangalore Division in the State of Karnataka (excludes the Greater Bengaluru Metropolitan area), with the quintessential idea being to learn and put together in perspective the concerns and suggestions of all the stakeholders involved in this Housing process. While the issues are fairly historical, they assume deeper significance amidst an unprecedented political economy bargain that places the'urban poor' population construct in a stifling paradox, along these key areas: (1) Availability of Land, Approaches to Housing interventions and the resultant implication for Urban poor in Slums versus Urban poor in Non-slum areas (2) Urban Poor Households' inevitability to access the Housing finance market versus their inaccessibility due to informality of employment and inadequacy of income, and (3) Program Entitlement issues due to non-clear land titles despite income and housing poverty. An attempt has been made to suggest some people-centred accessibility approaches and tools that may have room for policy and program improvements in Housing the urban poor.

Keywords Housing for all · Housing finance · Land for housing · Housing for poor · India

S. Maunav (✉)
Human Settlements Management Institute, HUDCO, Government of India, New Delhi, India

A. Kundu et al. (eds.), *Accessible Housing for South Asia*,
https://doi.org/10.1007/978-3-030-88881-7_16

16.1 Introduction

> "For how many more meetings do I have to come before my mother and I can live in our own house again? Please tell her that there are unsolved problems of the past and here she is with ideas for future", Nandita (name changed) intercepted, in no uncertain terms, an intense discussion on possibilities of translating house rent paid by the urban poor to mortgage payments.

More than five years of the Pradhan Mantri Awaas Yojana–Housing for All (Urban) mission has gone by since its inception in the year 2015, and stakeholder consultation for preparing 'Housing for All Plan of Action' for 61 towns of varying urban demography across 9 districts of the State of Karnataka was taking place in 2020. Was this only an opportunity to evaluate the program performance in retrospect or more? The mission was the Government of India's response to a rising urban housing shortage in India that was sharply skewed towards the Economically Weaker Sections and Low-Income Group Population. Set at the backdrop of the National Urban Habitat and Housing policy, 2007, that is dotted with focussed reference to 'the imperatives of inclusiveness, affordability and sustainability', the mission was designed to subsume every subset of the urban poor through four different verticals in a way that 'every citizen of India has a pucca house with water connection, toilet facilities, electricity supply and access by the year 2022 when India would be celebrating its 75 years of independence'. In keenness therefore, to locate the poor through the policy rhetoric and between the numeric achievements of the mission, I make an effort to take forward through a reflexive account, the lived experience of more than 13,000 Urban Poor Households; Representatives of the State Level Nodal Agency (SLNA) for Housing the poor; around 300 senior officials of Urban Local Bodies (ULBs) across functional domains and Slum Development Board; few Real Estate Developers and Representatives of Housing finance providers from Banks and Non-banking institutions. And that's what I understand would fairly encompass those stakeholders engaged in the micro-processes of the Low-Income Urban Housing eco-system. The macro socio-economic structure within which Housing is unfolding in the lives of the urban poor would deliberately remain outside the purview of this writing. The consultations which took place between October 2020 to December 2020 amidst the challenges of mobility and in-person interaction that the global pandemic overwhelmed all of us with, have much for understanding and insight. My locale since the last more than 22 years on a threshold, with an institutional role in program implementation on one side, and, my compulsive connect with the poor on the other cannot be completely left behind, and I am careful to have the readers know.

How this study was framed?

1. A people-centred approach has been adopted. While three key constituents that form the edifice of Housing access have been taken up for this writing, there is a skewed bent towards 'Demand-side Access to Housing finance for Low Income and informal sector households' due to its lighter presence in policy prescripts or academic writing.

2. With the easing of lockdown and corresponding mobility restrictions imposed due to COVID-19, during the period from September 2020 to December 2020, the author has visited 41 of the 61 towns in Bangalore Division, Karnataka –
    - Primary and secondary institutional data collected from Urban Local Bodies across functional domains, officers from Divisional offices of Karnataka Slum Development Board, members of City Level Technical Cell constituted under PMAY (Urban), few Real Estate Developers and Representatives of Housing finance providers from Banks and Non-banking institutions
    - Focussed Group Discussions in 2 slums and 1 non-slum area with identified beneficiaries of the PMAY (Urban) program in each of the 41 Towns.
3. For the remaining 21 towns, primary and secondary institutional data has been collected during the District level Stakeholder Consultations covering 38 towns across 5 of the 9 districts
4. A CAPI-based household level socio-economic survey was conducted through a hired agency covering 1,3000 households across 61 towns (5% of the beneficiaries identified by the State/ULB vide Demand Survey) between the period October 2020 to January 2021. Data were collected across 25 attributes and sample checks through telephonic contacts were conducted.

16.2 Uncovering Lessons Along the Contextual Narrative

Nandita's interception holds much merit both as an indicator of the contextual meaning of housing shortage in urban areas and for the provocation she provided for me to establish the links between the past problems and the future ideas. A student of Engineering, with her education being funded by a local NGO, Nandita lives with her widowed mother and a younger brother at a rented house and is taking rounds of the city office for the past three years to find out as to when the fund under PMAY would be released. The city officials, while appreciating her grit and tenacity, confess that they feel stressed at her very presence for she would not take any bureaucratic response for an answer. Her mother works at a local garment factory that fetches her around Rupees 12,000/- a month out of which they have been paying a house rent of Rs. 3000/- since the past three years. They have invested approximately Rs. 50,000/- from personal savings and chit funds towards laying the foundation of the house, and that was the average cost of the foundation, I learnt from the engineers. Nandita's mother could move up the construction no more. Now that they have demolished their earlier kutcha house, the stress on account of rent outflow and the likely escalating cost is burgeoning. As of mid-October, 2020, only 28.97% of the houses sanctioned under PMAY (Urban) were grounded for construction, and another 28.97% completed in the entire State of Karnataka. Of this, under the Affordable Housing in Partnership (AHP) vertical only 5.05% of the houses sanctioned were completed. Under the Beneficiary Led Construction (BLC), the figure was 41.67%. The corresponding figures for Credit Linked Subsidy Scheme (CLSS) and In-situ

Slum Rehabilitation (ISSR) verticals of PMAY (Urban) have far lesser significance to appreciate the numeric performance of PMAY since the 100% completion of project sanctioned under CLSS only means that subsidy has been approved for the number of loans sanctioned. Data shown under the In-Situ Slum Rehabilitation (ISSR) is a project taken up under Rajiv Awaas Yojana in the year 2014. This writing primarily encompasses urban poor households identified for housing provision under BLC and AHP verticals in slum and non-slum areas of the towns. There is no single project taken up under ISSR in Karnataka so far. Inadequate availability of land for affordable housing; Poor financial capacity of ULBs; Inability of urban poor to mobilize resources to pay their share in the cost of housing; non-lucrative land value for the private sector and the conspicuous absence of community participation particularly in slum rehabilitation largely explain the numeric lags in program output. To intensify the challenges, there has been a huge administrative delay in receipt of funds from the Government which the State renders to as a consequence of fund diversion to flood-affected areas in Karnataka during 2017–18. The problems so far appear historical by their nature if not in their intensity, and before I place the key challenges faced by the Government and the people, it is significant that they are located in the program structure and design. The Housing for All (PMAY-U) mission is pillared on four mutually exclusive verticals as the Government of India's inclusive approach to Housing intervention that addresses the diverse nature of Housing shortage. A 'Demand Survey' to assess the Housing requirement is mandated under PMAY(Urban) and the same was undertaken in all the 61 towns with varying levels of efficiency during 2016–17 in alignment with the structure and process prescribed by PMAY (Urban) guidelines. From the applications received, all Urban Poor households of the town who do not own a house in their name anywhere have been categorized as: (1) Households with sites (2) Houseless Households without Sites. Households with sites have been taken under Beneficiary Led Construction (BLC) under which a household receives grant assistance of Rs. 1.50 lakh from the Centre and Rs, 1.8 lakh (Rs. 2.00 lakh for SC&ST i.e. Scheduled Caste & Scheduled Tribe) for constructing a house from the State, and Households without Sites have been taken up under Affordable Housing in Partnership wherein the Government constructs a house with funds from Centre at Rs. 1.50 lakh per beneficiary, Rs, 1.8 lakh (Rs. 2.00 lakh for SC/ST) from the State and the remaining comes from the Beneficiary. This mode of implementation encompasses both the slum and non-slum areas of the towns in the State.

16.2.1 Availability of Land for Housing the Urban Poor

Barring the district of Bangalore Urban covering 6 towns, availability of land did not come up as the lead factor in explaining the implementation challenges. Not that the other factors particularly finance did not play a significant role, but the availability of land was more limiting in this district than elsewhere. It is pertinent to place that the Greater Bengaluru Metropolitan Area under the administrative jurisdiction of the Bruhat Bengaluru Mahanagara Palike (BBMP), with a population of about

6.80 million people spread an area of 741 sqm, did not fall within the scope of the study and therefore does not fall under the purview of this writing, lest the data gathered and lessons outlined, particularly regarding land availability, housing cost and value of house rent paid by the city's poor be generalized for the city of Bengaluru. While issues concerning land and demand-side finance were voiced as the key issues unequivocally by the city officials, a little dissection informed that the issue was more about the cost of land acquisition rather than its availability. And to keep from departing from the purpose of this writing, I shall not delve into the implications of acquiring fertile agricultural lands for urban housing. It was sufficient for me that I received an affirmative response from senior city officials to my stray curiosity. The actual financial cost of land acquisition for housing is much higher than the Government-approved rates. Incidentally, the rates received by land-holding farmers in the same area for other uses are almost two to three times the approved rates for housing. It has taken consistent efforts and time for the ULB/District-level authorities for negotiating with farmers to bring down the rates to a certain extent. The proposals were not approved. City officials felt that the rate of land acquisition should be concerning the location and not the use. A common pool of land must be made available to the Nodal Development agency of the city/region who should decide as to which parcel of land be put to what use. Well, the suggestion may not well augur with the Government for housing the poor given the financial returns on investment. A little further, data indicates that in many towns, while a huge demand for housing the non-slum urban poor households without sites is not being met for want of land, the Karnataka Slum Development Board (KSDB) is constructing houses for slum households in the Ground structure under the Affordable Housing in Partnership vertical. There is the absence of willingness of official Stakeholders to use available slum lands and for vertical expansion, i.e. G + 2 Structures that can accommodate the unmet demand, though however around 47% of the urban poor households have expressed acceptance for Ground + 2 structures should the Government provide good quality housing with ownership rights in multistoried structure (G + 2) with all basic infrastructure services The apprehensions of officials is well-founded for the initial challenges of moving from horizontal to vertical living is huge and may need to be addressed with participative interventions. Examples of similar approaches have been seen in the city of Tumkur in Tumkur district and Kanakapura town in Ramanagara district of the State in this study. The subject of participative slum housing interventions in mass housing programs within political timelines and targets is consciously kept outside the purview of this writing. The issue of feasibility of vertical expansion gets further reinforced with the Government's recent announcement to grant Title Deeds to site-less slum inhabitants. There is another dimension to the subject of land availability in slums and non-slum areas and this has to do with their respective socio-economic status. The income levels between urban poor houseless households in slums and non-slum areas being similar, it is evident that the slum inhabitants access to housing is better as eventually most of the slum households would have a site in their name and also be eligible to receive the Central and State share as per policy stipulations for construction of house under AHP by KSDB. In most of the towns, both anecdotally and by observation, the

Table 16.1 Approved land acquisition rates (Rs. in lacs /acre)

Town category	Govt-approved rates	Market Rates per acre
Town Panchayat (Class IV)	12.00	25–30
Town Municipal Council (Class III)	15.00	30–40
City Municipal Council (Class II)	22.50	50–100
Municipal Corporation (Class I)	37.50	75 to > 100

Note * Excludes BBMP at 75 Lacs per acre
Source Primary Data from ULBs and district authorities during town visits and district-level Stakeholder consultations

physical conditions of many slums were comparable to those of non-slum areas of the town. And yet, no efforts are being made to accommodate non-slum urban poor on available slum land (Table 16.1).

16.2.2 Urban Poor's Access to Housing Finance

If land was not the lead in determining the character of the way the program, what was it? The average beneficiary contribution for projects under Affordable Housing in Partnership (AHP) and Beneficiary-Led Construction (BLC) approximately ranges between Rs. 2.50 lakhs and Rs. 3.30 lakhs considering the average house cost at Rs. 6.00 lacs. And this is irrespective of the town typology. I distinctly recall the JNNURM times, when while appraising housing projects, I learnt that urban poor households from small towns more often than not could ill-afford to pay even Rs. 10,000 to 30, 000/- as their share of the housing cost. And where the Beneficiary Share had worked out to be very high, i.e. around Rs. 1.00 lakh and more, households fell into the debt trap of money lenders. While Nandita and her mother chose to live on rent, Begum Mehrunisa (name changed) could not hide her tears that slipped behind her veil as she appealed with folded hands to facilitate her receiving the Government fund. As the officials of the City-level Technical Cell spoke for her, I only heard her say "I cannot bear it anymore. Could you do something for me?" Mehrunisa has to pay Rs. 25,000/- per month for the coming 8 months for repaying Rs. 3.00 lakh that she borrowed from a local moneylender. She is the only earning member of the family and tailoring fetches her around 10,000/- to 12,000/- rupees a month. Her husband is ailing and her children are yet to complete their education. The delay in the release of funds has taken a huge toll on her finance and her family's well-being. About 61% of the 13,000 households have conveyed that there is a huge delay in receiving money from the government. As a consequence of this, 21% of them have borrowed money from money-lenders, friends and relatives at around 4–5% monthly interest rate to complete construction of houses on land owned by them. Those that have not borrowed live on rental premises and constitute around 35% of the households consulted. The remaining are residing either in kuchha houses on their site, or are sharing accommodation with relatives. There are still some who live in encroached spaces, public or private. Not all 13,000 households who were part of the consultation are yet selected for inclusion in projects taken up and sanctioned. They are part of the approximately 2.67 lakhs of households identified vide the 'Demand Survey' to be eligible for housing under different verticals of PMAY (Urban). Of the 13,000 households, around 20% did not have much to share about the delay in receiving funds since they are still waiting their turn for inclusion in a project. Prioritization of beneficiaries for inclusion in a project is done by the 'Ashraya Committee' headed by the MLA. In fact for projects sanctioned before 2018–2019, many beneficiaries are content. Devraj and his wife Manju (names changed) have left no effort to construct their dream house. While he lost his job as a chef at a nearby restaurant during COVID-19, he has started his own street food business. Manju supplements the family income with tailoring. While for many, the Government's support came as a big boon, for those who could not pay their share in the housing cost, their application got blocked or cancelled. Officials of the Urban Local Bodies are somewhat distressed with the situation getting unwieldy as 'beneficiaries' often gather in large numbers seeking to know as to when the Government fund would arrive or as to when they would be selected for a project. To worsen the situation, State Government has decided that the projects taken up after 2018 would receive only the Central assistance of Rs. 1.50 lakh per house. This, therefore, gets translated into an increase in Beneficiary Share by Rs. 1.80–Rs. 2.00 lakh adding up the Beneficiary contribution to more than Rs. 4.00 lakh. The disparity within and across towns gets too conspicuous with this and more significantly, people would not be able to mobilize such sums of money. Even with the State and Central share coming in time, people had a tough time mobilizing resources. Agricultural and construction wage labour, domestic workers, workers in private enterprises, street vendors - the monthly household income of the households irrespective of the town typology, ranges between Rs. 2000/- and Rs. 20,000/-. It's no more a question of whether the poor can pay or whether the poor will pay. They have to for such is the inevitability to access ownership Housing. Urban Poor households both by inadequate income and informality of employment remain from mobilizing financial resources to meet their contribution either from their savings or access to Housing Finance. Beneficiaries belonging to the lower subsets of the Urban Poor Category even lack the resources for investing in the start-up fund required to avail the Government fund, i.e. around Rs. 10,000 to Rs. 20,000 or the cost of foundation, i.e. approximately Rs. 50,000/-. The message of ULBs about their financial health is unambiguous and unequivocal. More than 65% of the total revenues of all the 61 ULBs are Central and State grants meant for various development programs and only 30% are from the ULBs' revenue. The dependency of the towns on the Central and State grants is very high and includes meeting its operational expenses even. They can neither contribute their share in the housing cost nor are they capable to raise resources from the market.

It's five years and more now. The Urban Local Bodies and State-level Nodal Agency have initiated the process to link Beneficiaries with Banks for payment of Beneficiary Contribution. Continuous follow-up with banks is also being made. Letters are being sent, workshops held, circulars issues and status reviewed, and well, a few MoUs signed. Amidst the pouring complaints and disillusionments from people and city officials during the consultation, a bank officer in one of the districts exclaims "we have burnt our fingers time and again". It is not a new finding that Banking institutions remain far from reaching Housing Finance to Urban poor Households due to restrictive regulations. There are perceived risks in lending housing finance and the absence of concomitant risk mitigation measures. The transaction cost for such measures would be too high for banks given the human resource, other bank services and products to be delivered across differential clientele categories. People are engaged in the informal sector as daily wage labour, domestic help, vendors, petty enterprise owners who do not have income documentation required by the bank. Banks take into account individual income and not household income to assess creditworthiness. As per banking norms, a minimum of Rs. 10,000/- per month should be available for meeting basic household needs after payment of monthly instalments. Urban poor households fail to comply with this. While some banks do accept Income Certificates authorized by Tahsildar/Revenue authorities, any income document showing an income that exceeds the income ceiling prescribed by Govt. of Karnataka ie an Annual income of Rs. 87,600/- for Below Poverty Line (BPL) would result in the beneficiary not getting the BPL entitlements. This inhibits them from providing any income details beyond the BPL ceiling. I may indicate at this juncture that as per the State policy of implementing PMAY (Urban), only households belonging to the BPL economic category are entitled to the State share. While the income figures provided by households during the consultation went up to Rs. 25,000/-, the reported incomes during demand assessment have been largely restricted to less than Rs 87,600/- per annum. Banks work on a Formal framework, i.e. Formal Property and Formal Income. Incidentally, the Beneficiaries of AHP get only an 'Allotment letter' and not an ownership document which may be mortgageable but not realizable by the bank in the event of default. In the case of Beneficiaries under BLC, the Title Deeds may not be mortgageable or the loan amount may be too small, and therefore does not meet the Capital adequacy norms of the Banking sector. The Banks are also reluctant to fund microloans to low-income households because of any loan below Rs. 1.00 lakh do not come under SARFAESI (Securitization and Reconstruction of Financial Assets and Enforcement of Security Interest) making recovery extremely wieldy or cost-inefficient. But then, we are aware that there is an emerging market for Housing Finance for low-income and informal sector population operated by few Housing Finance Companies (HFCs), Small Finance Banks (SFBs), Non-Banking Finance Companies (NBFCs) and Micro-Finance Institutions (MFIs). Their housing loan products, credit writing processes and recovery mechanisms are customized to the low-Income and informal households' profiles. Some such institutions are the Prime Lending Institutions (PLIs) under the CLSS vertical of PMAY (Urban). However, institutions are very few and far between, and they too have limited geography and insufficient resources to meet the huge demand. Interest rates charged by these institutions are higher than banks due to higher per client transaction cost inevitable due to an intensive client-centric process that ranges from loan origination to recovery. Some institutions work on partnership models with grass-root institutions on profits sharing basis. These institutions work on specific geographies and existing credit portfolios and may not have standardized operational methods to cover every region. All urban poor beneficiaries may not be successful in metamorphosing to Housing Finance clients even with the help of such institutions. But the market spares none. What then would be the outcome of those houseless-households who would not graduate to become a client in the housing finance market? What are the policy and program implications for this subset of the urban poor? What mechanisms did the State adopt to make adequate housing accessible to them?

The Karnataka Slum Development Board has initiated the process of linking the Beneficiary Contribution with the Building & Construction workers' Cess administered by the Labour Department of the State for providing interest-free housing loans (Rs. 2.00 lacs) to the slum beneficiaries. While discussions have been made and circulars issued, the proposal had not commenced as yet. The conditions to avail the loan mandate the beneficiary to have a 'Labour Card' and the requisite for the same is a minimum of 90 days of continuous work as construction labour. But all slum beneficiaries are not construction labour and all construction workers are not registered. Moreover, to be eligible to avail of the Housing loan, construction labour has to be registered for a minimum of 5 years go the stipulation. On another front, the Development Funds for SC/ST and minority population constructs are being accessed for payment of Beneficiary Contribution by some ULBs. However, the fund amount is too less and not always available. There may not be a single overarching solution to the ensuing issues in reaching Housing for All. The Government of India has made an appreciable effort to encompass the diversity of the housing shortage through its four verticals. Unfortunately, the urban poor population construct is far too heterogeneous. Policy and program intervention need to take cognizance of the fact that there are several categories of contestants to urban space within the construct of 'Urban Poor', who have differential access to material and non-material resources. If access to Housing Finance could be picked up as one of the key tools for the poor to access housing, the rent paid by the households offers a little way out. In Tier III and Tier IV towns, 38% of households living in rental accommodation pay a monthly House rent between Rs, 1500 to Rs 2500/-, and 45% of the households pay Rs 2500 to Rs, 3500/-. In Tier I and Tier II towns, 24% of the households living in rental accommodation pay a monthly house rent between Rs 1500/- to Rs. 2500/- and 59% of the households pay Rs 2500/- to Rs. 3500/- (Table 16.2).

Table 16.2 Equated monthly instalments for housing loan

Tenure	EMI for Rs 2.00 lacs at 10% RoI	Tenure	EMI for Rs 3.00 lacs at 10% RoI
10 YRS	Rs. 2643	10 YRS	Rs. 3695
15 YRS	Rs. 2149	15 YRS	Rs. 3224
20 YRS	Rs. 1930	20 YRS	Rs. 2895

Equated Monthly Instalments (EMI) for Housing Loans calculated for Rs. 3.00 and Rs. 2.00 lacs at 10% RoI with a tenure of 10, 15 and 20 years is distinctly indicative of the fact that the rental payments can be translated to housing loan repayments. This takes me back in time to the year 2015 to my short study of the field performance of the Rajasthan Affordable Housing Policy, 2009. The ticket size extended by Micro Housing Finance Corporation, Mumbai (Now Swantra Housing Finance Corporation) was about 2.60 lac rupees then, for a repayment tenure ranging between 10 to 20 years. The Loan To Value ratio (LTV) was around 70 depending upon the customer's credit profile and need. Amidst challenges, poor households continued to repay approximately Rs. 2600 to Rs, 4000/- per month. The present need is to set up viable, feasible and sustainable Institutional linkages with the Institutions that offer Housing Finance OR Housing Microfinance to low-Income and Informal sector households. The same should be anchored by SLNA and ULB /Implementing agency. The community institutional framework of Women Self-Help Groups (SHGs) and their federation under the National Urban Livelihood Mission (NULM) of the Government of India could be utilized for developing institutional mechanisms for Housing Finance delivery and collection of repayment. It may be noted that in the State of Odisha, women SHGs are involved in the collection of property taxes. The utilization of the SHG platform set up by the erstwhile livelihood program 'Swarna Jayanti Shahri Rojgar Yojana (SJSRY)' by the Directorate of Food and Civil supplies as the last mile connectivity to the Public Distribution System in the state of Chhattisgarh is yet another interesting example that I have documented myself in the year 2011. These practices can offer lessons that can be taken forward in the Low-Income Housing sector too. The involvement of SHGs should not be indiscriminate and only those SHGs that have exemplified good systems, better grassroots intervention and good enterprise management must be involved to link with. Such arrangements could be made sustainable vide a fee paid to the SHG Federation involved and be an additional source of income for the SHG women members. A couple of cities have expressed interest in the idea, and women SHG members have expressed their preparedness for such an endeavour during the stakeholder consultation. Development Institutions with an established history of grass-root penetration could be involved as facilitative agencies during the incubation period. Such measures have the potential to increase the creditworthiness of ULBs particularly in cash flow based funding.

16.2.3 Clear Title to Land & Other Issues

It is not only on the subject of finance that the program has been operating on a formal-formal framework, i.e. formal property and formal income as an enabling condition to own a house. Eligibility to be included as a beneficiary under BLC required that land titles be clear. Interestingly, some houses are kuchha and semi-pucca, meaning thereby that they require either enhancement of the existing structure or a new house, but the land ownership with clear title is in the name of the deceased parents/grandparents/older relatives of the family and other such conditions. While the houses are attributed both by factors of congestion and non-affordability which are constituents of Housing shortage, the present members are not able to avail the benefits of the housing program. The Government should possibly facilitate title conversion of such houses at a nominal fee as part of the housing scheme. In existing single-storey houses, where the title is in the name of father/head of the household, if the right to construct on the first floor is given to the ward who has an independent household, the new household could be considered under BLC (New). This would address the congestion factor and simultaneously reduce the burden of constructing a new house under AHP.

During the entire one-and-a-half months of travelling and talking to stakeholders, I cannot recall a singular passing reference to the program as a habitat intervention. I could not observe it either. There is a paradigm shift along the urban policy trajectory, a narrowing from habitat to individual house. How a beneficiary would construct new houses or demolish older ones without breaking the neighbour's wall who is not a beneficiary is not known at this point. The institutional processes got more entangled with time in the towns, the city officials never shied away from voicing that they added to the poor's burden, the number of times they cross-checked the data and geo-tagged those who had commenced construction, their VIGIL app and so on. The poor got photographed the fourth time before many could even see a brick laid, and this time it was for me.

References

National Urban Housing and Habitat Policy 2007, Ministry of Housing & Urban Poverty Alleviation (Now Ministry of Housing & Urban Affairs), Govt. of India.

Pradhan Mantri Awas Yojana- Housing for All guidelines, Ministry of Housing & Urban Affairs, Government of India.

Weekly progress report of PMAY-Urban as of 19.10.2020.

Chapter 17
Appraisal of Housing Finance in Pakistan for Low-Income Groups: Concepts and Processes

Sana Malik and Ruhizal Roosli

Abstract Housing finance is a specialized field of economics and finance, and its characteristics vary broadly across the globe based on the socio-economic profiles of the countries. Mostly, defined by mortgage markets, the housing finance market in developing countries like Pakistan is driven by underlying complex frameworks of social life and mindsets of the beneficiaries, making it a difficult subject to understand. Currently, Pakistan is facing a crucial shortage of 10 million housing units. Affordable housing projects from the public sector never worked massively due to payment deadlock from low-income groups as beneficiaries. The major reason behind this is their inability to pay the housing unit cost through down payments and instalments. This chapter describes important concepts and processes that operate the finance programs and products in the Pakistani housing market with key emphasis on the beneficiary's position. Discussions based on primary and secondary data unveiled the concepts and processes associated with housing finance mechanisms in the local context. It presents a complex synthesis of social underpinnings within the housing finance models and offers key suggestions for the way forward to achieve accessibility.

17.1 Urbanization and Housing Challenges

Urbanization is both a challenge and an opportunity, happening to the world simultaneously. In many developing countries, urbanization is transforming the megacities to a great extent over time, including employment opportunities and housing conditions. Pearson (2012) discussed that safe and secure housing is essential for good health, employment, education and community well-being. Without access to affordable housing, some people face homelessness or struggle to meet utility,

---

S. Malik (✉)
Housing Research Center, University of Management & Technology, Lahore, Pakistan
e-mail: sana.malik@umt.edu.pk

R. Roosli
School of Housing, Building and Planning, Universiti Sains Malaysia, Penang, Malaysia

A. Kundu et al. (eds.), *Accessible Housing for South Asia*,
https://doi.org/10.1007/978-3-030-88881-7_17

food and other basic living costs. Besides such multidimensional insinuations, it is becoming a global everlasting challenge with each day to provide access to affordable and adequate housing (Beer, 2007). In developing countries, slum dwellers, as well as middle-income groups within metropolitans, find it impossible to purchase an adequate housing unit for themselves without financial burden (Samad et al., 2016).

In the case of Pakistan, urbanization was mainly driven by migration, uncertainty and economic obligations (Rana & Bhatti, 2018). Since 1947 after independence, the country has faced rapid and inadvertent urbanization trends. The migration reached its peak in the past decades during military wars (1965 and 1971) because of the migration of Indian Muslims and in 1991, when Afghans migrated due to geopolitical factors (Haider & Badami, 2010; Kugelman, 2013; Mustafa & Sawas, 2013). Previous studies predicted that slum dwellers would grow up to three billion by 2050, following the current pace of urbanization (UN-HABITAT, 2010).

The housing challenges and issues are intrinsically locally driven for a given time and area. In the case of Pakistan, insufficient government resources led to the contested and inefficient housing market, promoting sprawl, land speculation, poor land records and weak finance systems (Hassan, 2017). Informal housing in the form of slums and squatters has become a global issue. Malik et al. (2020) argued that the recognition of this issue is not a new one and it has been associated with other global issues such as climate change and flooding, due to its broader impact on a local and national level. The presence of informal housing in form of slums and squatters indicates the poor government policies to provide accessible and adequate housing to the urban poor. A range of impediments including weak property rights, irregular construction frameworks, limited housing finance, inadequate taxation mechanisms and delayed land acquisition, exist to housing markets for efficient urban governance. (GoPb, 2015).

People invest in housing as a huge economic contribution from their income and savings, since it is a lifetime investment (Maliene & Malys, 2009). However, many Asian households are restricted to make such lifetime investments due to a lack of accessible and flexible housing finance, as such opportunities mostly exist for high-income groups only. In developing countries, high-interest rates and requisites for down payment limits most of the low-income households to avail of formal housing finance (Majale et al., 2011). This is why the high-income earners simply purchase their houses out rightly or via mortgage while some low-income and medium-income earners acquire their lands through savings and build their houses incrementally over some years (Fin-Mark Trust, 2010).

17.2 Housing and Financial Accessibility

The housing finance system is defined as a superstructure of laws, institutions and relationships between institutional and non-institutional units that facilitate the process of financial intermediation and capital formation in the Housing sector (Atamewan et al., 2017). Housing finance has historical tracks of deposit-based (such as loan associations or saving banks) and bond-based with different forms of state assistance for funding their urban expansions. In Southern Europe, the housing finance systems were featured through pervasive informal lending networks, not as institutionalized banking circuits. However, in the twentieth century, the deposit-based trend in housing finance was adopted by these countries to finance the urban expansions in cities (Blackwell & Kohl, 2018).

Studying housing markets in Asia, Cruz (2008) argued that a well-functioning housing market, together with finance, can help resolve these challenges. This argument corresponded well with the findings of Malpezzi's study (1990) that the housing units can be more affordable with deeper penetration of the national housing finance system of a country (Doling et al., 2013). The sustainable provision of housing can be successful through two key factors, i.e. availability and accessibility to mortgage finance. For attaining the sustainability of adequate housing for low-income groups, the continuous flow of funds is necessary for housing finance (Adedeji & Olotuah, 2012). The institutional context within the domain of property research enables the execution of affordable housing projects by providing: (i) administrative, legal and procedural support; (ii) access to finance; and (iii) access to land (Sukumar, 2001).

Stakeholder collaborations studied and exercised under FinMark Trust's housing finance, promoted innovative mechanisms of housing finance to enhance accessibility to the poor (Kalema and Kayiira, 2008). Studies like Drakakis-Smith (2012) and Moatazed-Kevani (1993) investigated such partnerships in housing development and concluded that public authorities usually supply appropriate land and tax incentives that facilitate the private firms in providing finance and construct housing units on these lands. The affordability constraint intrinsic in the mortgage instrument limits access by the low-income population to adequate housing (Atamewan et al., 2017). Housing can only be achieved provided if its within reach of beneficiaries in form of accessible and affordable finance. Few studies highlighted constraints that are faced in achieving housing finance, however, these are geography-specific but still, the primary causes are somehow similar irrespective of the context. In the case of Malaysia, the reasons behind the rejection of house loans for low-income groups included irregular income sources, lack of trustworthiness, weak capability for loan amount repayment and the poor capability of making down payments (Ebekozien et al., 2019).

In the Nigerian context, the main issues were revealed as shorter tenures around only 10–15 years, and a higher interest rate as of 22% for the inaccessibility of housing finance. Other challenges are macro-economic mainly high inflation; policy and regulatory (Land Use Act, Property Registration, Taxes, Stamp Duties); lack of credit enhancement vehicles (insurance); inadequate skilled manpower in the mortgage market; high cost of building materials cum over-dependence on foreign materials and inadequate infrastructure development (Fin-Mark Trust, 2010).

Urban management systems go parallel with fiscal allocations as part of financial programs of government and market sectors. Urban and financial reforms are purposeful in the sense that these are disguised by networks and interaction from the actors and not just a layer of rationalities. Housing finance work in fluctuating conditions like economic crises, currency devaluation, inflation, etc. that can be attained through urban-financial coalitions through ideas, interactions, events, documents, etc. (Socoloff, 2020). Previous studies argued that to scale up the housing finance provision to low-income and middle-income groups, it is important to support this sector by multi-faceted efforts. This issue becomes severe for urban housing development, due to the isolation of the urban poor within the real estate sector because of the speculative property business and price escalation factors. Isolated pilot projects cannot ensure the availability of affordable housing genuinely to the poorest groups of people, to scale up this cause, the state must provide subsidies in the housing sector besides the collective self-help attitude from target groups (Gillespie, 2018). Drawing on the literature of housing finance with perspectives of constraints and opportunities, it is important to overview the housing finance system in Pakistan for accessing the underlying key problems as well as opportunities for making houses financially accessible to low-income groups in Pakistan.

17.3 Housing Finance in Pakistan

Besides land, finance is a key part of the housing provision system, which is needed at different steps during the lifecycle of a housing project, i.e. for purchasing land, developing infrastructure and marketing the project. Homeownership could be possible for more people especially low-income groups, through taking care of housing finance. Developer finance is also a key part of this whole system by supporting the construction costs of housing units before being sold or rented out (Doling et al., 2013). In the housing sector of Pakistan, weak state legislation, onerous stamp duties, lack of standardized land processes, poor access to finance and limited opportunities of low-cost housing count for major issues of ineffective provision of affordable housing (Ghangro, 2018). A brief account of policy frameworks delivered the fancy dressing through macro initiatives for addressing the rooted issues of affordable housing provision despite adopting a proper planning process, summarized in Table 17.1.

This section is discussed in light of primary and secondary data. The descriptive narratives were extracted from in-depth interviews of key housing stakeholders in Pakistan. Besides state finance, other forms of mortgage include microfinance and mortgage lending for housing development are discussed in detail.

17.4 Housing Market Segmentation

Socio-economic brackets are associated with the monthly income defining different market segments of the housing sector. The housing market segmentation in Pakistan can be understood through different income levels. These income categories have distinct thinking patterns and housing issues. Mindsets vary among the people earning

Table 17.1 Federal policy framework for the Housing sector, Pakistan

Policy initiatives	Year	Main objective
Five-year plans	Every five year	Fiscal allocations for development projects
Housing Building Finance Company (HBFC)	1952	Housing loans and financial assistance to low-income groups
National Housing Policy NHP	2001	Rules and regulations framework
Housing Advisory Group (HAG)	2002	For enforcement of NHP
Vision 2025	2014	A 'Housing information system' for maintaining supply and demand database
PMRC	2018	Provision of housing finance with subsidized credit lines

Source adapted from Malik et al. (2020)

Table 17.2 Income-based market segments for the housing sector in Pakistan[iii]

Monthly income	Percentage in the total population
PKR 15,000	40% of the population
PKR 30,000–60,000	38%
More than 60,000	22%

below 15,000 PKR[1] and 30,000 PKR, it's not about education, it's about what people have and what they don't have.[2] Based on this logical pattern, the population of Pakistan is divided income-wise in Table 17.2. Builders and developers don't feel comfortable working with low-income segments of the urban society, except for political or philanthropic motivated projects. This area is a vacuum that is marked by a lack of demand-side segmentation (what are the income segments for low and middle-income housing and what is their financial capacity) and appropriate product offering is a noteworthy market failure (Ghangro, 2018).

The understanding of this income-based division of people is important for targetting the right users since monthly income has a strong relation with housing expenses as 30% of the whole income. Presently, households earning 60,000 PKR can serve as the sweet spot for government-funded projects for affordable housing. The reason behind this is that the sweet spot is comprised of 38% of people working in white-collar jobs (Table 17.2), who find it difficult to arrange finance for constructing their housing units.[ii] The low-income groups as the potential beneficiaries of the affordable housing market, being illiterate and uneducated, are not well aware of their rights for housing as well as for other social contexts like health, education, etc. There is

[1] Pakistani Rupee.

[2] Primary Data Source: PS1: Represntative from Lahore Development Authority (LDA), Paki-stan.

Table 17.3 HBFC loan products for the housing sector in Pakistan[iii]

HBFC products	Timeline	Salient features
Profit and loss scheme	1979 –1987	Its profit varies according to the area so, it almost 7–8% and revised every 3 years
Simplified scheme	1987–1989	It charges rent according to the locality
New simplified scheme	1989–1998	All the schemes were launched with the approval of the HBFC board. Federal Govt. has empowered the board to take any decision regarding HBFC
Ghar Asan Scheme	2001–2002	In between years, there is no lending process for two years, on the re-payment period
Ghar Pakistan	2002-Present	This rate of 16.75% is the floating rate and this is the market rate keeping the market trend of the time. Some banks give 17.5 and others 18%
Shandar Ghar Scheme (SGS)		for the renovation of houses

no guidance for them and they lack knowledge, and lack of awareness leaves most of them in illegal housing settlements.[3]

17.4.1 State-Based Finance

Under state-based finance, the government of Pakistan (GoP) has two major institutions, i.e. Housing Building Finance Corporation (HBFC) and Pakistan Mortgage Refinance Company (PMRC). Their roles and characteristics are discussed below.

HBFC Loan Products

The State bank of Pakistan (SBP) is steering as a regulator for the housing finance market to supervise the public and commercial banks. HBFC jointly owned by SBP and GoP, established in 1952, is the only housing finance institution in Pakistan with an agenda to serve low-income groups (Ahmed, Saleem, & Mojai, 2014). The national institution provides housing finance loans to low-income and middle-income people with interest rates. Although HBFC holds the largest portfolio of housing finance in Pakistan, still it does not fulfil the needs of low-income groups of accessible housing finance. Rizvi (2017) highlighted that HBFC has been previously issuing seven loans per day for house construction as a comparison to India's public financial institution providing 1000 loans a day. Before 1979, the interest on the loan was fixed-rate it includes both simple and compound interest. It was difficult for low-income groups to meet the conditions of housing loans. HBFC tried transformation of the loan products after 1979 to accommodate more people and facilitate mortgage to them (Table 17.3).

[3] Primary Data Source: PS2: Represntative from Housing Building Finance Corporation (HBFC), Pakistan.

Hashmi (2016) explained that HBFC faces difficulties such as political pressures for approving loans, delayed customer loan repayments, lengthy lawsuits with defaulters and recovery processes. Presently, HBFC being the state-owned department offers a flat 12% mark-up rate to the applicants earning 100,000 PKR and owning a plot size of 10 Marla maximum.[iii] In 2018, under the newly elected government of PTI,[4] Naya Pakistan Housing Program (NPHP) was launched to develop five million houses for low-income communities across the country. Following the rigour, HBFC plans to launch the loan products to facilitate the mortgage availability and making efforts to play role in NPHP as its key objectives in coming years.[iii]

PMRC

PMRC is another state company to facilitate HBFC and SBP for making mortgages effective and efficient for low-income groups. PMRC was established in 2018, with the partnership of the private sector, to enhance financial accessibility to the housing sector, as a key suggestion from the Housing Advisory Group (HAG) to implement National Housing Policy (NHP). The amount was lent by World Bank to improve the mortgage facility to low-income groups for buying houses. The institutional structure is yet to be framed, however, it started working recently with a portfolio of 8–10 billion and its fully functional.[v]

Securities and Exchange Commission of Pakistan (SECP) had housing refinance companies previously, but they have not been successful due to a lack of long-term finance. HBFC also making use of this as PMRC provides funding costs to the organization. The anticipations of stakeholders are considering PMRC induction into the housing finance sector as certainly providing uplift to the financial domain of the housing industry. The objective of PMRC is to provide long-term loans with a fixed rate, passing them to customers at the retail level (Ghangro, 2018). The scope of PMRC includes providing housing finance low-interest rates because they have subsidized credit lines.[5]

17.4.2 Commercial Mortgage

Income verification is an important part of availing mortgage finance for buying housing units. Unorganized patterns of monthly salary and its undocumented nature keep the low-income groups away from availing the facility of mortgage and loans for financing their houses. Low and middle-income groups face trust and documentation issues because and they don't have documented income. iii As documentation issue becomes prominent due to informal sources of income with no salary slips or appointment letters.

According to Table 17.2, Pakistan has a 40% population that earns below PKR 15,000 a month through informal sources. Hence, due to poor documentation, these

[4] Pakistan Tehreek-e-Insaaf.

[5] Primary Data Source: PS3: Represntative from State Bank of Pakistan (SBP), Pakistan.

Table 17.4 Mortgage models for Housing finance in Pakistan

Steps	Conventional Model	Islamic Model
1	Bank provides the finance for a mortgage. A transfer letter is issued to the applicant along with PTM (Permission to a mortgage)	The house is not transferred to you it transfers to the bank
2	Bank wrote to the liaison that after 5 years you clear the payment and then the house is transferred to your house	BOP is the owner of the house and they allocate you the house and you start to pay the payments on the unit
3	However, due to weak foreclosure laws, once you entered the house so it's really difficult for us to get out of the house	In Islamic mode, units are being made. they increase the percentage When you clear the payment, I'll transfer the house to you

people can't even take the loan. In such circumstances, such low-income groups suffer a lot when making efforts for owning or purchasing a house. it is important to identify these people including laborforce, maids, drivers, waiters, with undocumented income sources within cities. ii Housing issues occur severely for them and it would be favourable if the government develops a subsidized housing scheme for these poor households.[6]

In mortgage finance, payment plans follow the instalment package distributed over a timeline of spreading years and monthly payments. This implies that nothing is your property until you pay the whole amount. According to law, the property is not bought, it's just a piece of document as a legal promise that bounds you to make the full payment of property to earn its ownership.[ii] The value of money is the same for everyone and in every finance product either it's Islamic or convention.[7] In Pakistan, mortgage financing for buying a house contains two major models to follow: conventional and Islamic (Table 17.4).

In Asian finance Markets, it is a general perception that within 3–5 years either mortgage is settled down or default Paying the instalment is influenced by the thinking mindset of the payers, i.e. 'willing to pay' or 'thinking to pay'.[vii] Both salaried and self-employed persons have different attitudes since the former one is driven by his need and the latter one is motivated for its profit. From the field experience, it was argued that for making payments towards housing finance, low-income groups are proved to be 'good payers.[vii]

For the down payment, the attitude is also driven by a cultural mindset. A homemaker in the South Asian context, is usually interested in owning a house and can easily give up the jewellery and other assets for this purpose.[8] For the Ashiana Housing Project (AHP), being the only executed affordable housing project in Punjab, housing finance was devised by carrying out feasibility studies based on surveys of

[6] Primary Data Source: PS4: Local Urban Planner and Developer in Lahore, Pakistan.

[7] Primary Data Source: PS5: Represntative from Bank of Punjab, Pakistan.

[8] Primary Data Source: PS6: Represntative from Punjab Land Development Company (PLDC), Punjab, Pakistan.

Table 17.5 Financial plan for Ashiana Housing Project (AHP), Lahore, Pakistan[vii, viii]

Financial plan for Ashiana housing project (AHP) lahore (Launched 2010)		
Income criteria		PKR 25,000
Down payment		25%
Monthly instalment		
2 Marla		PKR 4500
3 Marla		PKR 7500
Tenure for payment		5 years
Housing unit cost		
2 Marla	Price	PKR 840,000
	Subsidy	PKR 162,000
3 Marla	Price	PKR 1,190,000
	Subsidy	PKR 195,000

low-income communities. This helped in formulating a payment plan that was affordable to the target groups (Table 17.5). In the case of AHP, this attitude was observed in the case of both monthly instalments and down payments. As mentioned earlier about low-income as good payers in comparison to high-income clients, it was proved from AHP as well where 615 loans were disbursed, out of which 200 loans are adjusted clearly while the remaining are regularly paying-off.[vii]

17.4.3 Microfinance Loan Products

Other than mortgage housing products, microfinance products in the housing sector are also playing their role. But the results are not that supportive due to high mark-up rates on the loan interests issued by micro-finance banks in Pakistan. Microfinancing is not mortgage financing and it provides loans for small businesses but on high return. Conventional microfinancing is done through specialized banks and has a very high rate of interest like 25–28%. For instance, Apna Bank, NSRS Bankm Finca Microfinance Bank, Khushhali Microfinance Bank and NRSP Microfinance Bank offer housing loans with a repayment period from 1 to 3 years maximum.[iii] It is very difficult to keep track of 20 years in the context of Pakistan due to poor documentation, hence banks especially micro-finance banks prefer housing loans with shorter tenure periods.

Microfinance Housing loans are usually out of reach from low-income groups due to high interest rates up to 17–18%. Microfinancing can be effectively done by following the model set by Akhuwat[9] due to its interest-free mode. Microfinance can be done effectively by charity organizations, i.e. the model of Akhuwat due to

[9] Lahore based Akhuwat NGO.

the nature of its business that is based on community-based learning and volunteer system.[iii] However, it is important to know that this type of funding normally applies to people who live in slums and squatters and build their houses on an incremental basis. Tariq (2012) established that it is also distinct from business micro-loan products, which most microfinance institutions use since housing improvement is the key objective rather than purchasing or building a new home. However, with the substantial increase in construction rates, now beneficiaries have started to demand a bigger loan size as the construction has been multiplied three times in the past decade.[10]

Akhuwat, due to its large portfolio across the country has recently caught the PTI's government attention for NPHP execution. The PTI government collaborated with Akhuwat for the disbursement of interest-free loans to low-income groups for house construction up to PKR 500,000. The project was of 5 billion rupees and 1 billion was released by the Government of Pakistan on 7th January 2020 and, it was distributed across Pakistan (rural and urban) till 31st January 2020.[11] To maintain transparency in this project, the amount was distributed in two phases, just to ensure adequate utilization of funds and transparency. Akhuwat Foundation has committed with GoP that in five years we will continue to revolve these funds.[xi] It is estimated that 10,000 houses will be constructed with the allocated amount for the affordable housing sector under NPHP.

17.5 Discussion: Ways Forward for Accessible Housing Finance

The provision of adequate housing cannot be achieved for low-income groups without making it affordable and loanable. On the contrary, the financial package also impacts the built environment of the cities. During and after the nineteenth century, the era of industrial urbanization, the proliferation of housing finance institutions played a major role in determining the patterns of city extensions and reconstructions (Blackwell & Kohl, 2018). In Pakistan, Government authorities must play their role by offering seed money to make public housing projects affordable in a financial manner. The kickstart for effective disbursement of funds can be initiated from 50 or 100 Billion (PKR), this would lead to better regulation of PMRC and releasing funds in other banks.[iii] The mismatch between the housing market segments and payment plans of projects convey the disconnection of policy-making processes from the ground realities of the housing sector.

This chapter provided financing models adopted for affordable housing for low-income groups. The unique characteristics of each model discussed conclude that understanding the market segmentation leads to the right selection of beneficiaries and feasibility studies lead to devising effective payment plans. Some of the key

---

[10] Room construction was approximately \$1000 (Rs.120,000 in 2011).

[11] Primary Data Source: PS7: Represntative from Akhuwat, Pakistan.

suggestions for achieving the accessibility of housing finance for low-income groups in developing countries like Pakistan are provided as follows:

(i) Strengthening State Legislation by Approving foreclosure law, to avoid the risk of being a defaulter
(ii) Maintaining the databases of low-income groups by local authorities to track the income sources, making the income verification process easier, transparent and speedy
(iii) Longer tenure periods must be offered with single-digit interest rates when offering mortgages to low-income groups
(iv) Salaried persons, as well as women, must be given priority for availing of a mortgage
(v) Interest-free microfinancing organizations must be introduced in each major city
(vi) HBFC must develop innovative products to attract more borrowers by maintaining an efficient and responsive mechanism of enhancing their capacity of daily loan.

References

Adedeji, Y. D., & Olotuah, A. O. (2012). An evaluation of accessibility of low-income earners to housing finance in Nigeria. *European Scientific Journal, 8*(12).

Ahmed, S., Saleem, M., & Mojai, A. S. (2014). Quarterly Housing Finance Review. Retrieved from http://www.sbp.org.pk/departments/ihfd/QR/Housing/2014/Sept-2014.pdf.

Atamewan, E. E., Eyo, E. E., & Efanga, M. E. (2017). Appraisal of availability and accessibility to mortgage finance for sustainable housing delivery in Nigeria. *European Scientific Journal, 13*(31).

Blackwell, T., & Kohl, S. (2018). Urban heritages: How history and housing finance matter to housing form and homeownership rates. *Urban Studies, 55*(16), 3669–3688.

Beer, A., Kearins, B., & Pieters, H. (2007). Housing affordability and planning in Australia: The challenge of policy under neo-liberalism. *Housing Studies, 22*(1), 11–24.

Cruz, P. C. R. (2008). Transaction costs and housing affordability in Asia. *International Real Estate Review, 11*(1), 128–150.

Doling, J., Vandenberg, P., & Tolentino, J. (2013). Housing and housing finance-A review of the links to economic development and poverty reduction. *Asian Development Bank Economics Working Paper Series*, (362).

Drakakis-Smith, D. (2012). *Urbanisation, housing and the development process*. Routledge.

Ebekozien, A., Abdul-Aziz, A. R., & Jaafar, M. (2019). Housing finance inaccessibility for low-income earners in Malaysia: Factors and solutions. *Habitat International, 87*, 27–35.

Fin-Mark Trust (2010). Overview of the housing finance sector in Nigeria. UK DFID; Bill and Melinda *Gates Foundation, 12*(1), 1–52.

Ghangro, A. A. (2018). The State of Housing Finance in Pakistan. Karandaz. Retrieved from https://karandaaz.com.pk/blog/state-housing-finance-pakistan/.

GoPb. (2015). *Punjab urban sector plan 2018*. Lahore: Planning and Development Department, Government of Punjab.

Gillespie, T. (2018). Collective self-help, financial inclusion, and the commons: Searching for solutions to Accra's housing crisis. *Housing Policy Debate, 28*(1), 64–78.

Haider, M., & Badami, M. G. (2010). Urbanization and local governance challenges in Pakistan. *Environment and Urbanization ASIA, 1*(1), 81–96.

Hashmi, S. M. (2016). *An Empirical Analysis of Low-Income Housing, Policies and Public Finance of Pakistan.* (Doctoral Dissertation, Yokohama National University).

Hassan, S. (2017, March 06). *A new paradigm for affordable housing.* Pakistan Economist. Retrieved from https://www.pakistangulfeconomist.com/2017/03/06/a-new-paradigm-for-affordable-housing/

Kugelman, M. (2013). *Urbanisation in Pakistan: Causes and consequences.* NOREF Norwegian Peacebuilding Resource Centre.

Majale, M., Tipple, G., & French, M. (2011). Affordable land and housing in Asia. *United Nations Human Settlements Programme (UN-HABITAT)*, 1–84.

Maliene, V., & Malys, N. (2009). High-quality housing—A key issue in delivering sustainable communities. *Building and Environment, 44*(2), 426–430.

Malpezzi, S. (1990). Urban housing and financial markets: Some international comparisons. *Urban Studies, 27*(6), 971–1022.

Malik, S., Roosli, R., & Tariq, F. (2020). Investigation of informal housing challenges and issues: Experiences from slum and squatter of Lahore. *Journal of Housing and the Built Environment, 35*(1), 143–170.

Malik, S., Roosli, R., Tariq, F., & Yusof, N. A. (2020). Policy framework and institutional arrangements: Case of affordable housing delivery for low-income groups in Punjab. *Pakistan. Housing Policy Debate, 30*(2), 243–268.

Moatazed-Keivani, R. (1993). The role of formal private building firms in low-income housing provision in developing countries: The case of Tehran. *Unpublished PhD Thesis, Development Planning Unit, University College London.*

Mustafa, D., & Sawas, A. (2013). Urbanisation and political change in Pakistan: Exploring the known unknowns. *Third World Quarterly, 34*(7), 1293–1304.

Pearson. (2012). *Access to Public Housing.* Victoria: VAGO—Victorian Auditor General's Office.

Rana, I. A., & Bhatti, S. S. (2018). Lahore, Pakistan-Urbanization challenges and opportunities. *Cities, 72*, 348–355.

Rizvi, Z. M. (2017). Affordable housing and importance of construction industry for economy at ABAD expo Islamabad. Shelter, p. 13.

Samad, D., Zainon, N., Rahim, F. A. M., Lou, E., & Abd Karim, S. B. (2016). Malaysian affordability housing policies revisited. In *MATEC web of conferences* (Vol. 66, p. 00010). EDP Sciences.

Socoloff, I. (2020). Subordinate financialization and housing finance: The case of indexed mortgage loans' coalition in Argentina. *Housing Policy Debate, 30*(4), 585–605.

Sukumar, G. (2001). Institutional potential of housing cooperatives for low-income households: The case of India. *Habitat International, 25*(2), 147–174.

Tariq, F. (2012). *Investigation of Incremental Housing Processes based on Microfinance: Implications for Policies and Practice.* (Doctoral Dissertation, North Carolina State University).

UN-Habitat. (2010). *State of the cities 2010–11—Cities for all: Bridging the urban divide.* Nairobi: UN-Habitat.

Chapter 18
Affordable Housing Policies in South Asia: Key Issues and Recommendations

Vineeta Hariharan and Sree Lakshmi Nambiar

Abstract South Asia is unable to realize the full potential of the benefits of rapid growth due to the messy and hidden nature of its urbanization. Messy urbanization is manifested in slum and squalor housing. In this paper, we review the policies for accessible housing in five cities in South Asia, and attempt to provide recommendations for enabling access to housing for all, which would reduce the impact of messy urbanization and foster economic growth and prosperity.

Keywords Accessible and affordable housing · Urban regulation

18.1 Introduction

The urban population of South Asia grew by 130 million between 2001 and 2011 and would rise further by almost 250 million in the next 15 years. South Asia is unable to realize the full potential of the benefits of this growth due to the messy and hidden nature of its urbanization. Messy urbanization is reflected in congested housing or slums and sprawl, which is growing in the peripheries of large cities not captured by statistics, giving rise to hidden urbanization. These constraints are undermining both livability and the agglomeration economies that can produce greater prosperity (Ellis & Roberts, 2016).

18.2 Scope

In this paper, we review the policies for accessible housing in two states of India, namely Tamil Nadu, Maharashtra, and three cities in South Asia namely Dhaka,

V. Hariharan (✉)
Senior Urbanisation and Public Policy Expert, New Delhi, India

S. L. Nambiar
Policy Student (Institute of Public Policy), Chennai, India

A. Kundu et al. (eds.), *Accessible Housing for South Asia*,
https://doi.org/10.1007/978-3-030-88881-7_18

Colombo and Karachi to understand their merits and demerits. The paper also attempts to provide recommendations for enabling access to housing for all, which would reduce the impact of messy urbanization and foster economic growth and prosperity.

18.3 India—Maharashtra and Tamil Nadu

18.3.1 Overview of India's Housing Policy

As per the constitution of India, both housing and urban development are in the domain of the state governments. The National Government, however, is mandated with the responsibility of formulation and implementation of social housing schemes. India has had a National Housing Policy in place and National programmes for the provision of housing over the several five-years plan in the country. However, since 2014, housing for all has emerged as a priority for the Government of India with the formulation of Pradhan Mantri Awaas Yojana, the Housing for All programme with a focus on private sector participation in the redevelopment of slums and provision of Affordable Housing. Here we review the policies of two of India's most urbanized states, viz. Maharashtra and Tamil Nadu.

18.3.2 Maharashtra

Maharashtra is faced with rapid urbanization and the ill effects of it, with an increasing housing shortage mostly manifested in slum housing. The State has framed several innovative policies to ameliorate the slum housing situation through mechanisms like Transfer of Development Rights (TDR) and also constituted the Slum Redevelopment Authority (SRA). The Maharashtra Area Development Authority (MHADA) and SRA together play a crucial role in the provision of housing in the State.

18.3.2.1 Maharashtra Housing Policy, 2021

Maharashtra continues to grapple with a mounting housing shortage, despite the initiatives, noted above. The state announced the new housing policy to fast track and address the housing shortage of 1.9 million houses by 2022, with the focus being on housing for the economically weaker section and lower-income groups (Government of Maharashtra, 2015). The key focus areas of the policy are as follows:

- Continuous creation of a land bank for affordable housing by using both Government as well as land belonging to the private sector.

- Increase the supply of affordable housing in the market leading to a reduction in price to the consumer. Optimum use of existing land resource by encouraging redevelopment.
- Improving the quality of life, overall living standards with due concern for the environment.
- Improve ease of doing business in the construction, building and housing industry

The new policy stipulates that the state will redevelop buildings on 7,000 plots in 104 layouts of the Maharashtra Housing & Area Development Authority (MHADA) in Greater Mumbai, making available as many as 30,000 new houses in Greater Mumbai (Table 18.1).

Table 18.1 Affordable housing in Maharashtra: key issues and recommendations

Key issues
One of the biggest hurdles in Mumbai has been the Rent Control Act, 1999, which allows nearly two million people to stay in homes almost free of rent. This proved to be ineffective as it completely protected the already housed people in Mumbai while excluding the migrant population. This Act has a detrimental effect on investments for rental purposes, and also negatively impacts the existing housing stock from the rental market (Government of Maharashtra 2015)
While vertical housing was aimed at a solution owing to land constraints, this has not solved the issue of housing the poor. Instead, it has contributed towards a surplus of empty flats along with a multitude of de-housed people
Speculative planning has resulted in a sharply divided cityscape with overcrowded tenements and vacant skyscrapers
Private builders make poor-quality houses despite being given incentives by the government. This leads to the resale of flats by the intended beneficiaries, as often their needs are not met, they face livelihood challenges and need liquidity
Key recommendations
The Rent Control Act must be amended as it has exacerbated the housing problem in the millennium city, and in fact, has proved detrimental to the positives of rental housing
A strong public–private partnership model (PPP) should cater to an inclusionary housing scheme, whereby those earning below the median income can be accommodated. Several countries like England, Canada, etc. require developers to set aside a portion of the total built space for inclusionary housing. A similar model can be considered here
Floor Space Index could be replaced by a new metric called crowding, defined as the number of persons per hectare for a particular urban use, be it amenities, open space crowding, street crowding etc. (Government of Maharashtra, 2015)
An efficient and sustainable land use pattern must be evolved and the Government should expedite the development of a Trans Harbour link that would open vast tracts of land on the mainland and make affordability a reality (Patel, 2013)
The increasing inequality in Mumbai mandates a prioritization of the housing needs of low- and middle-income groups over the profits of private developers. Despite laws that make it mandatory for private developers to allocate half the land of a slum redevelopment project for affordable housing at government-regulated rates, builders often stake claim to the majority of the project land—up to 70% or more—for their profits by selling those homes at competitive market rates (Johari, 2018)
Equitable land distribution pattern and a participatory planning approach hold the key for Mumbai's affordable housing to be a success (Government of Maharashtra, 2015)

18.3.3 Tamil Nadu

Nearly half of Tamil Nadu's population is urban which is expected to increase to 63% by 2030. An estimated 6 million people are currently living in slums (representing 16.6% of the state's urban population).

The Chennai Metropolitan Development Authority, Town and Country Planning Department, Tamil Nadu Housing Board, Tamil Nadu Slum Clearance Board, Cooperative Housing Society and Tamil Nadu Cooperative Housing Federation are the key agencies involved in the supply of public housing in Tamil Nadu. The policy on slums which is multi-varied has been taken up for review in this paper.

18.3.3.1 Slum-free Cities and Affordable Housing Policy in Tamil Nadu

The three-pronged strategies for developing or clearing slums followed by Tamil Nadu Slum Clearance Board are:

(i) In-Situ Plotted Development and Infrastructure Improvement

Wherever in-situ development is feasible, slums are identified and taken up for in-situ improvement for provision of basic facilities to make the areas habitable while providing tenurial rights to the slum dwellers after getting the land transferred to the Tamil Nadu Slum Clearance Board.

(ii) In-Situ Tenemental Schemes

The slums located in unobjectionable poramboke[1] areas, wherein the equitable distribution of space to all is not feasible, are cleared and tenemental schemes put up.

(iii) Rehabilitation and Resettlement Schemes

Wherever neither tenemental nor in-situ development is feasible, rehabilitation and resettlement in tenements in nearby locations with necessary infrastructure are taken up. The cleared site is then restored to its original use. Urban Renewal is being carried out by demolition and reconstruction of dilapidated Buildings.

The State Housing and Habitat policy of 2020 aims to ensure access to adequate, safe and affordable housing and basic services for all, and improve slum conditions by 2030. This envisages strengthening the role of the government as an enabler. In 2020, the Tamil Nadu government signed an agreement with the World Bank for two projects—First Tamil Nadu Housing Sector Strengthening Program of $200 million and Tamil Nadu Housing and Habitat Development Project worth $50 million—to strengthen the state's housing sector policies, institutions, and regulations (Table 18.2).

---

[1] Land not assessed under revenue records.

Table 18.2 Affordable housing policy in Tamil Nadu: key issues and recommendations

Key issues
The new Housing and Habitat policy of 2020, was criticized for its lack of direction and clarity and public consultation
A study conducted by the Madras Institute of Development Studies (MIDS) highlighted that the single biggest constraint to affordable housing supply in the state is the limited availability of land
The policy is silent on how the Shelter Fund will be managed and governed, how in-situ or proximate resettlement of slum dwellers will be achieved, and how the issue of basic amenities for slum-dwellers will be approached
The prime focus of the policy has been on rental housing. Other types of housing such as community housing programmes for vulnerable sections like homeless persons and trans persons have been ignored
Key recommendations
A robust system must be put in place to ensure land management and prices are regulated. The existing policy is silent on how land speculation will be checked, and on releasing of land for such housing. Land redevelopment must be followed wherever possible
The government should support developers with special funding for affordable housing and highly incentivize the buyer
Greater involvement of the intended beneficiaries (in the form of public consultation, stakeholder meetings) will promote cooperative action and strengthen decentralized governance
Greater plot sizes and lower plot coverage must be targeted
Financing of projects must be decentralized, and innovative methods of financing through Public–Private Partnerships must be encouraged
Highly-dense slums must be housed as far as possible in multistoried tenements

Source Thangavelan (2010)

18.4 Bangladesh–Dhaka

Dhaka is one the most densely populated cities in the world with almost 20,000 people per square mile. A fragmented housing delivery system and dysfunctional rental housing have exacerbated the woes of affordable housing, besides the pressure of rural-urban migration leading to high population density. At present, the government meets only 7% of the annual housing demand and relies heavily on the private sector to fill in the giant gap (Rahman, 2019).

The government has approved the 'National Housing Policy 2017' and emphasized affordable housing in the seventh five-year plan (2016–2020). National Housing Authority (NHA), with the World Bank's support, is undertaking a USD 50 million project to develop housing for the urban poor by 2021. However, the existing policy still has several shortcomings (Table 18.3).

Table 18.3 Affordable housing in Dhaka: key issues and recommendations

Key issues
Silos between public and private players have reduced cooperative efforts to improve housing capacity
Lower involvement of government—only as an enabler in the land market, loosening laws and regulations surrounding infrastructure investments have accentuated the housing crisis
Penetration of housing finance has been low outside certain central areas
Government schemes have suffered from a shortage of funds
Availability of land has been limited with large swathes of national parks and uninhabitable mangrove swamps
Key recommendations
Bangladesh needs a strong policy framework and transparent institutions. Projects need to be well-monitored and innovative initiatives must be widely replicated for which partnerships among government agencies, the private sector, and development partners are critical
Affordable housing finance schemes must be introduced 'Build Bangladesh-UNDP SDGs Impact Fund' can be a potential source for funding. Microcredit loans and savings must be tapped
The Municipality and private players must be incentivized to work together. For instance, in Gopalganj municipality, security of tenure was offered to 346 evicted families that resulted in their rehabilitation
The success of Community-based housing finance institutions can be replicated. In addition, rigorous consultative and participatory processes can enhance greater accountability amongst the stakeholders
Increasing the involvement of NGOs is necessary. ARBAN is one of the first NGOs to pilot a low-income, urban housing project in Bangladesh. They have built an apartment complex for 42-member households in Mirpur, Dhaka through community initiatives
Effective land management practices must be evolved and utilized to ensure planned development

Source: Synergy (2019)

18.5 Sri Lanka–Colombo

The 'National Housing Policy of 2014' aims at ensuring the "right to live in an adequate, stable, qualitative, affordable, sustainable, environment-friendly and secure house with services for creating a high living standard on the timely needs of the people". The government has been at the forefront of achieving well-defined development targets within a time frame. Sri Lanka is the only country in South Asia that has surpassed the Millennium Development Goals. It is not just a mere enabler but has also functioned as an effective regulator, financing agency, manager and infrastructure developer. Importantly, Colombo Municipal Council has been proactive in a housing development (Ministry of Housing & Construction, 2017) (Table 18.4).

Table 18.4 Affordable housing in Sri Lanka: key issues and recommendations

Key issues
Despite strong government interventions, shortcomings in terms of quality of housing ail the affordable housing segment. Low-quality construction material has led to substandard housing and is accompanied by unsanitary living conditions. For instance, in Matara, seventeen per cent of the housing stock is deemed to be unsanitary, due to the use of low-quality material and unsafe locations
Poor regulation and flouting of building safety codes have put the community at risk of disasters. Most of the low-income houses are located in flood-prone areas, and sewerage management and availability of drinking water continue to plague these homes
Despite having a multitude of government authorities steering the affordable housing segment, overlapping mandates and functionaries have made them inefficient owing to changes in governmental funding
Housing finance from the formal sector is limited to 15–20% of the planned settlements (UN-Habitat). Only 20% of low-income earners have regular employment- allowing them to access formal institutional credit
Lack of willingness and low community awareness has led to their exploitation by the authorities
Key recommendations
Proper regulatory mechanisms, checks on building codes and safety standards must be addressed to ensure safe and accessible homes to the poorest of the poor
Necessary institutional and policy changes must be brought in to cater to the existing demand for housing
Urban local authorities need to be equipped with enough power to ensure a performance-based housing management system
Sustainable finance must be focused upon so that formal institutional credit is used for availing loans
An efficient land management policy must be evolved
Innovative approaches based on community participation will ensure accountability among the stakeholders
The private sector must be incentivized to work in tandem with the government
Housing policy must be linked to broader issues of urban governance and other policy issues like disaster preparedness, sustainability and economic viability of the projects

Source Ministry of Housing and Construction (2017) and Asian Development Bank (2011)

18.6 Pakistan–Karachi

Pakistan is the seventh most populated country in the world. The urban housing demand in Pakistan is 350,000 units per year. Of this, 62% is for lower-income groups, 25% for lower-middle-income groups, and 10% for higher and upper-middle-income groups. The formal supply per year is 150,000 units. Unprecedented migration from rural to urban areas has led to a backlog of over 8.5 million units in the country (Hasan & Arif, 2018).

In Karachi, migration from the hinterlands, as well as population growth resulted in housing demand outstripping by supply. Informal settlements in the form of occupation and subdivision of government land (called katchi abadis or squatter settlements) and the informal subdivision of agricultural land (ISALs) located at the periphery of urban settlements have come up to meet the existing shortage (Table 18.5).

Table 18.5 Affordable housing in Pakistan: key issues and key recommendations

Key issues
The gap between existing housing supply and demand is ever increasing
The state is transferring its responsibilities to companies. Several municipal functions have already been transferred, including the collection of revenue in some cases
The government has transformed the former Housing Building Finance Corporation into a private company and has liberalized the loan process in terms of both procedures and packaging
Land use and its management remain a cause of concern. A myriad of state agencies controls the land, with little coordination with other authorities
Key recommendations
A strong regulatory framework is needed to protect the poorer sections of the population
Cooperatives or collective low-income groups could provide the poor with the means to own their property
Migration-related pressures must be solved cohesively—not only by addressing existing shortages but by solving rural livelihood problems
Vacant land under state governments can be used for planned housing settlements. Mixed land use must be focused upon
Planning rules and regulations set by the development authorities need to be revisited, building bylaws should encourage such spaces which are livable
Focus on 'vertical growth' for future cities
Microfinance institutions and incremental housing programmes will help low-income households to improve their access to affordable homes

Source Tariq (2019) and Aftab (2019)

18.7 Conclusion

The messy and hidden nature of South Asia's urbanization is reflected in the growth patterns of the countries studied in this paper. The policies in every country, are being designed more as reactionary rather than proactive intervention, to cater to the existing and projected housing shortage.

In India, the current affordable housing policy, at the National level caters to the provision of housing for the lower and middle-income groups. There is an urgent need for policies and programmes for slum housing wherein lies the actual housing shortage in the country. Every State must design policies and programmes, framed city wise, based on the nature of housing shortage and slum housing. Currently, rental housing finds a mention in all new housing policies of the central and state governments. There is an urgent necessity to ensure effective implementation of these policies and to take proactive steps to cater to the housing needs of the ever-increasing number of migrants and informal sector workers who throng to metropolitan cities for livelihoods. The associated policies to strengthen rural economies and peripheral urban areas to be able to cater to the livelihood and aspirational needs of the people, preventing distress migration, are equally important.

In Bangladesh, the issue pertains to stakeholder management. There is an urgent need for public housing to play a larger role in ensuring access and affordability of housing for all. The country could consider designing a National programme for the provision of housing for all, patterned around the PMAY of India, with clear roles assigned for all stakeholders.

In Sri Lanka, the issue pertains to the predominant role played by public housing agencies and low-quality housing being provided without adhering to building codes. There is also a need to have effective coordination between the various agencies and enhanced access to housing finance for all.

In Pakistan, indiscriminate privatization of housing provision has led to further marginalization of the poor. The policies here need to ensure stronger public participation and effective monitoring of housing provision for the poor. The problem of massive migration to capital cities for livelihoods needs to be addressed by building a strong infrastructure and provisioning economic amenities in rural areas to prevent distress migration.

To summarize the following interventions are required across South Asian cities to alleviate the messy and hidden urbanization and to ensure equitable housing for all.

i. Access to housing finance,
ii. Greater efficiency in Public Housing,
iii. Effective stakeholder management,
iv. City-specific policy solutions for slum housing,
v. Proactive affordable housing policies, Long-term strategies to cater to housing needs and prevent slums in future,
vi. Strengthening rural areas to prevent distress migration to urban areas.

References

Aftab, M. (2019). *How do we solve the housing crisis in Pakistan?*. The Nation. 18 March. https://nation.com.pk/18-Mar-2019/how-do-we-solve-the-housing-crisis-in-pakistan.

Hasan A., Arif H. (2018). The Crisis of Urban Housing. The Dawn. 19 August. Accessed May 9, 2021. https://www.dawn.com/news/1427893.

Asian Development Bank (2011). Impact Evaluation Study on Asian Development Bank's Assistance for Low-Income Housing Finance in Sri Lanka.Asian Development Bank. Independent Evaluation Department. August. Accessed May 9, 2021. https://www.adb.org/sites/default/files/evaluation-document/35045/files/ies-sri-housing.pdf.

Johari A. (2018). *Interview: Mumbai's dream of affordable homes is a real possibility, says urban planner PK Das*. Scroll in. 19 September. Accessed May 8, 2021. https://scroll.in/article/893561/interview-mumbais-dream-of-affordable-homes-is-a-real-possibility-says-urban-planner-pk-das.

Government of Maharashtra (2015). Maharashtra State New Housing Policy & Action Plan, 2015Government of Maharashtra. http://mohua.gov.in/upload/uploadfiles/files/Maharashtra%20New%20Housing%20Urban%20Policy%202015.pdf

Ministry of Housing and Construction (2017). *National Housing Policy. Revision of January 2017*. State Ministry of Rural Housing & Construction & Building Materials Industrial Promotion. Accessed May 9, 2021. https://houseconmin.gov.lk/regulation-and-polices-of-ministry/national-housing-policy/.

Patel S. B. (2013). *These 4 policies can rid mumbai of its housing problem.* First Post. 11 February. Accessed May 8, 2021. https://www.firstpost.com/business/economy/these-4-policies-can-rid-mumbai-of-its-housing-problem-620971.html.

Rahman A. (2019). *Housing solutions for the urban poor in Bangladesh.* UNDP. 10 April. Accessed May 9, 2020. https://www.bd.undp.org/content/bangladesh/en/home/presscenter/pressreleases/2019/04/07/housing-solutions-for-the-urban-poor-in-bangladesh.html.

Ellis P., Roberts M. (2016) *Leveraging Urbanization in South Asia : Managing Spatial Transformation for Prosperity and Livability.* Washington, DC: World Bank. https://openknowledge.worldbank.org/handle/10986/22549

Synergy (2019). *Housing the Urban Poor in Urbanizing Dhaka: Challenges of Access to Land.* Synergy: The Journal of Contemporary Asian Studies. 15 April. Accessed May 9, 2021. https://utsynergyjournal.org/2019/04/15/housing-the-urban-poor-in-urbanizing-dhaka-challenges-of-access-to-land/.

Tariq F. (2019) *Appraisal of National Housing Policy—A Case of Pakistan.* United Nations. https://www.un.org/development/desa/dspd/wp-content/uploads/sites/22/2019/05/TARIQ_Fariha_Paper.pdf.

Thangavelan, T. S. (2010). *Government of Tamil Nadu.* Housing and Urban Development Department. Accessed May 9, 2021. https://cms.tn.gov.in/sites/default/files/documents/housing.pdf.

Index

A. Kundu et al. (eds.), *Accessible Housing for South Asia*, https://doi.org/10.1007/978-3-030-88881-7

N

P

R

S

T

U

V

W

The manufacturer's authorised representative in the EU is Springer Nature Customer Service Centre GmbH, Europaplatz 3, 69115 Heidelberg, Germany. If you have any concerns regarding our products, please contact ProductSafety@springernature.com

Printed and bound by CPI Group (UK) Ltd, Croydon, CR0 4YY
30/09/2026
02225250-0009